COLLEGE LIFE IN THE OLD SOUTH

THE UNIVERSITY OF GEORGIA IN ANTE-BELLUM TIMES. (FROM AN OLD PRINT.)

COLLEGE LIFE
IN THE
OLD SOUTH

BY E. MERTON COULTER
HEAD OF THE HISTORY DEPARTMENT
UNIVERSITY OF GEORGIA

THE UNIVERSITY OF GEORGIA PRESS
ATHENS

Printed in the United States of America
BOWEN PRESS — DECATUR, GEORGIA

TO

GEORGE FOSTER PEABODY

PATRON OF THE
UNIVERSITY OF GEORGIA
FRIEND TO MAN

CONTENTS

ILLUSTRATIONS

PREFACE

PLANTATIONS and politics have been raised to such a high position in the civilization of the Old South that most people consider its history to be written when these institutions and performances have been set down and explained. Yet back of Southern development lay an institution whose effects were profound and widespread, even though it was not an institution of the masses. This was the college with the college community.

Leadership in the Old South was largely a development from the top downward rather than from the bottom upward. The sons of the more fortunate and ambitious classes attended college, where they came in contact with a social and intellectual system which largely remade them and which sent them back to the people as leaders in politics, religion, medicine, and in most other honorable activities—to the cities, villages, and the plantations. The college occupied the position of greatest strategy in the making of Southern leadership. It was basic and fundamental—not in the people it reached directly, but in the influence it exerted through its students.

The leaders of the Old South to a great extent were either trained in colleges, and for the most part in Southern colleges, or were in somewise identified with colleges and college communities. Robert Toombs left the University of Georgia stamped with the character he was later to fulfill as a statesman. As strikingly true was it that Alexander H. Stephens, the student, was father to the man.

Human nature was as intense in the college student as it was later when he became the lord of a plantation or a leader in statecraft. The student of the Old South took the business of going to school seriously, although he worked just as hard in doing mischief called forth by an educational system which took its students young and which in dealing with them considered them still younger. With all its imperfections the college of the Old South performed well the work it had resolved to do.

In my attempt to isolate and portray the atmosphere and accom-

plishments of the college in the growth of civilization in the Old
South, I have chosen the method of investigating and dissecting
one institution because this method leads to greater clarity, organization, and vividness. And just as plantations developed into
a type, so did the college and college community. To know what
college life was like in the Old South is to know truly what took
place at a typical Southern college. There were no fundamental
differences in what happened at the University of Georgia in
Athens, at the University of North Carolina in Chapel Hill, at
South Carolina College (later University of South Carolina) in
Columbia, at the University of Mississippi in Oxford, at the University of Alabama in Tuscaloosa, at Emory College in Oxford,
at Trinity College in Trinity, at Mercer University in Penfield.

I have selected the University of Georgia as the type because
through its early beginning it became co-extensive with that civilization which characterized the Old South. Also, the records of this
institution are more complete and more intimate as to every
thought and action of those who composed it than is true of most
other Southern colleges. In no other field of Southern activity
have the traces left been so reeking and redolent of the surrounding atmosphere.

This study has been considerably aided through the financial
assistance of the American Council of Learned Societies. The
substantial interest taken in this work by Mr. George Foster
Peabody of Saratoga Springs, New York, and by Mr. William C.
Bradley of Columbus, Georgia, has played a determinant part in
its appearance. I owe my thanks also to Professor A. K. Christian
of the University of Oklahoma and to Dean R. P. Brooks of the
University of Georgia for valuable suggestions and for proof
reading, and to Professor Merritt B. Pound and Professor William
Tate, both of the University of Georgia, for help in reading proof.

E. M. C.

PREFACE TO SECOND EDITION

As THIS book has for a long time been out of print and as there has been continuing interest in it by students in the University, by alumni of this institution, and by many other people concerned with the broader field of American history, a second edition was deemed desirable. It is republished, appropriately, it seems, as a part of the general program of the Sesquicentennial Celebration of the University.

As it was necessary to reset the type, the author suffered the temptation to do some revising of style and content and to bring the story down to a point nearer the present. He refrained, for this is not a rewritten narrative, but only a second edition. He made changes only to clarify ambiguities and to correct errors which came to his attention, and, also, to make the footnote citations conform to more modern usage. He slightly revised the bibliography, and he found it necessary to construct a new index to conform to a changed page numbering.

E. M. C.

CHAPTER I

A UNIVERSITY
IN THE WILDERNESS

IN THE straggling little frontier settlement of Louisville, saddled with the proud importance of being the capital of the State of Georgia, in the year 1801, a collection of respectable citizens bearing the extraordinary title of Senatus Academicus were contending with due parliamentary dignity, but with considerable animation, over who should have a coveted prize. The object of their desire was nothing more than a "college or seminary of learning," which the state had chartered sixteen years previously. Off and on for two years this unseemly contest had been going on among these sonorously titled gentlemen, during which time every county in the state outside of the "sickly coast" had been voted upon as a possible location. As each was conscious of the other's desire to possess this new institution they attempted to delay the final decision in their first meeting in 1799 (November 27th to December 2nd) by selecting a temporary site. This maneuver failed; thereupon the champions of Hancock, Wilkes, Greene, and Jefferson counties sought victory. None could get the required vote. Then an attempt was made to call the Academy of Columbia County the college, with the hope that it might sometime live up to its new name if given proper care. Failure again was written.[1] The meeting now adjourned in disgust until 1800, when the fight was begun over again with the same result. Finally on November 27th,

Greene County was triumphant and a committee was appointed to build there a "wing of the university" sufficient to accommodate 100 students.[2]

That things not settled right are never settled must have been the slogan of the opponents of Greene County is evident, for when the Senatus Academicus in their Louisville meeting (1801) attempted to get the institution started, these irreconcilables reopened the fight. After seven charges and counter-charges Greene County lost her prize to Jackson.[3] Would this decision stand? This was the third attempt of the ghost to take on corporeal existence, its first effort being when, only one year old, it was to be given joint abode in the new capital at Louisville, itself yet to be born in the wilderness.[4]

The plan of a college or university for the state was none of Georgia's making; it was imported. In her first constitution (1777) not a thought was given to a university, although the example of North Carolina providing in her constitution of the preceding year for "one or more universities" was at hand. During the years of the Revolution that followed, Georgia tried hard to take her own life with her Whigs and Tories arrayed against each other in a terrible carnival of murder and pillage, ever after known as the "War of Extermination." But the mountains and valleys and rivers and fertile plains were just as attractive as ever, and it did not take long for the news to get abroad that Georgia was distinctly the place in which to settle and grow up. Two classes of people took advantage of this opportunity. One group had discovered this El Dorado about the time the Revolution broke out, and following their vision they had begun to swarm over into the regions to the northward of the coast country and to settle in what came to be known as Middle Georgia. These people were the restless, land-hungry, gambling, hard-drinking gentry from as far north as Maryland, who had failed to be satisfied in their Maryland, Virginia, North Carolina, and South Carolina homes. Most of them had been driven out of Georgia during the war, but when peace came they returned with many thousands of their fellows, and before the end of the century they greatly outnumbered the lowlanders. They cared little for schools and had no conception whatsoever of a university.

The other group, not so large, who came prospecting to Georgia was not primarily looking for land on which to settle. Some would not turn away from such easy fortunes as could apparently be made in Yazoo speculations; but others were more interested in using their talents toward taking charge of this dynamic commonwealth, whose varied potentialities, with a vast domain extending to the Mississippi River, were likely unequaled in the whole Confederation. These newcomers drifted almost invariably into the settled regions—largely to Savannah and the coast and to Augusta. They came to be governors, politicians, lawyers, teachers in academies, and managers of whatever needed managing. And they were not disappointed. George Mathews came down from Virginia one year and was elected governor the next. But this group was made up largely of enterprising Yankees from New England. Their number was never large as compared with the influx into Middle Georgia, but their influence was far-reaching. The Colonial Georgians, among whom they settled, were of recent European origin, mostly from British dominions, but some of them were foregathered from the ends of the earth. The debtors and their descendants from the English jails were only a small part of the whole. There were besides them, other English, Jews, Greeks, Swiss, Salzburgers, Scots, Moravians, Huguenots, and Piedmontese.

Yale College graduates particularly early fell in love with Georgia and scarcely a class failed to send representatives to embrace her opportunities. Their activities and interests were varied; they turned their inventive minds to everything from cotton gins to universities. It was in 1783 that Abraham Baldwin, a graduate of Yale and a former teacher there, caught the Georgia fever from General Nathanael Greene, who owned a plantation near Savannah, presented to him by the state.[5] No doubt Baldwin expected to enter into some kind of educational as well as political work in Georgia, especially so since Governor Lyman Hall, another Yale graduate, had just been arguing with his legislature over setting up some "seminaries of learning."[6] The next legislature acted by granting in the law laying out Washington and Franklin counties, 40,000 acres of land (20,000 in each) to endow

not "seminaries of learning" but "a college or seminary of learning."[7] The influence of Baldwin may not have been lacking in
the change. The legislature was willing to do this small favor for
those who wanted a college, for what was 40,000 acres of land
when compared with the vast areas extending to the Mississippi;
and after all what was the price of land in Georgia!—any head
of a family who cared to settle in these same counties could have
a thousand acres free![8]

So it was, then, that the germ of a state university was planted
in these 40,000 acres on February 25, 1784, five months after the
signing of the treaty of peace granting Georgia her independence.
Endowing schools with land had long been a favorite method of
dealing with the question of education. Henrico College, a phan-
tom institution chartered in Virginia in 1619, had been given 9,000
acres, and William and Mary College received 20,000 acres with
its charter.[9]

There was little likelihood or expectation that a university could
be set up for some years to come, but at the same time the land
was granted, a board of trustees was named, who were to be little
more than landlords charged with the impossible task of renting
land where it was free for the asking. These gentlemen, eight in
all, including the governor (Hall), Baldwin, and ex-governor
Nathan Brownson, a Yale graduate, set to work to have 5,000-
acre tracts of "land of the first quality" surveyed and set aside.
Next, there should be a charter, but who in Georgia knew anything
about university charters? Even Baldwin and Hall, Yale graduates, knew nothing about such rare documents. Governor Hall
wrote Ezra Stiles, the president of Yale, inquiring about the mech-
anism of a university, and Baldwin asked him to send Yale's
charter down, or one of his own composition.[10] Armed with all
the information he could get and filled with the enthusiasm of a
builder, Baldwin set to work to convince the trustees and the legislature that a charter should be adopted immediately. He presented one he had worked out, and the legislature with rare good
judgment accepted it on January 27, 1785.[11] To John Milledge
and Nathan Brownson must also go part of the credit for developing the plan of a university for Georgia. Arguing the terrible

risks society undergoes from untamed barbaric nature, the charter calls for the molding influence of a university, to be managed and directed by two bodies, a board of visitors and a board of trustees. These two bodies meeting together were known as the "Senatus Academicus of the University of Georgia." This was an ingenious scheme for linking together the state government and the university under the direct management of one body. The visitors were at first the governor and the councillors, and later when the council was dropped from the state government, the governor, the senators, the superior court judges, and the president of the senate and the speaker of the house.[12] It placed the University under the watchful eye of the people's representatives, and it also gave the University a vantage point from which to argue for support. The trustees were composed of the old board of landlords with six new members added, making fourteen in all.

The scheme of education contemplated in the charter embraced elementary schools, academies, and the University at the top. The University was merely one wing of the beautiful structure, and the president of the University had the important duty of visiting the academies and supervising them. To emphasize the unity of education and literature in Georgia, all schools receiving state aid were "considered as parts or members of the University." Baldwin may have received some of his ideas from Jefferson, who had at least three years earlier suggested some such scheme for Virginia.[13] The essential elements of this plan were later used by Quesnay de Beauregard in his system worked out for Jefferson in 1788 and by Dupont de Nemours, for the nation in 1801.[14] South Carolina College followed the Georgia scheme in the latter year.[15]

As might be expected, Baldwin was elected president of this educational establishment (1785), whose worldly possessions consisted of two governing bodies, two academies, and the right to 40,000 acres of land. As supervising academies did not greatly appeal to Baldwin, he entered politics and left the trustees to collect the rents and do whatever else pleased them. They laid off the land into 100-acre lots and soon had a modest rent roll. Booming a town was early discovered to be a quick way to make money.

In 1786 the trustees began the town of Greensboro by selling the greater part of one thousand acres, incidentally reserving enough for another academy, a church, a courthouse, and a jail. Thus would they collect money for a university and prepare students for it.[16] New brooms sweep clean, but they never stay new for long. The task was difficult and the trustees soon tired. The President went away to Philadelphia to help save his country by helping to make a new constitution, and then he entered Congress. The Senatus Academicus continued to remain only a name—and the idea of a university came near fading from men's minds. Some of the trustees died, others moved away, and for eight years preceeding 1794 not a meeting was held. Four more years of inaction followed, and then life suddenly burst forth. Someone discovered that during the past thirteen years about $6,000 had accumulated —was it not time to start the University?

In 1798 the trustees met in Augusta and decided that another meeting should be held the next year at Louisville and that any trustee who was so careless as to be absent without a good excuse should be fined $20. At the appointed time a few stragglers met at the "Coffee House," called the roll, and found a quorum absent. They repeated this performance three times before they could assemble seven out of the thirteen.[17] As the Senatus Academicus had never yet shown signs of life, the governor prodded it with a proclamation calling it to awake and bestir itself.[18] Its first meeting was held in 1799, and all the latent forces of political bickering were let loose over the location of the University. In 1800 the legislature lent a hand by abandoning the Louisville site and limiting the location to the up-country.[19] And so in 1801, as heretofore recounted, the Senatus Academicus finally chose Jackson County.

But Jackson County was extensive in those days, indeed, as large as a half dozen twentieth century Georgia counties, and so the problem was only half settled until the exact spot was picked out. These Senatorial Academicians sublet this practical work to a committee of five headed by President Baldwin, whose duties as United States Senator were not engaging him at this time.[20] His campus had heretofore been the whole state; now he was at last about to get it concentrated within a few acres. In the midst of summer (1801) they set out into the forests to the northwest and did not stop until they had almost entered the Indian territory. The land was hilly and the streams clear and swift. Here at the last tavern, on the edge of all white habitation, they began the intensive search for the inevitable hill from which knowledge should go out to the people. After debating various eminences, they agreed upon a small plateau high above the Oconee River where it swirled down over some rocks near a clump of cedar trees.

This spot was known as the Cedar Shoals among the few frontiersmen who had wandered this far into the northwest, and here it was that Daniel Easley with a keen eye for business and a faith in the future had purchased almost 1,000 acres, and had directed some of the water to run a small mill he had built. Daniel Easley had been one of the commissioners appointed five years previously to locate a county seat for Jackson County, and the law was so unwise as to state that the business of the county should be done at Easley's house until a choice had been made. It may readily be guessed that the difficulties of finding the proper site were insurmountable. Those difficulties were never overcome until two years later (1798) when the commissioners were reorganized and Easley left out.[21] So when these five unsuspecting university promoters happened up on the wily Easley, their quest was at an end. Although the University owned a 5,000-acre tract nearby, Easley convinced this committee that his hill high above the Cedar Shoals was unsurpassed as a location for an institution of learning. He also convinced them that it would take at least 633 acres on which to build that institution. Here was the spectacle of the university organization, land rich and money poor, acquiring more land. John Milledge, one of the committeemen, and a friend and follower of Thomas Jefferson, who must have been particularly pleased with the hill and especially with the fine spring of water flowing out of the side, bought the land and presented it to the University. Easley was careful to reserve some of the most likely region near the river. What name could be more appropriate for the town that should arise here than Athens?— so Athens it became.[22]

Easley's persuasion had not been entirely responsible for this choice; this region was unquestionably beautiful in all its primeval glory, its undulating forests of pine and oak, its yellow jessamine and honeysuckle, and its streams of cool, clear water. Baldwin had long held that just such scenes should surround a college. At best there were great dangers "in the pleasing walks of science"; but if the location were unhealthful "it can be but an infirmary, a habitation of Diseases, rather than a seat of the Muses." Furthermore, there was none of the evils of town life here, and there was room aplenty in which a thriving countryside could develop to furnish the University fresh milk and butter and wholesome vegetables.[23] Such views were common in this age. North Carolina had already in 1793 selected much the same sort of spot for her university, and Thomas Jefferson had expressed exactly the same sentiments to Joseph Priestley in 1800.[24]

But even had such views not been held by the educational philosophers of the time, the up-country would nevertheless have received the University, for more Georgians lived in the up-country than on the coast and what good was a democracy if it could not prove that what fifty-one per cent of the people want is always right and that what forty-nine per cent want is always wrong? The small ribbon of old colonial settlers along the coast, hugging the Savannah up as far as Augusta, the colonial aristocrats, were almost ceasing to be of any moment in this new Georgia—the frontier Georgia. In 1790 there were fewer white settlers here than in Kentucky, and, indeed, the only excuse Georgia had for being a state was that she had been one of the thirteen colonies which had revolted. So apart from the coast the state was distinctly a frontier region with the same kind of Indian wars and Indian fighters as were to be found in the regions west of the Alleghenies. These hordes who swept in and seized the state were just as boisterous and wicked, as brave and hospitable, as inquisitive and reckless as any adventurers anywhere on the frontier from the Great Lakes to the Gulf. They had no ministers to pester them every seventh day; they had by design left Sunday behind. There was not an ordained minister in the up-country in 1784 "except 2 or 3 illiterate Baptist Elders," according to Ezra Stiles.[25] The Episcopal Church which had at one time been foisted upon the people as an Established Church had been cast out of the country with the other trappings of the King. Now, indeed, was there freedom from religion as well as from tyranny. For a generation to come they were to be illiterate, irreligious and happy.

Their occupations and pastimes were those typical of the frontier everywhere. Log-rollings, gander-pullings, shooting for turkeys and beef, heavy drinking, card playing, militia musters, and county court days gave them some outlet for their vigorous natures. They delighted in profane swearing and it went unchecked until the legislature in 1786 laid a fine of five shillings on any officer of the law who should emit an unholy oath, and two shillings and sixpence on the ordinary citizen.[26] The barbaric custom of gouging was particularly relished by participants as well as onlookers. But even in the wildest state of nature, protective measures must sooner or later develop. In 1787 the majesty of the law asserted itself by making it a high crime to "cut out or disable the tongue," gouge out an eye, slit the nose or lips, bite off an ear or nose, or in any other manner disfigure any member of the body. The first offense cost £100 and two hours in the pillory. A second offense carried death without benefit of clergy.[27]

To say that these people originated the University would be foolish. But since there was to be one they must be given credit for being wise enough to accept it as a gift. They had had neither education nor religion before coming to Georgia, as many had lived too far from the older parts of the Colonies where there was some little of both, and they were not very anxious in their new homes to depart from their old ways. Education for the masses had been part of the political philosophy and democratic dogma of the eighteenth century, which had led to the Revolution. The principles of a democracy must be protected from its own self, and educating the masses was an integral and indispensable part of this new democratic system. And furthermore the new order was to be built around the unlimited perfectibility of mankind.[28] The Georgia leaders were first to attempt to apply this doctrine in any American state, and the willingness of the Georgia people to allow this experiment to be made upon them is not to their discredit. Especially is this true when it is remembered that the start was made less than a year after the Revolution had ended, when the state was impoverished and almost ruined.

The lowlanders had stared with wonderment on this rampant barbarian invasion, which turned into unconcealed hostility when these rough frontiersmen began to seize every part of the government which the New Englanders had not got hold on. These up-landers first made a descent on Savannah and marched away with the capital up to Augusta, where they rested a few years before carrying it on to Louisville—so far into the wilderness that a town had not yet grown up there. But the *West* found it difficult to keep ahead of the *East;* so in 1807 these Westerners again carried the capital on to Milledgeville. The University was also legitimate spoils worth having, and, of course, the coast could not have it. The northwesternmost verge of white habitation got it. Savannah and the coast could make little complaint in losing it, as the coastal climate was undoubtedly deadly. In 1785 no less than three young Yale graduates had died in Savannah.[29] But nevertheless, there were many mutterings of dissatisfaction on virtually hiding the University up in the hills on the edge of the Indian country, and Governor Tattnall in 1801 admitted that a more central location would have been better. Before going out of office the following year he expressed the hope that the opposition would die down and that "the fabric of science, [would] rise rapidly into view."[30] The friends of the University, in defense, argued not only the beauty and healthfulness of the location, but called attention to the fine shad that ascended the river "as high as Athens in great perfection." As a further health item the rather strange phenomenon was noted that "what little vapour rises at any time from the river is always attracted by the opposite hills, toward the rising sun."[31]

After climbing the University hill and surveying the country undulating in every direction, Baldwin no doubt had a sort of feeling of sublimity, for choosing the site was the last of his official acts. He had now brought the Flying Dutchman into port and had anchored it. Being a United States Senator and the president of a university that must now be built up were incompatible. So at

the meeting of the Senatus Academicus when the committee had
been appointed to select the site in Jackson County he had resigned
the presidency into the hands of Josiah Meigs, another Yale graduate and former tutor there. Meigs had been instructed by Baldwin at Yale and ever after held him in high esteem, expressing the
hope later that it would always be remembered his appointment
had come through Baldwin's recommendation. In 1800 Meigs had
first been brought to the attention of the Senatus Academicus, when
he had been elected a professor with the understanding that he
would succeed to the presidency if Baldwin should resign.[32] He
was to have $1,500 a year, and $400 should be given him for his
expenses in reaching Georgia.[33] His acquaintance and standing
in New England were high. Among his classmates were Noah
Webster, Joel Barlow, and Oliver Wolcott.[34] Into his hands was
now cast the difficult duty of molding a university—a work the
gigantic importance of which he keenly realized.

If bricks cannot be made without straw, how can a university
be set up without money? The lack of money had been the cause
of the past sixteen years' delay. In 1798 Aquilla Scott, the treasurer, reported about $7,500 on hand, but when he was asked to
produce it the next year, the Senatus Academicus found that he
had peculated to the extent of more than $900.[35] But the Uni-
versity must have money if it was to arise—from whence should
it come? The state had given the charter and some land—was not
that enough? At least the University builders at this time were
afraid to ask for more. Instead they cast themselves on the bounty
of individual Georgians, circulating lists for subscriptions and
appealing for aid in the newspapers of the state.[36] The citizenry
were not greatly moved by such impractical causes as education
—all except James Gunn, a nephew of the Gunn of malodorous
Yazoo Fraud fame, who gave $1,000, with the feeling, perhaps,
of atoning for his uncle's evil doings.[37] The only hope remaining
was with hat in hand to approach the legislature with the established fact of a university building already begun and a prayer
for money with which to finish it. This body agreed to advance
$5,000 to be well secured and to be returned within five years with
ample interest.[38] The next year (1803) the state gave the trustees

permission to sell all their holdings in Hancock County and all that John Milledge had given, except 37 acres "for a college yard." These various maneuvers produced by 1804 over $30,000—no mean sum for higher education in those days.[39]

In the fall of 1801 President Meigs, leaving his family in Augusta, came up to Athens, the place in the forest where the University should be set up, and engaged lodging at Easley's home— the only dwelling "in town." Soon the woodsman's ax was busy clearing out a campus, and men with chains and pegs were staking off the sites for various structures. A dwelling for the president held priority and Easley secured the contract to build it. He also turned his home into a tavern for the numerous workmen who were attracted to this town in the building. A large three-story brick structure, patterned after the principal hall at Yale, began to arise on the crest of the hill. Here the University and all of its business should be housed. The contract went to David Gaddy and Jett Thomas, who promised to commence and finish it without delay. Armed with $1,000 they went to Augusta, a hundred miles away, for nails and lime. Also President Meigs called on his brother, the Indian agent at Hiawassee, Tennessee, to secure permission of the Cherokees to bring lime through their boundaries. Two miles from Athens they found fine clay which other contractors promised to mold into 300,000 or more nice red bricks.[40] The first college building south of Chapel Hill, North Carolina, now began to rise above surrounding shrubs and saplings. By 1805 the western half had been finished, which the trustees jubilantly named Franklin College in honor of honest Ben, who personified learning and wisdom and who had at one time endeared himself to Georgians by acting as their Colonial agent in London. The next year the building stood complete, all except two porches on the south side added six years later, and President Meigs proudly announced that "Better accommodations for students cannot be found in any College in the United States."[41] The friends of learning everywhere could justly greet this new edifice on the hill, which compared so favorably with other colleges of the country—even with Yale, its inspiration, which had at this time only two small dormitories and a chapel. Franklin College was decorated with shining "electric conductors," and an insurance policy in the Phoenix Insurance Company of London was taken out to give it further protection. A new sun had risen in Georgia.

CHAPTER II

THE FIGHT FOR LIFE

 PRESIDENT Meigs had not been idly waiting during these five years of building to begin polishing the minds of young Georgians. In fact he had laid the foundations of his student body before he had planned his collegiate building. He had gone out to the half dozen or more academies, branches of the University, to select his students, and he had collected them in Athens before the masons and carpenters appeared. He began to unfold to them the mysteries of knowledge, under the trees, in the tavern, in his own frame dwelling, and in a log building erected (after the first year) "for temporary school rooms at the seat of the University." What could be more in keeping with a frontier university than this: to hold classes in a log cabin twenty feet square, one and one-half stories high and costing $187.27![1]

The trustees ordered the plans of the University large enough for one hundred students, but whence such a number prepared for college? There were eight academies in the state in 1800, which, however, turned out few prospects for the University.[2] To intensify the search for learning the University voted to offer annually $50 in prizes for students in the academies. To take care of students unprepared for entering the University, the trustees ordered in 1803 the construction of a Grammar School on the campus, and by the end of 1804 the building had been finished. The

14

young Grammar School boys boarded and roomed with the regular college students until it was discovered some years later that their morals and industry were being ruined thereby.[3]

Within two years Meigs had been able to collect enough students to grade them all the way up to the senior class, where he lodged twelve of them. In all there were "between thirty and forty-five," studying "with laudable ambition and singular industry." Harvard and Yale, with all their age, had not many more.[4] He watched his students' health with as much keenness and concern as he did their scholarship. "We have had great health on this high hill," he reported in 1803.[5] The Senatus Academicus learned "with great pleasure the general health of the students" and noted with approval "their success in the pursuit of knowledge."[6]

There was an outstanding opportunity for this new University on the plastic frontier, unhampered by old traditions, to carry to completion the eighteenth century philosophy of both feeding the multitudes the bread of democracy and of determining that that bread should be wholesome and strengthening. Alas, Abraham, Josiah and all the other University pioneers ceased to think after 1800! They took the New England hard tack of classicism more than the luscious fruits of science and natural philosophy—and left it for Jefferson nineteen years later to give the Virginians the feast. They stamped New England on the subjects to be taught and on the manner of doing it. The first plan was to divide the college courses into six years, during every one of which the student was required to wrestle with the strange inflections and vocal intonations of ancient Latins and Greeks. His own native English he might "read occasionally at the discretion of the Tutor" during the first two years; he might peep into the English grammar weekly during the third and fourth years and write "a letter or some piece of simple composition"; and during the sixth year he might get acquainted with belles lettres. The six-year system never gained a foothold; instead came the usual four-class system with freshmen and sophomores and the strangely titled junior sophisters and senior sophisters. The studies required were much the same as in the six-year scheme, with the first two years almost absorbed in Latin, Greek, and mathematics and with the last two given over more largely to logic, natural and moral philosophy, belles lettres, and the laws of nations.[7] As an example of how busy a junior must have been, the following list of subjects was required: astronomy, determination of geographic longitudes and latitudes by observation of eclipses of the moon and by the use of the celestial globe, natural and experimental philosophy, chemistry, botany, "Cicero de Oratore," logic, Priestley's lectures on history, "forensic disputations," and composition.[8]

Yet there was much of the leaven of the new age at work here as readily appears in this morsel for the juniors. The atmosphere of this new institution was distinctly scientific rather than clerical, and no doubt Jefferson got in a few blows against the New England preachers at this time, for he wrote Meigs in 1803 congratulating him on being the head of "The College of Georgia" and reminding him that the hope for science lay in the South unshackled by the clerical chains of New England.[9] Meigs, a mathematician with strong scientific inclinations, needed little prompting. Before the University was actually begun he had secured permission from the Senatus Academicus to send to London for "philosophical apparatus and a small selection of books" which he believed would be at least equal in real utility to any equipment "belonging to any literary institution in the United States."[10] Soon he had the students at work making "projections of various kinds," and he may well be excused for his grandiloquent boast that he would "if it please God to spare our lives kindle a scientific fire on this Mount Pisgah, which will irradiate the Peninsula of California."[11]

Meigs seemed never to be quite content unless he were measuring something or seeking an explanation of some force of nature. He found out that the campus spring would flow 9,000 gallons of sparkling water in twenty-four hours in May, or only 7,700 gallons in January; he told his fellow Athenians how hail was formed; and he agreed to carry out for Congress a study of the variation of the magnetic needle.[12] But he reached the height of ingenuity and inquisitiveness when through the use of the formula for falling bodies he calculated how deep into hell the angels plunged in their nine days of mad flight. He found the bottomless pit to be 1,832,308,363+ miles deep.[13]

In 1800, before the University had been located, it had a president, Baldwin, and a professor of mathematics, Meigs. After Baldwin resigned, Meigs was left alone as president and faculty. By the summer of 1802, he determined that the dignity and finances of the University warranted at least one professor; so William Jones was added at $500 a year to teach the languages. After two years Jones was replaced by Addin Lewis, a Yale graduate, whose college background made him worth $800 a year. A division of labor was effected between Meigs and Lewis whereby the president took the freshmen and seniors—to initiate the newcomers into the ways of a college and to give them the finishing polish for the great world outside. In 1806 a new departure for an American college was taken when the study of the French language was added and Monsieur Petit de Clairville, a native Frenchman and a graduate of the College of La Flèche, was employed to carry on the work.[14] This development was in keeping with the democratic thought of the latter eighteenth century which had been so vitally influenced by the French. Baldwin had studied French while he was a chaplain in the Revolution; the aid France had given in that war was not yet forgotten; and the reaction against the French on account of the excesses in their Revolution had not influenced Georgia so much as it had other parts of the country.

At this time, five years after its beginning, the University was flourishing beyond expectations. There were seventy students in the college and forty in the academy. By his own intrinsic ability and his wide acquaintanceship Meigs had made the University known to the people of the state and had spread its reputation abroad. Joel Barlow, who had just published his *Columbiad* in 1807, called upon Meigs to review it, and to court the favor of the University he sent it a handsome copy bound in leather, containing 454 pages and eleven fine steel engravings, with the inscription "From the author to the University of Georgia, 1808."[15] Meigs, adamant when it came to saying things he did not believe, perhaps valued his friendship with Barlow too highly to review this grandiloquent poem; the University, less strict with its conscience, showed its gratitude by presenting Barlow with the LL.D. degree—yet a standard far higher than American universities were later to adopt for the awarding of honorary degrees.[16]

In the midst of this prosperity were fast sprouting the seeds of adversity. Meigs was plain in his speech—he never called black gray; he was uncompromising in his disposition—he never sidestepped the excitement of a fight. In fact he had left Yale for Georgia because he could not bring his republicanism into harmony with the arch Federalists, Timothy Dwight, the president of Yale, and Theodore Dwight, the future secretary of the Hartford Convention. Mrs. Meigs years afterwards wrote with some bitterness of feeling that the Dwight brothers had exiled her husband to the "backwoods of Georgia only twelve miles from the Cherokee Indians for no earthly reason but his stern democracy."[17]

So Meigs came to Georgia, an ardent Jeffersonian Democrat, and soon found himself in conflict with men of Federalist leanings, or men whom he chose to call Federalists and Tories. "What think you of Jefferson?" he wrote in 1803. "How high does he soar above the little sphere of his Predecessor in office—How beautiful is it to be honest and upright? His glory cannot be tarnished."[18] There were few simon-pure Federalists left in Georgia at this time, but the perversity of mankind will always breed contentions—in politics if nowhere else. By 1805 "Gladiator" had enticed Meigs into the arena and also "Aristides" was soon upon him.[19] The monster of religion in politics was about to raise its head. The dread of the rising Baptists was so keen in the legislature that it refused to grant them a charter for a college for fear that they might seize the state treasury for it.[20]

This unfortunate contest had its effect on the attendance at the University. By 1808 the students in the Grammar School had dropped from thirty to fifteen and in the college from forty to twenty-five. The trustees had also lost interest in the University; they made two attempts that year to hold a meeting, both of which failed. As the University was supported by tuition from the students, supplemented by the meager rentals from the land, it was soon upon the rocks of poverty. The trustees, finally succeeding in holding a meeting, began to inquire why the students had ceased coming; and the Senatus Academicus declared that if something was not done the University "may experience a relapse of fortune and reputation, which will blast the fondest and best hopes of the friends of Literature." The language professor was dropped; Meigs' salary was reduced from $2,000 to $1,500, and Petit de Claville's to $400. Finally in 1810 the Frenchman left the sinking ship and only Meigs remained.[21]

Attacks on Meigs came from various quarters, and an atmosphere of suspicion and intolerance—political, religious, and educational—enveloped him. "He saw men smile and smile in his presence and yet felt that it was not the smile of friendship," said a trustee a quarter of a century later.[22] Of this early fundamentalist onset, Meigs said, "I have always believed that knowledge pure and unveiled (whether politically or religiously) was the true basis of the happiness of individuals or nations. Idiots and fools alone will consent to unreasonable laws, and dishonest men alone will declare their belief of that which their judgment and conscience declare to be false. I have like all other public characters been a target for the shafts of those who dread the true light of science. I have in common with my fellow countrymen faults, but among them I defy them to find *hipocracy*."[23] Yet Meigs had not lost all friends in Athens, for he was invited to make the Fourth of July oration in 1810, and at the celebration this toast was drunk: "The University of Georgia—struggling against prejudice and illiberality—may its usefulness yet defeat the views of malignity."[24]

Meigs, frank soul that he was, resolved this very year to resign, a course of action which he had often thought of pursuing since the days of 1803, when he wrote that his labors of both body and mind were so difficult that he felt almost willing to quit. "The Crown of the President of a College," he added, "is indeed a crown of thorns."[25] He handed the University over to his critics, who immediately elected him professor of natural philosophy, mathematics, and chemistry, and he, left without any other livelihood, accepted. The trustees, done with scientists, decided that a preacher should be president, a decision from which they never swerved for the next hundred years. The Reverend Henry Kollock of Savannah was chosen, but he saw fit to refuse. The University was now left for a year without a president and with Meigs as the faculty. For a time he tried to be accommodating to all concerned, but his rising anger got the best of him as he saw the trustees trying to waste the land endowment (as it appeared to him). He called them "all a damned pack or band of Tories and speculators"—all except Peter Early. He had been demoted (this, despite the fact that he had resigned) to a professorship "and given . . . a poor, pitiful salary of twelve hundred dollars—damn them —he reckoned they would make him next professor of cabbages and turnips." So Augustin S. Clayton, who at this time liked him none too well, reported to the trustees. For such outspoken sentiments, Meigs was without further ado dismissed. Left with a family and no money, he was reduced to the straits of putting in a claim for ringing the college bell.[26]

The University had arisen, given great promise, and had now apparently finished its course—all within less than a dozen years. In the summer (1811) the trustees suspended the institution until the following December. When they attempted to meet again in November, it appeared that they, themselves, had become as moribund as the University, and the few faithful who did assemble resolved that members must attend or resign.[27] They had, however, found a president during the summer, and the suspension had been made to give him time to reorganize the college.

The man selected was a preacher and an Irishman, who had to his credit eighteen months of schooling and, no doubt, an equal number of fights, who spent part of this time seeking learning in the same school with Andrew Jackson, and whom the trustees found teaching in South Carolina College. He delivered the commencement address at Georgia in 1811 and was the next day elected president. His name was the Reverend John Brown.[28] At the same time the trustees elected to instruct in mathematics Henry Jackson, an Englishman and a brother of Governor James Jackson, who three years later went as secretary of legation with William H. Crawford to France, where he remained until 1817. The University, having no money, could not offer him a salary— instead they promised him his board and room. To carry out the French tradition M. Grivot was hired to teach his native language, and John R. Golding and William Green were chosen for other

subjects. The University hoped to happen on money in some way
to pay them.[29]

These new managers set to work with doubtless more fears than
hopes, and succeeded in completely realizing all the former within
five years. The beginning of the end appeared in 1816 when the
trustees reduced Brown's salary to $1,000 and the others to $600
each. The crash now developed quickly. There had been too
much moral laxness; the rules had not been obeyed; Green was
a chief offender and must go. There was no money left, and the
attempt of the trustees to borrow $3,000 from banks or individuals
sufficiently interested in the University to lend miserably failed.
Thinking to resign would be more dignified than to be rudely dismissed, Brown got out in May. A few months later the resignation
of the remainder was demanded—and for a second time the University reverted to a state of nature. To provide the appearance of
life Golding was put in charge temporarily.[30] Thus had the trustees laid violent hands on the University and forced its dissolution
—perhaps with sufficient cause, but withal a dangerous practice
and one hereafter to be employed more than once.

The University, which had been so anxious for the health of
its students, was now itself sick nigh unto death. Baldwin was
dead, the legislature was not interested and new friends had not
become enthusiastic or numerous. The only thing the University
had worth while was its land, and it was questionable whether this
property was any longer an asset. People had squatted upon it
anywhere they pleased, and the University made no friends when
it attempted to dispossess them. Many who were not squatters
were purloiners and pilferers of whatever they could carry off.
Even staid Athenians were so prone to make mistakes in cutting
down University trees that the trustees bargained with them to
furnish University wood at $8 a year for each fireplace. Rents
were small and hard to collect; fields were washing away; and
fences were falling down. The Senatus Academicus could think
of nothing better than to sell the land for what it would bring, and
they so recommended it to the legislature. Permission was granted
in the latter part of 1815.[31]

But the University's patrimony was never so large and so ex-

tensive as it seemed. It had no 40,000 acres, and never had had
so much. Not over 25,000 acres had ever been surveyed. Of this
amount 5,000 acres had been sold to provide money for a beginning, a like amount had been located on lands already granted
to the soldiers and sailors of the Revolution (and, of course, was
lost), and another 5,000 acres had slipped away to South Carolina in a boundary dispute.[32] This trouble arose over the failure
of Georgia and South Carolina to agree on the stream which
formed the headwaters of the Savannah River. The land lay between the Keowee on the east and the Tugaloo on the west, and, of
course, if the Tugaloo were agreed upon as the Savannah, Georgia
lost the triangle between the two rivers. When the dispute broke
out in 1787, the old Confederation Congress suggested that the two
states settle it in a treaty between themselves, which was done in
the Beaufort Convention of the same year. In the trade, Georgia
accepted the Tugaloo in return for South Carolina's withdrawal
of claims south of the Altamaha River, with the provision that the
5,000 acres might be saved for the University if it were recorded
within a year after the ratification of the convention. Five months
after the ratification by both states, Noble W. Jones was commis-
sioned to secure South Carolina's approval of the grant, but the
secretary of state, choosing to call the making of the treaty its ratification, refused to record the grant. This was in June, 1788. For
fifteen years nothing more was done and then in 1803 the trustees
applied to a South Carolina judge for a writ of mandamus to force
the secretary of state to record the grant. But fearing the hostility
of the judge, they also appealed to the South Carolina legislature
for redress, and sent Thomas Peter Carnes and two assistants to
Columbia as their agents. For some reason Carnes failed to bestir
himself, and the legislature failed to act. He was sent back to
the next session and the legislature refused redress. Georgia then
ordered suit to be brought in the Federal Circuit Court, but nothing
came of it. Tradition long afterwards had it that Carnes developed
so great a liking for South Carolina tavern life and liquids that he
forgot to present the petition of the trustees.[33]

For some years to come the University attempted to sell its lands
to the best advantage, only to find too often that it could not give

clear title to what it had thought to be its own. In time the legislature agreed to give the University $100,000 in state bank stocks,
to be fully paid for from the land sales. With the state bank prosperous the University received $8,000 annually in interest, and
thus gained its first element of permanency.[34]

But signs of this stability and prosperity did not appear at once;
six months after Brown had left, the trustees had become so moribund that the interested few who were able to form a quorum
provided for trustees *pro tempore* as a safeguard against extinction—this in addition to the aid along this line the legislature had
given in 1808 when it provided that vacancies by death or resignation should not be filled until the number had been reduced to
seven.[35]

Soon after the departure of Brown to a home he had secured
near Athens, the University was suspended until January 1, 1817,
and shortly before the reopening General Peter Early was appointed president *pro tempore,* with John R. Golding, a son-in-law
of Brown's, and James Camak, a graduate of South Carolina College, as the faculty. The trustees, beginning to cast around for a
president immediately after Brown's resignation, soon hit upon the
Reverend Robert Finley, a resident of New Jersey and a graduate
and trustee of the College at Princeton. They promised him a salary of $1,500, which William H. Crawford, who saw him in
Washington soon afterwards, assured him would certainly be increased to $2,000 within a year. As an additional inducement the
trustees agreed to pay the expenses of his moving to Georgia—
which amounted to almost a thousand dollars. Little was said
about a large number of students or handsome and useful buildings, but he was sufficiently informed that there were "few health-
ier spots in the world than Athens, although it be in Georgia." The
college was sixteen years old "and the grave of a student is not
to be seen." This information the secretary of the faculty guaranteed to be correct. A former resident of New Jersey informed
Finley that in January "Our mornings and evenings are like your
pleasantest weather in June; and it is not uncomfortable in the
middle of the day, unless exposed to the sun." The feeling seemed
to prevail in Athens that Finley was the last hope. Golding, Camak,

the trustees unanimously, and even Brown begged him to come. Henry Jackson, who had about finished his diplomatic work in France, was expected back at any time and would take charge of "Chemistry, mineralogy, etc," with about $2,000 worth of equipment which he was bringing back.[36]

Finley was long in making up his mind, and was never quite sure that he had really decided—even after the crown had been offered him three times. His friends, he thought, had overrated him and were inducing him to take some steps "which in the end would be unpleasant to them as well as to" himself. But he crossed the Rubicon for weal or for woe; he gave up his trusteeship at Princeton and received a D.D.; he resigned from the congregation he was serving and from the academy where he was teaching and set out for Georgia in May with many misgivings in his heart. The passage from New York to Savannah took two weeks and despite a terrible waterspout and the "awful thunder and lightning which lasted all night" off the North Carolina coast, he made the trip one day quicker than it took to go from Savannah on to Athens, a distance of only 200 miles. The stage that bore him onward passed over roads "hilly and rough, through a new country and dreary."[37]

But this was progress, indeed, to be able to reach Athens by stage at all. It bespoke the growing wealth and importance of the back-country. This new stage would "render the conveyance more easy to the Students, and enable others to visit the College more frequently than they otherwise would have done." Athens was yet far from being a polished town—only seventeen years out of the wilderness. It owed its beginning and continued existence, however, to the University, and therefore was somewhat better off culturally than its straggling sister frontier villages. Furthermore, it had been taking on some growth: In 1801 it had one dwelling house; two years later it had three dwelling houses, three stores, and "a number of other valuable Buildings"; while in 1806 it had ten dwelling houses and four stores. In the beginning it had made such a healthy start that the trustees were constrained in 1804 to lay out streets to direct that growth; and, of course, when it had reached the age of five it had reached the age of discretion; so it was now allowed to manage its own affairs through three com-

missioners elected by the people. The first stagecoaches had come
just in time to give Finley a rough ride up from Augusta, but
Athens had the promise of a wagon road as early as 1803 when
one was projected into this "Western Country" and on to the South-
west. By 1806 the post road from Washington to New Orleans
had been pushed through, and the intellectual standing of the
Athenians was greatly enhanced by a weekly mail. Athenians
might also communicate with Augustans once a week. A few years
later, people were talking about opening navigation on the Oconee
River to the sea.[38]

But as long as red Indians were around—the "savage Creeks
and the gallant Cherokees"—students and townsmen found it difficult to convince themselves that they were not in fact on the frontier. Indeed, strange noises were to be heard around the University, as incongruous to the redman as the war whoop should have
been to a university. It was the buzz of college life: "The high-
sounding song of Homer, the sweet notes of Virgil, the stirring
narratives of Xenophon and Caesar, the denunciation, the suasion,
and the arguments of Tully, heard no more in the native land of
the philosopher, were familiar sounds on the air of Athens." And
these same students "knew the rising of the Pleiades and all the
gems of Orion's belt and the whole train of Ophiuchus huge."[39]
In fact, "gallant Cherokees" now and then entered the seat of
knowledge that they might learn to solve these mysteries, but with
all the indulgence and consideration heaped upon them by students
and teachers alike they soon tired of white men's ways and returned
to their homes in the hills to the northward.

These were the days before Georgia was defying presidents and
supreme courts in her determined efforts to push the Indians beyond the Mississippi; friendship prevailed especially between
Athenians and the Cherokees. Indian squaws came down out of
the mountains trudging along with loads of moccasins, deer skins,
jerked venison, and cane baskets, and struck bargains with the
students when they were not reciting Homer or measuring the rise
of the Pleiades. One of the Indian traders had taken a fancy to
the thirteen-year-old son of President Meigs and had got permission to take the boy 150 miles into the Cherokee nation to Vann-

town on the Etowah River. After a seven weeks' visit young Meigs returned dressed in Indian stockings, with a belt of wampum and other Indian knickknacks about him, riding an Indian pony—and for a time the students had one more Indian among them.[40]

In the War of 1812 while "Old Hickory" Jackson was devastating the lands of the Creeks over in Alabama, the Georgia Creeks as well as the Cherokees remained friendly. But when the war first broke out no one in Athens could tell what the Cherokees a few miles away might do. Four months after war had been declared, the report reached Athens that a mighty force of 300 or 400 painted Cherokees bent on capturing the University and scalping the students and townsmen had crossed the Apalachee River near Hog Mountain on their way to carry out this mischief. Garrulous old George Gilmer, lovable and frank, in his later life told how he led twenty men from Oglethorpe County to defend this seat of learning. A panic seized the town as the time for the Indians to approach drew near; the women and children took refuge behind the brick walls of the college edifice, and there spent the night, while the students marched out to battle with the savages. As the excitement wore off toward dawn, some of these University warriors fell asleep at their post of duty, and all returned the next day as proudly as if they had won a battle. It was a false alarm. By 1819 the Indian boundary had been moved fifty miles away, so far that Athens was never to be afraid of the Cherokees again. But these same Cherokees never tired of visiting the University to trade with the students and shoot arrows for their amusement— until 1838 when they were forced to leave their home in the Georgia hills for the regions beyond the Mississippi.[41]

When Finley reached Athens he found it old enough to begin to have some self-consciousness and pride. Meigs had described the Athenians in 1805 as "rude, uncivilized, proud, jealous, etc." He related how he had recently "got an excellent bell, which is heard four or five miles around, and the Quadrupeds, and Bipeds, too few of whom ever heard a Bell before, prick up their ears in amazement at the Prodigy." Soon he was longing "to see the civilized part of the United States once more—I have now been five years on the forlorn hope in the most advanced part of the

Frontier of land and light and science and civilization." But the people were soon developing the feeling that it was the business of an Athenian to appear polite and cultured. And if Athenian women were to be so, there must be "Female Education" for them. To fill this need Harriet Allen, the daughter of an Englishman, came to Athens in 1810 and set up a "Female School" nearby, where she became the arbiter of good taste and horticulture. The men to further their culture organized a "Dialectic Adelphic Society" in which they regaled one another with orations. In 1807 the Reverend John Hodges had a press and type loaded on a wagon in Philadelphia and wheeled to Athens, where he edited a religious paper for a short time. The next year the *Georgia Gazette* began to inform the Athenians on how Napoleon defeated the Austrians, what the Chinese were doing, what Jefferson said in his message to Congress—but little about Georgia and practically nothing about Athens. Did not everybody know all the local news —and often long before the editor could find it out? The last editor of this paper was Samuel W. Minor, whose poverty was so abject that he cooked, ate, slept, kept his family, and printed his paper—all in one room. Unable at times to find out what was happening on the other side of the earth, he was forced to print what he himself knew. On one occasion he informed his readers that "our sow" had given birth to nine beautiful pigs and that there were now bright prospects of his gaining economic independence. It was the *Athens Gazette,* of higher standing, that told Georgia of Finley's coming.[42]

Athens and the Lower South at this time were in the midst of laying the foundations of that social order and culture, beautiful and polished yet seamy, captivating the élite Englishman and practical Yankee who touched it, the admiration of some, the curse of some—born of the same womb that bore suspicions, hatreds, and the horrors of civil war. The great swing around the Gulf had set in which was to bring into the Union shortly Alabama and Mississippi and spread the cotton plantations to the Rio Grande. There was developing a leisure class who might play because slaves worked.

The "fathers of the Revolution," while not having black slaves conspicuously in mind as participants in that freedom and in those natural rights which played so big a part in their philosophy, nevertheless, contemplated no system whose essence should be those things now so vigorously denied. In the excitement of the Federal Constitutional Convention, Georgia had stood for the foreign slave trade, but she no sooner won it than she freely flung it away.[43] In 1819 at a banquet in Athens this toast was drunk: *"The* [Foreign] *Slave Trade*—The scourge of Africa; the disgrace of humanity. May it cease forever, and may the voice of peace, of Christianity and of Civilization, be heard on the savage shores."[44] At this time the whole subject of slavery was discussed in the Georgia papers with reason and dispassion, and in 1824 the president of the University "heard the Senior Forensic Disputation all day on the policy of Congress abolishing Slavery—much fatigued but amused."[45] Apparently the students were doing some thinking also. The trustees were, likewise, not opposed to a possible disposition of slavery, for Finley, whom they had just elected president of the University, had been one of the organizers of the American Colonization Society. He was, indeed, present in Washington at its birth and had been made one of its vice-presidents; and so vital did his work appear to one friend that he later wrote, "if this colony [Liberia] should ever be formed in Africa, great injustice will be done to Mr. Finley, if in the history of it, his name be not mentioned as the first mover, and if some town or district in the colony be not called Finley." He, indeed, never lost interest in the project to his dying day—and then it "gave consolation to his last moments."[46]

The South was genuinely interested in ridding itself of this incubus, realizing, with Henry Clay, that Negroes freed and not removed were a greater menace than if they remained in slavery. On arriving in Athens, Finley wrote back to New Jersey, "With men of reflection the colonizing scheme is as popular here, as with you in Jersey."[47] But it was immediately evident to Finley that the urge in the South was toward slavery rather than away from it, and its baneful effects were already too plainly to be seen. "Slavery," he said, "chills every ardour and retards every improvement, and it will continue to do so, for a long time to come." He noted that the comforts of life were "not attended to, nor any of its elegancies, either in buildings or furniture, either in dress or table. Morals low, correct ideas few, manners coarse, and religious knowledge nearly nothing. Yet some of the people seem to be sensible of all of this, and desirous to have it all changed. But irresolution, arising from inexperience, and the indolence connected with slavery, will make changes slow, unless northern and eastern people come in to show an example and to take a lead." Not only did this newcomer think the Georgians had no culture, they had no sense about agriculture and the skilled trades. The land would raise good crops "and would continue to do so if the people had any idea of manuring. They have none, but being principally emigrants from Old Virginia, they wear out a piece of land and leave it." Everybody seemed to be bent on buying slaves and raising cotton. As yet there was but little thought of making any improvements, "the country being new, and what is worse, the population fleeing and constantly moving off to the Alabama Territory." The mechanics were few and bad—nothing being "done to the satisfaction of those who have seen anything better. A tanner and a currier might make a fortune in a little time in any part of this country. A man who could make boots and shoes might choose his own business and on his own terms. A carpenter and joiner, with a common blessing, might get rich as fast as labour could enrich any one."[48] Finley's first impressions were not his best, yet they were substantially true. "Immense sums of money" were being made on cotton plantations; each slave was worth $200 annually exclusive of his support. By 1838 the Indians had been cleared out of Georgia to make room for black Negroes and white cotton. Athens was in this broad sweep westward of cotton plantations, and it had enough slaves when Finley arrived to make necessary laws against their assemblying and trading.[49]

Thus was Georgia in the making; that uniformity among the well-to-do which was to be termed later the ante-bellum aristocracy had not yet crystallized out. There was already an aversion to labor, but the slaves were treated well—at least visitors thought so—and an "open and friendly hospitality, particularly to strangers, is an ornamental characteristic of a great part of this people."[50]

Finley arrived in June, 1817, and was immediately set to work presiding at a trustees meeting which was about to take place. In the latter part of July he managed the commencement and preached the sermon on "the intimate connexion between the growth of true science and the success of true Christianity." He pleased everybody by the grace and ease with which he performed. But his heart sank deep down within him when he looked for the soul and body of the University. He dolefully wrote a few days after arriving, "It would require a good part of the remainder of my life, to organize and put in motion the concerns of the College." The more he learned about the condition of the University the more discouraged he became. It was "at the last gasp—forgotten in the public mind, or thought of only to despair of—neglected and deserted—the buildings nearly in a state of ruins— and the trustees doubtful whether it can ever be recovered." It was "in the lowest state that is possible; the contempt of the enemies of literature, the scorn of its own particular enemies, and the pity of those who were once its friends." "This is a picture not overdrawn," he averred. Only twenty-eight out of Brown's forty students were left.[51]

But a small number might be best after all; better to educate a few than to ruin many. And, indeed, there was no fixed assurance that he would not wreck the few or get destroyed himself, for his demeanor was "stern and commanding; and he could assume a countenance, voice and manner truly terrific. He often presented himself to the indolent and refractory, with a dark and menacing contour. . . ."[52]

At this time it was not uncommon for people to turn to their religious instincts for comfort, and thus did Finley come to consider himself more missionary than schoolmaster—"to view the college as designed in the providence of God to militate the condition of man and direct his heart to heaven." His task to Christianize his students was as difficult as it was to educate them, for, although some appeared to be willing, too many declared that they did not believe in the Bible and that they had never read a chapter. He did not find an organized congregation in the whole town, but he succeeded in securing about a dozen villagers who agreed to come into a Bible class, which later he developed into a Presbyterian congregation. He preached in the town and out in the country churches with the fervor of a Peter the Hermit. He dealt equally in the terrors and mercies of the Lord, and when he pleased never failed to draw tears from every eye.[53]

Although the University was low, he did not think it was past mending. He told the trustees a better library was needed, more philosophical apparatus ought to be bought, a new building built, and the old ones repaired, and he suggested that the legislature be asked to pay for these things. In no way could he have shown more certainly his lack of acquaintance with Georgia. Speedily disillusioned he "voluntarily offered his own services in the delicate and ungracious business in courting public bounty." He set out on the dusty hot road, a footpad, an impecunious University beggar, into a half dozen of the surrounding counties—all in the "sickly season, and indeed, while a bilious epidemic was considerably prevalent in some of the lower counties," and thereby "imbibed the seeds of a disease that cut short his useful labours, and bereaved the institution of so valuable an acquisition in the very dawn of its prosperity."[54]

But this stern old Presbyterian had been begging people for their souls as fervently as for their dollars—gone six weeks, he delivered sixteen sermons, and left no account of a single dollar raised. He returned weak and languid, but he heard the cry of the Macedonians on all sides and he attempted to answer until he was forced to his bed where he died of a bilious and typhus affliction in the late summer of 1817. The going of Finley was lamented widely and in a genuine fashion. The trustees, "as demonstrative of their veneration for the lamented deceased and their regards for his respected family," gave his children their education free of tuition, presented his widow two town lots, and erected a $200 marker over his grave. The trustees here went far beyond cold business practice. In thus dealing with the Finleys, strangers in a strange land, they gave a concrete expression to that hospitality later to be erected into a tradition. With only a few months' labor done and a workable plan for the school's future growth developed, it seemed strange and mysterious that death should intervene—a fate against which the people should rebel had they known how. To Finley's New Jersey friends it was "awful and impenetrable to the view of mortals"; to a Georgia friend "No death was ever more deeply felt, or more generally lamented, in this region, than this." And now once more the University was left "to the dubious issue of wayward contingencies."[55] Finley had started to hold the University up before the people, display it as it was, beg them for contributions sufficient to keep it from starving; and doubtless he hoped eventually to convert the legislature through a backfire from the people—the true formula for any University of the people.

CHAPTER III

HOW THE UNIVERSITY WORKED

 WHETHER true scientifically or not, it is correct axiomatic lore that it is darkest just before dawn. Finley stayed just long enough to build up buoyant hopes only suddenly to demolish them by his untimely death. Some people doubtless felt that the Fates were against the University. For a year it staggered along without a head; then the trustees prevailed on the Reverend Nathan S. S. Beman, a Vermont Yankee, at that time conducting an academy at Mt. Zion in Georgia, to take charge, *pro tempore*, and offered him $500 for expenses in removing to Athens. Beman was hesitant and soon conveniently found that he could not come because his wife was "in a low and perhaps the last stages of a chronic affliction of the Liver." The trustees now elected the Reverend Ebenezer Porter of Andover, Massachusetts, who, however, could not be induced to accept. Henry Jackson, who was about to return from the French legation, might have had the job but he would rather be the professor he already was "because being less an object of terror to the students" he could "serve them and consequently the state the more effectually."[1]

Georgia was full of New England schoolmasters relieving the planters of the task of whipping their headstrong young sons, but the managers of the University trust seemed unable to induce these academy masters to try their hands at making those sons into men. Then in 1819, in November, the Reverend Moses Waddel was induced to give up the academy business and to take charge of the University. Ever since the age of fourteen (1784) he had been busily teaching and preaching himself into a fame that had by this time spread over the whole Southeast. He had taught John C. Calhoun and married his sister, and had started William H. Crawford and George McDuffie on the road to learning, as well as many other South Carolinians and Georgians. He had been born in North Carolina, had been educated for the ministry in Virginia, had preached in Georgia, and was at the time of his election to the University conducting his famous academy at Willington, South Carolina. He was the first native-born Southerner to fill the presidency, which is an important fact not because of any concern the South had for a person's nativity, but because the South had by this time progressed far enough intellectually to produce a first-rate educator.

Filled either with excitement or grim determination, he appeared before the Senatus Academicus and subscribing to the oath of office in the big minute book, bore down so heavily on the thick rag paper that he almost cut through the page. Jackson was soon to be back to join "in one more effort to raise the institution from its languishing condition." Alonzo Church, who hereafter for the next forty years was to become part and parcel of the ante-bellum establishment, appeared at the same time. Ebenezer Newton completed Waddel's first faculty. Now for the first time was the University about to impress itself on the state—to get talked about more widely, to win more loyal friends and more bitter enemies, to develop strength and boldness.[2]

How did this institution work? What was its internal organization? What did it teach and how? Baldwin, Meigs, Brown, and Finley had come and gone. How had they busied themselves? As previously noted, the Senatus Academicus was at the head of all the state's educational doings, a body of politicians coming and going with the elections, generally talking intelligently about education but never risking action, unwieldy from the start, and finally dying in 1859 a natural death. It elected the president, whereas the trustees might hire the faculty. Thus was the president put a

notch above the faculty and his authority over professors thereby
increased. The trustees were required to report annually "all
their actings and doings," to the Senatus Academicus.[3] More directly in control of the University were these trustees, who were a
self-perpetuating closed corporation. Even with such powers they
failed to develop much energy or many ideas—they did not often
feel important enough even to become tyrannical or troublesome.
They were long an easy-going hospitable assemblage, who had little
money at their command and were almost over-generous with that
little, providing for the widow and children of a deceased president or for the widow of a professor who was elected but who never
reached his post of duty. So neglectful did the trustees become
at times that the legislature stepped in to increase or decrease their
number—and in 1823 to pass a ruling that any trustee who should
be absent from two meetings should lose his seat. An institution
even no more complicated than this University must have wheels
and then other wheels within wheels, and so the prudential committee was evolved. A few of the trustees living in Athens were
so designated and were given the power and duty to wander
around the campus at unexpected times, to happen in on examinations and lectures, to inspect the library, to see that the buildings were kept in repair, to be a sort of real estate board to sell lots
in town, to hire servants and a tutor now and then, and to "have an
eye to the duties of the Faculty, touching the police of the college."[4]

The gates of knowledge were sufficiently guarded—principally
by Latin and Greek sentries. Those who would enter had to be able
"to read, translate, and parse Cicero, Virgil, and the Greek Testament, and to write true latin in prose; and shall also have learned
the rules of vulgar arithmetic; and shall produce satisfactory evidence of a blameless life and conversation." In 1822, George
Matthews passed his examinations on everything except character.
He was, however, admitted, but "with a warning that he should
be dismissed as soon as he manifested any signs of insubordination." It was soon discovered that "his character was not such as
can be tolerated by the officers of the institution"; so he was privately dismissed. No passports in these days were honored; all who

would enter should be examined, either privately or in groups, in the chapel at commencement times.   If any person should feel himself so advanced in knowledge as to want to enter a higher class he was required to stand an examination on all courses for which he sought credit and to advance all the fees he would have paid had the work been done at the University.   It was later provided that these fees should not be collected if he came properly recommended from a Georgia college.   To further protect its stock in trade, the University forbade a student receiving outside instruction without permission of the president and trustees.   Also any student who found himself suspended from college was compelled to pay tuition for the time lost.[5]

In the beginning a student might enter at the tender age of thirteen and thereby grow into an educated man at sixteen.   Discussion, vigorous and long, developed on this point.   The trustees decided in the 'thirties that the University was for young men— "not for the commencement of the studies of boys and the irregularities which must necessarily result, from having almost children introduced into situations where with half-formed judgments they are but too apt to run into excesses and improprieties of almost any kind."   They now fixed the age for freshmen at sixteen.[6]

There was an institution at hand which helped to solve this and other problems; it was Meigs' Grammar School.   When students were too young or unprepared for college, they might be kept here. The state gave $2,000 in 1819 for its better equipment, largely because it had been run free from tuition.   Its prosperity was proved by the seventy boys it had in 1821, all awaiting the proud day when they could enter the University.   The University students looked down upon these boys with contempt, and nothing could be more distasteful to them than for themselves to be sentenced to this ridiculous place.   This the faculty, soon discovering, used as a club to produce better lessons, and at times quite forgetful of their logic, to punish perfectly brilliant students for too much cunning.   The Senatus Academicus gave the faculty specific permission to banish "all and every refractory or negligent student" in the two lower classes to the Grammar School for not more than three months.   Anyone refusing to go should suffer expulsion.

President Waddel noted in 1825 that he had "recd 2 students from rustication in the Grammar School." This edifice became a special object of attack by the students, who battered it much and defiled its doors. In 1828 the prudential committee, while waiting for their mail at the post office, made rules to protect the building; but these campus managers were more prudent than watchful, for the next year the trustees were calling for the punishment of a student who had offered an indignity to the building—"to make a signal example of him." The school was finally discontinued in 1829.[7]

For the greater part of its ante-bellum life the University stuck to the beaten track of the classics. But, as previously noted, French early gained a foothold and hung on intermittently, and with the coming of independence to the Spanish-American countries the Spanish language loomed into importance. In 1826 the Senatus Academicus, moved largely by political sympathy for the new republics, argued strongly for the teaching of the Spanish language in the University, but it was never able to induce the legislature to appropriate money for this purpose. It was argued that recent happenings had "rendered the Spanish language more important even than the French." In 1831 the trustees decided that modern languages must be taught and they set out in search of a professor of Spanish, Italian, French, and German. They found William Lehman in Pittsfield, Massachusetts, a German Lutheran who had been educated at Bonn, Germany, and made him professor of almost all the languages of Babel still spoken. He remained for eleven years, and then for the next eleven years Latin and Greek held the field undisputed. In 1853 Emanuel V. Scherb came to instruct in French, and left the next year. Thereafter, until 1868, the modern languages rested. Much argument was made for this branch of learning, but it was never securely established in ante-bellum times.[8]

In the early 'thirties a considerable movement was started against the ancients and their worthlessness for modern people; but just as the Spanish-American wars had given the modern language protagonists an advantage, now the Greek revolt had turned the thoughts of the people romantically toward the splendors of ancient Greece. The students got so excited over the Greeks struggling so heroically against the terrible Turks that they organized meetings of sympathy among themselves and succeeded in raising $166 for the sons and daughters of Helen. About this time an actual Grecian named John D. Diomatari, born in Ipsara, drifted into Athens and entered the freshman class at the University. He was supported by the Presbyterian Educational Society until he was discovered deep in the pastimes of his fellow students —and then all aid from the churchmen ceased. He had been caught playing at the "unlawful game of cards"; and what was worse (which always followed cards) he developed fighting instincts. One day he attacked a fellow without proper provocation, and although he later apologized the faculty admonished him and put him on probation for twelve months. Ordinarily such offenses carried severer penalties, but in this case the faculty felt "disposed to look upon his conduct as arising from his imperfect knowledge of our manners and language, and from a highly sanguine temperament." Later he was fined $5 for being in a disorderly room, and he finally left the University in his senior year without standing his examinations. But the trustees could not forget that he was a native of a country which had given us so much; therefore, they remitted his unpaid tuition and gave him his degree. He later justified this confidence as American consul to Athens, Greece.[9]

But the combined sentiment for Greek and Grecian could not make many thoughtful people forget that the University failed to touch education at its most vital and practical points. There should be more about people and less about words. Why should the people not know something about their own history? The eighteenth century philosophers had given American history a permanent position. In 1837 President Alonzo Church called for the preservation of the early records of Georgia history and induced the Senatus Academicus to ask the legislature for $5,000 with which to do this work. It also asked for $4,000 more to pay for sending a trained person to London to get copies of the early colonial documents.[10]

In 1843 William B. Stevens was elected to teach belles lettres and rhetoric, and although he confined himself to these subjects, he was greatly interested in history. In 1839 he had helped to found the Georgia Historical Society and had begun to collect material for his *History of Georgia,* the first volume of which was published in 1847. He left in 1848 to preach in an Episcopal church in Philadelphia, and was later made Bishop of Pennsylvania. Richard M. Johnston in 1857 was made professor of belles lettres, evidence of Christianity, and history—marking the first actual recognition of history in the University.[11]

Efforts were made in 1838 to introduce political economy, without success; but the more practical subject of law was soon to be taught. Ed. Harden opened a private law school in Athens in 1840, and three years later the University promoted a law school under Joseph Henry Lumpkin, who two years later became the first chief justice of the newly-established State Supreme Court.[12] The interesting and practical 'thirties also saw an attempt to set up a school of civil engineering, but the legislature could not be prevailed upon to grant the necessary aid. The department of mathematics with its various instruments had long given a practical touch to its teachings—in 1818 James Camak of that department had been appointed by the state to help run the Georgia-Tennessee line.

But the most valuable aid the University could give the state would be along agricultural lines. The economic life of the South was one continuous series of exhilarations and depressions. Cotton was king, but too often were the people forced to reflect that they were his abject slaves. "The Red Old Hills of Georgia" might appear beautiful in song and poetry, but in real life they were becoming redder and poorer. Was there nothing in science and learning that could administer to the needs of agriculture? The state government was too deep in the eternal circle of debating to know or perhaps care, but William Terrell would make an effort to find out. In 1854 he gave the University $20,000 for the purpose of setting up a department of agriculture. Daniel Lee became the first professor, and to make life easier and more pleasant for him, he was relieved of all campus policing.[13]

Before the University had been actually founded, it was realized that one of the best ways to promote knowledge was through a library, and so in 1800 the trustees appropriated $1,000 for books and scientific apparatus. Meigs, with his mathematical mind, sent to London and bought more apparatus than books, so that the library was forced in 1806 to resort to the common device of a lottery to raise $3,000 for books. The legislature gave permission to hold the lottery, but there is no evidence that it was ever acted upon. The few books that were got together were of a scientific nature, conforming to the early atmosphere that pervaded the University. In 1812 the students were complaining that not a single historical book was to be had, and that the whole library was so insignificant as to be negligible. Two years later an attempt was made to borrow $2,000 from the legislature, but the value of books was too generally unappreciated and the spirit of being contented and even boasting over ludicrously small things was already too prevalent. The report went out in 1818 from a boasting Athenian that "the Library now contains more volumes of the most approved Historians, Poets, etc. than will be read by any student whilst in college."[14]

The University lent its aid to Jefferson in his attempt to have the tariff on books removed, and with the increase in the number of books being published and with the lowering of prices, the library began to make a respectable beginning. As the religious denominations began to grow in the South, the library started to fill itself up with theological works—to such an extent that the trustees in 1834 called for a halt and recommended that hereafter the president purchase more works "from other departments of learning and Science." Shortly thereafter Governor George R. Gilmer, a great friend of the University, gave the library a collection of bound newspapers which had accumulated in the executive office, and later willed the University his valuable private library. About this time the British government gave the library ninety volumes of the acts and debates of Parliament. In 1840 Franklin College, as the institution was generally known in ante-bellum times, had more books than any other college in the South or West excepting the University of Virginia and South Carolina College. In 1860 it had 13,000 volumes.[15]

The library was never considered important enough to have a building of its own; neither did it have a librarian. It was kept in some spare room in one of the college buildings and migrated around as necessity required. In 1830 it was almost completely destroyed in a fire which gutted New College. In order to provide for the expenses of the library, students were at first required to pay a fee when they used a book, and anyone who should do violence to a book should pay whatever damage the president might require. Freshmen and sophomores, who were considered as not yet having sufficient regard for books, might not remove them from the library; other students might not have out more than three at any one time.[16]

Closely allied to a library and generally kept close by were certain curios and relics. Meigs had begun the collection of a museum of natural history. In 1830 George I. S. Walker gave the University 154 gold, silver and copper coins of various nations; William Cumming gave sixty more of different kinds; and William Shields gave some "valuable antiquities of Greece and Rome." A few years later, when the missionaries had begun the conquest of the Hawaiian Islands, someone gave the University some "specimens of rare minerals from the awful Crater of Mona Loa in Owyhee." The fire which burned the library also destroyed most of the apparatus—philosophical, mathematical, and otherwise. Within a few years, however, the University secured again chemical equipment, geological specimens, and other laboratory fixtures, and in 1834 it purchased "a very excellent" telescope from London.[17]

Library, museum, and laboratory were not nearly so beautiful (and some people said no more serviceable) than the botanical garden. Baldwin, even before the University charter had been written, suggested the development of a plot of land where agricultural experiments might be made and observations on botany and natural history taken.[18] In 1833 the more ornate side of this idea was acted upon, and a botanical garden resulted. Two years previously Malthus A. Ward of Salem, Massachusetts, had been elected to teach natural history, and it was largely due to him that this interesting experiment was begun. John Bishop, a native of

England, was directly in charge. The trustees took a great interest in the garden, requiring an annual report on it and appropriating for its upkeep each year $600. It soon became the greatest attraction in town—a showplace which visitors must invariably see. It was a veritable Garden of Eden with hills and valleys, two sparkling brooks, a lake containing "a few perch and a harmless alligator," and over 2,000 plants, shrubs, and trees from every corner of the globe. The fame of the garden became widespread. Newspapers as far away as New York wrote descriptions of it;[19] the French government presented a cutting from the weeping willow at Napoleon's grave on St. Helena to William H. Crawford, which found its way into the garden and grew into a large tree;[20] two naval officers presented the garden a bunch of plants from the Cape of Good Hope; and off-shoots from the Washington Elm on Cambridge Commons and from the Charter Oak did honor to the nation's past.[21]

This beauty spot was not only a great aid to the students studying natural history, it was also equally valuable in lending charm to the romantic encounters of the students with Athenian maidens. It was the town's first and only park—"a favorite place of resort for the ladies." The trustees believed it to be of great esthetic value, uplifting and ennobling: "Its salutary influence upon the mind and heart will not be denied. Few, if any, instances can be cited of bad men devoted to the study of nature." It would help turn the minds of the wealthy students from idleness and vice. "Who," the trustees inquired, "would exchange the respect and veneration which the illustrious Humboldt secured by his study of nature for the homage which mere power can ever command?"[22]

As the garden grew in size it became more expensive, and by the 'forties the trustees were greatly troubled about the cost of keeping it going. Ward left in 1842; natural history was dropped from the curriculum, and talk of disposing of the garden was heard. In 1844 a committee reported that the funds of the University did not warrant the keeping of "this elegant and valuable appendage to Franklin College"; but it was seen that it could not be sold for anything comparable to what had been expended upon it; so the annual appropriation was cut to $300. President Church was greatly attached to the garden, and when no further money could be secured for its maintenance, he called upon a hundred old graduates to give $100 apiece to save it. In writing to an alumnus in 1854 he asked to be pardoned for "the zeal of the old man, who has been 35 years connected with the institution" and who felt as if he had "nothing else, of a worldly nature, to live for—and am conscious that what I do, I must do quickly." Two years later the garden was sold for $1,000—and, doubtless in the hope of pleasing the esthetic nature of the "old man," the trustees decided that the money should be used to erect a fence around the campus, to build a gateway, and to plant trees.[23]

What the students generally learned in the garden was not part of the prescribed course of study; yet without a doubt this pleasant retreat was a valuable laboratory attachment to the course in natural history as long as it was taught.

Another activity of the students more engaging and widespread in its interest than the garden was militia drill—the earliest example of military training in American colleges. Liberty won might not be liberty preserved unless there was eternal vigilance with it. Born at first of a fear of European nations and fed by the ever-present dangers of Indian raids, the feeling soon seized the American people that every man must be a soldier. Militia laws were among the first passed by the independent states and they were forever being tinkered with as time went on. In 1807, Georgia, fearing that another war with the British was inevitable, had pretty well codified her laws on the subject. Every man in the state, citizen or alien, between the ages of eighteen and forty-five, was held to be a soldier, unless he was a preacher of the Gospel, and was required to go through maneuvers and evolutions at least five times a year—one regimental muster for the whole county and four company drills for the militia district.[24]

All students who were eighteen and many who claimed to be got their notices regularly to appear properly armed and equipped for the various musters, and for positive enjoyment and rough hilarity nothing in a student's life could equal a militia muster unless it were, perhaps, a circus. Muster day became a great social institution in the life of the whole community, breaking the monotony of an age which knew not automobiles, moving pictures, and a hundred other excitements of the twentieth century. All the rowdies and rough characters of an unpolished age came to fight, gouge, and get drunk. The law attempted to preserve order by declaring that any by-stander who should "interrupt, molest, or insult" anyone drilling should be arrested and confined not more than a day nor less than six hours, and what was much worse should not be allowed during the time "to drink any spirituous liquors." Any soldier or non-commissioned officer who should "behave himself disobediently or mutinously" or should break ranks without permission, or should "appear on parade drunk," or should "quarrel himself, or promote a quarrel among his fellow soldiers" should be arrested, disarmed, and thrown into jail for a whole day, and besides be fined from two to ten dollars. The ludicrous situations that developed where untrained officers attempted to marshal in battle array a ragtag mob of rough merrymakers, may be readily imagined by those with a less fertile brain than an Augustus Baldwin Longstreet, who described a militia muster in one of his "Georgia Scenes."[25]

Naturally occasions which might draw such penalties would afford rare enjoyment to restless students bored by too many lessons and no end of rules. Students eighteen or beyond snapped their fingers at college rules, attended the musters as a patriotic duty, and when the annual general muster came, a holiday was likely to follow. This drill was always held at the county seat, and as Athens was long to give way to Watkinsville in this honor, the students had the additional thrill of leaving town. Now and then a literary society meeting would be largely broken up by the "unavoidable absence of most of the members on military duty at Watkinsville." There was so much fun attached to being soldiers that the students could not forego drilling oftener than five times a year; so they formed companies of their own to march around under the trees on the campus at spare times, to dress in blue coats, white trousers, big brass buttons, and high caps, and parade at commencement times and on the Fourth of July celebrations—even to march boldly up and salute old President Waddel.

By name they were the "Franklin Blues," the "College Riflemen," or whatever the whim of the day might suggest. On a campus tree or a building or in the town paper might appear such a notice as this: *"College Riflemen appear on parade in the rear of the Apparatus Room tomorrow at three o'clock, P.M. precisely."* Their elections for officers gave early and valuable training in the gentle art of politics, which they sometimes applied to the militia elections among the grown-ups in town. They would likely note the inevitable wooden soldier standing at attention in the town paper, with the high cap surmounted by a still higher plume, cross straps on his breast, white trousers, and polished boots, and the "broom stick" under his arm. This meant either a parade or a militia election—students liked both. In one instance they ran away with the election and chose as major Pack Wells, a livery stable keeper, all because they owed him money and thought by this compliment to get more time or absolution entirely.[26]

The wars the United States periodically found herself in produced real military enthusiasm on the campus. In 1812 a company of students formed and drilled with serious purposes in mind. An occasional Indian war lent zest to their drilling, and in 1836 Joseph Law, a senior, left for the Seminole struggle before his examinations. The trustees voted him his degree for this show of patriotism. This was the period in which the Texans were fighting for their independence—all surrounded by a halo of romance in the eyes of the Georgia students. They organized the "College Volunteers" and considered it so important an occasion that the literary societies for years afterwards adjourned on the anniversary to celebrate it more properly.[27]

From the very beginning it was quite certain that the professors would not look with equanimity on activities that gave the students so much pleasure, and especially when such activities led to the breach of two well-fixed rules of the College. In the first place the students were not allowed to leave town—and of all places, they were not supposed to go to Watkinsville, the county seat; and secondly, there should be no firearms in college. But for what use is a soldier except he have a gun—so the law thought, and the governor thereupon sent up a wagon load of rifles from Milledgeville and gave each student-soldier one. But students in those days were dangerous enough without such weapons—with guns might they not drive all the professors off the campus and even menace some of the townsmen? President Waddel was much worried. Reënforced by the trustees he called upon the governor to withdraw the deadly weapons, and save the school from serious riots. The faculty started a campaign to confiscate the guns and notified the captain of the student army "that every gun hereafter found in college will be taken by the faculty and will never be delivered up till they are called for by a legal officer to be conveyed to Milledgeville."[28]

To put a stop to these organized military raids of students over the campus and around town (drilling, they called it), Waddel and the trustees declared that there was "great evil, of compelling students of college to keep firearms, and perform military duty," and called upon the legislature to exempt all students of schools, public and private, from military duty in time of peace. Arguing further against military training, the trustees said, "They believe that the whole community, especially in a government like ours, has an interest in the Education of the youth of the country, which very far outweighs any benefit that can be derived from the military service of those who are pursuing their collegiate duties—and they think it cannot be doubted, that a participation in the ordinary parades of the militia, is calculated to distract the mind of the students, and to disqualify him for the performance of his peculiar duties." The legislature did not act, but the trustees proceeded in 1836 to abolish the volunteer companies (which were not protected by the militia laws), and set an oath which all students were required to take on entering college, that they would not join the old company or organize another.[29]

The students thought it an outrage not to be allowed to develop and grow into soldier patriots—they immediately petitioned the trustees for a volunteer company and were refused. They debated the subject in their literary societies and easily decided that students should be *compelled* to muster, that the militia system should not be abolished, even that the trustees should hire a professor of military affairs.[30] After the Mexican War, soldiering among the students gradually died out, until the profound emotions growing out of secession and war completely demolished the peaceful composure of the students.

War-making was never on the schedule to be taught the students; religion occupied a somewhat different position. Meigs was much like Jefferson in the belief that the University should not be tied to the religious chariot, as was the case with the other colleges of that time. And thus it was that the University started out more scientific than religious, but with the coming of Brown, it fell into the hands of preacher presidents from whom it was not to depart for a hundred years. As the separation of church and state was a fixed American contribution to statecraft, a state university could not be expected to deal directly with religious doctrines and teachings, but certain religious trimmings were added in the very beginning—borrowed from Yale College. The school day should break with prayer, and the sun should sink in the west upon the students praying. At six o'clock in the morning the prayer bell rang and again at five in the afternoon.

For the first half dozen years of its life, the University was forced to get along without a chapel, but in 1807 Hope Hull, a Methodist preacher and a trustee, offered to get a chapel erected on the campus if the trustees would give him $100. It was to be 60 feet by 40 feet and 18 feet high, connected to a belfry at the back. The chapel should be University property, and should not be used by one denomination more than by another. Hull found considerable difficulty in raising enough money to complete the building, but with a contribution of $50 from Major General Twiggs and another one of $200 from Peter Randolph and with $689 of his own money, he had it finished by the end of 1808. The trustees, who had expected to get a chapel for $100, now found that honor required them to reimburse Hull—and being honorable men, they paid him $689.[31] Though not being taught religious doctrines, the students were brought under religious influences at such unholy times as to cause them to greatly dislike it, as will amply appear hereafter.

The University was rigorous in its standards of scholarship and undeviating in its fixed scheme of operating. Students had no rights that need be respected—in fact they were not supposed to be important enough to have rights. They were in college for a definite purpose, which had been fixed. It was not for them to question—obedience should be their watchword. As a rule there was no cordiality between students and their professors; fear on the one side and suspicion on the other were the common relationships. If a professor was popular with his students he was likely considered a failure.

Knowledge was held to be a definite fixed quantity, and students must learn what was set before them. Student thinking was reduced to the vanishing point in the college scheme; but an irreducible minimum was forced into the student, of natural philosophy, of classical lore, of literature, and when he passed out into the world of affairs, he had something definite, however imperfect it might have been—and this certain knowledge did not fail to reappear in the careers of Southern leaders. The College was narrow and autocratic, but for that very reason it made a powerful impress on the students. Sharp instruments pierce deeper than blunt ones.

The art of orating was much with the students and they generally liked it. The climate, the social system, the college training made Southerners excel in oratory—florid and exaggerated as it was. Customs and rules changed, but at one time or another, two students from the three lower classes were required every evening after prayers to "pronounce pieces previously committed to memory" and receive instruction in elocution; "forensic disputation" was required of juniors every two months, and seniors should deliver orations of their own composition once a month. Throughout it all, they were supposed to learn what gestures were required to build Rome, destroy Carthage, how Regulus should address the Senate or Spartacus the gladiators, how Napoleon lost the Battle of Waterloo—or, indeed, how Patrick Henry chose liberty or death. At commencement times there were three long days of orating, declaiming, and "forensic disputing."[32]

There was no room in college for laggards; if a student should fall behind in his work, his professor should "admonish him of such deficiency that he may be incited to apply with greater diligence to study," and if for the next six months he showed no improvement he should "be degraded to next lower class, or dismissed from the College." Banishment to the Grammar School was another penalty that might be imposed, as previously noted. The three students highest in "proficiency in learning" were made honor students and had the pleasure of hearing their names announced at commencement. As further rewards for learning, shining pieces of gold were not considered worthy; instead, Cicero in ten volumes and Homer in four "handsomely bound, gilt, and lettered" were held up to be strived for. To the best students entering the University certain Greek, Latin, and mathematics prizes were offered with the additional honor of having their names and their academy teachers' names published.[33]

Various methods of conducting classes were used. Oral questioning was generally resorted to with freshmen and sophomores, while juniors and seniors were required to "take down in writing, the substance of all the principal points" in the lectures and these notes should afterwards "be exhibited to the lecturer for examination and correction." During their first two years the students had three classes a day, while during the last two, only two classes were required. The day began early with prayers at sunrise and immediately following (before breakfast!) the freshmen recited arithmetic, the sophomores wrestled with Horace, and the juniors dealt in logic. One of the most valued prerogatives of a senior was to have no classes before breakfast. In 1828, in a moment of weakness, the faculty abolished all classes before breakfast on Mondays.[34]

The calendar for the school year was made a plaything by the faculty, trustees, and the Academicians. In the early days they divided the year into four quarters, later they made three terms, and in 1861 they decided two terms were enough. Practically throughout the whole ante-bellum period, the three-term system prevailed. Georgia was unique in her vacation times. Illogical as it may seem, the year did not commence with commencement in August, but rather in January.[35] There was a long vacation and two short breathing spells. Every college in the country had a long summer vacation except Georgia; here it began in the first part of November and lasted until the middle of January. Following commencement "the students shall be indulged with eight days of relaxation," and in the first part of April between the second and third terms there was a spring vacation of about ten days known as senior vacation and participated in only by seniors. The most logical explanation of this winter vacation is the fact that Savannah and the coast country, largely dominating the University, ran the school in the summer when Athens was agreeable and the coast torrid, and closed school in the winter when the up-country was cold and Savannah balmy.[36]

Vacation times were great occasions in college life. According to the rules the faculty might pursue the students even into this period with books to read and subjects to study, but it is safe to say that these worthy taskmasters never stood on this right, for the students immediately fled town and gown on the first hint of freedom. The winter vacation sent them back home for two months and a half; the other two vacations, short ones, saw them going in every direction. These two vacations were looked forward to with greater eagerness, perhaps, than the winter vacation. A musing student wrote in 1857, "After several months of moderate drinking at the Pierian fount, we are again freed from College duties . . . to drink of the sparkling waters of pleasure and refreshment." Some went home, some heeded the call of the "girl they left behind," while some heeded the call of the girl they had not yet met, some went as far as Charleston, South Carolina, in their rambles, but most heard the call of the wild—and into the up-country they went, "rambling over the mountains and gazing with admiration upon the wild and romantic scenery of Tallula." Wagons and tents were engaged for this rough outing up to the Great Tallulah Falls and the gorge, to Mount Yonah and the Nacoochee Valley, into the land of Indians and romance and the beauties of nature. Another attraction second only to Tallulah was Stone Mountain with the high tower to be climbed, there to survey the panorama in all directions, of cotton plantations interspersed among the green pine woods—the Babylon-looking Atlanta had not yet crept up from behind the tree tops.[37]

Occasionally a few stray students and a professor, getting out of the beaten path, wandered into South Georgia, the land of sand hills and wire grass, where lived some of the most abject of all the "poor white trash." It was on such a trip once that a bunch of students and their professor-guide came upon a one-room cabin in the clearing at nightfall and finally after allaying suspicion were given sleeping quarters in one corner, curtained off by a sheet. The only cooking utensil was a frying pan which the house-woman used for frying meat, baking bread, and making coffee. They were almost horrified to see the same pan serving as a foot bowl after supper. The visitors decided on potatoes roasted in the ashes as their only food for breakfast.[38]

These trips were generally made during the spring vacation; the favorite pastime for "the eight days of relaxation" following commencement was to go to some of the watering-places—Indian Springs, Madison Springs, Franklin Springs—there to have a round of pleasure with ladies and gentlemen from far and wide. By 1830 stages were running to Indian Springs and Madison Springs and to the gold diggings of Habersham and Hall. Madison Springs was long a first choice for many reasons. One student (in 1855) liked it because it was "a nice quiet place—everything so cheap—I once bought a dozen large oranges there for two bits." These watering places were institutions of wide-spread influence in the South where family alliances were contracted and politics of national importance done up; and they were not half so quiet as the Franklin College student apparently claimed. They were "dens of iniquity and sin" according to the preachers who drifted there now and then for their health's sake. The Reverend Stephen Olin, a professor in the University, visited Madison Springs in 1826, and after enjoying it for some time came away uttering denunciations of it: "Here is a small village consisting of some twenty or thirty cabins and a huge boarding house. It is the great resort of fashion, disease, and sin; though the waters and the place do not cure, they aggravate two of the evils."[39]

Associating with interesting people at watering-places and enjoying the wild beauties of nature in the mountains, students were too likely to forget all about the re-commencement of school back at Athens. To spur them to return on time a fine of fifty cents a day was levied for each day's absence "without a substantial reason," and no fines were to be excused for less than a month's absence.[40]

Examinations were based on the assumption that the students had been amassing a sum of knowledge which tended to unify and coalesce into a related whole—not filling little compartments from textbooks unrelated and to be speedily forgotten when the crisis had been successfully passed. Therefore, the examinations at the close of the first two terms were mere harbingers of the seaching inventory to be taken at commencement times "on all the studies of the preceding year." The senior examination was guarded with particular care because the Bachelor of Arts degree was given those who were successful. This examination was "a general one, upon all the studies of both the two last and many of the preceding years," or as the rules ran, it should be "rigid, and extend to the whole course of collegiate literature" and only those found "well skilled in the liberal arts and sciences" should be given degrees. Following their vacation the seniors devoted their whole time to reviewing their past four years' work against the day of their examination, which was held from four to six weeks before commencement in order that they might have an opportunity to enjoy the beauties of an untrammeled existence before the greatest occasion in college life came—commencement. It was during this special senior vacation that some of the worst disorders on the campus occurred. The withholding of degrees was finally resorted to as a curb to over-exuberance of feeling and action.

"The test of the pudding is the taste thereof" is a saw honored with age and truth. Examination times were tasting times and this tasting should be done by more than the cooks only. In the original charter a board of visitors was established "to see that the interest of this institution is carried into effect," but its duties were so intangible that it never got out of the charter until someone discovered that attending examinations would be a befitting work for such a board. It first took on flesh and blood in 1811 when three trustees were named as visitors. Later the number was increased to fifteen and membership was not limited to the trustees. The most distinguished men in the state were generally named and urged to attend the senior examinations as well as the others. In 1855 among those composing it were Joseph E. Brown, Thomas R. R. Cobb, and C. C. Jones.[41] The lists were not closed against any persons who wanted to attend. In 1825 President Waddel noted with pride that "the Governor and many trustees" attended the junior class examination. In 1834 the University announced that the senior examinations would begin on June 23 "and continue from day to day until the Board of Visitors are satisfied." It added, "the College Faculty would be gratified by the attendance of Parents and Guardians, and literary gentlemen who may have it in their power to attend."

The board of visitors was not expected to attend the examinations at the end of the first and second terms. These were termed "private," but still they were to be "in the presence of such literary gentlemen as may attend." All examinations were oral and were conducted by members of the faculty.[42]

This University founded on the huntsman's frontier should not deal in intellectual food alone; it should also dispense the daily bread of life. It was well that it should be so, for to begin with, the town was too small to afford ample boarding places (and, moreover, the prices were too high at those it did possess), and, again, the faculty could keep better watch over the students if it did the feeding. So a commons or steward's hall was built almost as soon as Old College crept up. It was all so new to the managers that they borrowed *in toto* the eating rules used by Yale College—at least "as near as can be." Studying *à la* Yale required eating *à la* Yale. What a mob of hungry students might do in a dining room could not be predicted, but, at least, there should be present the restraining hand of the tutors and senior class. According to the rules, "in case of misbehaviour, disobedience or improper conduct, the offending Student may be turned out of the room, and lose his meal for that time."[43]

The old adage has it that hunger will tame a lion; but history says that hunger not properly satisfied will bring on the downfall of an empire. Franklin College required the steward to provide "victuals, after the manner of living in common Families" and threatened with expulsion any student refusing to be satisfied.

And he was voracious, indeed (or unduly fastidious and rebellious), who should go away from a Franklin College meal hungry. For breakfast there were "Good coffee and Tea, corn and wheat bread well baked butter wholesome bacon or beef." Dinner came at noon—not at night—and it eloquently bespoke the carnivorous appetites of young Georgians. There were corn bread, bacon "including alternately all the parts of the hog usually preserved," vegetables, beef, lamb, mutton, and shoat or poultry. If perchance no fresh meat could be had, then milk or molasses should be served with a second course of "confectionary." Under any circumstances, molasses was to be served every other day and soup twice a week, and the whole meal should "be well cooked and served up in a neat and cleanly manner." After consuming such a dinner who could want more for supper than corn and wheat bread, coffee, and tea "or coffee and milk and butter"?[44]

But students can never be satisfied, at least in the eyes of faculty and trustees. For this reason and others, steward's hall was abolished after a quarter of a century, and the students were allowed to board in town "except [at] houses of public entertainment and houses where spirituous liquors may be retailed." It took the trustees only a short time to discover that this arrangement was bad. It led to the student's associating with every tramp and politician who came to town, besides bringing him too much in contact with the village belles. They handed down the dictum in 1839 that a "student's business is with his books, and not with society, and every regulation which admits of too much social intercourse is unfriendly to his proficiency in his studies." They reiterated the rule that no student might board at a place where "a bar is kept, or spirituous liquors or wines are furnished." But conditions grew no better. In 1853 the trustees declared that "on the minds of strangers, it cannot fail to produce a most unfavorable impression of a literary institution, to find its students thronging the rooms of taverns, blocking up the sidewalks before them, and filling the air with the smoke of their cigars." From these tavern walls "there is no exclusion of vice provided it appear in a decent garb, and the young are constantly exposed to the contact with designing vagabonds who everywhere infest society." The next year they flatly forbade students boarding at hotels or taverns, and later re-established the commons.[45]

Just as the University should provide board for the students, it should also furnish them with rooms. In keeping up with the students, this arrangement was of first importance. At the beginning of the year the president assigned each student a room in the college dormitory, and anyone refusing to stay where he was put invited immediate expulsion. If at any time the dormitories should be filled, additional students might "reside among the inhabitants of Athens of a good moral character." The custom soon developed of the professors accepting two or three students as roomers—but it can easily be inferred that only the less virile ones would accept of such incarceration. Some of the Athenian families passing the test of "good moral character" in this respect in the 'fifties were the Barrows, Barrys, Baxters, Billupses, Brittains, Chases, Cobbs, Colts, Conyers, Coopers, Coppees, Cranes, Daniels, Delonys, Dents, Doughertys, Gerdines, Greers, Griffiths, Hardemans, Harrisses, Hemphills, Hills, Hodgsons, Holseys, Hugginses, Hulls, Lampkins, Longs, Lumpkins, Lyles, McCleskeys, Matthewses, Moores, Mortons, Nances, Newtons, Peepleses, Phinizys, Popes, Richardsons, Sansoms, Scudders, Shackelfords, Stones, Stovalls, Talmadges, Thomases, Vincents, Wares, Weatherlys, and Wrays. Each student in a dormitory was required to furnish a "bed, room-furniture, firewood, and candles." The only two dormitories were Old College and New College, and only juniors and seniors might have rooms in the latter.[46]

Tuition varied with the times. It was at first $6 a quarter, and then $8. Rooms were $1 a quarter and repairs and contingent fees 50 cents. A sweeping fee of 50 cents was levied on those rooming in dormitories, and a 12½ cent fee for those living in town. Besides a bell ringer there was an additional servant "whose duty it shall be, with the one already employed, to wait on the Students, clean their shoes and boots, to make their fires and cleanse the College Buildings." For this service $1 extra was levied. Each student was required to pay for all damage done to his room, and any damage happening during vacation times was assessed against the whole student body. In 1860 tuition for the

year, including servant's hire, library fee, etc., was $50. Board
ranged from $114 to $142.50, washing from $9 to $11, and fuel
from $5 to $10. The total required expenditures ranged from
$178 to $213.50. The students were subjected to various fines as
will appear hereafter. All money due must be paid before the
student was allowed to recite, and any professor who had too much
milk of human kindness in his heart to enforce this rule rigidly
found his next month's salary reduced by the amount due.[47]

As already noted, the University was giving its dying gasp when
Waddel began his ministrations. As the *Athenian* said in 1829, he
came when "nothing was left of the College but the name and the
buildings." To be more exact, according to his son, the president
found seven students "playing 'hide and seek' in the rooms of the
old College building." With great vigor he set to work, and within
three years he did a most remarkable thing—he produced 120
students where only seven had been before. Hereafter, during his
administration, he maintained by far a larger number than had
ever attended previously. He did more. Within two years he
had completed Philosophical Hall, and the next year (1822) he
saw the foundations laid for New College. It was completed in
1823. The corner stone was laid with Masonic rites and within
it were placed a small Bible, a few current coins, a glass containing "some of the most elegant manufactures of the present day,"
and a scroll containing the names of the president of the United
States, the governor of the state, the president of the University,
and the master of the Masonic Lodge. Augustin S. Clayton, a
member of the first graduating class and a trustee, delivered the
oration.[48]

Waddel was not without honor and appreciation for what he
was doing—and while he was doing it at that. The Senatus Academicus sang loudly his praises at almost every one of their
meetings. Within everyone's memory the University had "well
nigh languished to despair." "For a series of years," they said
in 1824, "it seems to have been visited by a wayward destiny,
which counteracted the effects of her most zealous advocates, and
reduced to a state of existence merely nominal in Form a condition so deplorable—so dampening to the ardour of patriotism, and

sickening to the feeling of philanthropy; an immediate and permanent relief was ardently to be desired."

"Happily for the present generation and for posterity, a period arrived which brought with it a combination of relief, most seasonable and efficient." By 1825 they had become actually jubilant— "We can confidently rely upon the annual overflowings of this Georgia Nile for the fertilization of our rising country."[49]

Waddel was an intensely earnest man, and seriously religious. He was the first president definitely to stamp religion upon the University. He was scrupulous and meticulous to a fault. He kept a diary and found nothing too insignificant to be recorded within its pages. One day "the 2 lost geese were found"; and then "Romulus [his horse] strayed away to-night." He "rectified" his watch, and one day "a Beggar called I gave him a coat and 25 cents." He was terribly impressed with the seriousness of life, and as is likely to be the case with such people, he was surprised each succeeding day to find himself still alive. He "coughed much"; he "took a Gambo pill." He "had a violent headache"; he was "giddy"; he called Dr. Gerdine, who "prescribed bleeding," and two days later he "got bled." He kept close watch for the first frost of winter and when it arrived he "put on Flannel." When the first violets peeped up in the springtime, he "changed drawers and stockings" to a lighter weight. By May 10 (1825) he reported the weather "clear and warm" and "shifted flannel," nine days later it was hot and he "shed flannel," and six days later he completed his transformation and "put on summer dress."[50]

He never felt quite sure that he should be a college president when there was so much preaching to be done. He began early to pine for his old South Carolina haunts, and now and then he got vertigo poring too long and intently over a map of the Palmetto, State. After five years in Athens, he definitely decided to leave and actually wrote out his resignation (1824); but all in authority fell to dissuading him and succeeded in changing his mind. He remained another five years, and then in 1829 resigned for good and all. He must go back to South Carolina to preach. As he mounted into his carriage to drive away, he was surrounded and treated to a farewell address by a respectful array of young Geor-

gians unwilling to see him leave.[51] He left behind an appreciation for learning and for religion that had not existed before. To
his memory, the town has called one of its minor by-ways Waddel
Street and has now forgotten him. The University has never seen
fit properly to honor its preserver.

JUSTICE IN THE HIGH COURT
OF THE FACULTY

HIGHER education was a new thing in the lower South when the University of Georgia began its existence. Yale men brought the idea in, and Yale men made the machinery and set it in motion. As already noted, how Yale College did things was of much importance in Georgia. The inspiration for the laws governing the students was also of Yale origin and was Puritanical and puerile after the most approved fashion of the age. It was anomalous indeed for the scientific Meigs to give way to this flood of petty restrictions and commands, religious and otherwise; but what else could he do—he who had known none other. Again was it even stranger that godless Georgia should embrace them so arduously and cling to them so tenaciously.

The first code of laws was drawn up by Meigs and adopted by the Senatus Academicus in Louisville in 1803, and thereafter they were codified and readopted at intervals—in 1811, 1816, 1823, 1827, 1834, 1854, and on down. Few laws were ever dropped; the changes were additions. These rules were the law of the land as far as the University was concerned and just as sacred. The student's passport to classes was a set of the laws signed by the president; he was given ten days to digest them and thereafter he fell hard under their inexorable pains and penalties. His every action was guided by them. A law got him out of bed and put him back again. He ate by them, he studied by them, he recited by them—they were with him always. He kept them close at hand, hardly knowing until he should consult them what he could do next.[1]

"If any scholar shall be guilty of prophaneness—of fighting or quarreling—if he shall break open the door of a fellow student—if he shall go more than two miles from Athens without leave from the President, a Professor or a Tutor,—if he shall disturb others by noisiness, loud talking or singing during the time of study—if he shall ring the Bell without order or permission—if he shall play at billiards, cards or any unlawful game—if he shall associate with vile, idle or dissolute persons, or shall admit them into his chamber,—if he shall instigate or advise any student to a refractory or stubborn behaviour—he shall for either of those offenses, be punished by fine, admonition, or rustication, as the nature and circumstances of the case may require." No student should "be allowed to keep any gun, pistol, Dagger, Dirk sword cane or any other offensive weapon in his room in College or elsewhere," and it was made plain that *elsewhere* meant *anywhere* in the world. Furthermore, he should not keep "for his use or pleasure, any riding animal or dog."

There were crimes even much more serious than these, and students must never be guilty of them, to wit: "If any scholar shall be guilty of blasphemy, fornication, theft, robbery, forgery, or any other crime, for which an infamous punishment may be inflicted by the laws of the State, he shall be expelled." Gentlemen out in the state might fight a duel and evade the law against it, but expulsion awaited the student who should settle his differences in such a fashion. Naturally students were forbidden to fight among themselves, but for fear of a misunderstanding that the law went no further, it stated plainly that no student might "strike, or insult any person not being a member of the College." And even yet, fearing his fighting instincts might seek to find other and unusual outlets, the law solemnly said: "If any scholar shall assault, strike, or wound the President, a Professor, or a Tutor or shall designedly break their doors or windows, he shall be expelled." Furthermore, admonition, suspension, or expulsion awaited anyone who should "lie, get drunk or be guilty of other gross immoralities."

All of the foregoing were crimes which the student should recognize without the authorities having to call them to his attention. For fear his conscience might not be active enough to suggest others, many additional prohibitions were laid down. If a student "shall frequently neglect the public exercises or if he shall spend the hours of study in idleness and manifest a prevailing inclination to a dissolute behaviour; or if he entice others from their studies and draw them into bad practices, he shall be dismissed from the College." He must realize that his time was valuable, and if he should ever "be so far lost to his own character or reputation as to be found in any public tavern, store, tippling shop or any other place where spirituous liquors are retailed," he stood in line for public admonition, and on a second offense, rustication followed. The student must properly restrain himself musically and otherwise. "Fluting, fiddling" or playing on any other "instrument of music in the hours of study and also on Sundays" was strictly forbidden.

He must be himself at all times and not attempt to imitate other people, fictitious or real, nor attempt merely to disguise himself. It was a grave offense to "come out in indecent dress or in woman's apparel," and any student who should appear "in any dramatic performance whatever in the town of Athens in term time or vacation" was inviting heavy punishment. Cleanliness was next to godliness: "If any student shall be deficient in cleanliness in his apartment the President or any officer may order all necessary cleaning done at the expense of such student." He should be clean in mind as well as in body and premises, and to help emphasize this fact the law set severe penalties for defacing the walls of the chapel or other buildings "by the drawing of grossly indecent figures, outraging alike religion and morality."[2]

But that which the students had least of was nursed and guarded with the greatest care—their religion. Colleges should be "nurseries of morality—retreats, where at least the outward forms of virtue and religion are to be found," and the faculty both by precept and example were required to display before the students "a virtuous and blameless life, and a diligent attention to the publick and private duties of religion." They should conduct various religious exercises in the University, and keep careful watch over the devotions of the students. Sunday was holy and made for rest; hence the students must "refrain from their usual exercises," including "fluting" and all other diversions on musical instruments. On this day, and on all others for that matter, they should not "go beyond the limits" of Athens. Later (1821) they were allowed a radius of one mile, "so long . . . as this healthful and innocent indulgence is exercised free from any conduct not violative of the laws of the College." In the early days before religion had come to the citizens of Athens, the students were required to attend morning and evening on Sunday devotional exercises in the chapel, conducted by the president or a professor, and later when Athens developed churches the students were forced to attend the church of their choice and to report that fact at their Monday morning class. But religion was not for Sunday only. As heretofore noted, there were prayers twice daily throughout the week.

All these rules and laws, commands and prohibitions, and many more, as will amply appear hereafter in the breach thereof, were written down—sixteen pages of them in a large ledger book—and yet it was not in jest that this elastic clause was added at the end: "Whereas the laws of the College are few and general" in cases arising not covered by the code the faculty "shall proceed according to their best discretion." It may well be inferred that the faculty was a high court of justice whose judicial duties were only second to its teaching business. Its sittings took place every Tuesday evening after prayers and were held in secret. No punishment was inflicted on a student without his notice and hearing, after which the faculty proceeded "deliberately and impartially, to decide on the case according to the laws which they are bound, by oath, to execute, according to the best of their judgment and ability." The law required the expulsion of any student who refused to testify. If any student should feel his punishment to be unjust he might be granted a rehearing within thirty days, and if he still felt aggrieved he had another thirty days in which to carry his appeal to the trustees. As has heretofore appeared, the penal-

ties were admonition, public and private, rustication (a trip to the
country or to the Grammar School), suspension, expulsion, and
fines. Fines were multifarious and shifting, constituting the whole
penalty or being added on to one of the others. At first the fine
for absence from prayers was 6¼ cents and for being late without
a good reason, or "egressing" (slipping out), 3 cents. Money was
too plentiful for such fines to be seriously regarded; so they were
later increased to 50 cents and 25 cents respectively. To leave
town or return to school late cost 50 cents a day. No fines could
be made more than ten dollars. In many instances, of course,
trials were not necessary and fines were inflicted by a professor,
if not over 50 cents—otherwise the case rested in the hands of the
president or the faculty.[3] In defending this code of laws the faculty
declared that better men than they believed "that the Laws of this
Institution enjoin no duties which are not necessary for good order,
for forming the best moral character, and for securing to the
Students the greatest possible advantages for a substantial and
liberal education."

Such a minute regulation of student life required an equally
laborious attention on the part of the faculty to see that the students were obedient. Unmarried professors and tutors lived on
the various floors of the dormitories to which they were assigned
in the rôle of spy, policeman, and judge. They kept strict watch
over the students during study hours, and went on patrol duty "at
frequent and irregular intervals." All of this solicitude was considered necessary, for "So many mere youths enter our college,
that it requires the vigilant and restraining influence of Professors
to Prevent those habits of inattention, which are so liable to be
formed, and which always result in disorder." The various patrolling professors, armed with all the authority of the law, went around
tapping on the doors to the students' rooms (and sometimes they did
not tap, for the law held that to forewarn a culprit was to forearm
him), and now and then they were greeted upon their first approach with that hackneyed expression "go to hell," despite the
rule which said students should "shew in speech and behaviour
all proper respect and obedience to the President, Professors and
Tutors of the College." Of course, the student always had ready

the defense that he thought the caller was his room-mate who was rapping. If an inquisitive professor were barred out by a locked door, he might batter it down and charge up the damages to the student.

This business of spying on the students was as distasteful to some of the patrolling professors as it was hateful to the students. The trustees often emphasized this duty of the faculty and chided the professors at times for being too lax in its performance. Other people expressed the hope that the trustees would be wise if they did not force the professors to "patrol the college into disorder and rebellion." Henry Jackson got partial exemption from this patrol work and soon became a favorite among the students. Charles Venable, an urbane Virginian, would merely knock on the door and inquire whether all were in and behaving themselves properly; while Joseph LeConte positively refused to busy himself with the puerile performance—and thereby and otherwise a young rebellion broke out which will find its proper treatment further on. Richard M. Johnston also objected to spending his time watching the students; he did not know this duty was required when he came to the University. Occasionally as an additional incentive in securing a professor, release from this work would be granted, as in 1831 when the trustees in trying to find a professor of Spanish, French, German, and Italian, promised that "No connection with the police of the College will be required."

Some members of the faculty, whether they liked this duty or not, became experts at finding the right student who had done the wrong thing. William D. Wash made himself a terror to evil-doers and yet he was respected, for he was absolutely fearless, in a day when young scholars were dangerous. Few ever successfully evaded him. Nahum Hiram Wood was neither liked nor feared, yet with all of his New England Puritanism and stiffness of manner, he had a sense of humor. When students got in the habit of emptying buckets of water on his head as he passed under their windows on his rounds, he adopted the simple device of carrying an umbrella and casually raising it when he came into the pathway of the descending torrents. But this same professor finally became tired of preserving order in a dormitory, and falling under the charms of a woman, married her; whereupon the prudential committee, which had been gradually taking unto itself more powers, made the marriage a success by allowing Wood "to lodge out of College"—"He having changed his condition from a single to a married life."[4]

These were the rules on student conduct and this their process of enforcement—rules from Puritan New England for the untamed South. The Southern atmosphere proclaimed the doom of the whole system from the beginning, but the educational managers never admitted it or receded for almost three-quarters of a century. Young Georgians at Athens, young North Carolinians at Chapel Hill, young South Carolinians at Columbia, young Mississippians at Oxford—all objected to such a system and in much the same manner. The sons of planter aristocrats hated restrictions, for they knew that only slaves were made to be ordered around, and the sons of the aspiring gentry had grown up in communities which recognized few men's authority and cared little for the law. Robert Finley hesitated much on accepting the presidency of the Georgia university, of course, on account of the "high responsibility" of the position, but really because of "the insubordination of Southern youth." To do as one pleased was liberty; to be restrained was tyranny. And besides, a peculiar sense of honor was one of their most highly-developed traits. A Georgia student asserted in 1855 that it was "mortifying to the feelings of the young men to have their words doubted, and must beget within them a sort of contempt and hatred for the Faculty. No graver insult could be offered to a gentleman than this."[5] It is also a common human trait to delight in doing those things forbidden.

Nature abhors uniformity, even to the extent of having fashioned some people into a spirit of conformity to the Franklin College rules. Alexander H. Stephens, never quite well and seldom weighing as much as a hundred pounds, left the almost impossible reputation of having received not one word of reproof from a professor. He was never absent from class without an acceptable excuse; he was never fined, and he never had a quarrel with a student. His physical make-up may have aided him in establishing this reputation. His half-brother, Linton Stephens, could plead no such infirmities, yet the only collegiate crime history holds against him was "playing the flute during study hours."[6] It was generally true that those students who lived in the homes of professors kept out of most of the mischief that continuously went on upon the campus.

The majority of students held firmly to the belief that the professors were the chief obstacle to their thorough enjoyment of life, and that, therefore, they were worthy objects of ridicule, scorn, and attacks. The professor was indeed a most colorless person who could not call forth a nickname from the students. Malthus Ward was always "Dr. Pegs" after the remark, "Words are only pegs on which to hang our ideas." James Jackson, the son of a former governor, was "the Major"; Professor William L. Broun was "Little Bruin"; President Waddel was "Old Pewt"; and Professor Hull was "Old Cosine." Benjamin B. Hopkins wore a long white queue. One day a mangey little pig with tail fashioned after the professor's queue appeared in the class—the laughter that followed set some of the students to crying. James Tinsley seldom failed to attract the attention of students when he crossed the campus with shirt-collar open and bareheaded. It sometimes happened that anonymous leaflets filled with ridicule of various professors made their appearance on the campus.[7] Stephen Olin, a New England dyspeptic, made enemies among students and faculty aplenty, but on maturer thought some looked back upon him as a masterful teacher. Charles F. McCay had a stormy career, but at least one student held that McCay was the only remarkable man on the faculty of his day. Henry Jackson was well liked over a long period of time, and even though this be a memorial resolution it is not without sincerity: "No man perhaps, was more universally esteemed and respected by his pupils, and yet more decided in his public disapprobation of everything derogatory to the character of the student."[8]

The attitude of students toward professors found a wide variety of ways in which to express itself, from mild dislike to malignant hatred, ranging from prankish indifference to deadly intent. They carried President Waddel's gate away and hid it near the post office without wishing their watchful teacher harm; but when they hanged

William B. Stevens in effigy in front of the chapel they were actuated by deeper feelings; or when they likewise suspended Nahum Hiram Wood from the Toombs oak, they were trying to show their dislike for his New England stiffness of manner and lack of sympathy. Contact with the professors in reciting lessons and making speeches gave rise to many troubles which made grist for the faculty meetings to grind. John Gardiner developed a dislike for declaiming and showed it by ridiculing the whole performance; he also "exhibited an insolence of manner and a great reluctance to perform his several collegiate duties of late"; therefore, it was "deemed that his further continuance in the institution would be worse than useless to himself, and pernicious to the College." John Crawford had "omitted to declaim publicly in the chapel, and as such neglect is (to say the least) very disrespectful toward the faculty as a body," he was given warning to mend his ways or leave. Another student hated formalities so much that he refused to march upon the stage to receive his degree. The faculty decreed that he should not receive it at all "unless a proper explanation and apology is made to the Faculty."9 When snow came to Athens the students celebrated by throwing balls of it in every direction, but principally toward any professor who might get caught out.

He was a fortunate professor who had no worries over order in the classroom. The boisterous manner of the students in answering the roll-call led to noting their presence by sight—a rule which placed certain near-sighted professors in a dilemma. One lively student was ordered by the faculty to desist from "the habit of laughing and making grimaces considered very silly." Another was an expert artist at drawing monkeys with the easily recognized facial expressions of James Jackson. The same professor was often sidetracked from any assigned lesson by some serious-minded student suddenly developing a burning desire to know more about the Yazoo Land Fraud. As the professor's father had played a big part in exposing this villainy and had fought more than one duel over it, the son's enthusiasm on the subject generally lasted the remainder of the class period. Classes were more than once set into commotion by cannon-balls bumping down the stairways and

landing against classroom doors. Make-believe goats were also
known to bleat at classroom doors, which would set the professor
into pursuit only to find the door locked. One Robert Harris was
showing only an early example of a common trait when he "be-
haved in a manner highly unbecoming during recitation by throwing a wad of chewed paper at a fellow student so as to make him
cry out." Arguments sometimes developed into fistic encounters,
as in 1856, when two students were fined ten dollars each "for a
fight which occurred between them in the recitation room of one
of the officers while the lecture was going on."[10]

The students were in their own estimation gentlemen and the
sons of gentlemen, but often they forgot these things and dealt
with their professors as their passions dictated. Thomas Beall
was found "guilty of a most flagrant act of contumacy in wilfully
disobeying and insulting an officer of the College" and was fined
five dollars for it. A senior in 1860, having completed all work
for his degree, made bold to express frankly his opinions of men
and things and declared that there was only one gentleman on the
whole faculty. This body at its regular weekly meeting being unable to agree on which one was the gentleman, expelled the senior
and refused to grant him his degree. A junior, Perryman by name,
was overheard one day engaging in the common pastime of cursing
the faculty. When he learned that he had been expelled for it,
he cursed them to their faces before he took his departure.[11]
Sometimes the students denied vigorously any implication in or
knowledge of attacks made on faculty members. In 1817 they
held a meeting relative to "a most wanton and disgraceful attack . . . made on the repose of one of the officers of the College"
and denied that they were in any way mixed up "in that foul
business."

It was not a common practice for a student to seek out professors to insult or assault; it was rather a case of running
up on them unexpectedly or getting caught by them. And then
dangerous encounters took place, whether it was at Franklin College, Mercer University, or the University of North Carolina. At
Mercer, in historic Middle Georgia, a professor was dangerously
wounded by a student. Old President Waddel on November 17,

1824, noted in his diary that he "awoke not refreshed by sleep having been interrupted by a disorderly company in the night who had music round the house." In fact, professors had a way of never appreciating the midnight serenades under their windows. One Andrews, who was caught by a professor under whose window he had been carrying on a serenade, was greatly surprised and hurt at his music not being enjoyed—and he so stated in his trial. But this defense did not serve to stay his expulsion, for he was guilty of many other crimes. He had a habit of engaging in "excessive constant and unconcealed profanity"; he had offered as an excuse one day when he appeared in class unprepared that "the President had been at his room and bored him for an hour and a half"; he had also been guilty of calling out at passing Negroes. In the light of this proved record, the faculty declared there "were strong reasons for thinking his habits were becoming bad." So they cast him out. Once President Waddel decided it would be wise to back down from a position the faculty had taken, when a student of desperate character, under the influence of liquor, planted himself in their pathway, arrayed in opposition. Subsequent knowledge of the affair showed the faculty the wisdom of Waddel's course.

The professors were exposed to the greatest hazards to life and limb while they were on police duty or in pursuit of mischievous students. One night in 1840 six drunken seniors began a disturbance which President Church, assisted by Professor Charles F. McCay, attempted to quell. The seniors laid down a barrage of sticks and stones which painfully wounded the President and badly bruised the Professor. An assault with a shower of stones was a favorite greeting to a patrolling tutor. William D. Wash went through experiences on the Franklin College campus which fitted him for leadership in the great Southern uprising of the 'sixties. One night the students attempted to drive him from the University by an attack on his room, which did not subside until every window-pane had been broken. On another occasion and with a different strategy, having securely fastened his door, they began an attack with stones from every angle. With considerable bravery Wash released the door and took the offensive.

He pursued a dozen of them to Old College and noted the doors through which they fled. There was a heavy docket at the next high court of the faculty. One night in 1858 Wash ran into a ring of students on the edge of the campus "singing obscene songs and using profane language." He gave chase, sending them toward their rooms, and being a fast runner he beat them in the race. Noting the vacant rooms, he brought charges the next day against the absent students. In 1854 twenty students began a riot, ringing the college bell and otherwise disturbing the peace of the sleeping town and campus. A tutor so rash as to venture out was attacked and driven into his room again, where he dodged the stones which were hurled through his windows.[12]

One of the most dangerous, determined, and best organized riots in ante-bellum times took place in the spring of 1832. Fourteen young rebels, disguised with handkerchiefs tied around their heads "in Indian style" and shirts over their clothing, set going a reign of terror at 10:30 P.M., which did not subside until 2 A.M. They made a great noise marching through the college buildings, breaking out door panels and window-panes, throwing brickbats against walls and floors, stamping with their feet in a terrific fashion, and beating with sticks and clubs. They carried away the chapel steps and planned an attack on the president's house. The faculty police were soon on the field, but so complete were the disguises that not a rioter could be recognized "though the moon shone with peculiar lustre, being nearly full." But the faculty espionage system the next day began to produce results, and before the same moon had waxed and waned again every rebel had been apprehended and expelled, and warrants had been issued for their trial in the courts of the land.[13]

Many student pranks against the professors had an innocent and harmless origin and an ending likewise devoid of guile. Not so with an affair which happened in 1839 in which Professor McCay was the chief sufferer. As has already been noted, McCay was active in police and disciplinarian work, and was pronounced by students after they had left college an outstanding teacher. One night while he was away from his room in New College, a mob of students entered it, gathered up his clothing, bedding, books, valuable manuscripts and lecture notes, carried them out onto the campus, and burned them in a bonfire. William Dearing, a prominent townsman, receiving an anonymous letter accusing his son of being the ringleader in the sorry business, assumed that McCay had written the letter and said gruff things about him. McCay considered himself insulted and on the advice of friends did what a gentleman was supposed to do under such circumstances—sent a challenge to William Dearing to fight a duel. Dearing, also being a gentleman, accepted the challenge, and it was reported at the time that the two did meet within sight of the college buildings, but were persuaded to desist. The facts seem to indicate that they never actually met on the field of honor. A furor arose in town and on campus; McCay had violated a state law in sending a challenge and should resign. He did resign, though from a desire to relieve the board of trustees from an embarrassing situation, and he thereby injected bitter discord into the deliberations of that august body. McCay soon repented of having resigned and let it be known that he would much rather remain at Franklin College. His enemies argued that if his resignation were not accepted the campus would soon be turned into a field of honor on which the students would be settling their every dispute with swords and pistols. Students were boys and should not be led to take on men's ways too soon. After numerous meetings and much discussion the trustees voted 8 to 7 to refuse to accept the resignation. In the meantime the faculty set its detective forces to work and promised to prosecute the students responsible for the outrage. Fearing certain detection and the wrath to come, the culprits confessed on promise of immunity from prosecution. They agreed to submit to any punishment the faculty might impose. Instead of becoming embittered by these experiences, McCay, pleased with the support he had received from the trustees, remained until 1853, when he removed to Columbia, South Carolina, where he soon became president of South Carolina College. He afterward settled in Augusta, entered the insurance business, became wealthy, and then spent the remainder of his days in Baltimore. Well versed in mathematics and insurance statistics, in 1879 he made a unique donation to the University. "For and in consideration of the affection and interest" he had for the institution he gave it $7,000 in railroad bonds (afterward converted into Georgia State bonds) to be held and the interest compounded until 21 years after 25 persons whom he named should have died. Based on the probabilities of human life and the rules of interest, calculations show the fund should become available about 1979 and amount to about $2,000,000. The interest is to be used in paying the salaries of professors.[14]

In the various disorders so far recounted, members of the faculty were either the direct object of attack or became involved in the disturbance before it subsided. Hereinafter will follow a glimpse into a side of student life which grew out of no dislike for professors but was rather an expression of that pleasure that comes from doing forbidden things—a situation which each succeeding generation beholds with alarm and declares to be a grave degeneration from the older days. There was the further element in the situation which the old rule-makers had apparently forgotten, that students were not machines made to run in a groove or on a pulley, but that they were rebellious sons of a rebellious generation, active, virile, boisterous. They were commanded to live their lives, every minute, according to a schedule. They arose early and went to prayers at sunrise and then to recitations or they must study until breakfast should be announced. At 9 o'clock they went to their rooms for study unless recitations occupied their time. They should go to dinner when summoned, any time between 12 and 2, after which they should return to their rooms to study until 5, when they returned to the chapel again to hear some professor pray for forgiveness for the many sins all had committed since the sunrise prayer. In winter they should return to their rooms at 7 and study until 9:30. At 10 they should be in bed. In summer (March 21st to September 21st) they were dismissed after evening prayers until 9 when they should return to their rooms and not venture out during the night.[15]

Thus it is seen how easy it was to break the rules merely on daily comings and goings. The accumulating weight of grinding tedium developing from this restrictive system generated riots and boisterous outbreaks otherwise unintelligible and senseless.

Some examples where professors were involved have already been described. Sometimes conspiracies were carefully hatched; at other times the movement developed by spontaneous generation, with a spring atmosphere always greatly aiding. In 1849 a student recorded in his diary, "I was pressingly urged to go on a spree, but declined." A May night of 1830 grew a young mob variously armed which began the evening's entertainment by doing such things "as pulling down fences, tearing up corn, blocking up avenues, drawing away a wagon and sulky and throwing them into the river and breaking off the railings of the bridge." The faculty assessed penalties from public confessions and expressions of regret to fines of $10.

On another night of concerted hilarity the program consisted of the following acts: One student was "disturbing the college with his fiddle"; another "rolling brick bats along the passage"; another "firing a cracker"; another "making loud boisterous, and strange noises with his voice"—and so the show proceeded. As usual, the actors were punished in various ways, but the crime of the one who had made the "strange noises" was aggravated by his "having disturbed the Grammar School by throwing pebbles at the children" (to show his contempt for people in such a low position). The most befitting punishment the faculty could think of for him was a sentence "to the Grammar School for three months" with the warning that immediate expulsion awaited him if he appeared on the College campus.[16] In 1857 a party of students drifted into the cemetery about 1 A.M. where a person dressed in a white sheet suddenly appeared. Various evolutions and movements followed, which finally ended in a general fight and contest at profane swearing.

Shooting pistols and carrying deadly weapons were practices which the professors long sought to suppress. President Waddel being a light sleeper was often awakened by shooting. On Christmas Eve of 1824 he slept badly, being much "interrupted by bell and shooting." At one faculty court he "arraigned nine boys for shooting." In 1822 a ring of students were fined, some $5 and others $2.50, for "going full in the face of authority, by shooting during the late Xmas holidays." Thomas Ligon for being "en-

gaged in shooting" when he should have been in his room studying was fined $3. Expulsion was meted out to some for carrying
deadly weapons. Bursting torpedoes, exploding crackers, shooting guns and pistols in 1824 were declared by the faculty to be
"not only destructive to the peace and quiet of the College but
dangerous to the lives of officers and students." The professors
gave warning "that they have come to the resolution that these disorders shall cease, whatever may be the diminution of members."[17]

Swearing, lying, and fighting were crimes duly forbidden but
frequently indulged in. Thomas Early was found guilty of "the
unprovoked use of profane language" as well as a constant practice of disregarding rules. He was expelled. Another student was
more lucky in suffering only private admonition "for using very
profane language," but two other students were privately dismissed for being "guilty of the enormity of deliberate and wilful
lying." Thomas Ware was suspended for "having been found
out of his room and heard to swear profanely."[18] Swearing and
lying may have been inborn traits in some of the students, but
President Waddel had reason to believe that they were acquired
in the case of others, for he noted in his diary that he "had trouble
with Sailor Jack whom I found swearing among the students."[19]

Where there were pistols, swearing, and lying there were likely
also to be fights. And so it was. In 1836 two students armed with
a pistol and a dirk in deadly and earnest fashion started about
settling their argument. One was stabbed near the heart and
dangerously wounded. Only by good luck did he recover. It was
also in the dangerous 'thirties that a senior entered another student's room and "with violent gesticulations" attempted to stab
him with a dirk. Other students rushed in and stopped his thrust.
As he walked away he said, "The damned scoundrel:—I'll be
the death of him before supper." In 1831 an argument developed
the following results: One student said to another, "If you will
go down into the woods, I'll whip you like Hell." The other replied
that "this is as good a place as any other," and the former agreeing
stabbed him. Both were expelled, but both being experts at the
art of petitioning and promising were able to get reinstated. A
favorite place for fights less deadly was in front of the chapel

after prayers, where each participant might display his ability before the assembled spectators. In 1855 two students fell to fighting on their way from prayers over an academic question— over the bounds and confines of a lesson they were about to recite. According to the evidence, "Cobb called him a 'damned fool.' Adams replied, 'You are another.' Cobb struck him on the head. Adams took hold of his collar—Cobb struck him again and the fight commenced." The records are silent on what took place in the *fight*. Cobb's aggressiveness cost him $5. Now and then fights were promoted by some sporting student, when ordinary contacts did not produce them. Cocke and Bunkley began a quarrel which, aided and abetted by interested bystanders, developed into a fight so ferocious that the faculty fined the participants $10 each and suspended them for a month and taxed the promoters $6 each. Cocke armed with a petition signed by the members of his literary society secured a release from his banishment.[20]

One of the most famous student fighters of the 'twenties and certainly the most famous of them all in later times was Robert Toombs. He entered the University in 1824, bold, vigorous, large of build, and full of life, fresh from a plantation and plantation ways. It took him only a short time to find out that the rules were entirely too many and senseless. With considerable blandishment one day he greeted Junius and Granby Hillyer, also destined for later fame, with their nickname, "Bull," and by way of throwing in for good measure "made it the occasion of various shameful and obscene remarks both to the said J. Hillyer and others." A fight ensued and according to Toombs both Hillyers jumped upon him "and beat him," but the Hillyers claimed that Granby was able to do it without help. Toombs did not propose to let the matter rest until he should come out victor; so he soon appeared at the Hillyers' room with a bowl in one hand and pistol in the other. He confused the enemy by hurling the bowl at them and made ready with his pistol, when other students intervening wrenched it from his hand. But Toombs was looking for satisfaction which he must have either severally or collectively. He next attacked Junius with a knife and hatchet, but bystanders thwarted his deadly execution again. Time seems not to have allayed Toombs' anger at having been whipped in an uneven match. Armed with a club and a pistol he next waylaid the road traveled by the Hillyers on their return to school after a visit to their home, and attacked Junius. Here was work for the faculty: The Hillyers were put under a bond to keep the peace henceforth and Toombs was "publicly dismissed from College"—Waddel carefully noting in his hungry diary for September 20, 1825, "dismissed Toombs."

Toombs was now to give early evidence of those qualities of a politician and statesman which were to be so completely identified with him later. To prepare the way, he acknowledged "the impropriety of his conduct," and then proceeded to hand to the faculty a petition from the Demosthenian Literary Society, of which he was a member, praying that he be taken back—and what was a much greater feat of statesmanship, he startled the faculty by producing a similar request from the Phi Kappas, bitter rivals of the Demosthenians. Unquestionably great things had to come from a student who could thus line up the whole student body to support his position in such a situation. The faculty must have felt so, for they received him back, adding the statement that their action should not be regarded as a precedent, for they still abhorred the use of deadly weapons in student relations.

The Hillyer brothers failed to keep the peace properly, and soon Toombs was delighted to see his bitter enemies lodged in the Grammar School for three months. He also learned that the tears of a Hillyer's mother were not nearly so potent as a Toombs' political stratagem. The Hillyers served out almost all their sentence, the faculty remitting the remaining few days on receipt of a "certificate from the teachers of that branch of the institution [the Grammar School] of their propriety of conduct whilst under their charge." Toombs went ahead enjoying freely his various contacts with a hundred young Southerners, indifferent and oblivious (not indignantly but naturally) to the rules and Franklin College proprieties, swearing, fighting a little, and drinking a little. Gentle Waddel records now and then how he "spoke to Toombs about swearing" and the faculty recorded in its minutes September 18, 1827, that "whereas Robert Toombs and William

Rembert have been in the habit of indulging in loud laughing and boisterous conversation in their room, and upon admonition waxed worse and worse," they were thereby fined $2 each. For almost three years Toombs had been adding to the strain and stress of faculty wrath, and then the crash came and as the first resolution of the new year, 1828, the professors dismissed Toombs and in reply to his letter begging reinstatement, entered the final verdict, January 2, 1828, "that the faculty could do nothing more in his case." Toombs departed, but there has grown up a wealth of legends concerning his mighty deeds—how he stayed around until commencement (from January to August was a rather long wait), and then, with burning oratory, drew the multitudes out of the chapel and away from the official program to a great oak tree near-by. As proof of this legend the tree was ever afterwards called the Toombs oak—until one day lightning struck the tree and killed it, and what could be more miraculous than the fact that Toombs had died the very moment before the tree was shattered! It is also told how years after Toombs had been driven from the campus and had attained fame, the University offered him a degree and how with malignant scorn he replied, "When it would have conferred honor upon me to have a degree from Franklin College you refused me; now when by accepting it I would confer honor upon your school you offer it. I will have none of it." This legend fails to take into consideration the fact that Toombs was an ardent friend of the University, became a trustee in 1859, and remained on the board until his death. Another story is told which Toombs relished and repeated, how on learning he was to be expelled he got a letter of dismissal and when Waddel began to address him for his crimes, replied, "Dr. Waddel, perhaps you do not know whom you are addressing in such language. I am not, as you seem to suppose, a student of this university but a citizen of the State of Georgia."[21]

As the students were sentenced by the rules to spend most of their waking hours and all their sleeping hours in their rooms, they naturally hit upon other and more effective means of entertainment than their books afforded. Much student life began and ended in these "dens of iniquity." Betting and card playing were diversions surreptitiously engaged in which thrived with much vigor from Saturday to Monday. The faculty long refused to admit that such a degrading diversion was being carried on in their midst but "with regret and pain . . . at length" (1823) they were "convinced that a number of Students have been engaged in the pernicious practice of card-playing." A student beginning this as an innocent amusement, the faculty declared, would soon be "tempted to engage in the criminal and destructive trade of the gambler whose life is the life of injustice and vice, and whose end is almost universally marked by the just indignation of a Righteous Providence." They started a crusade against card play-ing and wrung a promise from the frightened students to put down the evil. Those students caught in the net were punished variously according to their past records. The sentence passed on one un-fortunate required that he "remove his person and effects forth-with from the College edifice under pain of expulsion."

Another evil was blowing horns and making "unusual noises." For the former crime two students were fined $5 and $2.50—the amounts varying, doubtless, according to their lung power. One Foster was convicted of the latter offense in addition to "having slept out of his room contrary to law, of eating a supper and disturbing the College with the fiddle." He was dismissed from school.[22] Students caught sleeping in their rooms when they should have been studying were fined $12\frac{1}{2}$ cents for each offense. On a hot August day in 1832 a student amused himself by "catching pigs and pulling them up into his room, throwing heavy pieces of wood upon them, etc." For this "cruelty" he was repri-manded. And Albert Wray, having nothing else to do one Sunday afternoon, holloed "in a disrespectful manner, from the window of College . . . to a stranger peacefully riding through the cam-pus." This diversion cost him $2.

"Eating a supper" or "turkey feasting," as it generally was, constituted a serious offense in the eyes of the faculty, for it was an interference with studying and almost invariably meant the theft of the fowls, or their purchase from Negroes. Professor Richard M. Johnston's chickens afforded a source of supply until the professor's wife devised a scheme of inviting the main of-

fenders to her home and so generously entertaining them that
their gratitude gained immunity for her fowls. A standing fine
of $1 was announced "for purchasing anything from a negro in
College." Midnight feasts were often broken up and the participants fined $2 each. In 1825 a group of students were detected
"engaged in the degrading and contemptible business of bringing
into College and preparing for eating fowls which had in all
probability been unjustly obtained." For this crime they were
sentenced to the Grammar School for three months. One George
Walker gave a party to a large number of his friends one night
in his room "and after a supper, which the said George had
procured, were engaged in boisterous conversation, loud laughing and singing of songs." Spirituous liquors had stimulated
much of the hilarity. This method of dispensing Southern hospitality cost Walker $5 extra.[23]

Drinking whiskies and wines was, of course, a common practice
among students, as it was, indeed, among people generally. Moses
Waddel, who had a most exacting conscience, found wine and
brandy necessary for his health. The Athens liquor shops and
groceries displayed their "Malaga, Madeira, Teneriffe, Muscatelle,
Cherry-Bounce, Shrub, Claret—and Porter"—all of which they
sold "very low for cash." By 1858, the closing hours for the
town liquor shops had been forced down to 11 P.M. Drinking
could thus be carried on with such ease that drunkenness came
second in frequency among all the crimes committed by the
students—the indeterminate charge of disorderly conduct coming first. The faculty forbade student drunkenness and frowned
on any drinking whatever, and the trustees expressed their concern more than once at too much student drinking. Jeremiah
Wyche was charged in 1826 with "introducing into his room
spirituous liquor and making and permitting to be made a great
noise in the same." Wyche, knowing too well what the penalty
would be, denied the charge. He was given another hearing and
again he entered a denial. The faculty now informed him that
they had positive proof of his guilt, "and that he might think
upon the subject till evening." When evening came he admitted
his guilt and thereby made himself liable for two crimes, namely:

having liquor and lying about it. Wyche was fined $10. But he failed to mend his ways and ten days later he was expelled, and although both literary societies petitioned for his reinstatement, he was forced to leave. William Cocke about this time was found guilty of the "heinous crime" of drunkenness and received as punishment admonition by the president. Fines of from $5 to $10 were generally levied on students for drunkenness, but in aggravating cases expulsion resulted. W. L. Church, a son of President Church, was caught drunk in 1860 and expelled, and although the father thought his son should be given another chance, the faculty decided that "owing to the great prevalence of drinking in College, at this time" the boy must go. Much drinking went on in students' rooms and what followed inside and out afforded plots for the short story writers of the ante-bellum days.[24]

How should the faculty know when a student was drunk, or how even could a student know? This was an important question, as drinking was not necessarily punished unless it was done in a dormitory room or engaged in excessively. One Stanly in 1855 while visiting a young lady in town was accused by her of being drunk. He became indignant, and forgetting his chivalry, told her it was false. The case came before the faculty, and as the breach of Southern chivalry was not listed as a crime, he was tried for drunkenness. Stanly admitted drinking a third of a pint of champagne, but he convinced the faculty that it did not make him drunk. Dawson, one of the friends of the lady, considering that justice had not been done, assaulted Stanly, and a fight followed, costing Stanly $5 and Dawson $10 in the high court of the faculty.[25]

As billiards was a game unknown to the first lawmakers of the University, nothing was said on the subject in the early codes. In time the game reached Athens and enticed the students from their rooms many nights. In 1858 the town ordinances forced billiard halls to close at midnight, and when the faculty sought to punish students for playing the game at any time, they objected that it was not in the rule book. The rules were modernized in 1857 by including a rule against billiards. Kicking off the palings of the fence surrounding the campus was also made a crime this

year. President Waddel objected to students reading novels, and
one time when he caught some juniors reading in church, it fared
ill with them. C. M. Pope for writing threatening letters was
dismissed in 1850, and Joseph Stewart in 1857 was sent home
for having obscene books and pictures in his possession. Back
in 1813 a student was expelled for writing a scandalous note
reflecting on the faculty.[26]

The College bell had a very definite place in the student's con-
sciousness. Its notes " 'grate harsh discord,' or combine in sweet
harmony, as occasion summons us to, or to release us from our
studies." When it clanged out twenty minutes before sunrise and
then tolled six minutes as the rim of the sun appeared above the
Oconee hills, at whose last tap the students must be seated in
chapel—then was it "harsh discord." Originally the bell was
hung on crossbars between two trees in front of the president's
house, where it might be more safely guarded. Later it was
erected on a tower at the rear of the chapel, and here with less
protection it became a plaything for the students, once gently
tapping according to the appetite of a grazing calf tied to the
bell-cord, and one time being taken down and hid by the students.
But President Waddel, equal to any occasion, announced that
classes would be summoned "by sound of trumpet." The official
bell-ringers were generally the aristocrats of the campus. Two
stand out especially. Old Dick Corly was a venerable looking
Negro with white hair, well dressed, and wearing an air of
dignity in his every act. He refused to take orders from anyone
except President Waddel. Old Dick was in the course of time
succeeded by Blenham, who reigned for many years during the
presidency of Alonzo Church. He was a great friend of the students and won additional popularity by allowing them to use his
room (in the old Grammar School) for their midnight feasts
and frolics.[27]

Negro bell-ringers and other slaves were the only Negroes allowed on the campus. The University generally hired its servants
from their Athens owners at $100 each a year. The rule barring
Negroes from the campus was most likely the only one students
assisted the faculty in enforcing. In 1825 a number of students

"were engaged in chasing Negroes in and about the College
thereby making much noise and disturbance." For this excessive
zeal they were admonished by the president. John Clark, in 1823,
was not so refined in his dealings with Negroes. He was guilty
of "violently assaulting and maiming a negro without provocation" and was besides guilty "of cruel and barbarous treatment
to a poor deranged negro man." The faculty decided that President Waddel should "publicly reprehend and admonish said Clark
causing him to stand in the middle of the aisle [in the chapel]."
When Negroes did not come close to the campus, the students
now and then went to them. In 1853 a group of students were
fined $10 each for going to a Negro dance, and about this time
one Cone was expelled for "entering a private lot and attacking
a servant without provocation" and for the additional crimes
of "disguising himself and walking in the streets in a disorderly
manner on Sunday night and with drinking intoxicating spirits."
One of the most unfortunate cases of dealing with Negroes came
up in connection with W. T. Patterson, who went hunting with
a Negro slave. He became enraged at the slave for some cause
and started to attack him, but the slave put up such a show of
opposition that Patterson desisted. Patterson then reported the
trouble to the slave's owner, who had him whipped. When this
news reached the campus, one of the students with a Voltaire
complex remarked, "Any man who would hunt with a negro and
take exception at what he did and then use his privilege as a
white man to whip the negro, was no gentleman." Naturally a
fight resulted; Patterson was indicted. He fled the town to escape
arrest. In addition the faculty expelled him.[28]

As has already appeared, the students had very exacting duties
to perform for the good of their souls—chapel twice a day and
at most inconvenient times. There can be little doubt that prayers
thus carried on smothered out what little reverence the students
might ever have had. Evidence is ample that they hated all the
exercises connected with prayers and even the building in which
devotions were held. In 1855 they filed the bell-chain, tore away
the seats on the stage, and smeared tar on the seats on the main
floor. About this time they decided to mix a little fun with their

hatred of the exercises by answering the roll in the various languages they had learned, Greek, Latin, French, *et cetera*. President Church demanded that they stop it and soon found that his order "was almost universally disobeyed." Disorders during prayers were almost constant. Two students were expelled for this crime in 1827. One of them "deplored his error" and wanted to be taken back, but he who had shown no Christian spirit got no Christian forgiveness. Talking or kicking each other during prayers regularly carried a fine of $1, while throwing berries cost $2 for the first time, and if done a second time it became a "serious matter." In 1856, the whole sophomore class one day refrained from attending chapel and for this heathenish act were fined $2 each. Thereupon they petitioned to have the fine remitted as they had not combined to escape prayers. The faculty by a strange species of logic granted their petition if they disclaimed "any intention to violate law." There could be no person with a more supreme contempt for chapel exercises than William I. Vason, who in 1857 was guilty of "walking back and forth in an ostentatious manner with seeming contempt for the solemn exercises of the Chapel"; in addition he was guilty of getting drunk, playing off sick, fighting a citizen of the town, and "Finally after all this he danced in the Chapel during prayers." Students often showed by their hilarious conduct at the end of prayers their joy at the conclusion of the infliction. Bursting torpedoes as a method of announcing the end of the ordeal laid the student open to a fine of $1.[29]

Holidays during school terms were few and irregular. Washington's Birthday and the Fourth of July came nearest to producing a cessation of hostilities between the faculty and the students. As Christmas came within the long vacation it did not count in the holiday score. But during the 'twenties when school was made to reopen on January 1st for the second term there were many absences which parents, readily conniving with students, sought to have excused. At length, the faculty refused to take parents' excuses for late returns, and finally they decided the best solution was to reopen school on January 16th. The students maneuvered manfully each year to have election day made a holiday, but the faculty stood resolutely for the regular work of the day. By the 'fifties the students had developed such refined and romantic tastes as to be sure they must have May Day free. The faculty refused them again with the statement that they "had no power to make holidays, that these were fixed by the laws." As May Day came every year, there was always a chance to petition again, but something happened in 1829 which had never happened before and might never happen again—a son was born in Professor Church's family. This was truly remarkable, for all of his other four children had been girls. Nothing less than a holiday would do justice to the occasion. As this argument was unanswerable, the students had no classes on February 16, 1829.[30]

Now and then other special occasions induced the faculty to grant holidays, as in the case of the Clarke County Agricultural Fair in October, 1859. The students got a half-holiday to attend the exhibits, and the following day they demanded and got another half-holiday in order to see the premiums distributed and hear the speeches. T. Cobb of Mississippi enjoyed the relaxation so much that he got drunk "and rushed into the Campus and fired off a pistol," for which act he was in due time expelled. In the spring of the previous year the harshness of the faculty crumbled as the violets began to push up through their winter coat of leaves and the yellow jessamines began to festoon the forest shrubs. The professors now decided that the students might have April 22nd as a half-holiday to go on a "Pic Nic," as they "had been unusually quiet and attentive to their duties" since New Year—but the faculty added the warning that "this must not be taken as a precedent."

Springtime was the danger period for student holiday demands and takings. On March 4, 1853, 36 seniors, 30 juniors, 5 sophomores, and 2 freshmen decided that since they were unable to go to Washington to attend the inauguration of President Pierce they would at least attend no classes at Franklin College. For this species of patriotism they were fined $2 each—making the University $146 richer in one day. On April 30, 1855, the junior class declared themselves a holiday (for perhaps no other reason than that the weather was fine) and received as punishment a fine of $2 apiece. In 1859 the juniors and sophomores, not having the temerity to petition that April Fools' Day be made a legal holiday, declared it so as far as they were concerned, and were thereby assessed the inevitable fine of $2 each, which they were forced to pay as "It being the 1st day of April there was no doubt left but that it was by concert." Sometimes individuals who were bored with school wandered away, as did Robert Walker, and coming to themselves returned again to receive public admonition and to acknowledge a contrite heart.[31]

With the passing of time Athens grew large enough to have attractions which drew the students from their rooms and books— taverns, grogshops, billiard halls, strangers passing through, and disreputable hangers-on. Waddel often "heard great noise of students in streets," and in later days they had the "habit of going to the Post Office and sitting at the Tavern doors and on the streets during study hours." In fact, they were too much with the town. When the steward's hall was abolished they ate at the taverns and often got into fights, throwing food at each other at the table and now and then coming to blows with canes—and this happened at least once in the presence of ladies. The records of Joseph Ware show that he was guilty of having been "out of his room at an unlawful hour of the night—and also of associating with improper company, both crimes against the strict letter of college discipline, therefore resolved that the sd. Joseph be fined in the sum of five dollars and be subjected to a public admonition from the Pres." Peaceful citizens often complained of the intolerable disorders of the students, and the faculty would redouble its efforts to keep the students indoors. But the town was also to blame, for it allowed a section to be infested by certain fancy people who preyed upon the students.[32]

Athens was a larger town than any of its neighbors, yet Lexington and Watkinsville, especially, were continually beckoning to the students to come over. Militia drills, court days, and public speakings could always afford a sufficient excuse to leave Athens. William H. Crawford, Robert Toombs, John M. Berrien and other statesmen of the times seemed to have had an irresistible attraction for the students, especially if they spoke at some nearby

town. In 1855 seven students absconded to Lexington to hear
Alexander H. Stephens speak. When they were arraigned before
the faculty one of them said that he was of age and thought he
knew what was best for him, that he got much more from having
heard Stephens speak than he would have received had he remained at the College, that he considered Stephens a great man
and feared he might never have the chance to hear him again. In
the light of this argument, the faculty deferred action. But Watkinsville was nearer and received many more visits from the
students than Lexington; it was long the county seat of Clarke
County. Here militia regimental drills, elections, and court were
held—all so dear to the hearts of students. Here, also, they hoped
to escape the watchful eye of the faculty. In 1853 a bunch of
students who had stolen away to Watkinsville were charged by
the faculty with having got drunk and insulted a Jew. They admitted "having taken a little cordial" and that they had spoken
to a Jew not so respectfully and yet not disrespectfully and that
the Jew got mad and then one of the students remarked, "Come
away and let the stinking Jew alone." Many Jews were peddling
their wares through Georgia at this time—the father of Oscar,
Nathan, and Isador Strauss being among them. President Waddel was much opposed to his students leaving town, and to inform
himself better on their movements in this regard he would from
a vantage point sweep the horizon to the eastward and southward
with his spyglass. Now and then he would find his prey, and
quickly following after them, march them back, much to their
consternation.[33]

Many of the student trials were not without their element of
humor. Two seniors in 1830 were charged with going to Watkinsville to a ball. They frankly admitted it, "confessing that
as they left college after dark, and returned before light next
morning, they had hoped they would not be discovered." They
were fined $5 each for not being more clever. It was this same
year that a sophomore went into the country one Sunday and on
being discovered claimed that he had been given permission.
When every member of the faculty denied having given him
leave he "explained by saying he meant he had obtained per-

mission from himself." For this species of sophistry he "was admonished before the Faculty and fined three dollars." Joseph M. Shelman on being confronted with the charge of being absent from class too often offered no defense except "that he felt 'Lazy.'" A student in 1857 whenever called upon to speak in the chapel developed the habit of approaching the stage and then suddenly disappearing through a side door. He gave as his excuse that he was only "Fooling the boys." A student during the 'twenties offered irrefragable proof to President Waddel that he had not been playing "at the unlawful game of cards" because he did not "know the ace of jacks from the nine of deuces."³⁴

With all their supposed harshness and lack of sympathy, the faculty must have had much of the milk of human kindness in their souls. In 1829 a hilarious party of students were discovered in an unoccupied room where they "had cordial and wine, fowls and cake, &c. together with fiddling and noisy dancing and causing considerable alarm," and yet they were let off with an undetermined fine when they pleaded they were not doing it intentionally. Sometimes it may not have been the milk of human kindness but weakness on the part of the faculty that led to certain decisions. A. G. Browning was found guilty of the following charges: "1st Dancing on the Sabbath before the doors and in the passages of College. 2nd loud and vociferous whooping and yelling from time to time. 3rd. Sitting and lying in the Chapel during reading and Prayers. 4th. A habitual apparent indifference and carelessness respecting college duties, particularly a want of any proficiency in those studies to which the class is bound to attend." He admitted it all and the faculty resolved "that he remove himself from College immediately." Then he "most solemnly and unequivocally pledged himself" to do better and was readmitted. It was seldom that a student would admit his guilt, but James Thornton broke the rule again when being asked if "he knew anything about any 'game-cocks' confided that he did and likewise that, he himself had been concerned and interested in the cruel business of 'cock-fighting.'" Instead of receiving the reward of a George Washington for telling the truth, he was severely reprimanded and was ordered to be "separated from the institution and be no longer considered a member of the college."[35]

As previously noted, a student could appeal from a decision of the faculty to the trustees, but this was rarely done, and when it did happen the trustees generally disclaimed jurisdiction on some technicality. William Cocke, who was dismissed in 1827, appealed to the trustees and was informed that they could review a case only when the student was *expelled*—not *dismissed*. They, however, failed to explain the distinction. Later six students who had been *expelled* appealed to the trustees, but this supreme court again decided it had no jurisdiction, whereupon a petition from the student body was sent up. The trustees suggested to the faculty a review of the case, but made no order. This was undoubtedly the wise attitude for the trustees to assume, for otherwise they stood to do much mischief to the cause of maintaining order on the campus, as came near happening in the case of I. A. G. Bouchelle. This person was a student whom the faculty expelled and whom the trustees ordered reinstated upon his expressing regret and promising to respect the laws thereafter. The faculty resented this interference, and the trustees took pains to declare that they had no idea of showing a lack of faith in the professors.[36]

The ante-bellum college student was a rebellious, untamed spirit, who needed watching but who grew worse the more he was watched. Emerson said in 1837, "The Southerner asks concerning any man, 'How does he fight?' The Northerner asks, 'What can he do?'" There was a gentleman's agreement among the colleges (or a sort of protective league) against admitting students expelled from another institution. Sometimes a president forgetful of facts would in his report praise the conduct of the students. Waddel said in 1824 (at a time in the University's history when the students were exceptionally unruly) that they evinced "an honorable, and respectful submission to the Laws and authority of the Institution" and that they were "distinguished for a regular upright and exemplary deportment." An examination of the Inspector's Book and the criminal docket of the faculty for this period would show much damage done to property and to the integrity of the rules. An incomplete record for the forty-three years prior to 1873 shows the following dismissals—no regard being had for the almost countless lesser punishments: idleness and neglect, 16; drunkenness, 27; disorderly conduct, 50; gambling, 4; playing cards, 4; fighting, 18; stabbing and shooting, 7; disrespect to professors, 21; fighting chickens, 4; profanity, 1; cheating and lying, 1; indecency, 8; refusal to recite, 8; disturbing church, 3; and having firearms, 4.[37]

Verily, the college student of the Old South was a happy creature; he had so many rules to disobey and did it so effectively.

CHAPTER V

BETWEEN LESSONS
AND PROFESSORS

GOING to college gave a unique thrill to the boy of fourteen or sixteen on the plantation or in the small town. He set out for Athens by stage or steamboat (and after the 'forties likely by railroad), and long before he arrived he had likely met up with a half dozen fellows who were likewise going to Franklin College. If this was his first trip, there was likely nothing unusual in his manner; but if he had already spent some time at Franklin College he was a marked figure, receiving many a glance from his fellow passengers or stares from the passers-by along the road or hangers-on around the taverns and stations. In fact he was a smart fellow and knew it was so. By the 'twenties the humorists, of whom Georgia had a full supply, had appropriated the "college smart Aleck" and were making out of him a wonderful fellow among the unsophisticated—*hoi polloi.* "College boys are the most ingenious fellows in the world, . . ." said Simeon Black, the student, to Josh, the boy back home. "What? set up an old canvassing, legislature candidate, against a student for cunning! Ay! tell that to the marines, for the sailors won't believe it." "At your distance from us," he continued, "people seem to have a dreadful idea of College-boys. Did you ever listen to our tales how we treat the country people, and what pranks we play upon our school-masters, as they call the Faculty?" One countryman had passed the com-

ment that "them there College-boys is a dangerous part of creation," and Simeon Black admitted, "It is an indisputable fact,
that some among our members are wild fellows—real hair brains,
that would go all lengths for fun, and would as soon tar and
feather a man as to treat him but the number is not great. We do,
it is true, occasionally see a pile of wagons in the street, that have,
somehow, unaccountably, rolled upon each other and shed their
wheels during the night time; and we may even hear of a drunken
man's being spirited off to the river, and there scrubbed with sand
and brick-bats to give him colour; but what *very great* harm is
there if nobody is injured?"

A few hints were of great value to the over-awed young
prodigy who was thinking of cutting loose out into the wide world
to enter Franklin College. The wise student advised him to leave
at home "the old half-a-bushel go-to-mill hat, with which you
were accustomed to carry corn to your father's pigs." When he
came to college he must wear "a frock coat with pockets sufficiently
capacious to contain one hair-brush, one bottle cologne-water,
lots of smelling bottles (in case of swooning) and any quantities
of love sick ditties." He scarcely knew whether to tell the aspiring
youth that college life was sweet or bitter. "You may conceive of
our feelings every morning, while the prayer bell is ringing," he
said, "by supposing yourself to be slumbering in that delightful
region, half asleep, half awake, which connoisseurs in the art of
sleeping declare to be so exquisite and while in this sweet dozing
to be pestered, enraged, almost deranged, by having a swarm of
flies buzzing their serenades over your face, and tickling your
nose. No doubt you have often experienced this fly purgatory, . . .
and by it you may very easily imagine how, at least, sixty young
fellows here feel every morning. When the bell is about half
done ringing, we jump out of bed, in a tremendous hurry; haul
on our clothes, this way or that, no matter which, so that they are
on, and some neglect even this, but throw their thick winter plaid
over their shoulders, and off we dash for the Chapel, at which
we arrive sometimes just in time to hear our names—passed over.
When there we begin immediately to con over our lessons, to lean
our heads on the benches for another comfortable nap. After

prayers, we go to morning recitation. O! what dreadful conflicts we have there, between an inclination to sleep, and the fear of being discovered in the act, by the sharp-eyed man in the corner.—Nor unfrequently too, when we merely shut our eye-lids closely upon one another, to squeeze out, if possible, our drowsiness, and when we keep them so, for any length of time, thinking in the interim, about bright eyes, sweet cherry lips and angel forms, we hear a strange voice calling to us—'Next. Mr. P. or Mr. Q. if such and such things were thus and so, would this and that flow as a consequence, and why?' A considerable pause. 'I say Sir, if—why, Sir, are you asleep?' And then follows a provoking laugh." Then back to their rooms and they hurry to slumber until they are called for breakfast. "Then comes a scramble for the water-pan, then a flashing of the looking glass, and a quick brandishing of the hair brush."

With breakfast over, back to their rooms again they stroll. "There, for an hour or two, we act entirely as a notion strikes us—study, read, walk, play, make music or a noise.—During study hours, we generally read some useful work, such as an interesting history or a novel, till such a time as will just suffice us to get our lessons; then comes the tug, and whoever is quickest, is smartest."

But after dinner was the most enviable time. "You know how hot the weather is—enough to roast a pig that crawls out into the sunshine to pick up a plumb stone—and what an irresistible lassitude bears us down. We don't pretend to bear up against it here; not we, for that would rob us of our most precious luxury. As soon as we return from dinner, if you were to watch certain fellows to their rooms, you would see them lazily d-r-a-w-e off their coats, and throwing their weakly carcasses upon the bed, they would soon revel in as fairy a land as the one I described as belonging to the morning. But poor fellows! I have heard them give in some sad excuses for being absent from evening recitations:—they said that they had laid down to take a nap only for a minute, and when they woke up it was sundown. Between evening prayers and dark, we again spend a very pleasant time, and according to the advice given to us in a very valuable paper that is published here, we spend it mostly in the river. But Night! Night! above all other times, it is the time for us. Then it is that a College-boy is in his glory: give him night and good company, and he is as merry as a cricket. Then is the time for his carousing, for his story telling, for his joking, for his—let us not daringly withdraw that curtain which Nature has thrown over the arcana of a college life.—It would be sacrilege."[1]

Various styles of dress and affectations came and went. In 1829 it was the custom to wear beards and mustaches. Smoking cigars was considered a collegiate accomplishment. For the first half century there was no marked distinction among the four classes, which in the beginning were called freshmen, sophomores, junior sophisters, and senior sophisters; although the rules gave the last-named the right, as well as duty, "to inspect the manners of the lower classes and especially of the Freshman class and to instruct them in the customs of the College, and in that grateful and decent behavior toward superiors, which politeness and a just and reasonable subordination require." And it was added that "in order to preserve a due subordination among the students, the classes shall give and receive in the course of their collegiate-life those tokens of respect which tend to the preservation of due subordination." These instructions were largely forgotten by both students and faculty, and there was little that took place which could be called hazing. Now and then, when a freshman would appear on the stage to recite his declamation, the upper classmen would attempt to confuse him by scraping their feet on the floor and by applauding, but the faculty soon came to a decision that a continuance of it "will not be permitted."[2]

During the 'fifties the students, becoming more conscious of their college class distinctions, adopted a uniform cap and coat for each class. In order to prove to the Athenian populace that they were something more than mere children, they restored the old custom of wearing beards and laid down the rule that those who did not follow this practice, either through obstinacy or inability, should treat the others to ginger-bread as often as asked. By this time the "dandy," the "perfect lover," and other types had evolved, described thus by one of those who knew: "The

Lady's man courting his glass, and the *ladies* much more than his books, whispering soft notes of love into each one's ears, declaring to her that *she* is the little *angel,* sings charmingly, and performs admirably on the piano; the fashionable dandy, with his shining *goatee,* or *corked* upper *lip;* the idler lounging upon his soft cushions, frequently disturbing the quiet rest of the—mice by his loud snores; and last and least, what the world politely terms a fashionable drinker, reveling in bacchanalian indulgences." But "Emily," who also knew the Franklin College boys, was rather cruel in her opinions of some of their characteristics. She described the type as "a slave to the use of [tobacco] in three different ways, at the same time; with a breath whose fragrance would vie with the stale scent of a rejected pipe, teeth that might almost excite the envy of a Chinese, and a nose and upper lip bearing no remote resemblance in color, to a pair of buckskin slippers."[3]

Smoking never aroused more opposition than a blast from an "Emily" now and then, but drinking intoxicating spirits led to a movement, which had its ups and downs, expressing itself in many ways, but which never gave up its crusade against "demon rum." This feeling did not arise, however, until the nation had experienced a drinking fling of a half-century duration. In Georgia, as indeed elsewhere, drinking whisky was almost as common as drinking water. Around 1825 there were in Georgia 400,000 people including slaves; the amount of whisky drunk was 2,000,000 gallons. Thus, the average for each man, woman, child and slave was five gallons a year; but making the natural deduction that children and slaves did not get their proportional share, and being charitable to women, one must conclude that the men consumed on the average of near ten gallons a year. The early lawmakers had no feeling that the University and the University town should be legislated into an arid condition, but in 1822 Athens was given permission to tax the retailers of liquor 100%.[4]

Scattering sentiment for temperance, which had been springing up and attempting to organize itself, resulted in the formation of a State Temperance Society in 1828—the Baptists had organized themselves a temperance society the previous year. By 1830 there were sixty temperance societies in the state. In 1829, Joseph

STUDENT TYPES

Henry Lumpkin, later to become a lawyer and jurist of great renown, wrote an open letter to the students, begging them to quit their drinking parties and to organize themselves into a temperance society. There were so few societies for students to join in those days that their natural repugnance to temperance was overcome by their eagerness to join something. So the University Temperance Society was organized, and the next year some of the Athenian moralists started a society for the city. As far as the students were concerned their society became something much in their way when the thrill of joining it was past; and as for the grown-ups in the city and over the state, they soon decided that temperance societies must be wholly bad and the particular concern of the devil, for William Lloyd Garrison, who had run wild on abolitionism, was supporting them.[5]

So, during the awakening 'thirties Georgia slept on the temperance question and did not revive her interest until 1841, when she embraced the Washingtonian Temperance Movement. This new order, founded in Baltimore in 1841, was promoted largely by reformed drunkards, who sought to turn active drinkers away from their cups. Their pledge included also abstinence from wine and cider, which the older societies had not outlawed. But by this time the students had come to detest the temperance reformers and all their ways. The Phi Kappa Literary Society debated in 1840 the question "Are the temperance societies beneficial?" and decided emphatically "No."

By the by the inevitable promoter made his appearance in town (1842), seeking to make Washingtonians out of Athenians, and started his lectures in one of the churches. The students went the first night, listened, and made no trouble; the second night they went and there was no trouble; the third night they attended, and signs of an approaching storm were evident to those versed in student ways; when the fourth night came and it seemed to the students that there was to be no end to this temperance business, the fury of the storm broke. They came drunk and armed with pistols, which they fired, "whooping and hollowing in the streets . . . like a set of savages in a forest," attacked the church and drove the audience out—mothers and daughters screaming and fleeing amidst a fusillade of rocks, bricks, and other missiles. Alexander H. Stephens, now about to enter upon his career of national service, burned with shame and anger when he heard of the riot. He wrote his half-brother Linton Stephens, "Is this the effect of education—this the refinement of the schools—this the perfection of intellectual training—this the end for which so much time is lost and money spent? Oh, shame! That boys are not better taught—that they have no better minds to think and reason with themselves, and see the gross impropriety of such conduct." Four months later the same promoter of Washingtonian temperance appeared in Athens again to reap the harvest of his past sowing, and succeeded in inducing 300 Athenians to sign the pledge—though not without issuing a threat to some unruly students on the second night that he would thrash anyone who began a disturbance. The next year the city Washingtonians, hoping that the hatchet had been buried, invited the students to march in the parade celebrating their first anniversary. This the students refused to do. In this sorry story of student riots and hostilities to temperance, history should not fail to award credit to Henry M. Law, an eloquent senior, who in 1846 was called upon while drunk in a tavern to make a speech. He chose temperance as his subject and spoke with such power and pathos that he broke up the meeting and converted to the cause some of his most drunken hearers.[6]

The "Reformed Drunkards" were soon falling back into their old ways, but not before another temperance society had happened along in time to give them a chance to reform again. This organization, known as the Sons of Temperance, arose in New York in 1842 and made its first appearance in Georgia in 1845, when Macon formed the Tomochichi Chapter. This order differed from the others in its broader appeal and its benevolent features. Now for strange reasons or no reasons at all (or perhaps because camp-meetings had laid siege to the people), the students flocked into the society, organizing a chapter of their own, February 22, 1845, which embraced two-thirds of all the Franklin College boys. Soon the Sons of Temperance were begging for a spot on the campus where they might erect a building, but the trustees put them off with the excuse that they had no surplus land. Then they asked the

Phi Kappa Literary Society for the use of its hall, which was granted in 1850, and the next year withdrawn. Left without a meeting place, they appealed to the trustees again for a lot on the campus, and their plea was again rejected. This was strange usage from the authorities who had been so long and vigorously frowning upon student drinking.[7]

Athens had become a lively center of temperance influence. In 1854 the State Temperance Convention met here, and the students demanded two holidays as necessary for carrying on their part of the business. The forenoon of the first day was made a general holiday, and all Sons were allowed both days if they asked permission from their professors. During the early 'thirties the retailers of liquor were taxed $500 a year, and later for a time they were driven out of town, and signs like this one replaced the grogshops, "A. Brydie, Confectioner and Proprietor of the Temperance Coffee House and Bath House." In 1858 the "wets" and the "fogies" battled with each other for the supremacy of Athens and the former won.[8]

If the students were not to drink whiskies, they should have at least good water both to drink and to wash in. One of the important reasons for locating the University on the Cedar Shoals hill had been the presence there of bubbling springs of cool water; but as the springs were down the hill a way the students would not be satisfied without a well on the campus. In 1806 the trustees ordered Meigs to have a well dug "in the College yard," but the hill seems to have been too high for this feat of engineering to conquer, for in 1830 the trustees were again promising to sink a well and to put a pump in it, if it were not too deep. In the course of time a number of attempts to dig wells were made, but all resulted in failures, and the holes were filled up.[9]

The early Franklin College boys lived before water-works and bathing facilities had come to be a common possession, but some enterprising Athenian in 1810 got permission from the trustees to erect a bath house below the college spring, where he would provide two shower baths, "two plunging baths of cold water and six tepid baths." The rates were to be $6\frac{1}{4}$ cents for a shower or plunging bath and $12\frac{1}{2}$ cents for the tepid baths. Bath houses could not hope to compete with the Oconee River so near, especially since swimming there afforded additional amusement. The students got the reputation of spending most of their time in the river, and with it they did develop skill as swimmers. In 1852 Franklin Bryan, a senior from Florida, attempted to swim the Oconee in time of a great freshet, but the flood swept him to his death while many spectators watched unable to aid him. As the town grew larger, it became necessary to pass an ordinance prohibiting bathing in the river within one hundred yards of either bridge or 300 yards of a residence.[10]

With all the water in and around Athens, it was yet a common charge that the University was not conspicuous for its cleanliness. President Waddel wrote in his diary, November 12, 1824, "saw much filth in Old College," and two years later the trustees said, "The charge of the want of cleanliness is universal and may be well maintained against every room, in both buildings, as well those occupied by students as those reserved for purposes of recitation. In many instances this want of cleanliness is extended to a want of decency and filth is found to have accumulated, of such sort in such quantities as to be offensive and doubtless injurious to health." The trustees charged the faculty to use all efforts to instill ideas of cleanliness into the minds of the students. It now became the rule for students' rooms to be swept once a day and the walls whitewashed twice a year, and the passageways scoured four times a year.[11]

The trustees and faculty felt that student life should be confined to the campus or "College yard" as much as possible; they looked with suspicion on student activities out in town. Pride was taken in the campus and its beautification not only for esthetic reasons but also because of a desire to make it attractive to the students. In 1824 an investigation was ordered to determine the cost of planting three hundred trees and building a fence along Front Street—called Broad now. No great number of trees were planted at this time, but by 1833 a "strong and substantial" fence had been thrown around the campus—but not powerful enough to prevent students from kicking the palings off. In 1857 the campus was fortified with an iron fence, "made in Athens," which successfully resisted all assaults. It was about this time that the landscape artists planted hundreds of trees and shrubs on the campus to please old President Church for the loss of the botanical garden.[12]

Another move toward building up a campus community was the construction of homes for professors, near the University buildings. There was also in mind the very definite idea of concentrating the professors near the origin and scene of student disturbances. For many years the professors had been scattered around in town, but when President Waddel first arrived, insisting that he must be on the campus, he with his wife and five children lived in "Steward's Hall." A strong agitation for professors' homes on the campus arose in the early 'forties, and was based almost wholly on the idea of holding the students in check. It was planned to flank the dormitories on at least three sides with these watchtowers. In locating them little consideration was thus consciously given to the comfort and convenience of professors—though comfortable and convenient they were. Two costing $2,000 each were authorized in 1843 and were finished by 1846. Later others were built.[13]

The monotonous everyday order on the campus was broken by excitements other than fights and riots. A hailstorm swept over the college in the spring of 1831 and broke out almost five hundred window panes before it passed on. In the fall of the preceding year a disastrous fire visited the University and consumed almost half the entire plant—New College, which contained the library and mathematical and astronomical apparatus in addition to dormitory and classroom facilities. It was discovered aflame about 2:20 A.M. just in time for the sleeping students to be awakened and to scramble out half-clad. This was the first great fire to visit the town of Athens and thus it gave the newspaper reporter a chance to use unworked powers of description. "It was a fearful sight," said the *Athenian*. "The crackling and fallen timbers, the sheets of flames as they burst from one window after another, effusing their lurid glare around, and roaring fierce and frightfully, broke in upon the stillness of night with a sound that sent a thrill of horror through every bosom." The building was four stories high and burned for three hours. No evil is so bad as not to have some good mixed with it; as it was only three days until winter vacation, the students got this extra time. Good fortune which had saved every student from the fire did not hover over the ruins; the next spring Thomas W. Grant, a Grammar School pupil, was killed by a falling wall.[14]

Another excitement, this time followed with melancholy results, took place in 1824. It had been a long-standing custom among the mountain men to the northward to fill their wagons with apples, chestnuts, and dried venison meat, drive to Athens, and encamp around the college buildings, there to dispose of their products to the students. It was on a Saturday afternoon, when the students were resting from their week's labors, that two mountaineers drove up. The students began bantering them and holloing from the different windows, and the mountain men bantered back. Then in the midst of the noise someone blew a horn. The horses took fright and started to run wildly away, dragging the wagon over one of the mountaineers who attempted to stop them. There was much excitement everywhere and the rumor soon spread over the state that the students had murdered the man. An investigation was immediately made by the faculty, and Joel Leathers, the mountaineer who escaped with only a few bruises, laid no blame on the students for the accident.[15]

As for student sports, few things could be legally done except study and nothing had made its appearance to be commercialized. There were no college colors, no pennants, no yells. In front of the college buildings jumping rope, swinging on the rings, and playing town ball gave an outlet for pent-up energy which otherwise might have expressed itself in fighting and rioting. As early as 1831 efforts were made to erect a gymnasium, but nothing came from it. In 1849 the scope of the plans was widened to allow citizens of the town to exercise in the structure; but the plans were the only results that ever came from these efforts.[16]

In the very early times (before the common man or boy thought education was worth while) the University developed the reputation of being a school for rich boys and attended only by rich boys. Although students of moderate means and some very poor boys attended the University, it was only natural that the boys of considerable wealth, the sons of planters, predominated and gave the school its outstanding character. The student's almost unrestricted control of money added much to make him ungovernable. He could snap his fingers at fines, and always have enough money left to buy anything Athens had to sell. In 1830 the faculty dealt with an unruly junior by depriving him "entirely of the use of pocket-money." This was their last resort in an attempt to reform him. In 1836 the trustees ordered an investigation "to enquire into the nature & extent of the evils arising to the College from the extravagant expenditure of its students through large allowances of money to them by Parents & Guardians, and the extension of credit to them by merchants and shopkeepers of Athens." The faculty had already declared that "almost all the misconduct of Students at College, may be traced either directly or indirectly to the imprudent use of money." They also held that the less the money "the more secure their characters will be, and the more will they be guarded against useless extravagance, self-sufficiency and vice." Yet the merchants gave credit to the students to almost any amount and rarely lost at it. In 1831, however, an irate father refused to pay his son's debt of $260, on the ground that he had not authorized it. Most fathers, however, indulged their sons to almost any amount. As an example, a Houston County planter's son got $200 from home one day in 1849, and being an honest boy, he paid $170 of his debts immediately.[17]

With all the hilarity that went with student life there was considerable seriousness. The books they studied were difficult and dry. They had no choices—every course was fixed and had to be taken. In 1825 a group of students pledged themselves "to one another" to resist the faculty ruling that there should be two mathematics classes a day. Some of the rebels were expelled for this interference with the curriculum. Mathematics was considered especially difficult. The junior class in 1824 petitioned the faculty to excuse them from reciting "Cicero de Oratore" until they should have completed conic sections. The faculty refused. The students also disliked Greek, and hence they came up often with bad lessons. President Waddel noted in his diary, September 16, 1822, "bad Greek lesson"; the next day he recorded "bad Greek lesson again."

In 1849 a student who had just stood an examination in Greek wrote, "missed the contemptible little word"—and he still was unable to write down what it was. What the students studied seemed far removed from the life around them and equally as far away from any they might ever expect to see or experience. Yet the training they received was valuable. They took on attitudes and characteristics that made of them the chief leaders of the state, and some of them, of the nation.[18]

Student life at Franklin College had its pains and penalties, but with all of its rigors it afforded a rare experience to the sons of Georgia and of the surrounding states. Even while it was being lived it had a sort of daring wild charm about it, but in after years it took on a bewitchment irresistible. Indeed, distance lends enchantment to the view. The editor of the student magazine (the *Georgia University Magazine*) on taking up his duty in 1852 inquired what he should write about, and then immediately answered "We will tell you of ourselves, of our associates and of our beloved Institution, 'Old Franklin.' " And then the romance in and around "Old Franklin" flows through many of the pages of the G U M, as the magazine was familiarly called. Even so terrible a tyrant as the chapel bell called forth an ode:

> When Sol, from his couch in the East doth arise,
> Beams lightly on earth and mounts high in the skies—
> Loud peals of rich music his welcoming tell,
> All nature awakens with the "Old Chapel Bell."

The most hated and feared members of the faculty suddenly became likable and some of the suppers and entertainments the students received at the homes of the president and professors were pleasantly recalled. Alexander H. Stephens said the time he spent at Franklin College was "by far the happiest days of my life."[19] Many another man who had one time been a Franklin College boy felt much the same way about it.

CHAPTER VI

DISCIPLES OF DEMOSTHENES
AND THE FOLLOWERS OF
OTHER ANCIENT GREEKS

 ROCKS and trees gathered around Orpheus as he played upon his lyre in ancient Greece; wild animals and red Indians heard the young Franklin College boys as they poured forth their oratory in early Georgia, presided over by the spirit of another Grecian, Demosthenes. The school was hardly two years old when the juniors met on February 5, 1803, to organize a society "for the promotion of extemporizing, or extemporary speaking." Exactly two weeks later they turned on a flow of oratory that was to resound and reverberate for a century—that was to set up a custom and institute a method of popular control long to dominate the whole South. The first great question they attempted to settle was whether a monarchy was better than a republic.[1]

This society was named Demosthenian and its emblem was a golden key with clasping hands over an altar of friendship on one side and on the reverse side "the image of Demosthenes declaiming on the seashore." This was to be worn as a watch charm or pinned upon the coat; for formal occasions such as commencements and parades a silken badge with the same Demosthenes declaiming on the same seashore was worn. The Franklin College boys made much of Demosthenes; they studied his life, his speeches, and consciously held him up as their guide and hero. The emblems were sacred and none who was not a member might aspire to wear them. Once the society was thrown into a commotion by the report that a Negro boy was proudly wearing this decoration. A committee was appointed to investigate. It was difficult to keep the pins in the possession of the rightful wearers. In 1847 a friend of the Demosthenians found three of these pins in far-off New York City; he bought them, later sold two of them to lawful members, and offered the other to the society for $12. For twenty years the Demosthenians held their meetings in an old schoolroom and then in 1824 moved into their hall upon which they had spent $4,000.[2]

This sudden show of prosperity was born of a very certain cause. For some years before 1820 the society had grown lax and listless—and some members had almost forgotten Demosthenes. Then appeared in Athens a young ambitious college graduate, who once had been a student in Franklin College, but who departed for Princeton in 1817 when it appeared that Franklin College was dead. He was Joseph Henry Lumpkin, born in Oglethorpe County. He saw that only rivalry could put the spark of life back into orating and "extemporizing"; so he organized on Washington's Birthday in 1820 a new society which was called Phi Kappa. These two Greek letters stood for *Philo Kosmean,* but this was to remain unknown to all who were not members. The emblem was a diamond-shaped watch-key with the motto *Omoinia Kai Amoibos Philia.* Only the initial letters of this motto were to be exposed— the rest "to be kept a profound *secret."* Weak to begin with, and exposed to the sharp rivalry of the Demosthenians, the Phi Kappas were able to find no meeting place better than the garret of Parson Hope Hull's old chapel.[3]

But in 1836 they had succeeded in completing a hall of architectural dignity and beauty within and without, and on July 5 they dedicated it with pomp and ceremony. They became generous for once in their attitude toward the Demosthenians and invited them to the exercises, allowing them for the first time (and they hoped the last) to see within its mystic walls. There was prayer, an oration by William L. Mitchell, and music by the Athens Harmonic Society. In a befitting resolution they returned thanks "to those ladies who manifested so much good feeling and benevolence

toward Society in decorating the New Hall with flowers." A carpet
not to cost over $300 was to be put upon the floor, and the portraits
of all the presidents of the United States were to be hung upon
the walls. But the end of this rejoicing came when the slow process
of paying for the hall began. The old temporary hall which had
been occupied when the chapel attic was no longer tenable was
sold to the trustees for $400, and the honorary members, of whom
there seemed to be no end, were continuously being called upon
to help rescue the society from its creditors. At the annual meeting
following the dedication, held directly after commencement, an
effort was made to enlist the support of the Demosthenians in
inducing the legislature to pay for the hall. Being the first meeting of its kind in the new hall, it was memorable otherwise on
account of those who attended. John C. Calhoun was in the chair
and ex-President Moses Waddel was first assistant. Among the
other distinguished guests were Joseph Henry Lumpkin and Augustus Baldwin Longstreet, and among the members were the
Cobb brothers, Howell and Thomas R. R., the former delivering
an oration. But the request of even such an assemblage failed to
enlist the support of the jealous Demosthenians or to get the attention of the legislature. In 1838 Howell Cobb, John Milledge,
and J. P. Charles Whitehead together gave $1,000, and five
years later the hall was completely paid for—costing altogether
$5,000.[4]

The members of the two societies were proud of their halls and
zealous in the care and upkeep of them. When the planters of the
surrounding country brought their cotton to town and piled it too
close to the Phi Kappa Hall, a resolution was forthcoming requesting the owners of the cotton to remove it; and when the
"Dramatic Caps" in 1854, so forgetful of the dignity of the hall,
asked permission to practice their antics in one of its rooms, they
were given a quick refusal—although the Phi Kappas did allow
music lessons to be practiced there.[5]

The great patron of the societies, their aegis, greater even than
Demosthenes, was the goddess Secrecy. What could be more desirable, more interesting, more intriguing than to know something
that others did not know—to constantly remind them that there

were things they did not know! The secrets themselves might be
inconsequential; the fact that they were secrets was all-important.
The trustees refused to allow any other secret organizations on the
campus—notwithstanding the fact that during the 'forties and
'fifties the Mystic Seven held its meetings every seventh night,
opened the exercises with seven raps, did other things in the
rhythm of seven, and recorded its secret doings in the "Book of
Chronicles." Before Phi Kappas had built their hall, when they
were yet housed in one of the College buildings, they appointed
a committee "to write a letter to the Faculty remonstrating against
the Demosthenians roaming in Phi Kappa's end of the College
edifice." And when the time came to move into the new hall, the
troublesome problem arose of making the transfer without the
Demosthenians learning any of the secrets. A special committee
was appointed to supervise the moving of the furniture, and a
vigilance committee was carefully picked out and ordered "to
detect any person or persons who might be so injudiciously disposed as to be peeping into matters which do not concern them."
The Phi Kappas were convinced that their rivals were using every
resource to learn their last secret both in their old haunts and their
new. They were on the point of having the inner walls of their
old hall whitewashed to obliterate the secret writings that might
have decorated them when it was discovered that the "members
of the Demosthenian Society had already seen the inside of it."
And while their new hall was yet unfinished they discountenanced
Demosthenians entering it. They actually considered for a time
posting a notice ordering the Demosthenians to keep out. It was
considered the height of indignity for mere females to see the
inside of a society hall—this the attitude of those who in other
respects were "the flower of chivalry." According to the by-laws
of the Demosthenians, "No member, regular or honorary, shall
be permitted to bring a female or females into the hall at any
time, under the penalty of five dollars." Now and then they re-
lented to the extent of allowing "females" to visit the hall for a
period of two weeks, and on special occasions when decorations
were needed for the hall they were always willing to receive them
and to pass resolutions profuse in their praise of the *ladies* for

their valuable aid.[6] Thus did Southern chivalry shine forth.

Not only should the society halls and their precincts be kept inviolate one from the other, but especially should their proceedings be kept profoundly secret. The Demosthenian constitution of 1830 declared that no member should "divulge any circumstance which may tend to derogate from the dignity of the society, or any individual member of the society." So seriously did the Demosthenians take their secrecy that they refused to send a copy of their constitution to Randolph-Macon College in 1834, when young Virginians there were seeking to follow the common practice throughout the South in starting a secret society. To save the campus from a constant state of anarchy in Phi Kappa and Demosthenian relations, a solemn treaty was drawn up early in their history and revised and readopted at various times thereafter. A system of diplomatic language and procedure sprang up, as stilted, cold, and distant-like as an Algerian Dey or Turkish Sultan. But most controversies soon developed more heat than diplomacy. There was much need for this system, these diplomatic notes and missions, for the members of each society were constantly engaged in trying to find out each other's secrets—for what good were secrets if they were not to be found out![7]

The treaties concerned principally two points, questions of membership and the bounds and limits which guarded the sacred precincts of the two halls in time of meeting as well as in adjournment—the dead lines. Out of these two sources flowed contentions and misunderstandings without end. It was considered a *casus belli* for members of one society to walk under the windows of the hall of the other while a meeting was in progress. "Eaves dropping" and "pumping" were frequently charged by one society against the other, and a series of notes would follow between them ending in making the controversy more bitter. In 1833 the Demosthenians accused the Phi Kappas of taking into their membership two students, who had not, according to the treaty, resided in the College long enough. The latter made their explanation, to which the Demosthenians replied that if they had no better excuses than those offered they would like to know what apologies they were willing to make. The Phi Kappas replied in a tone which came

near causing a breach of diplomatic relations. In 1828 the Demosthenians accused "J. N. Waddell of eaves dropping and pumping."
The Phi Kappas immediately appointed a committee to investigate
the charges and the report followed that "no touch of guilt could
be attached to Bro Waddell." The high-flown diplomatic language
that invariably inaugurated any controversy dropped by the second
exchange to the level of such expressions: They had received "a
very illiberal and abusive letter"; they resented being addressed
"in so contemptuous a style"; "You have manifested nothing but
a determination to consider no excuse satisfactory"; they demanded
"an explanation of said epistle."[8]

The animosities that sprang up between these two opposing
groups of students were more than passing whims. They were
seriously bitter and lasted in some instances throughout the period
of college life and long thereafter. There are instances where
reconciliations were never made until old age had crept upon the
participants. The intense rivalry that prevailed between these two
societies is eloquent proof of the large part they played in the
lives of the students. For years the Demosthenians seem to have
been on the defensive, torn at times by internal dissensions, and
therefore likely to take as an offense the Phi Kappa happenings that might otherwise seem innocent enough. In 1833 they
accused Professor James Jackson of saying disparaging things
about them. He admitted saying that the Phi Kappas had more
members and were boasting about it, and he also admitted saying
that he had warned them that they would split with internal dissensions like the Demosthenians if they were not careful. It was
the custom for the students from Savannah and the coast (especially
Liberty County) to join the Phi Kappas, and so closely were society
lines drawn that it was something to remark about if a member
of one society had close friends in the other. In fact the groups
were so exclusive of each other that some of the wiser students
felt that they were being robbed of valuable friendships and
experiences.[9]

Strong rivalry marked almost every move these two societies
made with reference to each other, but along no line was it keener
than in scouring the earth for honorary members. He was indeed

an insignificant person who failed to be "taken in" either by one or the other of these two societies. They kept their sentinels on the watchtowers and whenever it was ascertained that the sun of any local politician or statesman had risen above his own local horizon, they sent him an invitation to become a member. Each society leaned strongly toward Whig politicians, and when in 1835 a Phi Kappa was so inadvised on what was proper as to propose Andrew Jackson, this rampant Democratic President of the United States was rejected, and a Dr. Richards was elected to the high state of honorary membership in Jackson's stead. Nine years later, when Jackson had become more respectable in the eyes of Phi Kappas, they elected him without opposition. At this same time they elected two other men who were later to become presidents of the United States, James Knox Polk and James Buchanan. In 1850 they elected the future president of the Confederacy, Jefferson Davis. In 1838 they recognized the coming greatness of the future secretary of the treasury of the Confederate States, C. G. Memminger, and added the luster of honorary membership in Phi Kappa to his name. In the same year they showed again the power of prophecy by electing John Tyler. Among other celebrated politicians and statesmen of their day who became honorary Phi Kappas were John J. Crittenden of Kentucky, Thomas L. Clingman, famous Whig congressman from North Carolina, Henry Dodge, senator from Wisconsin, Waddy Thompson, Whig minister to Mexico, John A. Quitman, fiery governor of Mississippi, Rufus Choate, famous in Massachusetts' Whiggery, Judge Beverly Tucker, Joseph R. Ingersoll, J. M. Legaré, J. L. Orr, R. Barnwell Rhett, M. L. Bonham, and Langdon Cheves. Some of the famous preachers of their day were not slighted, such as the Methodist Capers and the Presbyterian Thornwell, both of South Carolina.

In their haste to get ahead of the Demosthenians in chasing down honorary members, the Phi Kappas now and then ran off into pathways from which they later found it advisable to retreat. A certain person who bore a name, foreign and high-sounding, and who was important enough to have a page with him, appeared in Athens as a purveyor of sweet music, and was seized upon by the Phi Kappas and made an honorary member. His name was Baron de Fleur and his page was Charles Gunther. But mischief was abroad in some way or other shortly, for in 1841 they expelled both baron and page in the fewest words possible, not deigning to put the reasons down. Most likely it was found out that he was not really a baron. In 1845 a Mr. Brown was proposed for honorary membership, but when his character was held up for inspection it was discovered that he was an abolitionist, and, of course, rejection was swift. Was this a premonition of the John Brown of Harpers Ferry fame! They reached the height of their ambitions along the lines of honorary members when they placed the halo on Napoleon III, Emperor of France.[10]

The Demosthenians hoped to match Phi Kappa in every honorary member it should secure with one of their own of still greater fame. They showed presidential foresight when they elected Andrew Johnson, and although in securing Henry Clay they failed to add a president to their list, yet they had the only "Great Compromiser." They recognized greatness wherever it might rest; they would honor others than politicians and statesmen. True enough they elected William L. Yancey, the Alabama fire-eater, who thanked them for "this mark of esteem"; they chose Henry A. Wise, the Virginia governor, who accepted with thanks; and they enrolled Sergeant S. Prentiss, the magical orator from Mississippi. But they also found joy in recognizing such geniuses as the poet William Cullen Bryant, Richard Malcolm Johnston, the man of letters, who was much pleased to accept membership "in that highly respectable body," and Albert Pike, the greatest Mason of his day and no mean lawyer. David L. Swain, the president of the University of North Carolina, also passed the test. William Gilmore Simms was also so honored and seems to have truly seen the beauty and appropriateness of recognizing literary merit, for he said in accepting, "pride & pleasure are not a little heightened to my mind, when the compliment emanates from our own Southern region, where, perhaps, it has been our misfortune, hitherto, to have too greatly neglected this high moral interest." Others of less fame gladly accepted, proud to have their names inscribed in the records of the society to mingle "with many of the Great and Good."

Not only did the societies pounce upon all the great and near great they could find, they also packed their honorary rolls with all the local and state celebrities they could lay hands on. A new professor on reaching Athens would be lucky if he did not find himself in the midst of a riot between the two societies fighting over the question of which one should have him. President Lipscomb, who came to the University from Alabama, was seized upon by the Demosthenians and without blame on his part became the subject of a heated quarrel which resulted in the abrogation of the ancient treaty between the two societies. This happened in February, 1861. A Phi Kappa said in the presence of a Demosthenian that Dr. Lipscomb had regretted that he had joined the Demosthenians and that if he were free he would join the Phi Kappas. Lipscomb denied having made such remarks, and when the Demosthenians demanded that the Phi Kappas prove their charges a squabble developed which ended in the disruption of friendly relations.

Honorary members were valuable beyond the fact that they added luster to the society. The societies had a very definite notion that an honorary member at least owed the society something for the great honor that had been done him. Books were always acceptable and proper gifts—and each society secured many volumes in this way. They were also not averse to begging honorary members for money for special outlays, such as building halls and repairing them. Many of the honorary members, however, refused to take the hint at pecuniary and material gifts and instead in their letters of acceptance heaped praises on Phi Kappas or Demosthenians (whichever suited the circumstance), and now and then made large contributions of excellent advice. One fellow who had already been elected an honorary member by the Demosthenians was also elected to the same honor by the Phi Kappas unacquainted with their rival's action. He was so pleased with this additional mark of esteem that according to a Phi Kappa he said "as a candid Demosthenian he was obliged to acknowledge that our society was superior as a school for oratory."[11]

The societies held their meetings on Saturdays, beginning at nine o'clock in the morning, and the hour of adjournment was entirely problematical. There were no University classes on this day, and any students who were so devoid of respect for their own welfare as not to care to join a society were kept penned up in their rooms until noon. As a result there were few or no students who did not become Demosthenians or Phi Kappas. Now and then a student who found that his studies required more of his attention would be granted honorable dismissal, or merely a dispensation, if he asked for it. In 1836 Thomas A. Mitchell "was deficient in his studies & requested a dispensation from the Hall until August next." His request was granted. Besides the regular weekly meetings, special meetings were likely to be held at almost any time—to initiate new members, to answer some caustic verbal attack from the rival society, or as was the case with the Phi Kappas in 1845 to levy a special tax on each member to replenish a treasury which had just been relieved of $90 by some robber who got into it while the treasurer was sick.[12]

The meetings and general business of the societies were taken by the students with as great a seriousness as anything in their whole lives. Society affairs were no hilarious subterfuge for escaping college classes. But this fact did not prevent some playing with the subject of adjournment. Scarcely a Saturday came when a student out of deviltry or strong desire did not move an adjournment, giving some weighty reasons. So intent were the Phi Kappas on continuing with their regular business that in 1836 when an attempt was made to adjourn to attend a meeting "in behalf of Texas"—Texas, who had fired the whole South in her struggle against the Mexicans—the society refused. Yet under other impulses Phi Kappas and Demosthenians adjourned when affairs less weighty than the fate of Texas were involved. In 1849 there was a reawakening of religion on the campus, and the vote in the Phi Kappa Society was decidedly in favor of adjourning for the Baptist State Convention, which met in Athens on one Saturday in May, and for the celebration of the Sons of Temperance on the following Saturday—though in the latter case there may have been among some a resurging of the old feeling against temperance which had led to a few riots, which the students had enjoyed so much. Camp-meetings had an irresistible attraction for the Franklin College

boys, and seldom could a society meeting hold out against such
a counter-attraction. The same was likewise true of a circus. In
fact, the societies gradually melted away on the approach of so
overwhelming a disturbance as the latter. The Phi Kappa secretary
recorded in his minutes in 1849 that the meeting was a failure,
"most of the members having deserted the Hall to witness the procession of the Circus which was just entering town." The halls
were now and then abandoned "on account of the coldness of the
weather"; once the Demosthenians adjourned because of their
fatigue from the celebration of the Fourth of July the preceding
day; and once they adjourned (in 1831) to see "a grand solar
eclipse."[13]

There were the usual officers to be found in societies in general,
and others with strange and unusual names, such as clavingers
and censors morum. The presidency was naturally the highest
office and aspired to by all who were ambitious in the slightest.
Like the president of the United States he delivered an inaugural
address, which the secretary generally described in such a set
phrase as "a very fine, chaste & practical address." Benjamin M.
Palmer, later to become a famous preacher, had his inaugural
so described. But it was not always praise that got into the minutes.
Either through personal feeling or a desire to be honest with the
facts the secretary might become brutally plain. The secretary
of Phi Kappa in 1850 in describing the president's address said
it "was in reality a mock lecture, for he misrepresented many of
the best Members by accusing them of Malpractice in office. It
was fraught with the most absurd misrepresentations, and grossest
accusations against the individual characters of the members."
There is other evidence that there was not always the best feeling
reigning among members of the same society. Jabez L. M. Curry,
destined for a career of great usefulness, received an anonymous
letter from a fellow Phi Kappa demanding that he resign his clerk-
ship for the honor and dignity of the society. Curry, hurt by this
thrust, resigned despite the speeches that were made to dissuade
him. Yet Phi Kappas always used the term *brother* in addressing
each other or referring to each other in their proceedings, and
steadily refused to vote out the custom when assaults were made

upon it by those who thought it had been outlived. A candid and engaging glimpse into the Demosthenians in action was unwittingly left by R. T. Fouche, when, doubtless bored by the proceedings, he passed the time by writing on the fly-leaf of the Treasurer's Book this: "We are all . . . clever fellows. Fred is sitting up there as solemn as if his last friend were dead. Tom is looking around to report somebody. Billy is playing with a watch. Elic is considering whether a long concatinalion of bombastic diction should be tolerated in a forensic discussion. & *Barnes* is ranting condemning Louis XVI of France. *Pretty Good.*"[14]

The order of business differed somewhat between the two societies and each brought in changes as time went on. There was always a good supply of orations, which generally got described in the minutes as "exceedingly elegant and chaste." Then following the order used by the Phi Kappas in 1837, there were six members who were responsible for practicing at the art of letter-writing, six who should deliver declamations, and then came the main work of the society—debating. One person was appointed from each of the sophomore, junior, and senior classes for each side, to open the debate, and then the roll of the complete membership was called to give each person an opportunity to speak—on the side of his choice. Not once, but twice were the names called off, and sometimes a member either to show his versatility or to make merriment would change his side on the second roll call. Such a lack of sincerity was prohibited by the Phi Kappas in 1837. The quoting of the Scripture was also prohibited and the decision on the debate was handed down by the president or by a popular vote of the whole house.[15]

As already suggested the meetings were held on Saturdays, beginning at nine in the morning and continuing indefinitely. When the village tavern bell rang out the hour for noon dinner, the debating generally was scarcely begun. Sometimes the societies adjourned then, or, most likely to show how seriously they considered themselves engaged, they would wait until one o'clock. Back from dinner the debaters redoubled their efforts to settle the weighty problem before them, and frequently darkness crept over the campus resounding to the orators of future greatness. A motion in Phi Kappa made in 1840 to "adjourn hereafter at $\frac{1}{2}$ hour before sundown for supper" was defeated, and often the secretary recorded his minutes in this strain: The debaters "spent hour after hour in their intellectual conflict, till the shades of night came on." Some questions developed such heat and interest that the conflict lasted long into the night, disturbing the sleep of some of the villagers who lived near by. Kindly old President Waddel felt that his boys were staying up too late in their debating and told the trustees so.[16]

Debating was a serious business; the welfare of the country doubtless rested upon what the Franklin College boys did. A characteristic minute said the debate "proceeded with great warmth. It lasted long and strenuous were the arguments made on both sides of the question." But there were exceptions, and they were noted with characteristic vigor. Once the Demosthenians got through with their exercises about eleven o'clock in the morning and the secretary recorded in his minutes that it was "one of the most shamefully short and uninteresting debates that we have ever witnessed." On another occasion a Demosthenian secretary, thinking that there had not been sufficient fire and vigor in the debate, wrote that the "discussion was dry and exceedingly uninteresting, & but few participated, there seemed a magic spell which bound the members with much dulness. I humbly hope never to see such desertion and neglect again."[17]

The subjects debated were almost as varied as the thoughts of man; they embraced history, literature, philosophy, logic, religion, and a surprisingly large supply of current questions. As many of them were decided by a popular vote and the tally recorded, the decisions give an intimate insight into the actual thinking of Southern ante-bellum college students unusual in its exactness and vitality. Did college thought keep the same level set by the common mass as expressed in elections and the pronunciamentos of organized bodies such as churches, or did the colleges actually take the initiative and boldly develop sparks of thought which flew outward and upward? Some evidence should appear in these debates. True enough, with the renewal of one college generation by another and with the passing of time, which tended to change viewpoints on certain problems, some questions when debated over again under these circumstances won where they had lost before.

Vigorous thinking and some boldness cropped out in debates on religion and morality. In 1829 the Demothenians debated the question, "Which is most to be feared, religious or political fanaticism," and decided by a 19 to 12 vote that religion held more perils. The Demosthenians and Phi Kappas, both, decided that the immortality of the soul could not be proved apart from revelation, and the former decided that it could not be proved from the light of nature that virtue received its reward in this life. In 1836, long before Darwin had written his *Origin of the Species,* they rashly took up the question, "Laying aside all scriptural authority could we reasonably conclude that all men were descended from the same pair?" and decided by a 14 to 12 vote that no evidence could be adduced. They believed, however, that the Christian religion was essential to national prosperity, with 9 dissenting out of a vote of 27; and they also held that the Christian religion had contributed more to the world than science. Also the heathen would be saved without the Gospel. Their position was not definitely fixed on the principles of infidels. In 1838 they decided that students should not be allowed to read the works of infidel writers, but three years later they held that the law should not prohibit the dissemination of infidel principles. With the seriousness brought on by the Civil War, they decided in 1862 that such works should be prohibited by law.[18]

Infidel principles were generally held to be harmful, even more to be shunned than Catholicism. But the Catholic religion was bad enough, and according to a decision made in 1852, it should not be tolerated in the United States. This subject had long afforded queries upon which the societies had whetted their wits. In 1831 they had held that the Catholics were more evil than good, and a few years later they had spent a whole morning, the following afternoon, and much of the night in discussing whether Catholics should be allowed to enter the United States and to hold office. They decided 13 to 7 against it. When, after the fall of the Whig Party, political gropings were directed into channels of opposition to the Catholics, the most tenacious and long-drawn-out debates in the history of the societies took place. In 1854 the Demosthenians decided that the Know Nothing Party should not be encouraged, but the following year after two full days of debating they changed their minds. The Phi Kappas the same year debated the problem two days (consecutive weekly meetings) and declared in favor of the Know Nothings. Although the Franklin College boys never had much sympathy for Catholics, they had no great objection to the new-fangled Universalists—they at least decided that Universalism could stand the test of investigation. And they seem to have had no great horror of the Mormons, for in 1857 they held that Deseret (Brigham Young's commonwealth) should be admitted into the Union as a state.[19]

Concerning other questions of a moral character, the Demosthenians decided that there was no sensible reason why the mails should not be carried on Sundays (despite the belief to the contrary of certain societies which had sprung up); they could see no reason why students should not attend theaters even if the Methodists did not approve of it; furthermore, they believed that no one was likely to be greatly injured by reading novels. But they did not approve of lotteries. The Phi Kappas believed that the truth ought not "to be spoken in every circumstance." With the spreading of Methodists and Baptists over the land, and Presbyterians too, the preachers made their onslaughts on "infidel strongholds" and it was not difficult to see that they felt much concern for the religious sanity of the Franklin College students. In 1843 the Phi Kappas debated the query, "Did Deity display more wisdom or power in the creation of his works?" Thomas R. R. Cobb, a man of profound religious convictions, and perhaps an abler man than his more famous brother Howell, being "called on by the President . . . arose & suddenly a deathlike silence prevailed. For the space of half an hour, he held the hall in rapturous suspense. With his accustomed eloquence he demonstrated the wisdom of the Deity, then dilating upon his subject he descanted in glowing language upon his infinite perfectibility, his assimilating man to his own image & rendering him competent to enjoy the inestimable fruition of those bright realms where 'seraphs gather immortality from life's fair tree.' "[20]

The eternal and insoluble question of woman gave the societies many a tussle, and they attacked it and wrestled with it from every angle—from the impersonal and the general to the specific and the very concrete. The Demosthenians asked themselves the question, "Does refined female society exert a beneficial influence on male students?" and answered *yes* by a 17 to 10 vote; but the Phi Kappas, stating their question in a more inclusive fashion, answered it by declaring that woman exerted a baneful influence on society—a sad lapse from the standards of Southern chivalry. Women might or might not have a good effect on men; what about Franklin College boys and Athens girls? "Should Students in College visit the Young ladies?" or "Does Social Intercourse between the sexes benefit students?"—these things the Phi Kappas wanted to know. They decided in 1839 that the relationship was good. But too much intercourse leads to engagements and here developed a question of great profundity and complexity: "Does change of mind justify a violation of a marriage engagement?" The Demosthenians, 17 to 9, strongly believed it did. There were yet other possibilities concerning this subject: "If a young man, his truly affianced bride, and mother were sailing in a boat on a river, and the boat should overturn, which is he morally bound to save?" Inevitable logic could lead to but one conclusion—he should save his mother, for the laws of nature had not restricted people to one bride.[21]

There was a more serious angle than breaking an engagement or preferring a mother to a bride: "Should a man be compelled by law to marry the victim of his seduction?" The Phi Kappas thought that he should, while the Demosthenians decided otherwise. But after all the question of marriage itself was not a settled fact. The Demosthenians queried "Are all men morally bound to marry?" for in reality does married life afford more happiness than single? In the early 'thirties they decided in favor of married life, but in the 'fifties they voted for the single status. When it became a question of a choice between "civil liberty" and the "state of matrimony," they would always choose the former. But granting that marriage must come, "Ought Parents to regulate entirely the choice of their children in the all important subject of matrimony?" The Phi Kappas debated this weighty problem and left the decision to Alexander H. Stephens to decide, and this genius, who was destined never to marry, decided that children should have their own way. When the single status had been departed from there was no return. The Demosthenians held that divorces should never be granted—"after a cold and inanimate debate."[22]

The boys swept the heavens and the earth for something on which to whet their wits, and out of their endeavors grew a great multiplicity of teasing problems. Would the Dark Ages ever return—"no," said the Demosthenians. The Phi Kappas held that works of fiction should not be "propagated throughout the country." The Demosthenians would know "Which has the greater influence over man Booty or Beauty." They declared that ambition could adhere to honest principles, and in 1838, when overcome by a balmy spring day, these scholars had a lapse and declared that physical contest was more interesting than mental. Also being rather gifted in the art of spending all the money their fathers would send them, they naturally decided that a miser was much more injurious to society than a spendthrift. They also thought that the only way a gentleman had of settling an argument—dueling—should not be taken away from him. Though mental exertion might seem less interesting to Demosthenians (at least in springtime) than physical, yet they held themselves capable of pronouncing the dictum that American literature was inferior to European—and thereby sided with the host of English defamers of American things, who had long been storming the United States with their books of travels. The Phi Kappas in 1837 took an excursion into the realm of medical science and examined the question, "Should Botanical Steam Doctors be tolerated by law so far as to be allowed to practice and make charges as other physicians?" They granted them permission.[23]

History was a fruitful field from which to draw subjects on which to dispute—the grandeur of Greece, the splendor of Rome, the baseness of the barbarians, the darkness of the Middle Ages, and the power and might of the Modern Era. Caesar and Cicero, Regulus and Cato, Charlemagne, Alexander the Great, and Pericles frequently trod the halls of Phi Kappas and Demosthenians. The latter inquired in 1835 "Which made laws best calculated to subserve the interests of this country—Lycurgus or Solon?" This question "after a long and uninteresting and tedious debate was decided in favor of the negative." It was a great sweep of time down to the days of Warren Hastings. The fate of this unfortunate man was often considered and a verdict of condemnation generally handed down. But the most engaging and popular of all the characters of history was Napoleon. The debaters grew eloquent as they followed the astonishing career of the "Little Corporal" and with indignation they berated England for her ungenerous treatment of him. He was even brought forth one time to do battle with Washington for the crown of supreme greatness, but the "Father of his Country" won by a vote of 16 to 2. In 1861 the Phi Kappas debated the question whether it was right for Napoleon III to possess the crown of France, and decided in the affirmative.[24]

Although the utmost realm of human thought and imagination was the limit to which the questions for debate went, the United States and Georgia were most prolific in points to be settled. Questions of a political nature were most favored, though now and then problems of a fundamental governmental character or economic or social phase crept in. For example, the Demosthenians were at the forefront of the Jacksonian democratic movement, holding in 1834 that suffrage should be universal. Yet four years earlier they decided that there was no warrant for the assertion that a people are capable of governing themselves. It was at this time that the French were carrying forward the ideas of socialism under such leaders as Saint-Simon, Fourier, and Louis Blanc. The equalization of property had no appeal for the Demosthenians. Views were varying on the subject of war. The Phi Kappas debated the query as to whether war was ever justifiable, and showed that they had not yet become pacifists by holding that under certain circumstances wars were desirable. The Demosthenians believed in 1831 that the West Point Military Academy should be abolished; four years later they decided that military subjects should not be taught in a literary institution, but in 1838 they decided by a vote of 11 to 5 that students should not be exempted from military duty.[25]

In 1835 the Demosthenians held that immigration to this country should not be encouraged and that people who came should not have indiscriminately the right of citizenship. The prohibition of the sale of liquors failed to meet their approval by a vote of 20 to 13. On the subject of free schools, they took a position far ahead of the citizens of Georgia when in 1844 they held that such a system of schools should be established. The Phi Kappas also stood for this line of progress, but feeling that they were able to pay for their college education they took the position that the legislature should not support the University.[26]

Questions of an economic character also engaged the attention and interest of these embryo statesmen. In 1830 the Demosthenians entered into the land question discussion and sided with those who would turn over the Western lands to the states. In Jackson's quarrel with the Second United States Bank they took the side of Nicholas Biddle, but they stood by Old Hickory in his opposition to federal aid to internal improvements. In 1833 a company was organized in Athens to build a railroad to Augusta to connect with the Charleston and Hamburg, which had just been completed. The Demosthenians, not a one of whom had ever seen a railroad, discussed the railroad business at length and came to the conclusion that a railroad from Athens to Augusta would not benefit the state. There seems to have been some hidden prejudice in this society against railroads, for in 1857 they opposed the building of a railroad to the Pacific. But in 1836 the Phi Kappas fell in with John C. Calhoun's idea of a railroad from Charleston to Cincinnati.[27]

On the subject of national expansion, the Franklin College students showed a decided leaning toward Whig principles, although there was no absolute fixed uniformity in their decisions. In the beginning they held out much sympathy for the Texans, many of whom were expatriated Georgians. In 1830 the Demosthenians were in favor of having the United States buy Texas, and six years later when the Texan Revolution was on they thought Texas should be admitted into the Union if she gained her independence, but

in 1838 they changed their mind on this point. With the approach
of the war with Mexico, the Demosthenians felt that it would be
dangerous to the Union to extend the national territory, but the
Phi Kappas desired the extension of the Republic to the Pacific.
When the Mexican War was nearing its end, the Demosthenians
opposed the annexation of Mexico, and the Phi Kappas went further
by declaring that the United States should take no Mexican territory "as remuneration for the expenses of the war." But by the
'fifties when sectionalism had come into full play they followed
the South by holding that the war had been justified and that
Texas should be supported in her greatest boundary demands,
even to the extent of holding Santa Fé "in opposition to the general
government."[28]

On other points of national foreign policy, the Phi Kappas in
1826 thought that the United States should not enter into any form
of alliance with the South American republics, and a few years
later the Demosthenians did not think Canada ought to be annexed
if she should secure her independence from England. In 1835
when President Jackson had nearly maneuvered himself into a
war with France, the Demosthenians objected to the United States'
entering into hostilities. Years later when the Ostend Manifesto
was issued and it appeared that Cuba was to become a part of the
United States both societies opposed this Machiavellian movement—the Phi Kappas debating the subject for a whole day.[29]

The great slavery debate, which began vigorously in the 'thirties
and did not end until the Civil War intervened, was carried on
in the halls of Phi Kappas and Demosthenians scarcely less than
in the halls of Congress. Year in and year out the justification of
slavery was debated by both societies. The Demosthenians came
very near condemning it in 1833 when the vote stood 6 to 5 in
its favor. In 1827 the Phi Kappas set forth Calhoun's argument
that slavery was beneficial to the institution of government, but
the following year they boldly held that slavery was unjustifiable,
and again in 1837 they believed that slavery should be abolished.
Both societies often debated the query: Which has the greater
right "to complain of our inhumanity," the Indian or the Negro?
The Indian always won the decision. As the abolitionists waxed

hot and intemperate in their criticisms and now and then suffered
violence when they were so foolish as to be found in the South,
they gave rise to such queries as this: "Is the custom of inflicting
capital punishment without judge or jury upon abolitionists when
found in the South Right?" The Phi Kappas, who debated this
question, decided in favor of law and order. The Demosthenians
denied that slavery was a moral evil, but they believed, contrary
to the laws of the Southern States, that slaves should be educated.
During the last few years before the outbreak of war, certain ones
in the South argued for the reopening of the African slave trade.
In 1858 the Demosthenians decided in favor of it, but the Phi
Kappas after two days of debate refused their sanction.[30]

Resistance to the Federal Government and the disruption of
the Union were questions frequently discussed. Georgia's most
dramatic introduction to these eventualities first came in the
'twenties and 'thirties in her attempt to get rid of her Indians,
Creeks and Cherokees. The Demosthenians generally held that
the state had a right to extend her jurisdiction over these unde-
sirable peoples and that the United States should send them beyond
the Mississippi. In the early 'thirties the University campus was
the meeting place during commencement times of South Carolinians
and Georgians bent on resisting the tariff even to the point of
nullification. So it was doubly certain that the students would
take up the discussion which their elders were so hotly pursuing.
The Demosthenians were opposed to a protective tariff, were against
the encouragement of Southern manufactories which would take
advantage of this species of robbery, and on June 4, 1831, they
decided that a convention of all the Southern States should be
held to devise ways for resisting the tariff. For some time it appeared certain that Georgia would nullify the tariff before South
Carolina could act. The Demosthenians held that a state had the
right to resist a law which it considered to be unconstitutional, and
it favored the South's aiding South Carolina if she should secede.
But opinion was not irresistibly flowing in this direction; the
Demosthenians denied in 1831 the right of a state to nullify a law
of Congress, and the next year the Phi Kappas did not believe
that South Carolina's nullification would be beneficial to the Union.

Yet, in 1833, they condemned Jackson's treatment of the Palmetto State.[31]

For the next decade calculations as to the value of the Union were made as often as slavery was discussed, and the decisions generally were in favor of the Union; but with the crisis of 1850, the Kansas-Nebraska act of 1854, and the downfall of the Whig Party, the University debaters with seriousness and sorrow began to contemplate the parting of the ways. In 1854 while Stephen A. Douglas was maneuvering his Kansas-Nebraska bill through Congress, the Phi Kappas took up the debate and decided that the failure of the bill to pass would not warrant a break-up of the Union. And now with the Whigs fast disintegrating and yet with many Southern Whigs intensely hostile and contemptuous of the Democrats, the Phi Kappas decided that the South should nevertheless embrace the Democratic Party. In 1855 the Phi Kappas debated morning, afternoon, and evening the question, "Do present causes indicate a dissolution of the Union?" and came to the final conclusion that they did. And now, "Has a state the right to secede from the Union?" *Yes*, they decided on the anniversary of the Battle of Lexington, 1856; and *no*, they said the next year. The Demosthenians held as late as 1857 that there was no reason to suppose that the Union would be broken up, and that there ought not to be a Southern confederacy. But they decided frequently that a state had a right to secede "when she thinks her rights have been sufficiently infringed upon." In June, 1860, with the Democratic Party divided and running two candidates for president and with the Republicans solidly in support of Abraham Lincoln, the Phi Kappas queried, "Should the South secede if a Black Republican is elected President?" and the affirmative won.[32]

The regular weekly exercises, of which all this debating made up the greater part, kept the students constantly interested in their societies, but there were certain fixed occasions on which the Phi Kappas and Demosthenians displayed themselves before the world in all their power and glory. Naturally their birthdays were in their eyes events of outstanding importance, which must be properly celebrated and observed. The Demosthenians held their exercises on February 19th and the Phi Kappas on the 22nd. Each marched to the chapel in all their regalia and badges, with banners flying, there to listen to an oration delivered by one of their number. Then they returned to their hall to celebrate further through the resounding periods of a private oration. Occasionally the University paid them its respects by making the anniversary a holiday. The Athens newspapers in their early days when they found difficulty in filling their columns with material from Washington or London (local happenings they did not consider news) published the orations of these anniversarians and thereby made these young orators feel the full effect of their great accomplishments. No doubt some of these young students were given an urge which drove them far on the road to fame. L. Q. C. Lamar was the anniversarian for the Demosthenians in 1816.[33]

With the anniversarian exercises over, the next event to which the societies turned their attention was the Fourth of July celebration. In its young days the Republic observed its birthday with great enthusiasm and hilarity—as it became older it became more discreet. The societies took charge for the University. The orator was made to alternate between the two societies each year. The student military companies accompanied the orator to the chapel and after a resounding and patriotic oration had been spoken the meeting broke up with the older inhabitants (principally the grandees of the town) adjourning to a banquet and drinking bout, where toasts were drunk to all the Revolutionary heroes who could be remembered. With the coming of the temperance movement the toasts were abandoned and soon the townsmen had left off their banquets, and with the change went most of this show of patriotism. By the 'fifties the celebration was almost wholly a student business, attended only by students. The procedure also changed to the extent that the society which did not afford the orator provided a reader who labored through the Declaration of Independence. But the students were getting wiser. The celebration in 1856 produced an orator who soared well above the platitudes of the times, and a student complimented him for not being like many of his predecessors—fellows with "the same threadbare subject spoken in the same stale and threadbare manner . . . falling into the same old beaten track of the 'spirit of '76.' "[34]

There was no end to oratory in the ante-bellum South. The greatest time in all the year for this form of pastime was when commencement came. A whole day was given over to the juniors, called "Junior Exhibition," when the representatives from each society stood forth before the great multitudes who annually assembled to be regaled. To be a junior orator was one of the highest honors to which a Franklin College student could aspire. Then orators were elected by the societies, three from each one, and here was an opportunity for practicing and mastering all the art and trickery which man could devise for getting elected to something. A student confessed in his diary to one method of securing preferment in his society—in this case to win the honor of anniversarian. "I had done everything almost that one could do," he said, "to insure an election. . . . Then came the treat, 4 different kinds of liquors and cigars costing me something over two dollars. Some got drunk of course & it is somewhat a mournful reflection to think that I was the cause of it. No fighting however." The vigilant faculty, finding out what had happened, fined him $10 and put him on probation. So it was that many elections went, then as now, to those who were most expert in astuteness, rich in influence, and liberal in money. The professors were much opposed to this method of getting forward and were particularly anxious to remove the junior orators from the taint of electioneering. In 1832 they set out to bring about a change where "popularity is too often in the inverse ratio of merit." They charged that aspiring juniors assumed leadership of the freshmen and of the sophomores in their riots and disorders in return for their votes in the election of junior orators. The professors were also a little jealous of the part the societies were playing in the life and affections of the students—there was danger that the side shows were becoming more attractive than the big tent. Already they claimed the students had assumed the attitude "that the duties of college are of little importance in comparison with an attendance on the Societies."[35]

The professors appealed to the trustees for aid. These grown-ups, who had already graduated in the art now practiced by students, were immediately moved to put a stop to such unbecoming practices which, they said, constituted "a system of canvassing, treating & carousal, which must in the result be destructive to the interest of every literary institution in which it exists." Its evils were "incalculable, and in the highest degree alarming." Hereafter the faculty should propose five juniors in each society, and before the day was done, the societies must meet and choose three each. Indignation now ran high among those who had been acquiring some very practical knowledge which they knew would be valuable in the great outside world, but which they were now asked to cast aside. The Phi Kappas declared that the action of the trustees was "not only an arbitrary measure, but one highly injurious," and as for themselves they would forego the oration business before they would submit to such tyranny. Furthermore, if the faculty should go ahead and appoint orators, and there were juniors so devoid of the real honor as to accept this fictitious honor, they should "be prohibited from wearing the badge of the Association." Having appealed to the trustees once without success, they resolved that another effort should be made "and that they be conjured (by the esteem which they profess to feel for this and its sister association) to abolish a regulation fraught with so much injury." A motion introduced in the society to punish electioneering was voted down. Both societies finally bowed to the superior authority of the trustees, but never ceased to work for the old plan of election. In 1844 the trustees allowed each society one additional junior orator—making four each—and finally in 1859 capitulated and allowed the orators to have their way. But the juniors immediately showed that they had forgotten none of their old electioneering tricks, and so the next year the trustees restored the faculty method of selection.[36]

Commencement would have been robbed of its chief attractions without the societies. They not only afforded the day of junior oratory, but also each held on the last day its annual meeting. This day was without a doubt the grandest and most splendid in all the year. Now the old graduates came back to meet with their young brothers; they retailed mellow reminiscences to their young ambitious audience and fired them with visions of future greatness. The day began with the address to the two societies assembled in the chapel. The speaker rotated between the societies annually, and he was someone to whom the society considered they were doing a very great honor. He was always an honorary member of the society which selected him. These orators were invited from every direction and every profession, and the society never seemed to doubt that whoever should be the fortunate one would consider it so great an honor that he would lay all business aside and come a thousand miles (if need be) to make the address. L. Q. C. Lamar was invited by the Demosthenians in 1833 and he accepted, hoping so to act "as to sustain the well-deserved reputation of the society for literature and eloquence." They selected William Gilmore Simms in 1852, but he was forced to decline for "Recent premonitions of danger have compelled me to forego considerable portions of my labors & to back away from engagements that threaten to be hurtful." Generally the orations were pitched as high as Mount Olympus and scarcely ever did they fly down so near the earth as to consider the problems or thoughts of the common man. The oration was then handed over to the secretary of the society after a dignified and stilted letter asking leave to publish it had been sent out. Later it was generally published in pamphlet form to the number of a thousand. These long orations held out a particular terror to the secretary whose duty required him to copy them in the minutes. A long-suffering secretary of the Demosthenians, after covering sixteen pages of his minute book, finally reached the end and wrote "A hard task." A second inscription followed, "I know it by dire experience."[37]

After the oration of the day, the societies gathered in their respective halls in the evening where a private orator, who had also been picked from the honorary membership, engaged in more oratory. There were yet more honors to be passed around among the great who had come from far and near to the Georgia commencement; there were the presiding officer and his assistant. These honors were conferred with as great a seriousness as in the case of the public orators. The societies sometimes had difficulty in filling these offices. In 1838 the Phi Kappas chose James L. Petigru, Robert Y. Hayne, George McDuffie, Judge William Law, and George M. Troup, without an acceptance. Finally David

Campbell consented. Augustus B. Longstreet presided for them
in 1841. Orators were sometimes as difficult to get as presiding
officers. In 1836 the Phi Kappas selected Joseph Henry Lumpkin
and Herschel V. Johnson. The former refused, and finally William C. Preston, of South Carolina, accepted. In 1843 they honored George McDuffie and Richard Henry Wilde and both found
it impossible to come. The annual meeting had an additional
attraction for the students, for at this time each was awarded a
diploma by the society, signed by the presiding officer.[38]

The business of the societies was carried on with great seriousness; when members entered the dignified halls of these organizations they were expected to forget that one of their chief delights
in college was to break rules. Now they were living under their
own laws. There were no less than fifty offenses for which they
could be fined amounts ranging from five cents to two dollars. The
Demosthenians, unlike their more crafty brothers, the Phi Kappas,
set a fine of one dollar on anyone who was guilty of electioneering
for any office within the gift of the society. Gentlemen were expected to be dignified and circumspect in their carriage and even
more so in their sitting down. A motion to change the rules so
that members might make themselves more comfortable as they
listened to interminable speeches and orations, the Demosthenians
killed by a big majority in 1837. The purpose was to give members the privilege of "sitting with their legs crossed or with their
feet on the rounds of their chairs without being reported for sitting
in an indecent posture." And it naturally followed that "No member shall go to sleep or even lie down in the Hall or put his foot
upon the seats of the chairs or benches." Such a lack of respect
for decent behavior as to spit on the floor "or in a spit box which
may leak on the floor," was finable to the amount of fifty cents
with the additional duty imposed of clearing away "the blot from
the floor within a week" or suffer a standing fine of fifty cents a
week as long as the blot remained. According to the scale of
fines, to spit out of the window was just half as bad as to spit on
the floor. Smoking within the hall was strictly forbidden and to
smoke "within outer door" was punishable by a twenty-five cents
fine. Other finable offenses often committed were "applauding

twice," "not speaking," "talking," sitting or standing before the
fire, "spitting on the wall," "groaning," "eating chinquepins,"
moving seat, being out too long, going out without leave, spitting
on the carpet, not wearing crepe, laughing aloud, and pulling
the coat-tail of a member. Occasionally members were expelled
for such offenses as lying and stealing.[39]

But students were little more anxious to obey their own rules
than they were the professors'; in fact, these young debaters were
likely to leave a longer list of offenses against their society than
against their college. Future greatness was never to be discovered
in a Franklin College literary society, if correct deportment was
to be the measuring rod. Francis Goulding, who was destined to
write his captivating story of the *Young Marooners,* was in 1827
fined fifty cents for "disorder & lying on the bench," twenty-five
cents two separate times for simple "disorder," and twelve and a
half cents for being "out too long." Henry Timrod, later a poet
of no little renown and a victim of Reconstruction in South Carolina, was impeached for being absent three times in succession.
But be it said in deference to his memory that his excuses were
accepted and he was reinstated. Crawford W. Long, who discovered
how to put the world to sleep with his sulphuric ether, was, himself, convicted of "sleeping in the hall" and fined fifty cents. He
was also fined twice for "going out without permission," thirteen
times for being "out too long," once for "neglect of duty as
treasurer," and once for "loitering on the steps." John A. Campbell, who was later to dispense justice from the Supreme Court
of the United States, did himself feel the hand of justice, three
times for going out without permission, once for eating in the hall,
eight times for being out too long, twice for disorder, once for
moving his seat, and twice for reading in time of session. James
Jackson, who was honored with a similar position on the Georgia
Supreme Court bench, was fined by his fellow Demosthenians, six
times for going out without permission, once for "shooting paper
across the hall," once for being out too long, twice for "not speaking," and once for "creating a disorder."

But undoubtedly the terror of all the Demosthenians was Robert
Toombs, who broke practically all the rules the professors could

think of, and now naturally did not propose to let society rules go free. Within the period of a year and a half he got himself fined twenty-five cents for being "absent from tribunal," fifty cents for being "absent whole meeting," twenty-five cents for "going out without permission," one dollar for "not accepting clerk's office," twenty-five cents three times for "disorder," twenty-five cents for "reading in hall," twelve and a half cents for being "out too long," and an unstated amount twice for "eating in hall." His best enemy, Granby Hillyer, also accumulated a long list of offenses for which he paid the fines. Toombs' record also shows that he was an honest man, for the treasurer closed his account with the notation, "August 21 recd payment in full." Honesty was not a quality of which all Demosthenians could boast, for often claiming that they were unjustly fined or fined too much, they steadily resisted the collector and left school owing their fines. One Demosthenian refused to pay his fines in 1833 "until he gets his diploma." Phi Kappas were no better. Their treasurer in 1843 wrote, "Their debts of honor, are esteemed no debts at all; and never until we proceed to expulsion, or can get our society regularly incorporated, so as to give us the arm of the law, will we be able to check these swindling gentry."[40]

The fear which the professors sometimes had that the societies would make teachers unnecessary was no doubt heightened by the ever-increasing society libraries. The first floor in each hall was well-stocked with books which Phi Kappas and Demosthenians held to be a concern almost equal to their debating activities. And here there was much rivalry. Each sought to outdo the other in the number of books possessed and in their attractiveness and style of binding. There resulted much duplication for there was no borrowing by members of one society from the library of the other society until these rivals had reached middle-age. When they became more sociable toward each other and agreed to inter-change books, another Pandora's box was opened, for when Phi Kappas attempted to levy fines on Demosthenians, or *vice versa,* the matter developed into a first-rate dispute. Each society had a librarian who awarded a page in his book to each member. There he wrote down the reading activities of many who were to become

great. Jabez L. M. Curry always used up his page and had to
borrow from less industrious fellows; so did John A. Campbell,
unwittingly preparing himself for the United States Supreme
Court. Robert Toombs was much more successful in filling his
page in the treasurer's book of fines than in the librarian's book.[41]

These two literary society libraries played a bigger part in the
lives of the students than did the University library. By 1860 they
each had about 2,600 volumes. In 1843 the Phi Kappas, boasting
of their library, declared that they would soon have one "rivalling
if not surpassing any College in the Union." Many of these books
had been donated by honorary members, but also much society
money was expended in purchasing books. In early days the societies asked the legislature for appropriations to further their
libraries, but they soon learned that no money could be secured
from this source. The Senatus Academicus once begged the legislature to heed their pleas for at least $2,000 as it seemed the
society libraries were more useful and accessible than the regular
University library.[42]

Another literary work carried on by the students, though not
done through the society organizations, was the *Georgia University Magazine*, familiarly and affectionately called the G U M.
The first number of this publication appeared in 1851 and it
jogged along until the Civil War put a stop to it together with
the University. It began early asking the trustees for financial
aid and by 1854 had induced them to appropriate $100. In 1855
they made a similar appropriation. The aim, as expressed by the
editor, was "to convey stores of knowledge to the student, and
abundance of humor and wit to the gay, and gems of poetry to
the ladies." Historical and scientific studies, orations, fiction, and
poetry, dignified and ridiculous, blossomed forth in the G U M
pages. Not all that was submitted to the editor was accepted, and
the reasons for rejection were published for the good of all. In
rejecting the "Freshman's Lament," the editor said, "But if you
knew, lamented friend, what lamentations were called forth by your
'spavined dactyles' and jaundiced spondees, you would heartily
lament having put pen to paper. O for that lamentable lamenta-
tion—Try again, and don't lament."[43]

In an age when athletics and fraternities were unknown at Franklin College, the literary societies gave the students an outlet for their energy and interest which no other part of the University could command. These were little city states where students governed with dignity and success. They aided the needy student, they wore crêpe for thirty days when death carried away a member, and they passed long resolutions of praise for the departed brother. Committees of fellow society members conducted the corpse back to the bereaved family, or where distance was too great or transportation too precarious, the society buried its dead in Oconee Cemetery and erected dignified markers. But the rivalry of Athens and Sparta sometimes could not be allayed by death, as occasionally one refused to wear crêpe out of respect for the other's dead.[44]

Demosthenians and Phi Kappas might in the great world outside forget their old professors, their classrooms, and textbooks, but few ever forgot their old society halls. Scientists, statesmen, judges, preachers, planters, all agreed on this point. Joseph LeConte, years after his days at Franklin College, recalled in his busy career at the University of California that he had never seen literary societies equal to those of his student days. It took only a few years to develop romance, rich and mellow, in those student contacts and experiences in the society halls. Said one Demosthenian in 1839, "To me the name *Demosthenian* is fraught with the most happy associations, & the most pleasurable recollections of my life are identified with that *Hall*." In 1848, only four years after he had left Franklin College, Benjamin H. Hill said, "There, in that Hall, is the sweetest haunt of memory, and often will mind relax her efforts from the pursuit of worldly cares, and fondly ponder over the hours of youthful struggle and early contest. Times and things may change, but the heart will ever cling to the idols it once so fondly loved." Jabez L. M. Curry attributed much of the success that came to him in later life to the training he received in his literary society.[45] Truly, the literary societies, born of the students and nurtured by them, were mighty in the effect they had in the making of the ante-bellum college student.

CHAPTER VII

WHEN COMMENCEMENTS
WERE NEW

 PRESIDENT MEIGS had set his students to work on the high Oconee hill in 1801, but there were not many Georgians who knew that this plant had been set out. The *Augusta Chronicle* and, perhaps, one or two other newspapers occasionally printed notices about Franklin College having started, or about its plea for sustenance. Three years passed by and then the plant bloomed, and it continued thereafter to bloom every year. It was beautiful; the people who saw it liked it. They knew it was a mark of distinction to like such things. Those who made the plant bloom knew it was a mark of distinction to be able to produce so beautiful a flower. And thus the Georgia commencement grew and flourished.

Here in the wilderness blossomed forth classicism and never with such a brilliant hue as when the school ended, a time which by some strange form of reasoning is called commencement. What the University had to offer to the crowds who came to gaze and listen was the most incongruous product that ever a wilderness grew. But Meigs knew how it was done in staid old Yale at New Haven, for had it not been recorded that in 1778 "a cliosophic oration in Latin by Sir Meigs" had been rendered? Why should knowledge and approved ways of displaying it be different though it be in Georgia? Therefore, those who came to the early Georgia commencements heard such as these: a French oration, a Greek

134

oration, a Latin salutatory oration, a philosophical oration, and a scientific oration. The early Georgia audiences must have been long-suffering and courteous beyond computation, for it is recorded of the first commencement that a "numerous audience paid the most decent and pointed attention; and scarcely a symptom of riot or disorder appeared during the whole period of the public transactions."[1]

But it would have been nothing short of miraculous had such good order been maintained if unknown tongues had prevailed exclusively. There were some English orations spoken at these early commencements, a "Eulogy on Patrick Henry," "The Genius of Man," "The Potency of Mind," "The Inconstancy of Fortune as it Affects the Conduct of Men," "Freedom of Speech," "Liberty of the Seas" (spoken in 1807), an oration "in favor of liberty," virtue "and the necessity of enforcing it by example." But undoubtedly there were some spectators in these frontier commencements who came to see what the attraction was and who cared not for serious things. No doubt it was to keep them from rioting that such performances as these were given: "An ironical Oration in favor of monarchy," "A forensic dispute," "A comic Dialogue," "Poor Gentlemen," "No Song, No Supper." As a winning attraction for the commencement in 1815 it was announced that "A tragedy will be performed on Tuesday night." At the preceding commencement the "Tragedy of Cato" had been enacted. To add variety, a poem was occasionally recited and the Declaration of Independence read. There was always a great flood of declamations, and, of course, the commencement sermon. From early times music was used to enliven the crowds.[2]

As has appeared, oratory was the great stock in trade. For a day the junior orators reigned supreme, to be followed on the morrow by the seniors. Each graduating senior made his speech a parting to his University and a greeting to an expectant world. As the students increased in numbers, the time for each speech was limited to a correspondingly shorter period. In 1830 they were held down to ten minutes, and any who could not compress their burning messages into this allotment were required to pay fifty cents a minute for all excess time. As commencement approached each year, the orators began their practice, down by the Oconee River, deep in the woods, and now and then in the chapel they "blazed away in the dark."[3] Sometimes a senior, deciding that he had no message, either for his *alma mater* or for the outside world, would refuse to take part. The trustees decided that such rebellious conduct should be punished by withholding the degree from the guilty rebel. Tinsley W. Rucker suffered this penalty in 1833, "he having refused to comply with the Laws of College regulating the College exercises."[4]

The first commencement exercises (in 1804) were held in front of the rising walls of Old College out in the open on "a Stage under a spacious Arbor," constructed from boards found around Easley's sawmill and from boughs of trees found everywhere. Ten Bachelor of Arts degrees were awarded and one graduate of Hampden-Sydney was "admitted ad eundem." The diplomas were stiff paper written throughout by hand in Latin. But better days and more dignified were ahead; it was announced that the commencement in 1808 would be held "in a spacious new Chapel"—the same which Parson Hull had erected for less than $1,000. But year by year the commencement crowds increased, and "the horrors of a Commencement squeeze at Athens" became something to remark about. By the 'twenties not half of the crowd could get into the chapel and not half of those who succeeded in entering could hear the orators. An Athenian critic declared in 1828, "Confined in its limits, close and oppressive, uncouth in its architecture, unseemly in its whole appearance, it looks as if the chips of the College buildings had been gotten together at the close, and a chapel trumpt up by the carpenter's apprentices. Beside the neat halls of the Demosthenian and Phi Kappa Societies, it is perfectly contemptible, and wholly unworthy of the other buildings around it."[5]

The shanty characteristics of this chapel were indeed sadly out of tune with the splendor of the masses of people who tried annually to squeeze within its walls. All who loved a Georgia commencement went away determined to force the legislature to give money for a new building. The Augusta editor demanded a building four times as large. "The vast number of respectable, intelligent and distinguished individuals," he said, "who assemble here annually, from every section of the State, is the best evidence of the highest estimation in which this institution is held . . . ." The state must act. The polite and prudent Athens editor in speaking of the commencement in 1830 said, "We did not enter the execrable little coop, feeling it our place to give way to visitors." People began to fear that the old building would fall down upon their heads, and soon there was talk of returning to the old brush-arbor style of 1804. Finally the state acted, and in 1832 a new chapel of great architectural beauty and dignity was finished, costing $15,000. The trustees characterized it as "a tasteful & handsome building . . . apparently correct in its proportions . . . certainly elegant in its exterior appearance, and convenient in its interior."[6]

A century and a quarter later the same chapel, as beautiful and dignified as ever, is heroically attempting to do its duty to a student group increased more than fifty-fold. And yet in 1860 the trustees said this: "We think the College Chapel entirely too small for the use and purposes of the University—and the accommodation of the people on public occasions. We can but express the hope that the State of Georgia, with an ample and ever redundant Treasury, will at once remedy this want of the general people and enable the Board to erect a Chapel suited to the growing importance of the University, and the power and dignity of the State."[7]

It is possible that many of those who followed the high sheriff of the county in the procession up to the brush arbor to see the first commencement ever held in all the land from the Savannah River westward to the South Seas came to scoff at this new thing. If this be true they were sadly disappointed, for the Georgia commencement began immediately to grow and prosper and to find constant favor in the eyes of old and young, male and female, white and black, bond and free. The faculty delighted in it, for now they could show themselves off to the people and in the early days make plain to each other and to all others their respective ranks in "dignity and authority"—coming first the professor of natural philosophy and chemistry, second the professor of mathematics, and thirdly the professor of languages. "Everybody who

is anybody" made his annual trip to the Athens commencement—
the statesman, the politician, the scientist, "the industrious culti-
vator of the soil," "the blooming girl of seventeen, with all the
charms of youth, and innocence, and loveliness around her, the
gay coquette, the antiquated matron, and last and least of all the
dandy." In the eyes of a student in 1854, "Here is seen the learned
and the ignorant, the fashionable 'dandy' and the simple farmer,
the epicure and the peasant: and to crown all the rest," the beauty
of the land. But the happiest person of all, in his simple way, was
the black slave, who, if within a day's journey of Athens was
given a holiday. He came with his master and his master's family,
and there slipped in all the "poor whites" of the surrounding
country invading the town and campus with every form of conveyance which rolled on wheels or walked on feet.[8]

The tone of the whole occasion was pitched on a high plane,
and when it came to naming the visitors of importance the local
editor could not discriminate "where the major part were from the
highest ranks of society." The visitors came not from Georgia
alone but from the adjoining states, and occasionally a few would
drift in from afar. A stranger from the North happened in on the
commencement in 1830 and admitted that he was absolutely as-
tonished. He had heard of the splendor of the Georgia commencements but had never imagined what he saw. He soberly declared,
"I have never witnessed such a display of fashion, taste and refinement any where; and I have been at many of the Commencements of the Northern Colleges." South Carolina politicians and
statesmen had a strong taste for Georgia commencements and often
indulged it. George McDuffie came over frequently and John C.
Calhoun attended now and then. The latter was present in 1836
and after sitting on the stage for the exercises in the chapel,
attended the annual meeting of the Phi Kappas where "he deemed
it his duty & privilege to make a few remarks." And, according
to the minutes, he "enlarged upon the present state of our Country,
touched upon the abolition question, now so much agitated. He
then spoke of the probability of some of the Members of the Society
being called to act in this scene with their talents & perhaps with
their muskets, which last he said God Grant might never be."[9]

write plunder

A Modern View of the University of Georgia Chapel

Andrew A. Lipscomb
Chancellor of the University, 1860-1874

Moses Waddel,
President of the University, 1819-1829

The trustees attended in a body and always held their principal meeting at this time. The gentlemen who constituted the grandiloquently titled body, the Senatus Academicus, also lent dignity to the occasion and likewise held their annual meeting now. Among the interesting things done each year by the trustees was the conferring of honorary degrees. They started out at the first commencement by awarding five, all Master of Arts. Among those receiving the first degrees was John Forsyth, who married President Meigs' daughter and who was later Secretary of State. This dangerous power so easily and frequently abused in later times was now used rather sparingly, and the degree generally went to a worthy person. Some years none was awarded, and generally not more than two at any time. Joel Barlow, the poet and minister to France, was given a Doctor of Laws in 1809; Augustus Baldwin Longstreet, the Georgia wit and educator, was given the same degree in 1823; and George McDuffie was likewise rewarded in 1843.[10]

Commencements at Georgia began early to develop that source of support upon which the modern college commencement has come almost wholly to rest—the alumni. In 1828 the trustees ordered a catalogue of all the graduates to be prepared, and in 1834 the alumni did a more practical thing by coming together at the commencement of that year and organizing the Alumni Society. The main inspiration for this move came from the members of the first graduating class. Augustin S. Clayton was elected chairman; a constitution was formulated and adopted, and Clayton was made the first president. Their object was "to encourage education, promote the cause of science and literature, call the public attention to our State University, and annually renew the friendships of early life." Although the renewal of college friendships they doubtless expected to realize first and most often, yet they had in mind something much more substantial and valuable than a reminiscence of the past. Before the end of two years they had turned their hand toward the establishing of a magazine which they intended to call the *Athenian*, to be a literary monthly and to contain nothing "derogatory to religion, offensive to any denomination of Christians, or of any political party." They hoped to enlist the support of the literary societies and of the college community. This venture never succeeded, but they were soon bent on another. They decided to raise $10,000 with which to "purchase every thing relating to the discovery, settlement and history of the American Continent" and to present this valuable collection to the University Library. When venerable old Moses Waddel died in 1840, the Alumni Society set itself the pleasant task of devising some way by which their old president might be honored. They called on all old graduates to return for the next commencement and invited Augustus B. Longstreet to deliver an appropriate and commemorative address. An annual event of the commencement was now the alumni address delivered by some graduate of Franklin College, selected by the Alumni Society.[11]

As the University grew older it began to count its birthdays and by a simple mathematical computation it determined that in 1851 it would be exactly a half hundred years old—it could now have a semi-centenary, and what was more, it would. The trustees readily fell in with the scheme; they appropriated $100 for music and $300 for a dinner. A great crowd came together; the big dinner was held at the town hall where at least 400 people ate and talked, and a member of the first graduating class, Jeptha V. Harris, told how old President Meigs had held his first classes under the trees on the campus. There was much formal speaking besides the chatter around the tables. Short talks were made by the more prominent alumni such as Howell Cobb, and then Robert Toombs was called for. Toombs was quite sure that there was some mistake about his being an alumnus, for President Waddel had acted sufficiently vigorously on that point, but he thought it best to make no further allusion to his student days, and hoped others would not. But he was glad to see the University great and prosperous and broad-minded, having as its president a man from Vermont and prominent members of the faculty from Pennsylvania and Massachusetts. Other activities in connection with the semi-centennial were the alumni address by James A. Nisbet, of the class of 1831, and the appearance of the loquacious and lovable old George R. Gilmer, former governor of the state, who told disquieting secret after secret about the great and near-great under the guise of a lecture on "The Literary Progress in Georgia."[12]

Athens, with one or two small taverns, was forced whether she willed it or not to take the great swarm of ladies and gentlemen who came each year to the commencement as her own personal guests. Out of necessity to begin with and then out of the charm that went with entertaining when servants were plentiful, the grandees, the gentry, and the yeomanry of Athens opened up their hearts and homes. Athens was literally and physically crammed each year; the *Augusta Chronicle* said the people came "from every point of the compass till not a hole or crevice was left vacant in which a human being could find either comfortable or uncomfortable lodging." Everyone felt that the city should put on its best manners and act the part—even the butcher and the baker. Francis Waldron, the baker, put his notice in the Athens newspaper with the heading "GREAT DOINGS" and then told how "he intends baking a Commencement Cake weighing 250 lbs trimmed in a style that cannot be excelled." It was to be on display in his store for two days and then it would be cut to suit the taste of the most fastidious. He also had "Ice cream of a superior quality"—this was in 1840. Little wonder then that old President Waddel, after he had left Athens to retire to his Willington, South Carolina, home, drove all the way back to Athens over rough roads to attend commencements.[13]

There was much joy-making and fun connected with a Georgia commencement, especially so for those students who had been finding a reasonable amount of such entertainment during the regular school year. Complaints were now and then made of a lack of decorum and good order in the crowded chapel during the never-ending orations and declamations. In 1823 the trustees reported that "Discipline has evidently become relaxed, and a deplorable backwardness in enforcing it has but too plainly manifested itself." The custom early grew up of illuminating the college buildings in order that the crowds of visitors might come and look and be entertained. Too often unbecoming hilarity seized some of the students on these occasions, as for instance in 1831 when John T. Grant acted disrespectfully to President Church "in persisting to cut and exhibit at the illumination the words 'Gilmer and the gals.'" In the interest of good order, the Senatus Academicus passed the rule, "There shall be no parade, illumination or fireworks at the time of the commencement, but by the permission and under the direction of the President." And in 1832 an order went out against holding illuminations thereafter.[14]

But there was a much more refined and romantic side to the commencements than the disorders that attended illuminations. It was the "great *fair* for the proposal of hearts." Dancing and tuneful music and moon-lit August nights played their part. As early as 1809 dancing masters began to make their appearance in the springtime to teach the mysteries of their art "in the newest and most fashionable manner," and thereafter the coming of the dancing master was the surest sign of the approach of commencement. In the early times, dancing was considered a particular work of the devil by those who professed a great deal of religion. President Waddel had engaged in the practice when he was a young man, but he soon conquered the sin and never after departed from his resolution. During his presidency, dancing was strictly prohibited by the rules of the University. In 1823 he convicted a group of students for attending "a Ball or Dancing party" and promptly fined them one dollar each and informed them that a "similar violation in the future will not be treated with the same leniency." The permission he had given them to be outside their rooms was not "the slightest apology for attending said party." But times changed with the departure of Waddel, and quickly so, for in 1830 a commencement ball was held in Captain Brown's Assembly Room "where the Amateurs of refined pleasure" had an opportunity to enjoy themselves. It was held under the management of six seniors. By 1854 the scenes had shifted somewhat and now the ball was held at the Newton House Saloon where "fashion displayed her beauteous wand, mirth and hilarity beat high in every bosom; and a sound of revelry was heard." Dancing now was a fixed and accepted form of commencement amusement, at least among the Franklin College students. One of them bluntly declared in 1857, "We know of no more charming and harmless source of pleasure, despite of the numberless attacks which people who can't dance, aim against it." The commencement ball was

now given in the name of the juniors with nine junior managers
and nine senior managers. The invitation for 1859 read, "The
Junior Class will be pleased to see you at their Commencement
Ball given at the Lanier House on Wednesday Evening, August
3d." The trustees generally appropriated $100 annually for the
music necessary to enliven the various meetings of the commencement times.[15]

Georgia commencements were many-sided and attracted people
for many reasons. Following a custom which became common
among educational institutions of the period, the University provided an easy method for distributing second degrees—these were
not honorary degrees but deserts which could be claimed in the
course of time. Who could be so lost to that craving of appearing
learned as not to go to the trouble of returning to a Georgia commencement to receive a Master of Arts degree? Many were not,
and the list of gentlemen attending commencement was thereby
lengthened. In order to claim this honor, any person who was a
graduate of Franklin College, who was an alumnus of three years'
standing, and who could prove that he had not been in jail or had
not deserved to be, could come to a commencement and after having
paid $4, demand that he be made a Master of Arts "with all the
rights and privileges thereunto pertaining." As the rule had it,
"No candidate for the second degree may expect the honor of the
same, unless he shall have preserved a good moral character, and
previously to the commencement, shall have signified to the president, his desire of the same." Taking it for granted that all of
the graduates of the first class would want to avail themselves of
this honor, President Meigs issued this notice to them before the
commencement in 1807: "The young Gentlemen who graduated
in this University in 1804, are requested to attend the Public
Commencement, prepared for the exhibition of proofs of their
qualifications for the honor of the second degree." But in these
early days they were expected to contribute to the general entertainment "by the exhibition of orations or such other exercises as
they may judge proper for the occasion." This royal road to
learning, or at least to the appearance of it, was continued until
1870. After this time those who wanted the honor were required

to work for it by pursuing a course of study prescribed by the University and carried on on the campus.[16]

The Georgia commencement was not an educational exhibition alone; it was a political institution dear to the leaders and statesmen of Georgia and not entirely neglected by other states. In the days when travel was difficult and statewide congregations infrequent, nothing was so useful as a commencement—not even the meeting of the legislature. Here governors were made and unmade, political principles concocted and published, and animosities aroused and developed, which sometimes boded no good for the innocent by-standing University. Wire-pulling, log-rolling, and other variously named political devices were displayed before those students who remained over for such practical post-graduate work. Such learning would be useful thereafter.

Year after year the commencements served these useful political purposes, but those most outstanding and historic were the ones coming during the disturbances incident to the Nullification movement when Georgia came perilously near seizing the initiative and leadership from South Carolina. In 1828 Congress passed the "Tariff of Abominations" and thereby riveted onto the country as a fixed policy a kind of robbery which most people in the South bitterly hated and resented. The Franklin College students, who had seen almost everyone else passing resolutions against the tariff, decided in June, when the tariff was a little more than a month old, that it would be unbecoming for them to do less. They met on the twenty-sixth and resolved that although they might not be able to explain just how the tariff did all the evil things commonly attributed to it (others were doing that well enough), yet "let it not be supposed that we are unable to discover whether we are benefited or injured by it." They called on the faculty and the citizens of the state to combat the abomination by using only Southern products. The seriousness of this performance by youngsters who had the reputation of never being serious provoked the mirth of one Georgian and elicited the advice, "Boys, mind your books." But the boys maintained that the times were serious and they intended to be likewise, and that they resented such a silly exhortation. But the faculty was in complete accord with this student outburst; they immediately resolved to wear the manufactures of the state "so far as practicable."[17]

The state had become thoroughly aroused by the time the commencement in early August was due. Now there would be a chance for the older heads to come together; they would say what they thought about the tariff. Directly following the commencement exercises the biggest anti-tariff meeting that had ever gathered in the state took place. A thousand or more people crowded onto the campus; all the important leaders were here—William H. Crawford, Augustin S. Clayton, James M. Wayne, later to become Judge of the United States Supreme Court, John M. Berrien, soon to become Attorney General of the United States, Wilson Lumpkin, to be governor of Georgia within three years, George M. Troup, who as governor had a half dozen years previously threatened war against the Federal Government. Much oratory against the tariff resulted.[18]

Political leaders might talk if they chose that manner of procedure, but the students would act. They would not only advocate using Southern products exclusively, they would be more specific and practical. They decided to wear only homespun and appealed to the trustees to pass such a ruling. These censors of student morals were somewhat undecided on the wisdom of setting themselves up as tailors to the students. They laid on the table a resolution "having for its object the adoption of an uniformity in dress of domestic homespun for students," but they praised the students for their patriotism. They would not however force homespun upon those who did not care to dress in that manner. The students were resolved that they must have a uniform and that all must wear it. The literary societies took up the fight and on November 10, 1828, the trustees capitulated. Hereafter the students should dress in this fashion: "Frock coat made of dark grey Georgia Homespun, wool & cotton, the seams covered with black silk cord, or narrow braid, black buttons, and pantaloons of the same material corded or braided in the same manner." The students were given until April 15, 1829, to prepare their wardrobes. There was to be no departure from this order, but a month before the rule was to become effective the option of braiding or cording was allowed, but no other alterations were to be permitted.[19]

That students would suggest such an interference with the personal liberty of dressing as their tastes dictated and that the trustees would issue such a command show how deep the "Tariff of Abominations" cut. But the nearer the approach of the homespun parade the weaker became the students' dislike for the tariff. Were there enough tailors in all Athens to outfit so many students, and what funny figures they would cut in such garments? Then, without a doubt, there must be a sprinkling of non-conformists and rebels—those whose greatest relish in living was to disobey some rule. One student appeared in chapel with the curtain from his window pinned to his broadcloth coat, and when his time came to make his speech he recited the multiplication table with much seriousness and many dramatic flourishes—all in the presence of President Church. Then the village wits took to the lists and had their fun. "Aspasia," claiming to be a bewildered woman, wrote, "Hearing the College bell tolling very often of late, at an unusual hour, curiosity prompted me to enquire into the cause; when I was informed, it was for the last obsequies of those noble souls who inoculated themselves last summer for the 'American System,' with 'Anti-Tariff' homespun. . . ." A war of words followed until the students were ashamed to be seen in their new garbs, and then on August 3, 1829, the trustees came to the rescue and resolved that the students might "adopt what fashion they may severally prefer in the mode and making of their apparel," but they must not depart from the homespun cloth. A year later the trustees abandoned entirely the style-setting business. The students were in thorough agreement, for they found that homespun cost more than broadcloth, and they had also made a deeper study of the mysteries of economics and had discovered that their wearing homespun could not affect the tariff.[20]

Perhaps there was another reason why the students abandoned homespun. At the very time they were to appear in their new homespun uniforms, workmen set to building on the Oconee River near Athens a cotton factory. Augustin S. Clayton, a member of the board of trustees, was the chief moving force in this manufacturing venture. He was, he explained, not taking advantage of the tariff, he was engaging wholly in a defensive measure. His cloth might reduce the price of homespun or might perchance take the place of it altogether.[21]

But the abandonment of homespun uniforms did not mean that the tariff had become any more respectable, and the setting up of a few factories in Georgia did not make this method of enriching manufacturers less abominable. Calhoun's doctrine of Nullification thrived west of the Savannah no less than east of it. In July, 1832, a new tariff law was passed differing nowise in principle from the "Tariff of Abominations." It was now time to act in Georgia, and what could be more serviceable in the crisis than a Georgia commencement! But by this time moderation had ceased to be a possession of a great number of anti-tariffites, and to the anti-tariff men of calmer judgment it seemed that the state was heading directly toward bloody civil war if a law of Congress were to be nullified. At the end of the commencement exercises in 1832 the following notice was posted on the campus: "The friends of Gen. Jackson, and those opposed to the *Protective System,* and opposed to a redress of Tariff grievances by *Nullification,* as the mode of relief, are requested to attend at the New Chapel, To-Morrow, at 4 o'clock, P.M." The Nullifiers, who were in a great majority in town, on campus, and among the commencement throng, immediately resorted to a stratagem and issued another notice for a meeting at the same time and place to all "persons whatever who feel interested in the subject, without regard to any party or present opinion. . . . " The first faction appeared early and, with William H. Crawford in the chair, started on their deliberations when they were stormed by the Nullifiers, who, under the leadership of Clayton and Berrien, seized control of the meeting and voted through a set of resolutions bitterly condemning the tariff and calling for a convention to meet in Milledgeville in November. For the next three months the state was torn and perplexed by Nullifiers and Anti-nullifiers, and when the convention came together Georgia missed by the slightest margin doing what South Carolina did a few weeks later. Thus was the new chapel, just finished, dedicated by a meeting which narrowly escaped leading to a bloody baptism later.[22]

The University commencement in the ante-bellum days was itself an institution in the state. It had its attractions for the educators, the politicians and statesmen, for the business men, the farmers and the planters, for the poor whites and the slaves, for the fine ladies and gallant gentlemen, for the giddy girls and the foppish dandies. It was an educational, political, and social force of no little influence.

THE COMING OF RELIGION

THE frontier knew no restraints, legal or religious. Those who fled the "hell-fire and brimstone" eruptions of the Jonathan Edwardses of the older settlements were not anxious that the religion they had left behind should soon catch up with them. Drinking, gambling, cock-fighting, and such-like frontier pastimes had at least their bright sides for a time—something that the kind of religion they had known had none at all. The democracy they stood for did not of itself call for the admixture of any religion, for else why had the church and state been so rigorously separated?

Georgia at the beginning of the nineteenth century was as godless as any part of the booming frontier, and was long to remain so. A Georgian wrote in 1819 that religion was "but little thought of here except by a very few." He added, "I doubt whether a more proper field for Missionary labours can be found in the world."[1] How seriously true his statements were may well be seen from the religious situation that still prevailed a dozen years later. In 1831 there was only about one-tenth of the people who belonged to any church whatsoever. There were about 32,000 Baptists, 27,000 Methodists, 3,000 Presbyterians, and a few Christians, Episcopalians, Roman Catholics, Lutherans, Friends, and Jews. All the other Georgians belonged to no Christian church even as the heathen Chinese—451,000 of them went about their

149

business, taking no time to worry about their souls' salvation.[2]

Even this small sprinkling of Christian church-going Georgians was the feeble result of the hard and arduous circuit riding of Methodists from the year George Washington first swore to uphold the Constitution, of the passionate preaching of Baptists for almost as long a time, and of the infiltration of pious Presbyterians. Methodist circuit riders, generally with all their earthly belongings in their saddle-bags, preached their way through Middle and Upper Georgia and long wandered over rough roads before they became important enough to be allowed a station where they might settle down. Lorenzo Dow passed up and down this region in his wanderings, announcing his next coming a year hence and invariably riding up at the appointed time. Francis Asbury came this way now and then, sowing the seeds of Methodism. In 1808 he held a conference in Greene County. The voice of John Major, of Richard Ivy, and of Hope Hull, each was heard crying in this wilderness, and indeed Hull felt his religion so enthusiastically that he once said if he had some good friend to help him he could shout a mile high. This religious dynamo happened up on Athens before it was out of its swaddling clothes and immediately became identified with the University in 1802 as a trustee and remained so until his death in 1818.[3]

James Russell, the wonder preacher of early Georgia Methodism, became so worked-up in his business of spreading religion that at times he excitedly leaped from the pulpit crying, "All who want religion, follow me," and the congregation by this time stirred with emotions as deep as his would follow him into the woods. Such movements were only the less exciting manifestations of the Great Revival which swept over the frontier around 1800 and of the camp meetings that followed for a century. Wicked frontiersmen were suddenly stricken by the awful feelings of the immensity of their terrible lives of sin, and in the temporary derangement of their minds that followed they swooned away and lay for hours in the straw prepared for those "smitten of the Lord," or they started suddenly to flee away and fell prostrate as if shot down by a sniper, or they took suddenly to jerking with apparently every muscle in their bodies until it seemed they would be torn to pieces or converted into rigid marble, or they shouted and talked in unknown tongues, or indeed sometimes they chased with scourges the devil into the forests and lashed the trees in their zeal to utterly destroy him.[4]

Though the University was stamped with Christian principles, no minister presided at its birth. It came before the preachers had appeared in Georgia in sufficient numbers to have a voice in affairs; it was to be a torch of science and learning held high over a darkened land, and it was not placed in the hands of a preacher. In fact Meigs agreed much with his friend Jefferson in educational matters as the latter subsequently presented them to Thomas Cooper in describing the ideal at the University of Virginia. Jefferson said religion had been purposely left out of his University for "by bringing the rival sects together and mixing them with the mass of other students, we shall soften their asperities, liberalize and neutralize their prejudices, and make the general religion the religion of peace, reason, and morality."[5] But with the coming of camp-meetings and emotional religion the preachers were soon turning upon godless education wherever it might be found. Said one, "The zeal of infidelity has descended into mines, has dared the terrors of volcanoes, has dived into the ocean, has ransacked and examined every accessible part of the world for the purpose of proving that no reliance ought to be placed on the revealed promises, no dread ought to be entertained of the threatenings of the Almighty."[6]

The politicians were able to destroy Meigs before the preachers had had a chance. His successor, John Brown, was a fervent preacher but a weak educator, and he soon gave way to as vehement a man of God and a more able teacher. Finley unfortunately died before he got well started, and he left the task of stamping religion upon the University to Moses Waddel. As has already appeared, Waddel was profoundly religious; he conceived of his duty toward the University as being largely an opportunity of turning people to God—in reality only the continuance of the ministry he had left, over in South Carolina. When Waddel took up his work in 1819, he found that religion had begun to make some impression upon the University and its organization. While Meigs

was president, Hope Hull had attempted to look after the spiritual
welfare of the institution and in his campaign for the souls of the
students had secured the erection of the first rude chapel on the
campus. He frequently preached to the students, and apparently
became a bore to some of the more wicked sons of wicked parents,
for Welden Jones, who had just passed his examinations in 1812
and who saw his Bachelor of Arts degree awaiting him, used one
day out in the yard in front of the chapel "highly insulting language & conduct" toward Parson Hull for certain observations he
had just made in his sermon. For his frontier rudeness Jones was
forced to apologize in the presence of the faculty and students
before he was allowed to receive his degree.[7] Hull, as previously
noted, was a Methodist. The Presbyterians were also early in the
field with the University as a particular object of missionary zeal.
In 1811 the Hopewell Presbytery celebrated the first Lord's Supper ever to be held in Athens, and significantly enough it took
place in the college chapel.

Waddel could never conceive of education divorced from religion. His religious activities were as evident during his ten years
at the University as was his educational work. He traveled all
over the surrounding counties preaching to those who would come
to listen; he organized the first Presbyterian congregation in
Athens in 1820 and was its minister for the next ten years;
he was the first vice-president of the Presbyterian Missionary Society of South Carolina and Georgia; in fact, wherever there were
prayers to be said, blessings to be asked, or funerals to be preached
Waddel was a valuable man to have nearby. In 1825 he carefully
noted in his diary that "at noon funeralized Mr. Davies Griffin
in chapel."[8]

Dominated no doubt in this regard by Hope Hull, the trustees
in 1817 offered a half-acre lot to the first denomination which
would build a church in Athens. Hull's Methodists seized the opportunity and a few years afterward chapel exercises were being
held alternately in the Methodist Church, to continue "so long as
the same may be found useful to the Institution & the harmony
of Religious worship." The Methodists hoped thus to gain an
advantageous position in their designs on the University—a posi-

tion at least as strategic as that held by the Presbyterians. By
1830 Methodism had gained a secure hold on Athens and the
surrounding country. In this year James O. Andrew, famous later
as the bishop around whom the Methodist Church split, moved to
Greensboro, from which place he drove up to Athens twice a
month to preach. The next year he moved to Athens and stayed
until the Conference transferred him in 1832.[9]

Denominational rivalries and hatreds soon made it necessary
for the trustees to make further grants of lands—religious hostility
was too violent to be lightly courted. The Presbyterians were
granted a lot; they slipped by the gates and pitched their tabernacle
on the campus. The Baptists, who by 1828 were the most numerous
denomination in the state, now demanded their lot. The trustees,
with fear and trembling, gave them the choicest corner on the
campus. Athens had now become "respectable" enough to attract
a few Episcopalians and of course a mere gesture from them was
sufficient to secure their heritage. This was in 1837, six years
before they were able to form a congregation. Finally in 1843
they succeeded in getting a member of their church elected to
the University faculty in the person of William B. Stevens, who
became their first rector in Athens. But one important element
in the Athens population was still unrepresented at the University,
where were encamped Methodists, Baptists, Presbyterians, and
Episcopalians. The Negroes would also worship the white man's
God, and a few years before the Civil War those who worshiped
according to Baptist ways were rewarded with the old church on
the campus, which the Baptists had deserted for a new one. Here
Lewis Phinizy, as black as his congregation, preached every Sunday evening. Almost all the time there were professors or students
present, fulfilling the law which required the presence of a white
man at Negro gatherings. In 1860 the trustees decided that the
African Baptists should evacuate the campus.[10]

Although the covetous desires of the various denominations to
seize control of the University may not be to their credit as Christian people, yet the situation has a certain element in it that
recommends more than it condemns. For, indeed, it marks an important advance in the mentality of the pioneer churches from the

low level where a substantial element had frowned upon all learning as displeasing in the sight of God, to a point where they now
thought education was not only to be tolerated but even to be
encouraged. The Baptists were the greatest early offenders; a part
of them held that education disqualified a preacher, for it interfered with the message that the Lord prepared each Sunday to
deliver through the mouthpiece of His minister. The Presbyterians
were of the principal denominations the least contaminated with
this doctrine of the perfectibility of illiteracy. By the 'twenties
they had organized the Georgia Educational Society for the purpose
of aiding their ministerial candidates in securing an education.
For years after this time there were to be found always in the
University a few students who were receiving aid from this organization. Alexander H. Stephens was helped by this society
when he first came to the University. The light of learning also
broke in on the Methodists and soon they also had a society for
helping those students preparing for their ministry.[11]

The Baptists were not greatly concerned with spending money
for education at this time, especially if they could secure a lodge-
ment and a stronghold in an institution which they might influence
for their own purposes. As they grew stronger in the state and
came to have more members than any other sect and as they became better informed on the situation at the University, they
suddenly came to the realization that the state's jewel of education
was in the keeping of the Presbyterians—an outrageous and pre-
posterous situation, for there were eleven Baptists to one Presbyterian in Georgia, and yet the Baptists did not have even a solitary
representative on the board of trustees or on the faculty. *Per
contra* every president of the University except Meigs had been
a Presbyterian; in 1829 three out of the twelve professors were
Presbyterians (the others belonged to no church except one Episco-
palian, a Methodist, and a Congregationalist); and six out of the
ten tutors were Presbyterians—the others being unattached.[12]

An opportunity for the fight to be brought out in an open issue
came in 1829 when Waddel, after having announced his intention
to resign year after year, now, no longer able to resist his burning
desire to devote his whole time to the ministry, carried out this

intention. Immediately the trustees elected Alonzo Church, who had taught mathematics in the University for the preceding ten years and who had been an able second to Waddel. But Church was another Presbyterian, and certain Baptists were now more convinced than ever before that the University had been sold out to that denomination. Their anger and disappointment were keen and biting—almost devastating. Here was the most damning and transparent evidence that "bargain and corruption" had crept in to keep the University a closed corporation securely lodged in the household of the Presbyterians. The country had been treated only recently to an example of scurvy trickery which had kept Andrew Jackson from the presidency of the United States; now Georgia was witnessing the same kind of corruption which kept the Baptists out of the University. The precipitate haste in naming Church was positive proof. The Baptists had hoped to secure the election of William T. Brantley, formerly from Philadelphia but now a minister in Augusta. To rouse up further enmity against the University they showed also how the Methodists had been given no consideration, how William Capers had been rudely passed by—this despite the fact that Capers was not a candidate![13] According to one of the outraged friends of education, "Are the Methodists and Baptists *all* such traitors to the principles of our Constitution, that they cannot be trusted with the tuition of a class of young gentlemen? Or are they such ignoramuses that they cannot furnish a Professor or a Tutor?" Brantley, said the Baptists, was the most capable man in the United States for the position, and if the Baptists were to be thus treated and denied a part in the University it were better that the institution be blotted out of existence. They charged that Waddel had publicly advocated in the chapel infant sprinkling and had attributed ignorance to the Baptists for not agreeing with him.

The friends of the University were quick to answer these charges. Church and his faculty vigorously denied that the slightest religious disputation had ever entered into the instruction of the students or into the contacts of the professors with the students. As to the qualifications of Baptist candidates, none had been put forward who was suitable, and as for Brantley, he had been a Federalist and had opposed the United States in the War of 1812 against the bigoted British. And indeed, the question was asked, had the Baptists been sufficiently appreciative of the value of education to develop men intelligent enough to teach in the University? Brantley might be well enough educated, but he was no product of the Georgia Baptists. A Baptist of the better class decried this narrow sectarianism. "Discard forever," he said, "this vile principle of sectarianism, as the greatest bane to peace, prosperity, and high-minded philanthropy." Indeed had sorry times overtaken the state, said another friend of learning, when Georgians should advocate the closing of the University simply because Baptists or Methodists happened to present no qualified candidates for professorships. What would they have, he asked. "Destroy our literary institution at home, send our youth abroad to imbibe infidel, Unitarian, Universalist and anti-tariff beliefs and doctrines?" Away with all this narrow un-Christian religious prattle, anyway! What right had any religious denomination to control the University or to have any close concern about it! In 1830, all combined, there were only 75,000 Methodists, Baptists, and Presbyterians in all Georgia. Belonging to no church were 533,000 Georgians or six-sevenths of the people. Was it not barely possible that the University belonged to them as much as the other one-seventh? If it happened that there were more Presbyterians serving the University than any other denomination, might it not be that they were better educated and that they came into their positions through merit? Thus argued one Georgia Baptist.[14]

But the Baptists must be pacified; they would not be put off. In fact they might not acquiesce in the election of Church. The legislature could increase the number of trustees; it might call for sixteen new members—"all Baptists." The next year James P. Waddel, another Presbyterian and a son of Moses, was elected to teach ancient languages. This was flying in the face of an already outraged denomination; it was a crime they must not stand. There was the Reverend James Shannon of the Augusta Baptist Church, who was a master of the languages of all the Ancients—or at least of all those tongues that should be used to confound Georgia students. He must have the position. Waddel, who had no taste for such an unseemly squabble as was about to arise, withdrew, and the Baptists secured the election of Shannon. This educated Baptist remained at the University until 1835 when he left to become president of the University of Missouri. Waddel, who had so gracefully stepped aside, was now re-elected and he served for twenty years.[15]

The threat of the Baptists to secure control of the University through political action was dangerous and ominous and boded nothing but disaster for church and school if persisted in. As it happened at this time the political elements in the state were so disposed as to make it possible for this religious disturbance to be eagerly embraced and used. During the "Era of Good Feeling," when all the people were supposedly agreed upon correct principles of government and party action, the Georgians, who were never happy if not disputing, fell out over something no one was ever able fully to discover, and calling themselves "Troup men" and "Clark men," carried on the well-established pastime of abusing each other as they sought to get elected to the offices. Sagacious old Hezekiah Niles, up in Baltimore far from the conflict, who appeared to know a great deal about everything and regularly told it to the public in his *Weekly Register,* had no end of trouble trying to find out what "the shooting was about" in Georgia. Finally he made the honest admission as to the "Troup Party" and the "Clark Party": "We do not know what they differ about— but they do *violently differ.*"[16] The principles that separated the two parties might have been a well-kept secret, but the character of the people who composed each group was fairly easy to ascertain. In general, the Troup men were those who had started out to follow George M. Troup; they liked to think of themselves as aristocratic and cultured. The Clark men followed John Clark, who had been a backwoods son of a backwoodsman; they were more apt to be small farmers and men of few pretensions.

As it happened, the religious denominations were not the only groups who hoped to control the University; Troup men and Clark men were equally as covetous. For a half dozen years prior to this time (1830) the former had been in the ascendency in the state, and had come almost completely to dominate the University.

The Clark Party claimed that all the trustees and faculty were Troup men and that they taught the students to be Troup supporters. The Clark men and the Baptists thus had this in common: neither controlled the University and yet each fervently desired control. It was also undoubtedly true that the Baptists now combined their forces and prejudices. In fact the Clark men encouraged the Baptists in their raid on the University and took advantage of every move to oust the Troup men. A graduate charged that certain politicians had always been opposed to the University and that they were now taking advantage of the sectarian dispute to crush the institution. "The Clarke party will spare no pains," he said, "to widen the breach, and they will spare no pains to overthrow the College." The Baptists and the Clark Party joined forces and influence in the legislature in the session of 1830 and laid violent hands on the University. The board of trustees, which had heretofore consisted of seventeen members, was now increased to twenty-eight, and the additional eleven named by the legislature were all Clark men. Thus did the University become the victim of political exploitation and of religious bigotry—a precedent which was to plague the institution more than once thereafter. Augustus B. Longstreet described the onslaught as resulting in the College losing half of its sovereignty and thereby stirred up a dispute from which he had no inclination to run away.[17]

The purpose was to equalize the Troup and Clark men on the board, a desire laudable enough in itself but dangerous in the manner of its execution. Soon after the board had been reorganized, a resolution was passed prohibiting students engaging in politics or political disputations in any of their speeches or orations at commencement or at other times. This was perhaps a wholesome move to free the University as far as possible from the danger of becoming the spoils of politics, but evidently it was impossible to divorce the minds of the students from the great and glorious pastime of their fathers. The Clark Party might have an equal voice in the management of the University, but it would not thereby make Clark supporters out of the sons of Troup fathers, for only the more wealthy Georgians had the means or desire to send their sons to the University, and thus did the general sentiment of the students long continue to favor the Troup Party. As previously noted, the students during the Nullification controversy became bitter opponents of the tariff, and when President Jackson threatened to coerce South Carolina, they, siding with the nullifying Troup men rather than with the union Clark men, made an effigy of "Old Hickory" and burned it.[18]

Alonzo Church gave promise of a long life, and thereby left no comfort to the Baptists in their desire to secure the presidency of the University. They and all the other designing religious denominations were soon to understand that this institution could never be seized and used for the purposes they had in mind. In fact it would be better to retire from the struggle and set up colleges of their own. The Methodists and Baptists would leave it to the mercies and management of the politicians, the Savannah supporters, and of the Presbyterians. In this manner they could sap the strength of the state institution and get their revenge. They professed to fear the infidel character which they claimed had fastened itself upon the University, and by setting up colleges of their own they could better fight state support for higher education. Apart from these rivalries, ambitions, and hatreds, the dominant churches of the South had reached the stage in their development where their appreciation and pride of learning were being felt. During the later 'twenties and the 'thirties they set up colleges in almost every Southern state. In Georgia the Methodists secured a charter for Emory College in 1836, the Baptists followed the next year with Mercer University, and the Presbyterians (who as a religious organization had no more control over the University than had the Baptists), determining not to be left behind, started Oglethorpe University in 1838. Every one of these colleges had grown out of, or had combined with, manual labor schools which they had set going not long previously as the cheapest approach to an entry into the field of knowledge.[19]

That the University ruined young men was a favorite argument against the institution, perpetual and never to be shaken in the eyes of those who were so blind they would not see. Chancellor Henry H. Tucker, in 1875, found this form of hostility to the

University still strong, and he took occasion in an address before the legislature at that time to say: "It is said that many young men have been ruined at the University. It is not said how many have been ruined at home, and who, perhaps, might have been saved if they had been put under the fostering care of the University of the State. But it may be well to look among these ruins, and take account of the damage that has been done at this notable place. There is where William C. Dawson was ruined, and there is where Eugenius A. Nisbet was ruined, and there is where Iverson L. Harris was ruined, and there is where Hugh A. Haralson was ruined, and there is where Judge John J. Floyd was ruined, and his classmate, Judge Junius Hillyer, was ruined at the same time and place. There is where Bishop George F. Pierce was ruined, with his distinguished classmates, Dr. Nathaniel Macon Crawford, and Dr. Shaler G. Hillyer, and Bishop Thomas F. Scott, and Dr. John N. Waddell, Chancellor of the University of Mississippi. These five classmates, Pierce, Crawford, Hillyer, Scott, and Waddell were all slain at one fell swoop by the arch destroyer. They were all ruined at the University in the class of 1829. Ebenezer Starnes met his fate at the same place, and so did Henry L. Benning, both Judges of the Supreme Court. Howell Cobb and Herschel V. Johnson, both Governors of Georgia, were classmates, and both fell together, and at the same time and place fell Judge Augustus Reese. Francis S. Bartow and Junius A. Wingfield were classmates and met the same doom. Judge James Jackson and Judge David A. Vason, and David W. Lewis, for fourteen years a member of this body, and Governor John Gill Shorter, of Alabama, were classmates and met a common catastrophe. Professor Shelton P. Sanford, William Hope Hull, Isaiah Tucker Irwin, once the Speaker of this House, and Professor John LeConte, of national reputation, and Rev. Dr. Benjamin M. Palmer, of New Orleans, were classmates, and the splendid galaxy all went down together. Alas! for the class of 1838!

"His Honor of the Supreme Court, Judge Robert P. Trippe, and his Honor Judge Alexander Speer, were in the same class, and met together the ruin which is so common at the University. This was the class of 1839. Professor Joseph LeConte and Thomas R. R.

Cobb fell together. Dr. Felton and General Garlington were in the next class. Jabez L. M. Curry, Judge E. H. Pottle, and Judge Linton Stephens were in the next; and Peter W. Alexander, Henry H. Jones, and last, but not least—I say last, but not least—Benjamin H. Hill were in the next. Just look over the list—and the list might be indefinitely enlarged, for I have named only a few as specimens of the many—and see what we have done!"[20]

Propelled by the pride of ownership and by their dislike for the state University, these denominational colleges thrived from the beginning. It was easy to make of each preacher an agent for the college of his church and an enemy to the state institution. A good Baptist should go to Mercer University and a good Methodist must attend Emory—it naturally followed that the University could not be entered without great danger to their souls. There now grew up the perpetual myth that morality and religion could be found only in the denominational schools. By 1844 Emory was graduating almost as many students as was the University. Many Georgians charged that sectarian bias, not scholarship, was one of their greatest elements of strength. In 1857 Richard Malcolm Johnston refused the presidency of Mercer University to become a professor in the University because, as he put it, the University was a more intelligent institution, not held down by religious dogma and not requiring such strict and narrow rules of discipline. Though the disintegration of the University had been freely and gleefully preached from the time the denominational colleges arose, a friend of old Franklin College wrote in 1855, "Notwithstanding the predictions of some, who thought that, with prophetic vision, they saw the time when our College would decay and crumble, rapidly approaching, we yet see no signs of the coming fall. It has weathered more than one storm, and its timbers are yet sound; and the day is far distant in which, decayed and worthless, the props shall give way, and the stately edifice fall in shapeless ruin."[21]

President Church was a minister, and took his mission from God as seriously as he did his commission from the state of Georgia. The religious character previously given the University he well maintained. In fact a critical "Plain Sense" claimed that

Franklin College was priest-ridden. There were too many preacher-professors to please him. According to his observation, "They live well, say long prayers, talk a great deal about the poor 'Heathen,' quit the College, and wind up by marrying a fortune."[22] General Edward Harden in 1848 attempted without success to pass a motion through the board of trustees forbidding professors to become pastors of churches while they were connected with the University.[23]

Such was the position the University as an institution had assumed in the jig-saw puzzle of sectarianism. There can be no doubt that the faculty was much more religious than the citizenry of Georgia, but what about the students? Recurrence to Waddel's religious concern for the University is again necessary. One of his important reasons for accepting the presidency of this school was to make it a bulwark of Christianity against the atheistic tendencies imputed to quarrelsome old Thomas Cooper, the president of South Carolina College, and to Thomas Jefferson, the moulder of the University of Virginia. With a fatherly concern he watched after his students. One day he was somewhat upset when he "heard unexpectedly of a female Deist in town"; what action (if any) he took, he failed to record. Camp meetings had early made their appearance in and around Athens, and Waddel had encouraged them as far as possible. Once he dismissed school from Thursday until Monday to let the students attend a Methodist camp meeting. In 1826 a fervent revival, which became particularly intense in the Athens region, swept over the state. At Washington, forty miles away, every person outside the church was converted except two or three, and at Athens forty students joined the Methodists, Baptists, and Presbyterians. In writing of this religious triumph, Lovick Pierce said much fear was felt that the summer converts who should go home during the winter vacation "while mingling with family and other irreligious friends, . . . might lose some of the heavenly fire, which all believed they carried away with them, but to the praise of God's grace be it told, they returned fervent in spirit, serving the Lord." It was a great outpouring, the most remarkable he had ever seen. "No sooner are the regular college duties disposed of," he said, "than the pious

students are engaged in singing, praying or relating to one another
the experiences of the past week, or day—or, what is a daily
practice, talking to and praying for the penitents." Three-fourths
"of the members of college" were doing this, he declared—and
what was even more extraordinary there was none to scoff or
deride.[24]

From this time on for many years camp meetings became one
of the greatest attractions and excitements in the lives of the students. This form of religious manifestation appeared generally
in the late summer and continued on into October. In 1830 thirteen
were announced for the regions tributary to Athens. As long as
the president and professors thought the students wanted to attend
for their religious good they were liberal in abandoning University
work, but there were too many attractions other than the exhorta-
tions of the ministers that appealed to the students. They sought
religion as an excuse, but in fact many of them enjoyed more the
freedom from school work and the pleasures of a camp meeting
crowd. In 1830 a two-day vacation was allowed; some of the
students remained four days, and for this over-abundance of
religious enthusiasm they were fined one dollar each. Another
student who went to camp meeting without permission was fined a
like amount. In 1832 a student who tried to persuade the faculty
that he must have religion was refused permission to attend a
camp meeting; he disregarded the faculty advice in the matter
and went. The faculty, considering this zeal out of all proportion
to reason, expelled him.[25]

The students could not always induce the professors to give
holidays for camp meetings, but when such attractions conflicted
with their literary societies they could adjourn, as, for instance,
the Phi Kappas did in 1840, "on account of the religious excitement." It was during this year that another revival visited the
University, bringing into the church many students. Among those
led to join a church was Joseph LeConte, who became a Presbyterian. A few years later the Demosthenians adjourned, as the
students and citizens of Athens were "under a state of religious
excitement." Perhaps the most intense and severe revival which
ever spread over Athens and the University came in 1858. It was

a deep and silent searching of souls, accompanied by little that was spectacular or boisterous; the culture of the University community had by this time banished the noisy and uproarious antics of earlier times. Beginning in April it ran for more than five weeks, stopping only when the populace became "worn out with fatigue." The University was the very center of the disturbance. It was reported that when it started only two of the professors were members of a church, and only "one seeker of religion among the students." Two and three meetings were held a day, in both literary society halls and in the churches of the town. President Church and members of his faculty aided the regular ministers in the preaching. At the end of the fifth week the Methodists had gathered in ninety new members, the Presbyterians fifty, the Baptists forty-one, and the Episcopalians eleven. The excitable and inflammable nature of the Negroes was fired; they joined in and ran on indefinitely. By the end of May they had added more than a hundred new converts to their churches.[26]

Less evanescent emotionalism and more permanent conviction characterized this turning for consolation to the highest and finest feelings of the innermost being. After the major outburst had spent itself the people still found themselves on a higher plane than formerly. In September (1858) meetings for mutual consolation and rejoicing began to be held throughout the community. The first one began in the law office of William W. Lumpkin, where the business men met daily. The excitement of the times and the almost melancholy drifting of the country toward war, kept the religious fervor high during 1860. In September "due to the religious feeling pervading the whole community" and on account of the desire of Thomas R. R. Cobb to encourage it, the Phi Kappa Literary Society abandoned its meetings for a time and gave over its hall to the preachers. Since the middle 'forties, when both the Methodists and Baptists split their church organizations in the sectional struggle, religion had been booming in the South. Both of these churches doubled their membership during the next fifteen years. The situation at Athens and at the University tended to become typical of the whole South.[27]

The University of Georgia was not conspicuously different from the state of Georgia at large in the amount or quality of religion that obtained there. Without a doubt during and following revivals it forged far ahead of the state. Many students were sons of irreligious parents for whom the University was not responsible. The situation was almost humorously recognized in Lovick Pierce's fear that some recently converted students might have a terrible back-sliding on an approaching vacation, "while mingling with family and other irreligious friends." The University and all its official doings had a distinctly religious flavor, much beyond what could be found in a twentieth century state university. It regularly taught "Evidences of Christianity" and "Moral Philosophy," and every president it had from its foundation down to the twentieth century, excepting Meigs, was an ordained minister, and some of them preached about as much as they taught. Learning of the Franklin College variety was not atheistic, despite the denominational colleges' charges to the contrary. Joseph LeConte, whose keen scientific and analytical mind made him one of the greatest geologists of America, was led to join the church while a student. But some of the professional religionists, who claimed to be the sole keepers of truth, interpreted Christianity to a not-very-discriminating people in such a way as to arouse a feeling which harmed more than it helped the University. The finest and noblest sentiments that human nature falls heir to come from man's honest search for his Infinite Maker—the search at Franklin College was as honest and as earnest as at any other educational community in the Old South.

THE UNIVERSITY
AND THE STATE

It was through no popular demand that the University came to Georgia in 1784, when it got the promise of 40,000 acres of land, and in 1785, when it received its charter. A small group of men, some only recently arrived in Georgia, were responsible for presenting this institution to the Georgians, the mass of whom being illiterate but reasonably happy and yet not unduly suspicious of learning. Only a few of the common people recognized the full meaning of this attempt to promote education, but they opposed it with all they could command. The constitution under which they were living at this time had been made in 1777 in the stress of war, while yet the more enlightened Savannah and Coast country prevailed, and it had required that schools be set up in each county "and supported at the general expense of the State." By 1789, when the next constitution was made, the swarms of frontiersmen, who had come into the upcountry, were influential enough to cause the constitution-makers to forget entirely about education. It was not even alluded to in this document—perhaps this was a partial answer to those educational promoters who had tried to set up a university five years previously. Then, in 1798, the third constitution, more mindful of the arts and sciences, declared for their promotion in "one or more seminaries of learning," and called upon the next session of the general assembly "to provide effectual measures for the improvement and permanent security of the funds and endowments of such institutions." The educational managers were at work again. The general assembly was finally prevailed upon to lend enough money to set up the University three years later.

Education was no vital concern of these tens of thousands of people flocking into Georgia; why should it be? They had not come here seeking learning nor the expense that went with securing it. They had left behind much better educational opportunities than they could dream of finding here. They had come to get better land and more of it than they had ever had before. They wanted to clear fields, build themselves homes, raise cotton and make money, now that Eli Whitney had invented the cotton gin. Material and practical things concerned them now; perhaps, when wealth and social position came, they would become interested in intellectual doings. Westward from Augusta they spread out through Middle Georgia, laying out broad plantations worked by gangs of slaves, driving some of the small farmers farther on or pushing them up into the hills and mountains or down into the sterile pine barrens and wire-grass country. This rich red cotton land the planters must have. If the Creek Indians were in the way, they must retreat—even to the extent of Governor Troup threatening war against the United States, which was inclined to uphold the treaty rights of the Creeks. The Cherokees also must vacate— by 1838 Georgia had cleared out the last of her troublesome Indians.

The planters through Middle Georgia grew and prospered. They cleared more acres, bought more slaves, and sold more cotton. The price of their commodity generally had them running around in a vicious circle, trying to get ahead of low prices with more bales. But the more fortunate and more ambitious planters were able to save from their running expenses enough money to build their fine old white-columned homes, set back from the roadway in tasty surroundings. They were fast becoming gentlemen, planter aristocrats, with easy manners and correct judgments. Visiting Englishmen began to recognize them as the élite Americans. The furnishings in their homes bespoke culture. On the walls were paintings done by Stuart, perhaps, or by some wandering artist of no lesser fame than a Chester Harding or a Saint Memin or Thomas Sully. The library was well stocked with books, Shakespeare and Dickens certainly, and Sir Walter Scott's novels as fast as they came out. Actually carloads of books rolled southward to the plantation homes. Leisure, begot by wealth, a lazy climate, and servants on all sides, set the planter and his family to reading these books. Out of it all was distilled a certain unassuming culture which has ever after set a sort of romance on the ante-bellum South.

But all Southern people were not so fortunate, so intelligent, and so cultured as these planter aristocrats, living in their fine old mansions. The Southern gentlemen and their gentle ladies were far too scarce to make this picture typical of the Old South. In 1860 there were 118,000 white families in Georgia, whereas only 41,000 held slaves. But the old plantation, mellow in fiction but too scarce in fact, could blossom forth only where there were about twenty or more slaves to do the work. Now in Georgia in 1860 there were only 6,363 families who could qualify, and credulity should not be stretched so far as to assume that all of these families lived in delightful mansions and read Shakespeare and Scott. The sad but inevitable conclusion follows that about 112,000 Georgia families were not presided over by Southern gentlemen and their accomplished ladies. Thus, for every family that might qualify for the planter aristocracy, there were about nineteen who had to be content to remain in the respectable middle class of farmers, tradesmen, and professional men—if indeed they were able to escape the fate of being "poor whites." Without a doubt the great majority of Georgians of ante-bellum times belonged to the middle yeomanry class, who were neither rich nor yet so very poor; and at one extremity was found the finest product of Southern civilization and at the other, the scum and dross that nature and nature's laws have decreed shall ever attend the forward march of the human race.

It is ever true that the most ambitious, who may be the most intelligent and educated, and also, perhaps, the most crafty and cunning, strive for leadership and generally secure it. It was, therefore, natural that the planters should gradually assume control of the state and largely dominate its politics. What would they do with the state's educational theories, a heritage laid up by Baldwin and Milledge and Few and the early Coastal leadership? The political philosophy soon grew up that it was no business of the state to provide free education for the people. The leaders definitely held that the constitution called for no such interpretation, and they strangely failed to read into the requirements of a successful and efficient democracy an intelligent electorate. The only departure from this position was a half-hearted attempt to provide a fund to be used in paying the tuition of the very poor and indigent and the establishing of academies, aided by grants of land and by an inadequate endowment.[1]

If the general educational foundations were thus dealt with, what would be the attitude toward the cap-stone? The state had given the University its charter and 40,000 acres of land—here the Georgians of the ante-bellum times thought the generosity of the state should stop. Those who wanted an education and were able to pay for it should provide the running expenses. But, even then as now, tuition could not run a university; so the trustees were driven to the resort of selling the land and thus gradually using up the endowment. An act of the legislature in 1815 deposited with the state the notes from the sale of these lands, and two-thirds of the proceeds were to be advanced to the University. The amount of $100,000 was agreed upon, but as the state did not deliver the money it assumed a perpetual debt to the University of this amount, invested the money in bank stocks at 8 per cent, and began paying the University $8,000 a year as interest.

With the new enthusiasm incident to the coming of Waddel and to the gratitude over the saving of the University from the decay that seemed inevitable a few years before, the trustees in a tone of apology and with an attitude of one who was fearful that he was about to commit a grave crime, called on the legislature to come to the rescue of its own. The legislature in 1821 caught the vision of a greater University, and did for the institution a service which won it this praise: "With posterity it will be accounted an honor to have been a member of the Legislature of 1821." It declared that the annual income of the University should always be $8,000 even if the bank stock should fail to produce the promised 8 per cent; the state would make up the deficit from the public treasury. It also appropriated $15,000, to be secured from the sale of University lands, and $10,000 additional from the sale of fractional surveys already made, both sums to be used in the construction of new buildings.[2]

The friends of the University now made the natural mistake of believing that the state would grant substantial support when substantial needs could be shown. In 1824 they asked for $3,500 with which to build a home for the president, and thereby uncovered a withering prejudice that had been growing up against the University. A legislator, who seems to have been a fair representative of his fellows, declared that he was tired and worn out with hearing the University begging for money. According to the report, "if an institution so old as this is cannot support itself he would let it fall." There was no need for a president's house. If the legislature should give money for this purpose, then immediately the demand would arise for a home for each professor. After all, the University was for the rich; the poor got nothing out of it. The bill was killed. Afterward it was easy to arouse prejudice against the University, and against education generally, by merely referring to the attempt to build the president a "mansion." Asbury Hull, secretary and treasurer of the University for almost half a century, was defeated for the legislature in 1828 because he had introduced the bill for the president's home. It mattered not if the president were even forced to pitch a tent on the campus—what business had the state spending money on a rich man's school? A friend of the University wrote in 1830, "Ought not shame to burn the cheek of every Georgian, when he is told, that, for the President of their College to live in, there is nothing better than Easley's old log house patched up—nothing better than Easley's old barn to worship God in—and not the sign of a house at the public expense for a professor."[3]

The break of the 'thirties ushered in, indeed, a notable era in human affairs, almost as wide as the world. The spirit of change, revolt, suppression, and hope touched also Georgia and the University; the agitation stirred up by religion and politics has already been noted. An inextricable part of the whole movement was the attempt of the University at this time to drive the state to a proper support of its educational institution. Beginning about 1829 the friends of the University entered upon the most determined and prolonged campaign ever attempted up to that time to settle definitely the policy of the state toward the promotion of higher education—and incidentally to fix the position of Georgia along the lines of general intellectual and cultural progress. Waddel was leaving; Church was coming in—what was to be the future outlook for education and the higher feelings of life in Georgia?

All the prejudice and ignorance that grew up naturally in the state or could be engendered by religious bigotry or political trickery were thrown into the fight. One of the most powerful weapons yet devised among politicians was to array an imaginary poor against an imaginary rich, and then call for the vote. It was easy to say that Franklin College was attended only by the sons of the rich, and what was more, it was alarmingly true, if by the rich was meant the well-to-do. It required no detective skill or power of divination to discover and establish this fact. Who but a person with means could attend a school which was forced to charge tuition in order to exist, where board was to be paid for and a room too, and where a certain state in life (beyond that on a farm) was required. Furthermore, there was another sifting process which kept out the poorer boys: only parents with means could prepare a son for entrance into the University, in Georgia, where education, both primary and secondary, was free only to the very poor, who were too proud to profit by it. The accompanying maps show that the counties sending most students to the University were the richest parts of the state. But it does not follow that only the sons of planters with a thousand slaves or ten thousand acres attended the University. The well-to-do middle class were able to send their sons to the University and many of them did so. In 1829 "the decent annual expenses of a Collegian at Athens" ought not to have exceeded $400, and it might have been much less without great inconvenience. Alexander H. Stephens spent on the average $205 yearly. Some students were aided by private individuals or organizations, and it was not an unknown occurrence for students to withdraw for want of money. Now and then a college story ranged around a rich student and a poor one, as was the case in "The Contrast or the Man of Gold and the Golden Mind," which appeared in the *Southern Literary Gazette,* and the poor student generally came out the hero.[4]

The friends of the University did not deny that as a rule only the substantial Georgians could afford to send their sons to college, but they could not see the logic of demolishing the University for that reason. "We should not be jealous of the University because the sons of wealthy men are educated there," said Augustin S. Clayton. They would attend universities outside the state if there were none in Georgia, and they would bring back foreign and dangerous notions. This argument became more potent and compelling as the slavery dispute began to tear the sections further apart. "A Friend of Learning" said, "I have no doubt that more than half of these young men, never would have received a liberal education had there been no College in our State." He maintained that "most of them are young men, who have come from the plain substantial farming class of our citizens." "Quintillian" admitted for the sake of the discussion that only the rich attended the University, and argued that they would be much more considerate of the poor for having had an education.[5]

Yet the argument was nevertheless cogent that if the state should spend great amounts of money on the University, it would be taking part of the poor man's taxes (however meager they were) and expending it on something which would be enjoyed for the most part by the well-to-do. The perfect answer to this argument at this time was that the state was expending no money on the University. It also followed with compelling force that the expenditures of the state could not be resolved into a simple analysis of benefits conferred on certain classes of the people, and only in connection with the University had the question been raised. Whom had the state's entry into the banking business with hundreds of thousands of dollars helped? Or what of the millions in aid of railroads and internal improvements—especially in comparison to the few thousands asked by the University? But the poor-boy

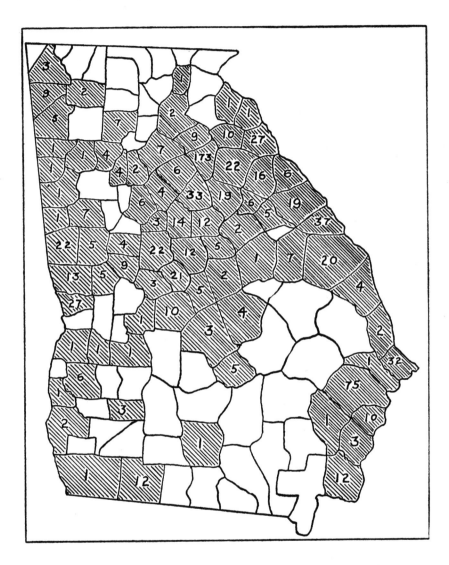

STUDENT ATTENDANCE AT THE UNIVERSITY OF GEORGIA BY COUNTIES

The numbers give the total registration of students for the years 1828, 1834, 1836, 1838, 1840, 1844, 1851, 1854, 1856, and 1860.

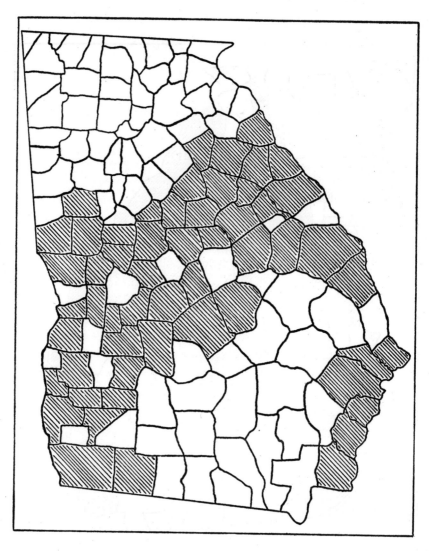

PLANTATION GEORGIA

Counties having in 1860 fifty per cent or more Negro population are shaded. Naturally, this belt was the plantation region. Counties containing large towns had either an equal division of whites and blacks or a majority of whites. Note how closely this map coincides with the one on student attendance.

argument had long worried the trustees and they had sought to answer it in various ways.

In 1822 the University sought to gain a point with the poor boys and the churches by deciding to admit free of tuition annually five ministerial students "pious and meritorious and unable to defray the usual expenses of education." This was good argument as far as it went, but something more would have to be done if results of any practical value were to be attained. George M. Troup, previously governor of the state and now a trustee, hoped to link up the Poor Schools with the University and down forever the charge that the poor boys could not attend the University. True to his political bringing-up and training, he said, "The poor are, and will, I trust, continue to be the governors of this country," but the University was too poor to educate them unless the state should come to its aid, for "the poor cannot give alms to the poor." It was only by supporting the University in order that it might admit the poor free "that the institution can permanently be secured against those political and religious jealousies which constantly threaten it, which disturb and weaken it, and which must finally destroy it." The Senatus Academicus greatly admired "the elevated patriotic, & truly republican sentiments of that distinguished Citizen," and referred the idea to the legislature with the recommendation that a law be passed setting aside a sufficient amount of money to pay for the education of the poor boys who should seek to enter the University. The trustees adopted the definite plan of limiting the bounty of the state to one poor boy from each county and of calling for an annual appropriation of $15,000. These poor boys were to be entered in the Grammar School in Athens when necessary, and they were "to be taught, clothed and boarded at the public expense, until they shall have completed the full course of studies taught at the University." This plan was wholly feasible, was just and far-sighted, and might have worked a wonderful change in the character of the state. It seems to have been honestly desired by the friends of education in the state, despite the fact that they were charged with crying out against "this attempt to contaminate the aristocracy of Franklin College with the sons of Plebeians!" What happened will shortly appear.[6] Free tuition was later to solve this problem.

These ideas were being agitated in 1829 preparatory to the University's campaign for adequate support. The definite wants presented to the legislature this year were: $5,000 to be used in buying books for the library, which would help poor boys unable to meet this expense, $2,000 for a cabinet of minerals, $18,000 for six new faculty homes, and $8,000 for a new chapel. For maintenance $2,100 annually was requested, out of which was to come the salaries for two new members of the faculty —one for Spanish and one for natural history.[7] The University proponents hoped that the legislature would see the wisdom of this needed expansion. Placed on a purely mercenary basis it would be a good business move, for more and more students from other states would be attracted to the University and each would bring to Georgia an average of $300 yearly. The amount already being brought in through this means reached $4,000 or $5,000 yearly. South Carolina was giving her College an annual appropriation of $10,500 yearly, and Alabama, an offspring of Georgia, was giving her University $16,000 a year. And Virginia was soon giving her University $15,000 a year.[8]

A determined effort by every known means was made to awaken the state. The educational crusaders held up the state in shame; they sought to touch its pride; they played on the tightening sectional string; they appealed to sordid money-making proclivities. One editor declared that the University had been "considered as an illegitimate child of the State—toward whom the most stinted parsimony has been practiced—while thousands have been lavishly spent on the Penitentiary—an institution productive of endless mischief to the social relations of our people." It was sad but true, he held, that the average Georgian was not intelligent enough to appreciate the value of a university and of education. Perhaps the only remedy was for the missionary to try to blast the people out of their stupidity. "There is here," he said, "as rich and wide a field open for him as ambition needs to toil in."[9] Augustin S. Clayton hoped that he might make the state hang its head in shame and force it to help the University as the only road to an easy conscience. "Shall this state, one among the first, the

wealthiest and most patriotic in the Union," he queried, "evince to
the world that it has less use for knowledge, less taste for literature,
and less regard for the moral character of her citizens, than did
our ancestors in the earlier and ruder settlement of the country?
Shall fifty years' experience profit us nothing, add nothing to the
refinement of our character, the improvements of our morals, the
enlargement of our judgment, the liberality of our sentiments, and
the exaltation of our pride?"[10] Even the students were wise
enough to see the sorry position their state had assumed and bold
enough to speak their minds. One of them wrote, "The parsimo-
nious course which Georgia has pursued with regard to this College
is sufficient to brand us with contempt in the eyes of the world."[11]

Indeed, according to the Senatus Academicus, Georgia was already receiving widespread reproaches on account of the low state
of her University.[12] This body put in the further dignified plea:
Shall it be said of Georgia "that while she is expending annually
thousands, from the public Treasury, to improve the physical condition of the country, she refuses to be equally liberal with her
neighbors, in discharging that most important of all duties, that
can devolve on any government, namely, to provide for the moral
& intellectual improvement of her Citizens?"[13]

The enemies of the University aroused all the prejudices of
religious intolerance and political deception, arrayed the poor
against the rich, decried the value of a University education as
only filling the heads of boys with the indigestible lumber of
Latin and Greek,—"how are the people to be benefited in a
pecuniary point of view, by giving the people's money to support
a set of lazy professors?" as a Georgian queried a few years
previously.[14] The University should be moved from Athens to
Milledgeville, where the legislature could watch it more closely,
if indeed it should not be discontinued. More than once this
strategy had been suggested—in fact it was very prominently advocated in 1818 when the University had almost ceased to exist.[15]
The move was now urged more to destroy than to help, the leader
being E. J. Black, a representative from Richmond County. Some
of the students, ready for their fun even in so serious a matter,
wrote him sarcastic letters, purposely disguising themselves in

crude language and misspelled words. He now in stentorian seriousness used these letters as further evidence of the utter worthlessness of the University.[16]

The legislature of 1829 was too much busied with other matters to give the University little more attention than to curse the day that it was ever born. It had no money to spend on such absurdities. Said the indignant editor of the *Athenian,* "How any man pretending to an enlightened and liberal mind can oppose judicious appropriations of this nature . . . is beyond our comprehension. . . . We confess that with such legislation, and with such legislators (we know not and care not who they are) we have no patience, and, if we can get no men of better sense or more patriotism, and who are less under the guidance of their passions and prejudices, instead of annual session, we think it would be more to their honor, and more to the character of the state abroad, if we had a session but once in four or even ten years. They would thus be prevented from doing harm at least."[17] The more he thought over the situation, however, the more he saw to be thankful for. The legislature had actually resented the humble petition of the University in presuming to ask for aid, and the *Athenian* editor now realized that the legislators were not as bad as the Goths and Vandals had been, for at least the buildings of the University were left standing. It seemed, however, that it would be more honest for the state to admit "that we see no great use in this thing called learning. . . . We could then, like a good old grandma, send our youth to our juvenile offspring Alabama, or to the young and thriving west, for an education, where such subjects are considered worthy of attention, without being reproached with having a College at home."[18]

The fight grew hotter and more complicated at the next meeting of the legislature, 1830. By this time the Troup and Clark parties were quarreling about the University, and the Methodists and Baptists were charging the Presbyterians with having secured control. So the University supporters were beset on all sides, but they seized the initiative and fought for what they had lost in 1829. The Senatus Academicus showed not only how the legislature had not given deserved support to the University but also how it had actually withheld $40,000 due from the sale of lands. How had the mighty fallen when a sovereign state was proved to have plundered a defenseless stepchild! They begged for this money, theirs by right, and told how it would place the University "upon a footing with any Institution in the United States."[19] About this time New College burned and with it was consumed almost the last hope of the friends of the University. The legislature was now asked for $10,000 to be used in rebuilding the structure, and in addition, for an annual maintenance fund. Again the Senatus Academicus pleaded with the legislature and besought it to see the light of reason: "By every consideration of the blessings of knowledge to every community—by all its advantages in the support of our civil & religious priviledges [sic]—by the respect due the character of the State, both at home & abroad, and the implied pledge, to our Sister States that we will promote everything that will strengthen our Union, increase our affection for each other, and add to our reputation in foreign countries, so much opposed to our growth, in useful literature & refinement, the College of Georgia ought to be liberally supported with one heart and one mind." The state could not plead poverty; its resources were ample.[20]

The University won the fight, but it was a confused and mixed victory, won not on merit but through compromise. Instead of giving the University $10,000 for a new building, the legislature loaned this money and carefully provided for its repayment. It did the handsome thing of appropriating $6,000 annually, but made no settlement on the $40,000 it was withholding.[21] But, for these benefits the legislature reorganized the board of trustees, adding eleven names to this self-perpetuating body. Furthermore, it did deliberately or through a pernicious accident a trick calculated to damn still further the University in the eyes of the common people. It, purporting doubtless to be following the recommendation of the trustees of the preceding year, charged the University with educating free from cost for board and tuition one poor boy from each county, to be met by funds thereinafter mentioned— but the joker was that the legislature had directed the University to educate the poor without thereinafter mentioning any funds.

To carry out this clause would have bankrupted the University; the trustees disregarded it, but by so doing they were turning away (at least in principle) poor boys—and thus did the enemies of the University secure more argument.[22]

Within a year New College arose again, costing $12,349, and the trustees were busily gathering together $1,000 each year with which to satisfy an exacting legislature. Shylock must have his pound of flesh! Nevertheless, a year or two later the guardians of the state's sovereignty and of its treasury were feverishly investigating the use to which the University was putting the meager sums it had received and determining the amount paid back of the $10,000 borrowed.[23] It was doubtless with some regret that they found everything appertaining to the college finances regular.

The University had now, for the first time, secured an annual fixed appropriation as a gift from the state. It could feel stronger and more permanent than ever before, but at the same time it knew well that its position was not impregnable before an attack of the combined forces of ignorance, illiteracy, and bigotry. For fear of precipitating an attack the trustees re-emphasized an old rule concerning student expression. All student orations at commencement times must be censored by the faculty, who were required to exclude from them "all political matter involving the party politics of the day."[24] The various University authorities had long had the feeling that students could not be trusted with their own thinking. One of the early rules ran, "All the students are strictly forbidden to exhibit any performance on the stage which has not been examined and approved by a member of the Faculty."[25] Back in 1809 the Demosthenians had engaged in politics, considered of the patriotic variety, when they dressed in homespun as a protest against England.[26] Again in Nullification times, homespun was in good repute, as has already appeared. Students might wear their political opinions, but they might not speak them, as the Senatus Academicus definitely stated in 1825 that "the students in all public exhibitions, be required to refrain from the expression of any sentiment of general or local politics."[27] The Phi Kappas seized this as a subject for one of their debates, and decided that the Senatus Academicus was not justified "in restricting the students, from expressing in public their political Sentiments."[28] If a student might not express his political opinions, might he run for office? One in the 'twenties decided to see. He ran for Congress on the Clark ticket for the state at large, and seems to have been making some headway when his opponent maliciously wrote a touching obituary of him and glowing tribute to his sterling qualities, bemoaning his untimely death, and sent it to an Augusta paper. It was published, and as the student had no quick way, before the days of telegraphs and railroads, to deny that he was dead, he was "unanimously defeated."[29]

But the actions of students were sometimes more eloquent than their words. In 1831 a group of students burned in effigy Thomas Haynes, an inconsequential aspirant for governor.[30] In 1841, when President William Henry Harrison died, the Whig proclivities of Athens and of the University prompted commemorative exercises for him, but when Jabez L. M. Curry later hurrahed for Tyler, who was soon disowned by the Whigs, a Whig professor fined him one dollar.[31] Partly on account of fear of the political and religious elements in the state, and partly through the feeling that it was not good for students to do a great deal of actual thinking, the University authorities became more insistent on curbing the mentally alert. But there were limits to which a majority of the trustees would go. In 1833 they refused by a vote of fifteen to six to pass a resolution prohibiting all students from engaging in "party or sectional politics or political discussion . . ., either oral or in writing, or publishing, or any other display of emblems of personal indignity to public characters."[32] The modified prohibitions as they stood were too severe to please the students. Quite often they inserted new material into their speeches and orations after the faculty had passed upon them, and now and then they substituted entirely new speeches. In 1834 the trustees were rather critical of the faculty for having permitted students at the commencement exercises to speak on topics which they adjudged to be political. But a resolution to censure the faculty failed to pass the board.[33] Sometime later the trustees decided to withhold degrees from any student who should deliver a speech without having first submitted it to the faculty. Whether a Franklin College student had a burning message to deliver or not, he was likely to resent such close mental tutelage and to sidestep it, one way or another. In 1856 the faculty reported, "Several ridiculous speeches, calculated to produce disorder in the chapel, have been spoken lately on the stage." They also reported that this practice had to stop.[34]

The attempt to control student expression was not called forth wholly by the feeling that students should be interested in nothing except their lessons; the fear that they might awaken the dormant hostility to the University was ever present. In fact the institution had been too prosperous following the support it had received in 1830 to escape attacks. During this period its total annual income was generally about $20,000—for the dispensers of light to have this much money at their disposal was dangerous. The legislature was incredibly slow in learning this fact, but in 1842 it realized how negligent and wasteful of the state's funds it had been. It now snatched away the last vestige of the $6,000 annuity, and relegated the University to the position it had occupied in 1801. When President Church heard that this was about to be done he hurried to Milledgeville to stay the disaster if possible, but when he saw the sons of the University itself leaders in the camps of the enemy he burst into tears and retired. The educational leaders of the state stood almost aghast at this boldness of the legislature.[35]

Yet the trustees were themselves not without a certain pugnacious narrowness with regard to possible sources of revenue for the University. In 1847 they refused "large quantities of land in the County of Rabun," offered them by Colonel Leonidas Franklin—for what reason they did not record, but most likely for the same reason which impelled them to refuse a like proffered donation from William A. Carr, namely: that he be given two scholarships *in perpetuo*.[36]

If the University were to continue, it was now necessary to reduce salaries and expenses everywhere possible. Already it had been starving its professors. In 1829 the Senatus Academicus had suggested that the politicians were receiving more than the professors "for services perhaps not more arduous or useful." The president was receiving $2,200 a year, the professors $1,400, and the tutors $700. In 1837 the salary of the president was increased to $3,000 and of the professors $2,000; now it was necessary to drop back to the old scale, and to dismiss two professors who for eleven years had faithfully served the University. They were Malthus A. Ward and William Lehmann. The faculty now consisted of four professors and one tutor.[37] To insure the value of the money actually received, the trustees now resolved to accept for the payment of college dues no "wild-cat" or depreciated bank notes.[38] Two years later (1844) the foundations of the University had been so shaken that the trustees debated long and vigorously on a complete reorganization of the institution, which called for the resignation of all the faculty and of the president.[39]

From this time on, the University struggled with poverty and prejudice, hoping each year for aid, but never again even down to 1875 would the legislature be so foolish as to waste the state's money on such an absurdity as higher education. All the old pleas for support were revived; the state was begged and besought in vain. One of the arguments used most consistently, but to no avail, was the danger of sending Georgians to Northern universities. Back in 1819 Hampden McIntosh wrote a University professor about entering his son in the Georgia institution, observing that the "want of good schools in our state is one of the greatest evils we have to encounter. . . ."[40] As the sectional argument became more bitter, the friends of the University felt that there might be some good in the dispute, for surely Georgia would come to the support of her school as against the education to be had in the abolition North. Said the Senatus Academicus in 1827, "Intelligence is of but little consequence without principles—intellectual cultivation can never compensate for the want of patriotism. . . ."[41] It had also recently said, "This Board can not but feel and believe that nothing can be so important to the good people of Georgia, as to have their youth educated among themselves, and as long as knowledge is strength, and absolutely necessary to all the departments of government, to the council and to the field, to the literary reputation as well as political character of the state, so long will it be necessary to cherish and diffuse its blessings, throughout this rising and flourishing country."[42] The Civil War drew nearer and the trustees three years before it broke out warned again: "Whether the state will furnish the means to enable our youth to qualify themselves for the various avocations of life, or be content to remain in a condition of dependent vassalage upon Virginia, Massachusetts and other communities, some of which are hostile to our best interests and jealous of our prosperity—it is for the proud and patriotic people of Georgia to determine."[43] Also, if they must come to such an argument, it would be good business for Georgia to keep her students at home, for each carried from the state $400 or $500 a year. It was hoped that the churches might be won over when the radical religious departures in the North were fully exposed. Surely the conservative, God-fearing Georgians would not want their sons to come in contact with such religious heresies as existed in the North. The total result of this sectional argument was to restrict the area from which a Georgia professor could come—by the 'fifties scarcely from beyond the limits of Georgia—and to reduce the Georgia students in attendance at Harvard, Yale and Princeton from 35 in 1850 to 13 in 1860—or more strikingly, to reduce the 28 Georgians at Harvard and Yale in 1850 to 2 in 1860.[44]

The pent-up feelings of an outrageous fortune began to express themselves with greater force during the early 'fifties. Why was it that Georgia was so illiterate and enjoyed it so much? A determined effort was made at this time to convert the state to a free school system.[45] The friends of higher education also entered the arena again. The pity that the two campaigns might not have been united! The *Rome Courier* said in 1853, "Franklin College was sparingly endowed by the State Legislature, and even that small fund was given grudgingly and in a churlish spirit. The annual appropriation was a few years since refused, in plain violation of the State Constitution, and has not, we believe, been restored. Franklin has had to combat a thousand difficulties, and petty Demagogues have made a merit, before ignorant constituencies, of their avowed hostility to this institution. We grant that she has triumphed over all opposition, but who can estimate the good that has been left unachieved by reason of the short-sighted parsimoniousness of our Legislative worthies?"[46] Georgains here and there began to speak out the shame they felt. Said J. R. Sneed, of Washington, "This is a reflection and a dishonor to which a liberal and enlightened people should never submit; and for one I shall not be content until the blot has been wiped from our escutcheon."[47]

In 1855 the trustees and supporters of the University organized the most systematic and logical campaign for an endowment that had ever been attempted up to this time. At a large meeting of the board in November, where were present such leaders as Wilson Lumpkin, George R. Gilmer, Howell Cobb (all former governors of the state), Joseph Henry Lumpkin, and Herschel V. Johnson, the governor at that time, a memorial to the legislature was unanimously adopted. All the arguments heretofore used were repeated and emphasized, and to meet the poor-boy argument the plan was advanced of educating at the University free from all necessary expenses five poor boys from each congressional district. In a tone of humility and trustfulness they asked how a state could deny a few crumbs when it was so amply able to provide.[48] They believed that the time had come "when an earnest & united effort, should . . . be made to obtain from the Legislature a large & liberal appropriation for the endowment of the College—upon a scale adequate to the enlightened views of its founders. . . . We should not rest satisfied until an honest effort is made to make Franklin College what it was intended to be—a blessing to the state & to the whole country."[49] Wilson Lumpkin was put in command of the campaign. He got his documents and pamphlets together, and distributed them through the legislature and scattered them over the state—he used all the means known from a long and wide political experience to influence legislators to support the University. He forced through the house a measure to endow the University, but lost his fight in the senate. According to Lumpkin, "The Legislature of Georgia is a numerous and unwieldy body, and from custom we have a greater amount of Legislation than any other State in Christendom. And no gentleman seems to be willing to return home to his constituents, without claiming the

honor of being the author of one or more Legislative enactments."
"The measure has many insidious enemies," added Lumpkin.[50]

The poor-and-the-rich trick had been largely responsible for this
last defeat, but the trustees refused to be discouraged. They resolved at their next meeting to take "fresh courage to persevere
in our efforts until they are crowned with success."[51] Although
receiving nothing from the state and, therefore, being a private
institution in everything except control, the University now agreed
to give free tuition to all students studying for the ministry and to
one student from each of the ten congressional districts and to
two from the state at large.[52] In 1860 the trustees were laying
plans to make another onslaught against an overflowing state
treasury, now that the state-owned Western & Atlantic Railroad
was sweeping in a large surplus. They were planning to ask for
$100,000 annually for five years for a permanent endowment,
but the malignant distempers of the time soon made educational
institutions the least concern of a sorely beset people, North and
South.[53] When war intervened, there was more promise of
Georgia's ultimate awakening to a proper support of her University than had ever appeared before.

Governor Joseph E. Brown, in his last regular message before
the outbreak of the Civil War, argued valiantly and sincerely, but
in vain, for an intelligent attitude toward the University. He begged
the legislature to appropriate $500,000 in five annual installments
for an endowment, and showed that "a dime and a half, for five
years" would be all that was necessary from those who paid taxes
on a thousand dollars worth of property—all "for the purpose of
building up a University which would place Georgia in the very
front rank of all her Southern sisters, where the young men of
the South who, in future, are to conduct its government, direct
its energies and defend its honor, may be educated, without assist-
ing, by their patronage, to build up, elsewhere, institutions at war
with our dearest rights." In fact, the people need not be taxed at
all; returns from the Western & Atlantic Railroad would be sufficient. One poor boy from each county should in return be educated
free, with the understanding that he should teach in the state as
many years as he had been maintained at the University. "That

contracted policy which is ever standing at the door of the Treasury, with a flaming two-edged sword," he exclaimed, "is but little better than moral treason to the Constitution, which, for more than a half century, has been pleading for conformity on the part of those who swear to obey. . . . Away, then, with that narrow stinginess which begrudges a dollar to such a cause, while it is often wasteful of thousands upon objects that possess little or no merits."[54]

There was, indeed, much darkness before this possible dawn which the war drove back. The number of students had now dropped to less than a hundred, and it seemed that the politically-minded press of the state was generally against the University. President Church complained of the crumbling buildings, the lack of ordinary comfort, bad ventilation in worse classrooms. He was always haunted with the feeling that he could detect an unpleasant surprise on the countenance of visitors when they entered his office and saw the depressing poverty and dilapidation that stared at them from every corner.[55] It seemed that Georgia's University was being deliberately destroyed when the institutions of other Southern states were going forward. Twenty years previously Georgia had been abreast of them all in attendance; now the University of North Carolina had 460 students (with 178 from other states), and it had just finished two large buildings. The University of Virginia had almost a thousand students. But alas for the University of Georgia, despised among its own people![56]

There could be no doubt that Georgia was less appreciative of higher education than other Southern states. During the decade directly preceding the Civil War, the South as a whole made greater progress in giving an education to her sons than any other part of the United States. She sent twice as many students per thousand white population to her own colleges or to Northern universities as were sent to college from any other part of the country.[57] And Georgians were not wholly backward in sending their youths to colleges. Young Georgians went to Emory, Mercer, Oglethorpe, Wesleyan, and to institutions outside the state, but they seemed to be taught to despise their own University. Yet there was no more heroic fight by any institution in the South to do a work and accomplish a mission than was waged by the University of

Georgia. By 1865, 2,500 students had sought its help and 800 had departed with degrees. They had become leaders in every field of work. For example, the class of 1829 graduated seven ministers, college presidents, bishops, and professors, five physicians, five lawyers and two planters. The University had had efficient and worthy servants—Josiah Meigs, Moses Waddel, Stephen Olin, Joseph and John LeConte, Alonzo Church, Richard M. Johnston. In intelligence and accomplishment they could compare favorably with Jonathan Maxcy, Thomas Cooper, Francis Lieber, and William C. Preston at South Carolina College, with Alva Woods at Transylvania College and at the University of Alabama, with F. A. P. Barnard at the universities of Alabama and Mississippi, with the peregrinating Augustus B. Longstreet, with Josiah C. Nott at the Medical College of Alabama and the University of Louisiana.[58]

Wars are unique contests in that no one wins. The Civil War rudely brushed aside this outstanding surge of the South toward higher education; it also smothered this preparation for the blossoming forth of Southern letters. The South was just approaching the point where it could produce and appreciate. In statesmanship and oratory it had long excelled, for the populace was born to listen to political disputation and to play in politics. Education was necessary for literature. Men of letters might arise, but they would long remain unappreciated. True enough the planters could read and appreciate, but they were too few to encourage a Southern literature. Intelligent Georgians had early detected the trouble. In 1821 the trustees of the University in urging the legislature to give them support had said, "Let us no longer be reproached from abroad with the odious assertion that Georgia is 'missionary ground,' a term implying the absence of moral and intellectual refinement." A few years later the students took up the idea; they formed a club and began to fight and fuss. "Cervantes" said it was plain that Georgia was ignorant; she had no Irving or Cooper. "Where is the Georgian who has ever made any figure in the empire of letters?" he asked. "But I awfully fear too many inhabitants of Georgia, who have arrived to years of discretion, scarcely know that they are American Citizens, and I will hazard the assertion, that many there are who know not the first principles on which our noble constitution is based."[59] As late as 1855, the students were still regretting the fact that the South refused to encourage its own literature, but, instead, subscribed for *Harper's, Putnam's,* and for other Northern productions reeking with abolition poison. They neglected their own *Southern Literary Messenger.*[60] Not only did they let the *Messenger* languish; they starved many another ambitious attempt. The *Southern Literary Gazette* began publication in Athens in 1848, but the next year it moved to Charleston. It begged the people to form literary associations, as existed in many parts of the North, which by studying and reading Southern literature might promote it. "We mourn that the South," said the editor, "preëminent in physical beauty and resources, is, beyond cavil, behind the North in intellectual development and cultivated taste. The confession is indeed humiliating, but who will dare to disclaim it?"[61]

Again, why did the Georgia legislature refuse to support higher education and promote literature, duties required by the constitution; why was it not forced to carry out the constitution? A Georgia editor was unable to answer in 1850: "Why it is that our legislature takes so little interest in the matter we cannot conceive."[62] It was almost the case that the meeting of a Georgia legislature was feared by the friends of education more than it was welcomed. It was not uncommon for a Georgian to thank God that the legislature had adjourned. One of the last acts of the senate, said one, "a redeeming feature amid deformities and enormities of the winter," was to kill a measure "which proposed to prostrate the literary honor of our State by striking a death blow at Franklin College." In part it was the same cause that made all legislatures disappointing bodies, something that Thomas Jefferson had early discovered. His hopes of developing the University of Virginia were qualified by his suspicion of legislative intelligence. In a letter to George Ticknor in 1817 he said, "My hopes however are kept in check by the ordinary character of our state legislatures, the members of which do not generally possess information enough to perceive the important truths, that knolege is power, that knolege is safety, and that knolege is happiness."[63] More than a quarter of a century later the Georgia legislature was described as "busily and solemnly at work bringing the whole Legislative power of the Empire State to bear in changing the name of John A. Smith to John B. Something Else," where " 'State glorification' speeches were the order of the day, bringing into play Legislative wisdom that never looked intelligently into the spelling book as far as Baker!"[64]

But why should the Georgia legislature, time after time, resist what appeared to be plain reason, and what appeared to be an insistent demand of a substantial element of the intelligent people of the state? Besides reasons already suggested, it was a powerful fact that the University did not closely touch the lives of the vast majority of the people. Ten lists of students made at about four-year intervals from 1828 to 1860 show 50 counties from which not a single student attended the University and 81 counties sending students. But the great majority of the students came from the Middle Georgia plantation region and the Coast country. Nine counties actually sent a majority of the students counted in these ten representative lists.[65] It thus happened that out of the 131 counties in the state in 1860 there were representatives from 50 counties whose constituents had come into contact with the University in no way and there were 43 more counties which had sent five students or less to the University.[66] There were great regions over the state where the University was not of vital interest to the people. But add to this situation the fact that the state government was not truly representative, and it is easy to see why the legislature could disregard the pleas of the friends of higher education, even if they had been in a majority. By the constitution of 1798 each county was entitled to at least one representative and not more than four, which was a fair proportion before the concentration of population. But in 1843 an amendment was added which gave every county at least one representative and no county more than two. Between this time and 1860, 30 new counties were created, which unbalanced the representative principle still more, as the populous counties were not necessarily the ones which were suffering mutilation. Thus did a minority of the people, and by the force of circumstances the least able to rule, seize control of the government of the state, never to relinquish it.

Plantation rule could succeed in Georgia only along the lines where the prides and prejudices of the people could be touched, in politics and around considerations of color. Education and religion, progress and poverty were issues which the most successful politicians and leaders generally eschewed. However burning might be their arguments for education before intelligent audiences, the Georgians who made politics their business were too likely to forget their zeal when it came to the practical manipulations with the voters and the legislators. They could never quite make it an issue on which they would rise or fall. Wilson Lumpkin, George M. Troup, Howell Cobb, Eugenius A. Nisbet, Thomas R. R. Cobb and many other Georgia notables made excellent records in speaking and writing for education, but their actual accomplishments were negligible. Yet these same men won their victories before the people and the legislature in other fields. Lumpkin and Troup and Howell Cobb became governors; Thomas R. R. Cobb stampeded the state into the most gigantic decision it ever made—secession; Nisbet was equally successful along political lines. When it came to arguing for the University before the legislature it was more often praised than pitied, and almost invariably dismissed as the state's "proudest boast." Shortcomings and poverty were covered up with senseless and mocking praise. Governor Gilmer, who was as true a friend to the University as a political leader thought he could well afford to be, neverthless in 1830, when the University was on the verge of collapse, gave in a twelve-column message to the legislature a fourth of a column to education—uttering the pitiably false platitude, "The flourishing state of our College shews the disposition of our people to support it liberally."[67]

For the reasons that have appeared the University of Georgia was in fact a private school in its greatest need—private in support and public in control. In 1855 the suggestion was made by some friends of the institution that the alumni take control and run it, relieving the state of a burden which it apparently so utterly detested that it had tried to starve the institution to death.[68] The argument one time ran that Europe thought rulers were born and America thought they were made. Was Georgia measuring up to the American doctrine? European rulers had encouraged and preserved art, literature, and education, but they had not made it possible for the masses to learn to appreciate and enjoy them; the rulers of Georgia had refused to do either.

CHAPTER X

REVOLT AND REORGANIZATION

At Franklin College the last five years preceding the Civil War were stormy and devastating, and, as has appeared, it seemed that the situation might finally hit the rocks. The immediate cause of the trouble was not the niggardly course the state was pursuing toward higher education, nor was it related to the impending sectional struggle. There had been gradually growing up a conflict between two systems of thought and reason and now the tilt was about to be engaged in. Franklin College had been growing, not in size but in mentality; the old order was coming into conflict with a new order that was striving to be born. The revolt cannot, therefore, be attributed to one simple cause, but rather to the spirits of two ages, each made up of many elements.

The University had its traditions and its keepers of these traditions. It had its charter, its usages and customs, and there were those who had been put in charge to preserve and carry them on. Men might come and men might go, but if they were true to their oaths, the soul of the University must go marching on unsullied and unchanged. There are always two types of leaders and preservers of palladia, those who believe that things as they are are best, and those who believe that the heritage of the past should be considered subject to change, and be made to conform to the best the present has to offer. Both kinds of leaders

191

may be equally honest and each convinced that what his opponent
stands for is dangerous. The very nature of authority and responsibility tends to lead to the first type. The troubles of the 'fifties
were based on the essence of this conflict.

For the first seventeen years of its life the University had
three presidents; during the next forty years traditions were made
and carried on by two men, both of whom came at the same time,
the one, therefore, serving as professor and president the whole
period of forty years. Waddel came in 1819 and gave real being
to the University, and when he left ten years later Alonzo Church,
who had been professor of mathematics during this time, became
president and carried on the traditions for the next thirty years.
Church was a native-born Vermont Yankee who graduated at
Middlebury College, and like many other graduates of this school,
came to Georgia to teach. He taught in Eatonton Academy, married
a planter's daughter, and soon transformed himself into a Georgian.
Then he came to the University to teach such exactitudes as mathematics. He always had a rather Puritanical disposition and outlook on life. Rules were made to be obeyed; life was not a
haphazard existence. When he was elected president in 1829, an
admiring friend said, "We are told that he failed but once punc-
tually to meet his class at recitation during the last Collegiate
year, notwithstanding he has preached almost every Sunday during
this time, either in Athens or its vicinity."[1] With his stern
honesty and fixed convictions he appeared to a more critical col-
league, Joseph LeConte, as "a bigoted, dogmatic, and imperious
old man."[2] His health was not uniformly good (he was granted
a half year's leave of absence in 1843); the effect of health on
history is profound but difficult to measure. Nevertheless, Church
ruled his faculty and the trustees too, and the students of evil
inclinations looked upon him with fear and dread. He had keen
and piercing black eyes and a quick temper.[3]

He stood for the order of things as they are and he found con-
soling sentiment even among young people now and then to back
him up. In the annual report of the Phi Kappa Literary Society
for 1838 appeared the following: "The spirit of reform, which
may well be termed the *Demon* of the age has not made us wiser

than our Forefathers; & we are left to follow peacefully & confidently the path which conducted them to honor & Independence."[4] In 1854 one of those artists who picturesquely wandered through the country in those days strayed into Athens, and who would be a better subject to paint than President Alonzo Church? This artistic vagabond persuaded the senior class that this was true; the painting was executed, and President Church and his family were glad to receive this token of respect from the students.[5] The students collectively undoubtedly thought well of Church, but sometimes individually their opinions were not very complimentary. A student up before him for punishment in 1849 "found the old fellow as surly as a restive bull."[6] His combative disposition early in his presidency cropped forth in connection with a dispute with Stephen Olin, another New England Yankee and a classmate of his at Middlebury College. He, too, had come South, had taught at the University a few years, and had now recently departed. The roots of this quarrel went back to the charge that the Presbyterians controlled the University, and its branches ramified much into politics and personalities. It was claimed that Olin had under the name of "Friend of Equal Rights" attacked the University in a letter and had had copies laid upon the desks of the legislators; and it seemed to have been proved that Olin, although a minister of the Gospel, had at the University failed seventy-four times to attend morning prayers and forty-eight times, evening prayers. Before the quarrel was over, Judge Augustus B. Longstreet, in his *States Rights Sentinel,* came to the rescue of Olin and incidentally enjoyed the fight.[7] With all his faults Church was a learned man and a zealous scholar; his address before the Georgia Historical Society became well celebrated.[8]

But the world was moving, even in Georgia, and more than President Church realized. During the 'forties and early 'fifties new and younger teachers were filtering into the faculty, and by the middle of the 'fifties they were formulating ideas and expecting to be heard. Such men as John and Joseph LeConte, William Leroy Broun, William L. Jones, Charles S. Venable, William Henry Waddel, John W. Park, Charles F. McCay, and Emanuel V. Scherb were creating an atmosphere which was somewhat obnoxious to President Church, William T. Brantley, and to those who enjoyed most the aromas of the past uncontaminated by present stenches. Many newspapers that had a chronic grudge against the University soon began their chorus of denunciations of Church for driving away from the University his professors of greatest merit. In 1850 James Jackson resigned; in 1851 Nahum H. Wood tired of his mathematics; in 1852 William L. Jones departed; in 1853 McCay accepted a position in South Carolina College; in 1854 Scherb went; and in 1855, as a sort of stunning climax, came the resignation of John LeConte. Why this trickling away of the best blood of the University—the life and strength of the coming years? Various factions had various explanations. Many who were enemies of the University under any régime blamed Church because they hated the University; others who were the best friends of the University blamed Church because they loved the University. When McCay left, quite a flurry was created, and when his supporters suggested that it might have been worth more to the University to have retained McCay and dispensed with Church, the friends of the President proved rather conclusively that Church had not been the cause (that the trustees could get his resignation any time they pleased), but that South Carolina had more dollars to offer McCay than had Georgia.[9] The greatest blame that can attach to Church here was in his contention that the University professors were not too poorly paid—that a professor got $2,000 and a superior court judge received only $1,800.[10]

The nature of the issues between the old order and the new became clearer in the resignation of John LeConte in 1855, and in the going of his brother Joseph the following year. John LeConte had been elected professor of natural philosophy in 1846, and immediately his work had called forth the praise of Church. He developed a laboratory and, what was more, he evolved the enthusiasm of his students. Here was a teacher who made them think and who caused them much joy in the doing of it. He won their hearts, and his going was much regretted by them. "The resignation of this distinguished professor is now universally known and lamented," said the *Georgia University Magazine*.

"He has been universally beloved and esteemed, by every member of our College—while all will remember the eager solicitude and kind anxiety with which he guided his pupils in their pursuit of scientific knowledge."[11] A wordy newspaper controversy immediately developed which did no particular honor to either contestant, but which justified itself by preserving for posterity a knowledge of what it was all about. LeConte declared that his main reason for resigning was the domineering, petulant, and tyrannical disposition of Church. "He is irrascible in temper—" he charged, "overbearing and arbitrary in his intercourse with his colleagues,—and at times, discourteous and ungentlemanly in his deportment and language." The president was elected by the Senatus Academicus; the faculty, by the trustees. In this situation Church thought there was an especial virtue and authority for himself. He insisted that LeConte should patrol the campus and visit the student rooms. LeConte held that the five or six hours extra he spent in his laboratory excused him from this annoying puerility, and he thought that Church and the trustees had so understood it. President Church defended himself against the slurs of a domineering attitude by quoting expressions of esteem and good will from letters written by Jackson, Jones, and Wood on their departure. He also claimed that LeConte had taken advantage of the University by resigning just before school was scheduled to begin, instead of giving the six months' notice required by the rules.[12]

Regardless of the merits in the dispute, there could be no doubt that the University was disintegrating rapidly. The work of John LeConte had to be dispersed among the various professors until a successor could be found, but Joseph LeConte, who had been elected professor of chemistry and geology in 1852, refused to accept the duties that his brother had performed. Soon Charles S. Venable, an amiable Virginian, was secured to carry on the work of natural philosophy, which John LeConte had abandoned, but he immediately joined the camps of the enemy and gave President Church additional concern. The session of 1855-1856 was characterized by almost continual wrangling and disorder between the faculty and the president. Joseph LeConte and Church became bitter personal enemies, each mutually repulsive. LeConte charged, in a letter to the newspapers, that Church was "oppressive in his official conduct"; they both carried their troubles before the prudential committee, which declared that there was no evidence that Church had "in any matter or manner oppressed the professor."[13] LeConte lost his appeal in this case, but there were more matters under dispute. Joseph, like his brother John, refused to engage in the spy business, and he had as allies in this little rebellion Venable and Broun. They flatly refused to visit student rooms or to help to preserve order on the campus, and once LeConte refused to stop a student riot in his own yard. Although secretary of the faculty he attended few of its meetings. Again did LeConte appeal to the prudential committee for an interpretation of the rules on policing students. Again this committee acted and declared that the duties required by President Church must be performed and that no relaxation or dispensation could be granted.[14] The president clearly stated his position in the dispute, and his ideas of an ideal University faculty: "With our small faculty we need men who are willing to labor—and who will submit to the drudgery of instruction, and to the disagreeable service of sustaining the discipline of the institution."[15]

This revolt against a system of petty rules was only a symptom of a much more fundamental contention of the young rebels. They were contending for a real University, using university methods and management to supplant the outgrown wornout detention station called Franklin College. They wanted the students to be regarded as young men, and the honor system to be instituted. They wanted the courses of study to be wholly revised and the "standard of attainment for graduation" raised. Church maintained that a revision would be "wholly inconsistent with the good of the institution."[16] The trustees answered the other contention with the amazing rule that a student should not be kept from rising with his class if he failed in his effort to pass merely in the courses of mathematics and the sciences—this, provided he was diligent, studious, and good in deportment. The young rebellious intellectuals rose up in a faculty meeting soon thereafter and, seizing control of the meeting through the majority they

held, passed a resolution begging the trustees to repeal their recent
rule striking at intellectual integrity and honesty, lowering the
scholarship of the University, and placing it in an unenviable
light before the other Southern universities. They declared that
one-third of the students' time was given over to the study of the
sciences. Those who voted for the resolution were LeConte,
Venable, Broun, James P. Waddel, Park, and William H.
Waddel.[17]

An additional significance must be seen in the attempt of the
trustees to belittle and destroy the sciences at the University.
Scientific methods of securing knowledge and adding to it might
possibly conflict occasionally with certain religious sects' interpre-
tations of the Bible. Joseph LeConte had back in the spring of
1845 read *Natural History of Creation*, which gave him his first
introduction to the doctrine of evolution. Later, when he became
a professor in the University, in order to conform to the rule
of giving the boys as much theology as possible on Mondays to
prevent them studying profane subjects on Sundays, he discussed
the "general laws of animal structure as evidence of a divine
plan."[18] LeConte in all his subsequent work and investigations
found no reason for changing his mind on this fundamental thesis.
He remained a Christian throughout his life. But there were those
in Athens and at the University who held that the LeConte brothers
were evolving dangerous monstrosities in their laboratories—
perhaps a Frankenstein would rush out of a test tube and lay waste
on all sides. Harry Hammond, who later followed LeConte, con-
tended that the earth was 22,000 years in the making, which
period left a yawning chasm in time when compared to the con-
ventional six days taught by Patrick H. Mell of the ethics and
metaphysics department. Some of the students, somewhat confused by this discrepancy, went to Judge Joseph Henry Lumpkin,
long the distinguished chief justice of the state supreme court,
for a final decision. Judge Lumpkin declared that six days was
correct and that those who thought otherwise were losing their
faith in Holy Writ. Thomas R. R. Cobb, another learned man of
Athens, concurred.[19] President Church, almost as much preacher
as teacher, who taught the Greek Testament on Monday mornings

to silence the criticism over the state that the University had no religious instruction, naturally looked with feelings of hostility on the LeContes' evolution theories, yet he did not drive the brothers away from the University on this ground as is often stated.[20]

Church saw his faculty disintegrating and his students melting away, until at the beginning of the session in 1856 the number had dropped to 79.[21] The latter situation caused him as much worry as the former, and he took occasion often to account for the small numbers. He laid the trouble largely to the church schools which had grown up and to their policy of attacking the University, offering cheap board, and catering to big numbers. "A degree rather than an education is too often the object sought," he said. The University might have fewer students than some other institutions, but with fewer students it could do better work. The University should work for "higher advantages [rather] than larger catalogues." Of course, it took the revenues from about a hundred students to keep the University running. This situation ought not to be; the state should endow the University and free it from any consideration of numbers.[22] Good work should always be the test of the value of the University, for "one educated young man from its halls will be more useful than twenty who may have spent their four years within the same without any considerable efforts to secure the advantages which it offers."[23] These were sentiments which the most ardent of the intellectual rebels could endorse, and they were undoubtedly called forth by the revolt. After John LeConte had left, President Church also said concerning the espionage system, "I believe a few general rules are better than a large number of specific enactments. Students should be required to conduct themselves in an orderly & gentlemanly manner & attend to their College duties industriously."[24]

As already stated, the fall term of 1856 began with few students and many storm clouds. The trustees at their meetings in August had talked plainly. There was "a lamentable relaxation in the discipline of the College. The proof is as overwhelming as it is mortifying—this must not be." The professors were given the plain understanding that they must attend morning and evening prayers, that they must be in their rooms during study hours, that they must preserve order in the dormitories, on the campus, and in the town. If the situation did not mend, the trustees would investigate. They begged the faculty to stand together and support the president. At this time (August) Church resigned and declared that he would not reconsider. Nevertheless, he did reconsider with the above-mentioned storm clouds blowing up.[25] In October the trustees, having reached the end of their patience and resources, called for the resignation of all the professors and the president, and advertised for a new faculty. Church was re-elected president and Brantley, Lee, and William H. Waddel were hired again. The others were sent on their way—LeConte, Venable, Broun. Waddel stayed until 1860; Lee, until 1862; Brantley left the next year to preach in the Baptist Church in Philadelphia, now secure from the reach of University trustees. LeConte went to South Carolina College to join his brother John, and after the Civil War both departed for California to build one of the greatest universities of the country; Venable became General Lee's adjutant during the Civil War and then professor of mathematics in the University of Virginia; Broun returned to the University in 1866 to teach natural philosophy, later became president of the Georgia State College of Agriculture and Mechanic Arts of the University, left for a position in Vanderbilt University in 1875, and ended his wanderings as president of the Alabama Polytechnic Institute. Now came Patrick H. Mell, John D. Easter, the first doctor of philosophy to grace the University, Williams Rutherford, and the year following (1857) appeared Joseph Jones to succeed LeConte, and Richard M. Johnston, who was later to become more famous as an author.[26]

The same conditions that were being sensed by the LeConte brothers as needing attention were also attracting the notice of others. Undoubtedly the agitation of the LeConte group had its effect in stirring up the other members of the faculty and the trustees. The general tendency of the University to decline relatively during the 'fifties was, of course, enough to set those in charge of the institution to thinking about causes and remedies. The trustees in their meeting in 1854 had instructed the faculty and prudential committee to study the problem. The result was a rather long comprehensive report, adopted unanimously at their meeting on November 9, 1855, at which were present three ex-governors, Wilson Lumpkin, George R. Gilmer, and Howell Cobb, and Governor Herschel V. Johnson, Judge Joseph Henry Lumpkin, Col. William H. Jackson, Judge Junius Hillyer, Dr. John Wingfield, Col. Absalom H. Chappell, Dr. David A. Reese, Dr. Leonidas B. Mercer, and William L. Mitchell. This report was directed as a memorial to the general assembly. The University was declining because the state had failed to support it, because denominational institutions under vigorous sectarian patronage were forging ahead, and because the University, in fact, was not a university. It ran in part, "From first to last, the grade of scholarship in this Institution has been gradually advancing, and our object in coming before the Legislature, is not to ask for aid to maintain our present ground, but we think the time has arrived when our great State should have something more than a respectable College, and should aspire to the accomplishment of the objects which our wise predecessors had in view by the establishment of a University, where learning and knowledge, which qualify men for all the varied avocations of useful human pursuits, may be acquired. Why may not Georgia, the central State of the South, hold out inducements to her surrounding sisters, which may obviate the necessity of sending our Southern sons to Massachusetts, or even to the Old Dominion, for the purpose of acquiring any knowledge which can be obtained from men or books."[27]

It advocated an endowment, free tuition to all students who would promise to teach, and free necessary expenses for five poor students from each congressional district. Franklin College, at this time, was not teaching all the varied subjects necessary to free ambitious Georgians from servitude to outside institutions. It ought never to be true that Georgia should be unable to supply her sons with every form of human knowledge and training desired. The future growth and usefulness of the University lay in supplying these needs. The University must, therefore, be enlarged along the following lines: A professorship of modern languages must be established, which would give practical training in German, French, and Spanish; there must be a school of agriculture; a school of applied sciences should be set up; and a law school should be developed.[28] As has already appeared, the legislature was too busy discussing the outward forms of politics to give any attention to the development of the soul and genius of the people.

But the agitation, once started, would not subside. It spread from the professors and trustees out over the state among Georgians who were given over to the practice of thinking about and discussing other subjects than politics. It engaged the attention of people who might never be greatly interested in the abstractions of education. German and French and Spanish smacked of the commercial world; applied sciences had a practical ring; agriculture was the foundation of the state, and even the law was not to be despised. The University was about to convince the state of its practical value, of its right to exist and even to be supported by public funds. The old University was organized under a régime "when eis and ous, kou and kous, were the tests of college excellence," said the *Federal Union*. "We are now living in a different age, an age of practical utility, one in which the State University does not, and cannot supply the demands of the State. The times require practical men, civil engineers, to take charge of public roads, railroads, mines, scientific agriculture & etc."[29]

Those directly in charge of the University seemed to be convinced that the institution could be saved only by a radical reorganization. In 1859 William L. Mitchell, chairman of the prudential committee, formulated a program which made a complete break with past arrangements. He was much obsessed with the idea that the students coming to Franklin College were entirely too young and "that the foundation of failure, if not ruin, is laid in the Freshmen and Sophomore years of College life." He would therefore abolish these two classes in Franklin College, and transfer the work to an institute which "might be properly ranked as a gymnasium," where the youths should "be watched over night and day, till fully prepared for the Junior Class" in Franklin College. The old university idea would be incorporated into the new organization. There was to be the college proper, consisting of only juniors and seniors; and the following University schools should be set up: the Medical College of Georgia, the law school, the agricultural school, and the school of engineering and applied mathematics. An additional feature was the encouragement to men of wealth to establish scholarships, fellowships, and professorships. The following degrees should be granted: Bachelor of Arts, Master of Arts, Bachelor of Laws, Doctor of Medicine, Doctor of Philosophy, Doctor of Divinity, and Doctor of Laws. This array of schools with twenty professors would "exhibit the University of Georgia before the public in an attitude altogether desirable."[30]

The trustees accepted this plan in 1859, and the next year changed the title of the chief executive of the University to chancellor. This officer was to have as his assistant the "President of the College" (later termed vice-chancellor) who should look after the University while the chancellor was making himself generally useful throughout the state, for it was now to be his duty not to spend his time teaching classes but to awaken the state along the line of education, and to become a leader of statewide influence— as indeed had been the intentions of the founders of the University. He was to pursue wealthy citizens until they should give donations to the University, and he was to attempt the impossible—to get money from the legislature by visiting it and conversing "freely with the members." For fear that this last duty might not be proper, the trustees later excused the chancellor from visiting the legislature—although he was not prohibited from doing so if he chose.[31] There was much reason, at this time, to feel that the enlarged and vitalized University would recommend itself to the state and soon secure ample support from the public treasury.[32]

President Church was growing old and tired; disputes with his faculty had not helped his health. In November, 1858, he resigned and asked to be relieved of his duties at the end of the school year. The institution was now on the up-grade again— "discipline, morals, & attention to studies have never been better since my connection with it."[33] The trustees accepted his going with regret and extended their appreciation of his long and zealous service. As a mark of esteem, they respectfully invited him "to take a seat on the stage in the College Chapel during the public exercises of this and each ensuing commencement during his life." He died in 1862.[34]

The University was now in need of a chancellor. Thirty years previously when there had been a vacancy in the presidency, candidates were numerous and backed by determined denominations. Now the churches had colleges of their own and no one seemed to care to be chancellor of the University. The trustees elected Henry Hull, but he declined. Henry R. Jackson was then elected; he also refused to serve. The trustees now decided on Joseph Henry Lumpkin for chancellor and Patrick H. Mell for vice-chancellor. Lumpkin declined, but Mell accepted. Then their attention was directed to Andrew A. Lipscomb of Alabama; he was elected and he accepted the position in 1860.[35]

It seemed that the University was about to enter into a new life, with a new organization, a new director, and a new system of rules, for the old rules were greatly amended by this time. The demerit system was adopted, whereby students might be made to see their approaching doom from afar if they continued in their evil ways. Nine demerits meant suspension. If a resident of Athens, a suspended person might not enter the campus; if he lived outside the town, he was given forty-eight hours to depart. John R. Crane, a sophomore, inaugurated the new system by groaning in chapel and receiving therefor seven demerits.[36] To carry out the new frame-work of the institution the law school was set up in 1859, and the "Collegiate Institute" was fast nearing completion by 1860.[37] The prospects for the new University were now different from what they had been a half dozen years previously, and, therefore, they must have been brighter, but the Civil War was now rapidly approaching to cut short this as well as many another hopeful development in the South.

WHAT A COLLEGE TOWN
THOUGHT ABOUT AND DID

 THE founders of the University, in keeping with the views of educational leaders of their day, held that town life was incompatible with, if not destructive to, all the higher intellectual virtues. For this reason they placed the University as far away as they could get it from a town of respectable size. Even Watkinsville was avoided to the extent of ten miles of trackless forests; though not large enough to be incorporated for six years to come (1806), it was the county seat and was too large and too wicked for the Muses of Learning to thrive in. Yet reason early made it clear that the conveniences of living in a college community must breed a town of some sort, but that same reason held that towns could be molded, developed, and influenced scarcely less than individuals who constituted them. So those in authority who made the University also made the town, and the life of the one was peculiarly and inseparably entwined and enmeshed with the other. No town was ever more completely the creature of an educational institution than was Athens and the character of no town ever more deeply partook of its creator.

A few rods north of the University structure a street was run and called Front Street, and on this thoroughfare and in all the regions beyond, the town was given the right to grow and thrive— but only as the trustees of the University should permit and direct through the sale of lots; for the two grew up on the land which John Milledge had originally given the University. One of the early duties of the prudential committee was to manage this business, and in the exercise of this authority it prohibited the sale of "spirituous or vinous liquors" in any buildings erected on Front Street, and, furthermore, declared that only stone or brick buildings should be erected on that street.[1] Now and then squatters crept in and even sat down on the campus itself. By 1824 a prosaic blacksmith shop had slipped almost into the shadow of the University buildings and was entertaining the students with the rhythm of its clanging anvil. Only when the trustees threatened to charge this worker of Vulcan rent, did they rout him from his classic surroundings.[2]

Athens, lying in the path of the surging westward movement, soon found itself surrounded by plantations busily engaged in raising cotton with their gangs of slaves. The town grew rapidly at the start, and in 1806 it was incorporated and given the right to elect three commissioners who should be its rulers "with full power and authority, to make such by-laws and regulations, and inflict or impose such fines, penalties and forfeitures, and to do such other incorporate acts, as in their judgment shall be conducive to the good order and government of the said town."[3] With its planter background and early turn toward an affluent population the town early developed and continued to maintain about as many slaves as white people. In 1828 there were 583 whites and 517 Negroes; ten years later there were 1,102 whites and 905 Negroes; and when the town marshal took the census in 1852, he found the total population to be 3,462.[4] Athens could not hope to surpass Savannah or Augusta as a city; but among the rest of the towns of the state it had a distinct feeling of superiority. The editor of the *Athenian* in 1829 decried the custom among some people of referring to the "village of Athens." He informed the public that Athens was no longer a village, that it was one mile square, had 1,300 people, and was laid off as a town. He continued, "We issue this our protest in the name of all the good people, forbidding henceforth and forever the use of the word village when applied to Athens—Let it be called a town."[5]

Although Athens' greatest ambition was to appear cultured and intellectual, and although it attained considerable renown in these respects, yet material progress could not be neglected. The town really assumed a sort of industrial leadership in the state remarkable for its broad and daring vision. The first cotton factory of any importance in Georgia was set up near Athens in 1832, and was promoted by Augustin S. Clayton, a graduate of the University and a watchful spirit over it for forty years. By 1842 there were three cotton factories in the town, each employing from 80 to 100 workmen, about equally divided between slaves and whites little better off in life.[6] It early developed connections by stage-roads with Augusta, Milledgeville, and by a national road with Washington and New Orleans.[7] And when the practicality of a railroad was forcefully presented to the South in the Charleston and Hamburg Railroad, running to the Georgia line across the Savannah from Augusta, it was Athenian energy and capital that gave to Georgia her first railroad. This was the Georgia Railroad, chartered in the very year the South Carolina road had been finished (1833), begun in Augusta in 1835, and finished to Athens in 1841. James Camak, a former professor in the University, was the first president. It had the same bizarre history that all railroads had when they were new—it had its first wreck, which killed two people and which determined the company to run no more trains in the pitchy darkness of night, and it used horse-cars at first. The fact that Athens had been built on the western hills of the Oconee River left the town for forty years without the distinction and noise of a train within her actual borders, for the difficulty and cost of bridging the river were considered too great.[8] And so it happened that the students who came by train were forced to climb the hill to Athens, afoot or in the town hack. A telegraph line was built from the city in 1852, but it proved a failure when a message which had been sent over it was not heard from for three weeks; the next year successful service was established which continued until raiders in the Civil War cut the wires.[9]

A town with such daring energy as Athens had could not long remain content to grope in the dark or stumble through the night

with sperm oil lamps or tallow candles. A certain Athenian by
the name of A. Jones proclaimed the startling discovery that the
despised chinaberries which rolled around on the streets of the
town or were thrown by the village urchins at their elders, could be
distilled into a brilliant illumination gas, which he predicted
would soon light the progressive towns of the South. About the
same time Professor Denison Olmstead, at the University of North
Carolina, was extracting a gas from cotton seed, which he declared
was better than coal gas. He predicted that the cotton seed annually
thrown away in the South would produce enough gas to light
fourteen cities as big as London.[10] Athens was never lighted by
chinaberry gas, but in 1850 the town was supplied with a gas
made from pine wood. This experiment was not a success, as the
supply of gas was not constant, and often on the most important
occasions the lights flickered out. The danger of being plunged
into darkness at the evening church services gave additional excuses to some of the townsmen to remain away, and also afforded
merriment in the Methodist Church on one occasion, when the
preacher announced the next service and innocently added, "There
will be plenty of gas." By 1859 gas lights in Athens had become
dependable, and the editor of the *Southern Watchman* informed
the public that the streets would be lighted and would "be rendered passable the darkest nights."[11] Athens kept up with progress
in adding to the comforts and luxuries of life. Plenty of ice was
for sale to those who could buy it, and fresh Norfolk oysters could
be had in season. As early as 1844 Talmadge advertised his cold
drinks and ice cream, and announced that he had fitted up rooms
especially for the ladies. Alexander had soda water and lemonade
with plenty of ice for sale at $6\frac{1}{4}$ cents the glass. He proudly
announced the fact that he had just received a machine for making
"Aerated Soda Water."[12]

But Athens had no ambition to become an industrial metropolis;
it was a college town where culture and refinement must be bred
and developed—it would be called the "Classic City." It em-
bodied the fine metal smelted from the rough ore of Southern
plantation economy, of Southern slavery, and of Southern illiteracy. It was the fellow, if not the superior, of that crystallization

of gentility and culture induced in North Carolina by the University at Chapel Hill, in South Carolina by the College at Columbia, in Virginia by the University at Charlottesville, and in Mississippi by the University at Oxford. Like begets like and attracts like. Athens was a cultured community, was born so, grew up so, and profited much from its cultured immigrants. People with money and a love for respectable and intellectual leisure moved here, built their white-columned homes among the green groves, and unruffled by the prosaic business of striving to make money, helped make the finest product of the civilization of the Old South. Doubtless not less than half of the white families living here had fixed incomes. The lowlanders moved here away from the hot summer months on the coast, and some of them became permanent residents. The University attracted families with sons to educate, and the society of the town drew in others.[13] Other states and even foreign countries contributed their numbers, attracted not primarily by Georgia, but by Athens. Ben: Perley Poore came down from Massachusetts to grow up with the town, soon purchased the *Southern Whig* to edit, became too friendly to abolition ideas and too prominent in Negro society, and left with no love and little respect for a community he did not understand.[14] Madame Govain, whose complete name was Rosalie Renie Marie Claudine Josephine Yvron Vincent Dennis de Kedron de Trobriand Govain, a close friend of Empress Josephine and an aunt of Simon Bolivar, came to Athens to live, built her terraced home on the slopes of the Oconee, and drew the lines along which the élite society of the town should develop. She had been persuaded to exchange her West Indian sugar plantation for a large tract of land in Clarke County, which had been granted by the State of Georgia to Count d'Estaing in recognition of his services in the Revolution. Here she reigned until her death in 1866. She was succeeded by Madame Sosnowski, the daughter of a court physician to the Duke of Baden, who had married a Pole. She set up a school where she dispensed chiefly the social graces, including a little music, some drawing, and the French language. O. A. Lochrane, fresh from Ireland, happened into Athens, without standing or influence, and by a fiery speech for temperance in

1844 won helping friends, who induced him to study law. He later became an outstanding chief justice of the state supreme court. John Howard Payne, of "Home Sweet Home" fame, came to Georgia to commiserate with the Cherokees, but found his way to Athens and fell in love with Mary Harden. Thus it was that Athens become uncommonly cosmopolitan. The French influence began early and long played a very noticeable part in the social and intellectual background of the Athenians. In 1845 a "French Boarding House" was set up by G. L. Jules d'Autel, where he promised all boarders an opportunity to learn French. He added that he had employed a good French cook. This same Jules also informed the public that he had set up as a "Watch Maker and Manufacturer" and that he was "from Paris."[15]

This Athenian community undoubtedly had a sort of bewitching charm, which it cast over those who stayed long enough for its full effect to be felt. Students, professors, and visitors were of one accord in their praise. Professor Leroy Broun, whose experiences at the University were not wholly unruffled, remembered Athens "as a most charming place, with charming society all through the town."[16] Richard Malcolm Johnston, at one time a professor in the University, who wrote much on the South and knew his subject, declared that the social and cultural standards in Athens were probably equal to those in any town throughout the whole South.[17] John N. Waddel, another professor in the University, thought Athens was "one of the most elegant and attractive places in Georgia, and indeed of the entire South," and in his later life longed to return to his Athens surroundings.[18] This outcropping of the best in the Old South did not appeal only to those who were part of it; foreigners came to America with critical and discriminating views of all things west of the Atlantic, but on reaching Athens they were carried away by the atmosphere they entered. James Silk Buckingham of England, an extensive traveler and a prolific writer, visited Athens in 1839 and was completely captivated. He saw a town, "picturesque and romantic," perched on a hill with no painful regularity of streets and buildings, but instead with great columned homes painted white with green blinds, with porticos and piazzas, peering at him from various angles through the forests of trees. He had scarcely reached the place before he was ushered into a "very elegant and highly intellectual" commencement party given by President Church to the senior class, where about 200 guests practiced at their social graces and intellectual accomplishments from 8 o'clock until midnight. He declared, "I do not remember ever to have seen a greater number of beautiful countenances than among the young ladies of this party; their ages ranging between fifteen and twenty. The style of beauty was like that of Charleston, Savannah, and New Orleans; small delicate figures, fair complexions, but not so deadly pallid as at the North; great symmetry of features, brilliant black eyes, finely arched eyebrows, and full dark hair.... The ladies, though so young, appeared to have more resources for conversation, and more power, as well as ease or freedom of expression, than ladies of the same rank or class in the North. Their manners too were more frank, cordial, and warm, which contrasted agreeably with the seeming caution and frigidity of the Northern ladies. A group of sisters sang and played more agreeably and with more accuracy than is generally witnessed in American parties...." He was equally pleased with the gentlemen: "In general appearance and manners the gentlemen of this party were superior to those usually seen in such assemblages at the North, and their conversation was quite as remarkable for its intelligence. I doubt whether any town in England or France, containing a population of little more than a thousand persons— for that is the extent of the white inhabitants here—could furnish a party of two hundred, among whom should be seen so much feminine beauty, so much general intelligence, or so much ease, frankness, and even elegance of manners. If the Athens of Georgia shall continue to retain these features of superiority as it increases in size and population, it can hardly fail to exercise an Attic influence on the surrounding country, which in time may rival that of the Athenians of Greece over the people of the Peloponnesus." He found his lectures on Palestine and Egypt, which he gave in the Methodist Church, attended by a bigger proportion of the people than was the case in any other Southern town, including even Charleston.[19]

ATHENS AND THE UNIVERSITY OF GEORGIA IN THE 'FORTIES
(From a contemporary painting in the University of Georgia Library.)

PORTRAIT OF ALONZO CHURCH

There was a genuine ease and gentility of manners among many Athenians which was not marred either by an artificial assumption of a superiority that did not exist or by jarring attempts to patronize prominent visitors. Yet no community could be without its imperfections and cheapening artificialities, and Athens had much of these things. Athenian critics, themselves, were well able to sense them. One declared in 1829, "The display of ostentation in Athens is celebrated, I have never seen or heard of a place of its size to equal it." He saw it displayed in the old and the young, in their family pretensions, in their dress and manners, "but most of all, by dashing to church in a fine carriage. . . . A lady cannot do without one, to walk fifty or one hundred yards is utterly out of the question."[20] The hospitality of the people was becoming a tradition by the early 'thirties, which had a striking exemplification in the refusal of the Athenians to exact room rent from the students who were suddenly thrust upon the bounty of the town in 1831, when one of the University dormitories burned. As soon would they make charges for any other guests in their homes. Yet claims were made that Athenian hospitality was much more evident in the attention the women gave to visitors of their own sex. As for the gentlemen strangers, a critic declared, "They come here strangers and they go away strangers." They leave and speak "of the haughtiness and proud-purse feelings of our community; of our cold and hollow-heartedness, and inhospitable manners." But it seemed that such gentlemen strangers had failed to understand the etiquette of Athenian hospitality—they were expected to call on Athenians uninvited. But the best of Athenian manners seemed to be corrupted by a false modesty which led the local clergy to substitute *stomach* for *belly* in the Biblical passage, "On thy belly shalt thou go"; and Athenian pronunciations were not according to the best usages, as when the *a* in *prepared* and such words was given the broad sound.[21]

It marked an epoch in the lives of the Franklin College students to be impregnated with this Athenian atmosphere for four years, and for many of them it was their remaking. They not only came into contact with the prominent families, the Cobbs, the Lumpkins, the Doughertys, the Claytons, and many others and saw much of such visitors as Alexander H. Stephens, Robert Toombs, George M. Troup, Benjamin H. Hill, and many other famous Georgians; but what was more pleasant and thrilling, at the same time they had rare and romantic associations with the daughters of these same families, and many of them succumbed for life. Joseph LeConte, looking back on his student days at Franklin College, declared in his old age that the girls of Athens were "celebrated for their beauty and refinement" and that the students regarded it a great honor to visit in their families.[22] A self-elected connoisseur of beauty said, "We venture the assertion that Athens has *more* pretty girls than any other town of its size in the United States or—anywhere else."[23] The students often went out on serenading parties—especially into Cobbham, the western extension of the town. The girls considered such attentions an honor worth remembering, and after the music had ceased they would invite the students in for refreshments. The rules for conquests in this realm allowed callers to enter at sun-down and remain not later than 9 o'clock. The greatest occasion for appearing together in public was on their way to church and back—the rules again requiring that the two should separate on entering the building, the girls sitting in the center and the boys on both sides. This parting of company at the church door held for adults as well.[24] One of the Franklin College students committed to his diary in 1849 the information that after returning from church he sat down on the steps in the moonlight, and "then for three hours in the full tide of enjoyment I lingered, and at the lapse even of that time I was loath to leave. Tell me not that woman's power to effect good is limited, when I must write that I promised & have fulfilled the promise of reading a chapter in the Bible every night." Another night he was not under the influence of the moonlight, but he "Told everything that I should [have] kept to myself, being partly under the influence of some wine."[25]

The girls kept albums and often coyly exacted a sentiment from their student visitors before they were allowed to leave. They were otherwise well versed in the art of getting on in the world along the lines fixed for the girls of the Old South, but they were not without their critics, who saw little worthwhile in the empty and useless

lives they were living. A critic of the reform school bluntly in-
veighed against the frivolity of their conversation. He described
a typical scene thus: "After the usual salutations, proceed remarks
about the state of the weather, which by the way are not always
correct—at one time mistaking fair for cloudy—at another representing an evening as fine, which in reality it is anything else—
then upon the fashions, courtships and marriages, neighbors'
foibles, and finally, it is to be feared, in some instances, to down-
right slander." Some excused the ladies by holding that the rules
of etiquette gave the gentleman the right to pitch the conversation,
but others held that if more elevating subjects were introduced
the ladies would be unable to proceed.[26] Another reformer, a
nineteenth century Justinian, hiding under the name of "Philo,"
would legislate into existence the girl of his dreams: "I would
revolutionize the customs of the ladies. . . . I would make them
more docile in their manners, more tractable in their dispositions,
and some I would obliterate from existence or make them more
constant in their affections—I would strive my utmost to make them
rational creatures, or at least, to conform to reason, as far as possible—I would discard the harp, and institute in its stead the use
of the needle—I would exchange the piano for the wheel, and
break every looking-glass and destroy every toilette and give them
healthy exercise in the room of *paint*, and an industrious disposition instead of pretty looks, pretty clothes, and almost fainting
exclamation—I would burn every rag of muslin for winter's wear,
and give them good comfortable thick dresses to exclude the cold
damp air—I would throw away every pair of prunelle shoes, and
furnish them with good thick calf-skin boots in their stead, and
then I should not be disturbed with barking coughs, nor weak and
feeble constitutions that grow sick at every change of weather."[27]
    If the reformers would dress the ladies in calf-skin boots, they
would be compelled first to drive out of town the beauty shops,
which shod and clothed the Athenian women. Miss Mankin, in
announcing the opening of her shop in 1836, listed some of the
beauty-provoking garments she offered for sale. She had "Oriental,
Florence, and English straw Gypsies" as well as "Silk hats, Artificial flowers, Ribbons, Laces, Caps, Capes" and many other things

whose proper use was known only to women. "Mr. John Truelle (From Paris)" came to Athens in 1840 and informed his prospective customers that he would always have on hand "a large and general assortment of fashionable WIGS, CURLS, FRONT PIECES and New Fashioned Plaits and Hair Bands." He also announced "Old Hair repaired with neatness and dispatch."[28]

Perhaps the reformer of woman's ways was unduly hard in his criticisms of the Athens girls; perhaps he should have criticized the schools which they attended for not teaching them useful knowledge, since "female academies" early got their start here. True enough they were of uncertain value at their best, and one Athenian mother declared openly in 1854 that a few years of primary instruction "with a few music and French lessons" were all the girls could get in Athens and that if more were desired they were forced to go to some Northern city or to some other place than Athens to secure it. Yet if music was their ambition Athens afforded a respectable offering. By 1827 John F. Goneke had a music school started, and later Professor Hoffman announced that he was prepared to teach the use of thirty wind and string instruments "in a scientific and comprehensive manner," and guaranteed to make artists of even those "who think they have no ear or taste for music." A Vocal Music School was by 1830 attracting much attention and securing a large following. Soon the ladies of the town were using the college chapel for singing concerts, and the Athens Society for the Improvement of Sacred Music was giving performances to raise money which should be used in buying Bibles for the poor. In 1830 this organization announced a concert in which Mr. Goneke would direct the instrumental part. It hoped all "lovers of harmony and Christianity" would attend, and it particularly sought to enlist in the movement "the Christian, the moralist, the philanthropist and the politician." By 1836 the Athens Harmonic Society was in existence—"a Society that is doing much to produce a correct taste, and elevate the standards of sacred music in our community."[29] Truly there was music in the souls of Athenians!

The University gave ample educational opportunities to the boys of Athens, but the strictures of the Athens mother on the

opportunities for girls still held. An answer came in 1858 when
Lucy Cobb Institute was set going, a school which soon developed
into great usefulness to Georgia and other Southern states. There
were yet members of the Athens community who were not being
reached by the molding influence of education from the University,
the "female academies," or the various private schools run at one
time or another—the poorer children. In 1833 an evening school
running from seven to nine o'clock and teaching drawing, writing,
and arithmetic was organized, and in 1850 Athens established her
first free school.[30]

Not all of the young men in Athens were in the University nor
were any of the older ones, yet they would not be denied a part
in the intellectual feasts that were going on. In 1837 M. Bauge,
"the champion of Paris," came along and set up a fencing school
ready to teach an art "which no young gentleman should be
without," and within two weeks he had a school full of young
Athenian gentlemen busily learning how to become more genteel.
The older men set up in 1834 a lyceum, where learned lectures
were read every Thursday night, to be followed ten years later by
the Athens Independent Lyceum, which regularly held its anniversary meetings in the town hall. There was also an Athens
Debating Club organized by the more contentiously inclined aristocrats of leisure, which met now and then in a room over the post
office in the afternoons, from 3 o'clock to 7. Most of the members
of this club bore such titles as general, major, colonel, and judge.
Their hall was well supplied with newspapers from widely over
the nation. At a meeting reported in 1839 they debated with
spirit whether the state should educate its children, and decided
that it should. Even those who were not aristocrats felt the urge
of assuming to be intelligent and so the Mechanics' Association
organized itself in 1837, and regaled its members with an oration
once a year. Athenians had a mania for organizing. The Bachelors'
Club sprang up in 1831, and held its celebrations and gayeties
generally about the time when the University commencement took
place. The town also supported a school of penmanship, run by
Professor J. Tucker, who guaranteed to teach the "plain and ornamental branches of Penmanship"; and there were enough people

in Athens who considered their importance or beauty sufficient to make steady work for W. M. Brown, who made it his business to paint portraits and miniatures.[31]

The industrial and agricultural interests of the town were organized with an educational slant and were displayed before the public in fairs and shows. In 1831 William H. Puryear was a moving spirit in the organization of the Fairfield Jockey Club for improving the breed of horses and for conducting racing. Three years later the Athens Cattle Show was held "on Tuesday before Commencement." There was also an Athens Fair Society, which exhibited now and then the "production of their own industry, and ingenuity"; and a Young Ladies Fair, conducted by the ladies of Athens Female College, gave exhibitions during the early 'forties of things they had made, hoping to sell them for money with which to relieve the poor.[32]

The community spirit prevailed to a remarkable extent, not only expressing itself in groups of closely related interests but also in ways representative of the whole town. The celebration of the Fourth of July was an event looked forward to continuously by the young and the slaves and relished almost as much by the older people, not so much for the exuberance of any conscious patriotism as for the good fellowship and good eating and good drinking that went with it. Due to this latter factor it was often found desirable to hold the celebrations in two divisions, with one crowd composed largely of University interests, but not because toasts could not be drunk by this group, for in 1830 it was reported that many toasts were drunk "with a hilarity of feeling which nothing but wine and Independence could inspire." Before festivities had got too far, it was customary to have the Declaration of Independence read. At the celebration in 1831, "a few of the venerable remnants of the revolution graced the board; and peace, harmony and patriotic joy held their pleasant reign." It was on this occasion that an otherwise obscure man named S. S. Jack made himself famous by this toast to the bachelors: "May their food be thunder and their drink lightning; may their beds be made of thorns and their pillows of cuckleburs; may every whisper of conscience be like the sting of a scorpion, and every ray of beauty like the blasts of death, until they repent of their evil doings, and bow submissively at the shrine of love." As the springs of Bacchus were gradually dried up in Athens by the activities of the temperance societies, patriotism of the variety expressed in the Fourth of July celebrations died down, and for years Athens let the day go by without notice—until indeed a sort of unconscious urge developed near the outbreak of the Civil War and set the people to celebrating again.[33]

For the first quarter of a century of Athens' existence Washington's birthday was likewise honored, and the signal for getting ready was generally given by the students the night before. President Waddel noted in his diary February 21, 1825, "noise in streets by fife & tin-pan & trumpet." More genuine feeling for the subject of the occasion was seen in funeral processions for dead national heroes. In 1845, on the death of Andrew Jackson, the town, joined by the Phi Kappa and Demosthenian societies, formed a procession and marched to the chapel, where funeral services were held.[34]

In 1832 some Athenian discovered that Georgia would be exactly one hundred years old that year, and since the celebrating zeal was early running high and since the occasion would take place in February (five months from the Fourth of July festivities), it was resolved that the state's centennial should be properly observed. In the morning at 9:30 o'clock the militia company assembled on the parade grounds and marched to the Baptist Church, where the audience had assembled. "The Throne of Grace was addressed in a fervent and patriotic prayer," after which "a chaste and beautiful oration" was delivered. Someone read Washington's Farewell Address, and then the militia company "retired, and after performing various evolutions, and firing several salutes," those Athenians who were respectable or fortunate enough repaired to the Georgia Hotel where they more agreeably celebrated the state's birthday with "Bacchus the while shedding his generous influence from many a flowing glass." This patriotic performance continued until nightfall, during which time many toasts were drunk "amid loud and repeated cheers, intermixed with the firing of musketry, and the music of the drum and fife." To General

Oglethorpe: "The enterprising founder of Georgia, and the early advocate of American Liberty—One hundred years ago he planted the first white settlement west of the Savannah." Silent honors followed this toast. The pent-up fervor of generations of Southern chivalry broke out in this toast: "Woman!!! The center and circumference, diameter and periphery, sine, tangent and secant of all our affections—Can two circles have the same center and components and yet not coincide? Vide Plafair!" This sentiment was vociferously agreed to by the emission of twenty cheers—eight more than were given to any of the patriots and heroes introduced in the other toasts.[35]

It was well to celebrate heroes of the past, but it was better when possible to honor those yet living. Such an occasion presented itself in 1819, when President Monroe, on a Southern tour came through Athens. The whole town and countryside gathered in and about the college chapel to await his arrival. As he approached Athens he was met by the principal men and escorted into town, and after showing himself to the multitude he was conducted to his hotel by President Waddel and ex-President Brown. Waddel made a speech of welcome to which Monroe replied, and then followed a dinner, at which the visiting President gave the following toast: "Success to the University of Georgia." In the evening the University was illuminated with almost a thousand lights, and the students entertained him in their best fashion.[36]

Other appropriate ways by which the town expressed itself were in fire companies and guard companies, both of which belied in their names their chief purpose for existing. The guards were a lingering suggestion of the old militia musters, which had long ago been mocked out of existence. They grew up as a counterpart in the South to the various Zouave companies in the North—both being showy organizations which grew up for the purpose of displaying their members in gaudy uniforms and, although coming only a few years before the Civil War, having no origin in any bellicose feelings. The fire companies existed chiefly for "evolutionary purposes," and in 1858 they with the guards took control of the Fourth of July celebration. Ultimately they became useful as fire fighters, especially after they bought a fire engine. It was only after a long argument that the decision was made to take this step, for the opposition argued that someone would set the town on fire to see how the engine worked. And true to predictions, soon after this engine, named the *Relief*, arrived a fire broke out under suspicious circumstances. Finally the *Relief*, itself, was consumed by the enemy it was supposed to fight, as it sat helplessly in the engine house, and thereby arose one of the chief claims of Athens to fame—for was it not the only town in the world to have its fire department to burn![37]

Athens liked no less being entertained than she liked entertaining, and thus it was that traveling shows, menageries, hurdy-gurdy performers, lecturers, tricksters, magicians, and hawkers and walkers of every description thrived when they came to Athens, even as they did wherever else they wandered. Elephants and other "monstrosities of nature" early made their appearance in Georgia, and in 1812 Athens was honored by the visit of a tiger. The attraction was announced thus: "A COMBAT The curious are respectfully informed there will be a combat between an Asiatic TYGER and a large ferocious Georgia Bull. It will be in a pen in the enclosure at half past four. This will be one of the greatest curiosities ever witnessed in America. The beauty of this uncommon animal—his immense strength and great ferocity, will be seen in all their grandeur. Admittance One Dollar—Children half price."[38] This was bull-fighting according to the Georgia method. In later years a merchant kept a bear near his establishment, where he used to afford amusement by turning dogs into the pen, but bear-fighting was not so interesting or exciting as the traveling circuses which began to make their appearance in Athens by the 'thirties.[39] Before the days of the railroad they traveled in great caravans over the rough and muddy country roads from town to town. Athens was a good circus town, and never failed of at least one circus a year. The procession would be well organized some miles out and as it would enter town it would afford a spectacle irresistible to the ordinary mortals. In 1850 the Welch, Delevan & Nathans' National Circus entered Athens with "The Great Armamaxa, or Imperial Chariot" drawn by "30 elegant horses." Occupying this vehicle was the Knickerbocker band, "who will perform all the most fashionable and modern airs of the day."[40] The Spaulding & Rogers' North American Circus introduced itself to the town by the blaring trumpeteers in the "Appolonicon," drawn by forty horses. Another followed its "Music Chariot" into town.

The show itself, in the big tent, generally opened with some "grand and stupendous spectacle," allegorical or historical, where all of the performers filed in. The Spaulding & Rogers "outfit" presented the "Spirit of '76!" in which thrilling scenes and patriotic heroes of the Revolution were introduced, such as "Old Put! General Washington! and Mad Anthony Wayne!" Its conclusion was a tableau "in which the 'FATHER OF HIS COUNTRY!' Mounted on his Charger, is borne aloft, in triumphal procession, on a Platform, on the shoulders of his brave Continentals!" Another circus made its grand entrée into the arena as "Turks upon the Danube," and another presented the "Crusaders," and the "Nymph of the Floating Veil" with La Petite Maria, eight years old. Then followed the most extravagantly described and varied kinds of attractions, acrobatic, equestrian, legerdemainic. A circus in 1852 announced that "Mirth, Music, Majic Melo-Drama, Equitation, Spectacle; Pantomime, Farce and Tragedy, mingle, bubble, effervesce, and burst upon the eye and ear, alternately bewildering and delighting the spectator." Another show offered more specifically the following: "Gymnastic Feats, Bottle Tricks, Globe and Barrel Exercises, Vaulting, both single and double Leaping, Equilibriums, Tumbling, Pyramidical Devices, Posturing, Comic Singing, Dancing, Comic Berlettas, Interludes, Farces, Promenades, Cavalcades, Masquerades &c." It also had the only four-bottle magicians in the world—"all others who may attempt these feats are *complete Humbugs*." To reach the climax it had "the clown of clowns, his equal never yet found or known the world over." Robinson and Eldred offered the spectacle of a man walking on the ceiling with his head downward, also a Georgia mule, "Sancho," ten years old though no larger than a dog, also "Thunderbolt," the performing horse, and "Damocles," a trick pony, and Herr Spooter, the great bugler. They offered $5,000 to anyone proving that Master James Robinson was not "the best rider in the world," and his brother John Robinson offered a standing bet that he, himself, was the best rider in America. "The Great Combined Gymnasium and Zoological Arena! of A. Turner & Co." advertised its vaulter who would "throw a somerset over the Elephant," and announced that its clown would "give his private opinions respecting the Maine Liquor Laws, and other groceries in general." There was also another circus with "the nearest human of Brutes, the Talking Horse, HIRAM"; and Bailey & Co. offered the attraction of Antony and Cleopatra, two elephants that stood on their heads, played musical instruments, ascended inclined planes, and went through all the operations of the most accomplished acrobats. The W. Waterman & Co. had a youth of six years "whose performance has astonished every beholder." The Stone and Rosston Combination Circus and Murray's European Circus had its "comic mules" and a gymnast who has been applauded "with enthusiastic frenzy and colossal shouts of admiration." The Great Western Circus in 1850, which had neither wild Indians nor cowboys in it, turned out to be only the revival of "the ancient sports of the Olimpiad." The first real "Wild West" show to reach Athens appeared in 1855, Mabies Menagerie, Den Stone's Circus and Tyler's Indian Exhibition United. They had their "superb Music Chariot" and there were the "Chiefs, Braves and Sages of the Seneca Indian Tribe!" in their original costumes with weapons. These "Wild Tenants of the Forests" entertained with a buffalo hunt and staged a "pastoral scene," "The Corn Gathering," a "Bird Dance," a "Thanksgiving Dance," scalping groups, war songs, and the tableau "Pocahontas Rescuing Captain Smith," all "interspersed with Grotesque Dancing, Singing, Whooping &c."[41]

An even greater "stupendous and fearful attraction" than the contortionists and freaks were the "ferocious monstrosities of the brute creation." Robinson and Eldred's Great Favorite Southern Circus and Sand, Quick & Co.'s Stupendous Collection of Wild Animals carried with it a "terrible curiosity . . . , a White or Polar Bear, weighing 700 pounds, white as a snow drift, more ferocious than even the Tiger, and untameable as the Hyena," the elephant Bolivar weighing 14,000 pounds, captured by the British army in the Punjab, a grizzly bear, "wonderfully ferocious," "the greatest variety of mischievous Monkeys and Baboons ever exhibited," and "the wonderful nondescript, half leopard and half Tiger—a huge animal of tremendous strength and fierceness." Another circus had a giraffe, "stupendous, majestic, and beautiful, . . . the greatest wonder of the animal kingdom, . . . tallest of all known creatures, . . . rarest and most singular." The Raymond & Ogden's Menagerie carried "the most rare and gigantic assemblage of WILD BEASTS and BIRDS ever exhibited in the United States," rhinoceros, elephant, camel, lion, tiger, leopard, puma, cougar, panther, ocelot, condor, pelican, macaw bird, parrot, bear, wolf, ichneumon, and "a wilderness of the MONKEY and BABOON Species." Many other animal circuses came with their specimens of "wild ferocity." Robinson & Lake's Great Southern Menagerie and Circus featured "THE HORNED HORSE. THE LAST OF HIS RACE. THE PERPLEXITY OF NATURALISTS. THE WONDER OF THE AGE."[42]

Franklin College students and Athenians generally flocked to these attractions, and soon stirred up the censors of public morals to such an extent that they sought to prevent further attendance on these "dens of monstrous iniquity." The University faculty forbade the students to attend a circus, but found great difficulty in enforcing their decree. Some of the students disguised themselves as Negroes and sat with the slaves. A circus in 1847, either ignorant of its repute in Athens or bent on affronting the University prudential committee, asked permission to show on a vacant college lot. This request was "promptly & unanimously rejected." The following year another circus sat down uninvited on a college lot. The trustees ordered it to get off instanter. The clergy of the town, especially the Methodists, thundered their condemnation against the iniquity of circuses. The Methodist minister warned his flock against such evil practices and read them this resolution passed by the church: Resolved "That we regard it very inexpedient and dangerous that any church member should attend a circus, and deem it no place for them; and therefore affectionately recommend our members to abstain from going to one."[43]

Forced to combat the growing opposition of the churches, the circuses began to change their announcements to show what great moral agencies they were. Robinson's declared that there was nothing in the show which would offend the most fastidious; Stone & McCollum's Mammoth Great Western Circus announced that they did nothing "immoral or objectionable," but that on the contrary they had been awarded "the palm above all others for propriety, decorum and order"; and G. F. Bailey & Co. announced that La Petite Maria, eight years old, would go into a cage with a leopard and thus prove the passage from Holy Writ that the "lion & lamb shall lie down together and a little child shall lead them." A great "Zoological Exhibition," after enumerating the "wondrous works of nature" in its cages, said, "The moral and useful purposes which an exhibition like this can serve, are perceived by all, and acknowledged by all moralists; the exhibition serves to entertain and instruct in the wondrous works of the Supreme Being, and is particularly impressive on the minds of youth."[44] As the hostility of the South toward the North became more pronounced and ramifying, circuses found it convenient to forearm themselves by adding Southern or the name of some Southern city, as New Orleans, to their title. In May, 1857, the "Great Southern Circus. Southern Men, Southern Horses, Southern Enterprise, against the World!!!" came to Athens, and two weeks later G. N. Eldred's Great Southern Show appeared, claiming to be "The only Southern Company now travelling in the South."[45]

Many other traveling groups and individuals peddling their amusements, generally of a character to escape the bans of the clergy and the University prudential committee, appeared in Athens. Signor Blitz appeared in magic, ventriloquism, "diablerie," and trained bird performances, and Dr. H. Rosenbu gave a lecture on ventriloquism, imitating the singing of birds. He announced that persons of every religion should come "as the object of the Lecture is not to amuse the vulgar, but to gratify the learned." In 1856 some wild men were exhibited in the town hall for two days, really wild according to the local judges of ferocity. One observer said every Athenian should see "these novel specimens of humanity." There was much singing done for a price in Athens, ranging from the Tennessee Minstrels with its

Negro delineators and the additional attraction of Monsieur Haller, "the great South American Magician" in his "Temple of the Sun," to the more élite and classical performances. Mrs. Keppell, "Late of the Italian Opera, Havanna, and St. Charles Theatre, New Orleans," gave her vocal and instrumental concert; Sieur and Madame Canderbeck gave on the German harp and violin "Grand Battle Pieces, Concertos, Duetts & & "; M. Le Baron De Fleur, "Pianiste to the Emperor of Russia," gave a concert in the college chapel at the commencement in 1840; the Rasche Family gave a "Grand Vocal and Instrumental Concert" of a "chaste and purely moral character"; Henry Squires and "little Mary McVicker" gave a violin concert; Madame Siminski played a flute to great perfection; the Columbians gave selections of "Songs, Glees, Duetts, Trios, Quartetts &c" and met with great favor "in more than half of the States of the Union"; the Estelle Troup sang and danced; Mr. Hart's Theatre Company and Messrs. Carter & Morton's Theatrical Company variously amused their audiences; and the Swiss Bell-Ringers performed in Athens in 1859 and brought forth this remark from one of the local editors: "As one of the novelties worthy of special notice may be mentioned the fact that tolerably good order was preserved." An attraction of great interest was Blind Tom, who performed here in 1858, a Negro boy nine years old "and but one degree removed from idiocy." He played in a style "which would put to the blush many professors of music." Yet he had no teacher "but the birds." He was a Georgian. Among the last musical concerts to reach Athens before light-heartedness and smiles were banished by the alarms of war were Bailey's Troup, "which broke the dull monotony" of the town, and Old Folks Concert, in which the characters were dressed in "ante-Revolutionary costumes."[46]

Some of the traveling attractions that came to Athens were considered culturally valuable, and thereby certain Athenians were given a chance to enjoy openly shows which they could not afford to see as long as the name circus was attached. In 1830 a "Grand Solar Microscope" made its appearance in town. The public was "respectfully informed that this astonishing Instrument, *Magnifying* MINUTE INSECTS, *more than Eight Millions of times their natural size"* was the wonder of the age. One could see through it in vinegar *"living eels* from 4 to 10 feet in length, their muscular contortions and death agonies, some of them perfectly variegated with *spots,* and others *striped."* It was claimed that this instrument would show that the fuzz on a fig was "living insects from 2 to 5 feet in length, . . . climbing, fighting, and running in all directions" to escape the sun which kills them. The point of a needle looked like "the rude end of a beam." Traveling picture galleries often made their appearance here. In 1838 a collection of paintings "representing Burning Mountains, Conflagrations, Battles, Cities, Shipwrecks, &c" were being exhibited. The "Grand Cosmorama" also came along, consisting of a collection of paintings of "new and rare" animals. President Waddel in his day went to see the "Portrait Gallery" of paintings, and the year before the Civil War broke out a "Bunyan Tableau" showed the progress of the Pilgrim in pictures. The least spectacular of the attractions, but perhaps little more dependable, were the lectures delivered by wandering savants. In 1831 Professor Wheeler gave in the college chapel a lecture "illustrated by the Globe, Orrey, and illuminated Diagrams," and drew a large crowd; in 1840 Professor Richards afforded "Scientific Recreation" in the Baptist Church by expounding the mysteries of pneumatics, electricity, electro-magnetism, and various other related subjects; and four years later Dr. Lardner lectured on the moon, sun, stars, comets, steam navigation, the compound blowpipe, and many other scientific subjects.[47]

With all the attractions and entertainments dispensed by the hawkers and walkers, magicians, and circus masters of ante-bellum times, life in a college town of the Old South was not without its excitements. The students of the University did not fail to take advantage of all the attractions the town had to afford, and often they lent a hand in the merriment. In 1851 they were busily preparing for a sham exhibition, but the eyes of the professors hit upon them and they were forced to desist on the peril of dire punishment. But an indulgent faculty for years allowed "Fantastical exhibitions" or "Fantastiques" in which the students disguised themselves in various fashions much to the merriment of the Athenians. The parade held in 1858 was considered "the most grotesquely ludicrous" that the town had ever seen. But it seems that the limits had been overstepped, for the faculty resolved this year that the "Fantastiques" must cease thenceforth.[48]

Athens had its own local characters, who often threw the town into laughter or amazement. There was G. W. Barber, the wit, who advertised his Oconee hill for sale as choice bottom land, and when confronted with the charge that it was a rocky hill, he answered that it was bottom land as the rains had washed the top off. There was also the idiotic slave who for years annoyed the townsmen, until the city council threatened to fine his owner fifty cents for every time the Negro was caught wandering on the streets. And again there was the beggar Gulley, who developed begging into a science and made a good living out of it. But a character more remarkable than all others was John Jacobus Flournoy. Though well educated, he drifted into poverty, wore a long white beard, and allowed his snowy white hair to grow to whatever length it desired. Clad in an India-rubber overcoat in summer and in winter, fair weather and foul, he rode a mule in his interminable peregrinations. He had a mania for writing letters for the newspapers on morality, religion, slavery, government, and all other subjects he could think of, and for advancing ideas more fantastic than the tales of the *Arabian Nights*. He regularly announced his candidacy for the legislature for half a century, and sometimes received as high as a dozen votes. When the newspapers refused to accept further of his strange correspondence, he paid for its insertion. He also developed the habit of writing long and rambling letters to many of the prominent men of his day. In May, 1865, he wrote Andrew Johnson, who had just assumed the presidency, a long, rambling, and largely meaningless letter of eleven oversized pages, and before mailing it he added a postscript of two full pages. Oliver Wendell Holmes in his *Professor at the Breakfast Table* gives some attention to this remarkable character, and James Silk Buckingham, the English traveler and writer, takes up some of his views in his book, *The Slave States of America*.[49]

Colonel William H. Jackson was neither a wit nor a crank, but he won fame for himself and set the lawyers a problem by deeding a tree to its own self, according to tradition, because he had often enjoyed its shade. He incidentally gave Athens an additional claim to fame in the boast that it was the only town in the world to have a tree which owns itself.

The gentility and culture of Athens had many qualifications, which were, however, generally common to the age. The same gentlemen who graced President Church's commencement party had the sloppy habit of chewing tobacco almost incessantly, in church and almost everywhere. Buckingham, the English traveler, who wrote in such high praise of Athenians, nevertheless, said, "In the churches, at public lectures, in private parties, or in public assemblies, you hear every minute the sound of the labial ejection, and its fall upon the floor; while the chewers roll about the offensive and blackened mass in their mouths, as though it was all that was worth living for." The same cultured ladies went to church and in finding their seats, stumbled over sleeping dogs, and at those church exercises the children romped around, whispering loudly and scratching on the backs of benches; and the larger boys who were fast becoming Athenian gentlemen, combed their hair sleek down on their temples and invariably came into church late to be certain to attract notice. And when services were finished they hurried out, and lining themselves up, stared steadily at the ladies as they debouched. The apologists for this condition declared that the starers were mostly "rude boys and unpolished mechanics." At the theatrical performances and other public assemblages there were generally a "clattering of tongues, and unceasing, senseless giggles," which made it very difficult for people to hear. The boys appropriated the best parts of the streets for their marble maneuvers, and as the ladies passed by they reluctantly stood aside, stared, and asked, "Who is that?" The local editor maintained that indulgent parents suffered "their children to grow up like heathens and vagabonds."[50]

Athens was undoubtedly a beautiful town, unmarred by too much regularity in its streets, with its green trees and the tasty architecture of its homes. But again its beauty was qualified. Its streets were muddy and sometimes almost impassable; the editor of the *Southern Watchman* declared in 1860 that he "saw an empty wagon with four horses attached to it 'stalled' on a dead level." Not until the 'fifties was the freedom of the streets taken away from the dogs, cattle, and hogs. Although a city ordinance in 1839 authorized the town marshal to kill all dogs "whenever they shall be found making any noise or disturbance," yet soon thereafter a visitor staying at the Planters' Hotel complained of his night's rest being almost continuously disturbed by the nightly prowlings of no less than one hundred each of dogs, cows, and hogs, barking, lowing, and grunting, each according to its own nature. City ordinances, passed at various times, to abate the nuisance were never observed or enforced—in 1867 an ordinance was passed inflicting a fine of $1 on every owner of a loose animal captured by the marshal on the streets. It was a custom of most of the gentlemen who rode horses to hitch them on the sidewalks, which often forced the passing ladies out into the mud.[51]

As the ordinances of Athens were observed chiefly in their breach, a perusal of those things prohibited should give a fair picture of what Athenians did from day to day. Wagoners were not allowed to encamp on the streets, nor should they ride horses or drive wagons on the sidewalks; to block the sidewalks unless attendant on an auction was finable to the extent of $5; no persons should "appropriate the side-walks of the city, or the doors of cellars opening upon said side-walks, for sleeping purposes" unless they stood ready to pay the fine of $1; the speed limit for riding horses through town should be no "faster than an ordinary gallop," excepting physicians going to a sick bed; persons found drunk or disturbing good order were subject to arrest and incarceration in the guard-house; to throw rotten fruit, carcasses, and other rubbish into the streets "in such quantities as to become offensive" was punishable to the extent of a $5 fine; no one was allowed to build fires on the streets; no gun or pistol should be fired within 300 yards of a house or street; no fireworks of any kind should be indulged in; no kites might be flown; vacant lots should be kept free of stagnant pools; and playing ball and marbles in the streets was not permissible. Athens had long had a large supply of loose hogs since the days when Mrs. Meigs' pigs in 1805 ran wild over the campus. In May, 1854, the city council decided that all hogs must be taken off the streets within five days. Immediately the protagonists of freedom for hogs objected and cited the danger of fever breaking out in the town if the scavengers were removed. The council reconsidered and decided that the hogs might have the freedom of the town until October 1st. As the day for their incarceration approached, the marshal inserted in the town papers a neat picture of a sleek hog surmounting the warning that the hog law would be enforced strictly after October 1st.[52]

The slaves of Athens, who constituted generally about half of the population, were given the right to roam the streets until 9 o'clock in the evening, when the town bell was rung for their especial warning. If a slave were found rioting or breaking the peace he was subject to ten lashes, and if he were convicted a second time the punishment was twenty-five lashes.[53]

The most glaring example of Athenian neglect of a public duty was the town cemetery. A visitor in 1839 noted that this cemetery was the only one he had ever seen unenclosed, and it appeared to him to be "the most neglected spot in all the settlement"; twenty years later, reports showed that its dilapidation had gone on unimpeded; soon the young ladies were resorting to it to sit on the tombstones and make merry—"a duced shame," to put it mildly, the *Southern Watchman* editor declared. Then it became a camping ground until the city council placed a charge of $5 for every offense of lodging in the graveyard.[54]

Athens being long the only town of any importance in northern Georgia attracted as frequent visitors not only the immediate countryside but the countrymen from all the surrounding counties. It, therefore, drew people who were not of Athens, and who did not partake of its traditional gentility. One such person was a woman desperado who made her appearance on the streets in 1851, "pointing her pistols and brandishing her bowie-knife" at a terrified townsman. She was arrested after the marshal had executed some strategic maneuvers.[55] Whether Athens was a Mecca for women who ran away from their husbands or not, a Rabun County mountaineer thought it would do no harm to insert the following notice in the town paper: "TO THE PUBLIC I was once ready to exclaim with Campbell,

> Without the smiles from partial beauty won,
> Oh, what were man, a world without a sun,

And married my present wife Elizabeth; we lived together as we
should have done for some time, when she began to be obstropolous,
so much so, that I soon was convinced of the truth of this couplet
of Pope's,

> Oh, woman woman! whether lean or fat,
> In face an Angel, but in soul a cat.

And now to cap the climax, my said wife Elizabeth has left my
bed and board without any provocation, I therefore forewarn all
persons not to trust her on my account, as I am determined to pay
no debts of her contracting. I am not anxious for her to come
back, and shall not enforce the law against any one for harboring
her.

JESSE CRAIN

Of Rabun County."[56]

The absence of close and stifling competition gave the newspapers of Athens a respectable position in Southern journalism.
The most important ones were the *Georgia Express*, the *Athenian*,
the *Southern Banner*, the *Southern Whig* and the *Southern Watchman*. Personal vituperation was remarkably absent in all of them,
and most of them took a literary trend. This was especially true
of the *Athenian*. It was not uncommon for them to use a fourth
of an issue in printing the oration delivered by some student in
his society hall. All took an interest in the University and defended it against the attacks that too commonly emanated from
the newspapers in other Georgia towns.

Although the hospitality of Athens early became a tradition,
yet this social generosity did not extend to the point where hotels
and taverns were superfluous. There were generally two, whose
standing was sufficiently high to work no social disadvantages to
their guests. In 1830 there were the Planters' Hotel and the Globe
Tavern. There was also at this time the Franklin Hotel, which
had formerly been the Athens Hotel. In 1831 its name was changed
to the Georgia Hotel and the new manager proudly announced
that "The Female Department and Table are under the manage-

ment of a lady whose taste and manners cannot fail to please all classes of the community. The Bar and Stables, it is also hoped, will be kept under a sound and satisfactory régime." In 1838, when the railroad from Augusta was appreciably nearing Athens, this hotel being closest to the proposed terminus changed its name again to the Rail Road Hotel. It later went under the name of the Lanier House. Athens hotels were not considered fit places of abode for Franklin College students; neither should students take their meals there or loiter around them at all. Nevertheless, few students attended the University who did not develop mellow memories of escapades which had one of the town hotels as a prominent feature in the background.[57]

Among the towns of the Old South, Athens undoubtedly stood near the top in culture. The social graces and amenities were well and consciously developed here. Its educational background, as well as the prominence of its citizens and visitors, was equaled in few of the Southern towns. It was preëminently the social and cultural center of Georgia.

CHAPTER XII

IN TIME OF WAR

 THE will to live is a human character-
istic as reasonable and as natural as the
urge to satisfy hunger or to love or to
hate, and war affords no exception to the
rules. A minority of the people of the
United States took advantage of a long-
growing bitterness of the two sections
toward each other to finally catapult the
whole population into a war which the
majority had unwittingly let itself make
possible, but which it had not desired. In the election of 1860 a
majority of the people, North and South, voted in such a way as
to indicate they wanted a peaceful course pursued by those in
authority. Abraham Lincoln was a minority president, just as
John C. Breckinridge was a minority candidate in the South. John
Bell and Stephen A. Douglas, representing the parties for moderation, received a majority of the votes in Georgia by more than
2,500. The vote in Athens was: Bell, 383, Breckinridge, 335, and
Douglas, 41; in Clarke County it was, respectively, 695, 451, and
51. The educational and cultural center of Georgia was, thus, for
peace, and the surrounding county was even more pronouncedly
for the same course.[1]

But even the most peaceably inclined heard with dread and
almost consternation that Lincoln had been elected—a "Black
Republican" and purely a sectional figure about whom much was
thought to be known in the South but nothing commendable. Lin-

coln meant to Athenians the triumph of John Brown of Harpers
Ferry infamy, and there was a fear as devastating as it was un-
warranted that a servile insurrection would take place if heroic
measures were not adopted. How miserably the two sections misunderstood each other, and how little each knew even of themselves!
A panic seized Athens, and on November 10 the town authorities
called a mass meeting for the purpose of better organizing for the
protection of the inhabitants. More patrols for the town were
organized, and the captains of the county police were warned to
be doubly on guard. Each planter was advised to personally patrol
his own slaves and premises. A Vigilance Committee, prepared to
act on an instant, consisting of twenty members with twelve as
a quorum, was appointed to investigate any attempts at insurrection and to bring "to summary and condign punishment, all persons convicted of such offenses before them." Was this not a
strange delegation of governmental power unknown in the law?
This meeting bitterly condemned the election of "Black Republicans to the Presidential offices" and solemnly declared its "determination never to submit to their rule, if our state will authorize
us to resist." On this committee were put many who should have
known better than to assume such fright before further investigation
could be made—Thomas R. R. Cobb, Wilson Lumpkin, James
Camak, W. S. Grady. At this mass meeting, Cobb made "an impressive and eloquent speech in favor of a dissolution of the Union."
The spell of the occasion brought a unanimous adoption of the
proceedings. But all Athenians were not so easily frightened, and
they doubted whether the leaders of this meeting were as terrified
as they appeared. Some *"furious* communications" about the
meeting "denouncing its proceedings as 'monarchial,' " were sent
to the *Southern Watchman,* but they were said to be too inflam-
matory to be printed.[2]

The feeling was soon uppermost that the country was alive with
spies, abolitionists, and Lincoln incendiaries. An inoffensive native
living about four miles out from the town was heard to express
free soil sentiments. He was immediately arrested, brought to
Athens, taken to the town hall, and "tried by the crowd present,
acting as a committee of the whole, the Intendant presiding."

Trembling with fright, he explained that he had meant no harm. This explanation was accepted after Thomas R. R. Cobb had made a reassuring speech to the crowd, and the prisoner was released with the warning that the next offense would produce a hanging, "without the intervention of judge or jury."[3] The panicky conditions showed no abating and soon the largest crowd that had ever assembled in Athens came together, many from the surrounding counties, and demanded that a state convention be called to coöperate with other states in forming a confederation "on the basis of our present Constitution." The demands met with unanimous approval. The masses were gradually, through expert direction, coming to believe that their only salvation lay in severing their connection with the "Black Republican" North—honest sincere feelings engendered by honest sincere leaders, yet based on insufficient evidence.[4]

The next month (December), South Carolina took the course that led to four years of bloody civil war, followed by a longer period of a more devastating peace, and Athens applauded with the energy born of a long pent-up feeling. She fired fifteen guns at noon, and in the evening of the following day a torch-light procession paraded the streets in honor of the approach of what they thought would be a bright and untrammeled future for the South. Some of the more enthusiastic Athenians "illuminated" their homes that night, and the orators repaired to the town hall to make speeches. Other states followed South Carolina, and in January (1861) Georgia sent her statesmen to a convention in Milledgeville to decide what was best for the state to do. The University had trained the leaders who were now to wrestle with the problem and solve it. Howell Cobb, his brother Thomas R. R. Cobb, Robert Toombs, Francis S. Bartow, and Eugenius A. Nisbet were sure the solution was simple; South Carolina had already shown the way. Alexander H. Stephens and Herschel V. Johnson, who had studied under the same teachers at old Franklin College, were quite sure that the remedy was not so simple, and in a test vote they convinced 130 delegates out of a total of 296 that secession was no remedy. By a later vote secession carried 208 to 89, and to show the "Black Republicans" that the majority still ruled in Georgia and that the state was a unit now that the act was done, every member of the convention solemnly filed by the speaker's desk and signed the resolution—and the contagions of the times carried even Stephens off his feet. If South Carolina's act was worth fifteen guns in Athens, what Georgia did was worth one hundred, and the Troup Artillery had the honor of firing them.[5]

The new Confederacy, which so many had been dreaming of but the meaning of which they had not clearly sensed, was now to become a fact. On February 4, one month before Lincoln should assume control in Washington, Jefferson Davis was inaugurated as president of a new nation in the Western firmament, and it seemed that the "Colossus of the New World," which Spain had early foretold and dreaded and which England had not relished, was now to be recorded along with Rome and the other fallen nations of the past. Again was the hand of the University evident in the works of the sons she had been training for the past half century and more. Of the ten delegates sent by Georgia to the Montgomery Convention, eight had received their training at the University. Thomas R. R. Cobb was a chief force in the making of the constitution of the Confederacy[6] and it seemed that Robert Toombs would have been chosen the president of the new government had his constitution resisted the refreshments at a state reception as well as many others who imbibed as freely. He received the first place in Davis' cabinet, the secretaryship of state. Howell Cobb became the first speaker of the Provisional Congress, and Alexander H. Stephens, who had worked feverishly to prevent a confederacy, now became its first vicepresident. Francis S. Bartow, Eugenius A. Nisbet, Benjamin H. Hill, Jabez L. M. Curry, W. P. Chilton, M. J. Crawford, W. P. Harris, and A. M. Clayton helped Thomas R. R. Cobb frame the new constitution, and Herschel V. Johnson, J. G. Shorter, L. J. DuPré, J. H. Echols, L. J. Gartrell, D. W. Lewis, and Robert Trippe became members of the Confederate Congress. John A. Campbell resigned his position on the United States Supreme Court bench to become assistant secretary of war, and Philip Clayton became assistant secretary of state. Indeed had the University wrought much, for good or for ill.

The Unionism of many in 1860 and their subsequent doubts for the future soon vanished in the almost universal enthusiasm for the new age that engulfed the South. On March 9th the first Confederate flag was raised in Athens. For months before, military companies had been forming, ready to receive the flag which they were to carry into battle, if necessary. By June, 1860, four months before the election of Abraham Lincoln, the Athens Guards, the Oconee Cavalry, and the Troup Artillery were parading.[7]

Athens was thoroughly aroused; the past products of the University had been heard from; what of the students and professors of 1860-1861? The glory of fighting for a long-standing ideal and against despicable traducers appealed with almost irresistible force to the ardor of college students. Swayed by the natural impulses of youth, the Franklin College students had often, in their society halls and out, championed the new and independent South. To act was much more romantic than to sit still and accept the malignant calumnies of the supercilious abolitionists. When Preston Brooks used mercilessly his cane on Charles Sumner in the Senate, the students of Franklin College applauded and promptly held a meeting to raise money for another cane to be sent him. Six months before Lincoln was elected they petitioned the faculty for a holiday that they might attend a target-shooting contest. The ardor of youth, the spirit of adventure and romance, and the counsel and advice of outstanding Southerners made secessionists and activists out of the Franklin College students. Calhoun and McDuffie had told them of the days of glory to come and of possible disasters, and many other well-wishers had either in person or by letter kept the thought before them. An honorary member of the Demosthenian Society wrote his colleagues in 1854, "I like to see the young men of the South training themselves for the future. That future will be full of glory and danger; it will require considerable sagacity to avoid terrible disasters." As *The Day* approached, Athenian sentinels on the watchtowers took to rousing the students. Thomas R. R. Cobb, almost mystically religious and sincere, lectured to the students on slavery and left the distinct impression that it was worth the price of the dissolution of the Union. Joseph Henry Lumpkin, as learned in the law as any

Georgian, lectured to the students on the United States Constitution and more particularly on the "Glorious South, cut loose from
the North, with King Cotton and Free Trade"—and in the words
of a student who heard him, "how we were thrilled and wished to
get at the invader!" Now and then Robert Toombs came through
Athens and struck the same chord.[8]

As a result of this expert tutelage the hated Yankees dwindled
into pigmies too insignificant to be regarded at all, unless with
contempt. Yankees knew nothing about guns; Southerners were
born marksmen. Franklin College students were equal to Athenians
in enthusiasm for the future. Then early in the morning of April
12th a Charleston battery fired a shot which swept across the sky
and landed on Fort Sumter—and the war began. The South had
been maligned for a quarter of a century; the North had been
profiting from Southern industry, and had resolutely refused to
compromise the points under dispute; the Lincoln Government
had delayed and equivocated over the Fort Sumter issue—now
the South would have its independence, and if the North wanted
war the South would accept it. The University campus had never
before known the intensity of excitement that now swept over it.
The students seemed to feel that if they did not immediately leave
and enlist in the armies of the Confederacy, the war would be
over without their having had a part in it. One of them declared,
"I remember the first time I heard 'Dixie,' felt like I could take
a cornstalk, get on Mason and Dixon's line and whip the whole
Yankee nation." On April 15th they petitioned the faculty to
be allowed to form a military company and begin training, and
G. P. Bennett and J. O. Waddel immediately joined a company
and left for the war. The Cobbs, and Toombs, and Lumpkin, and
other outstanding leaders might be for a quick and precipitate
course, but the Franklin College professors would have the students remember that their first duty at that time was with their
books, and that the war could either be won or lost without their
aid. The University notified the parents of Waddel and Bennett
of their departure "and of the Faculty's disapprobation of the
same." Fundamentally the background of higher education in
the South was hostile to secession and the war that seemed sure to

follow. The majority of the students came from the planters; the planters had been predominantly Whigs, and leading Whigs had consistently denounced secession as inopportune, and even some, as unconstitutional. Old President Church had made the students desist in their resolution to send Brooks a new cane, and now Chancellor Lipscomb tried to allay the excitement and keep the students at their books. Richard M. Johnston was opposed to the whole secession movement. He refused to "illuminate" his home when Georgia seceded, and at the end of the term he resigned from the University in order to escape from the war excitement that pervaded Athens. If forced to fight, it was only natural for most Southerners to enlist in the Confederate armies, but the conspicuous example of one former University student failing to choose the Confederate side was Stephen V. Benet, of Minorcan ancestry, who came to the University from St. Augustine, Florida. He became a brigadier general in the Union army and was made chief of ordnance.[9]

The Franklin College students, believing that their professors understood little outside of books, paid scant attention to their views on the subject of going to the war. Soon after Fort Sumter, determined that the Confederacy could not do without them, fourteen juniors left school "alleging that the excited condition of public affairs prevented them from studying." Before leaving they met and sent to the faculty their request for honorable dismissal, with this introduction: "Whereas the present disturbed conditions of our political affairs demands an exercise of patriotism, thereby rendering preparation absolutely necessary and rendering us as members of the University of Geo. totally unable to comply with our duties or to pursue our studies to advantage. . . ." In answer to this request, the professors resolved "That the students be informed that the Faculty feel themselves bound to the law that no dismission shall be granted except upon the written application of the parent or guardian." The students in the Lumpkin Law School, without further ado, organized themselves into a company and notified the governor that they were awaiting his call. So thoroughly had the students been prepared for these distempers of the times by Lumpkin, the Cobbs, and

Toombs that truly could they not fiddle with their books when the nation was afire. The faculty recognized the fact to the extent of allowing any senior in a military company called into service to receive his degree at the August commencement. A month before the term had concluded, only 75 of the 123 students who had been here at the beginning were left. Augustus B. Longstreet, at South Carolina College, took the same attitude assumed by Chancellor Lipscomb, and had the same trouble with his fiery South Carolinians.[10]

Not all the professors were impervious to the swirl of the tides around them. The Vice-Chancellor Patrick H. Mell resigned and organized his Mell Rifles, and William D. Wash, who had long been a terror to the mischievous students, left to enlist in a Mississippi company. He later joined John Morgan's famous cavalry, was captured in 1863, and was imprisoned at Camp Butler, Illinois, where he died. One of his comrades, in notifying the University of his death, declared that Wash "knew no fear, nor have I any hesitation in saying that he was the bravest man I ever saw." There was now much talk of converting the preparatory department ("Rock College") into a military academy.[11]

But Chancellor Lipscomb decided that he would put the University on a wartime footing and keep it open throughout the war if humanly possible. The trustees agreed with him, and reduced by 20 per cent the salaries of those professors who remained. He believed that the very opportunity which Southerners had long been praying for had at last arrived, and to abandon the educational field at this time would be the height of folly. Southern students who had been attending Northern institutions had now returned and none would go back. Southern colleges would now fall into this heritage. The South, long bound down by Northern hostility and aggression, was at last free to expand and to develop that being and genius which Nature and Nature's laws had always intended. "We are now undergoing a transition," said Chancellor Lipscomb to the trustees in 1862, "from a state of things that interfered with our legitimate progress, and particularly tended to restrain and thereby impair our intellectual growth. Under our former political relations, none of our interests suffered more than those of education. But we have now entered on an era that will communicate a new and mighty impulse to the mind of our people." With many other seers of his day he prophesied the renaissance of the arts, trade, commerce, industry, and agriculture, and he expected the University to stand in the forefront of this development. He continued, "The industrial interests of the Confederacy will necessarily stimulate this department of professional life in an unusual degree, and, hence I do not know a better service you can render the state than by immediately adopting measures for the organization of a school of engineers."[12]

But his Greater University and Greater South were already crumbling as surely as were the Union troops battling with the Confederacy and destroying her defenders. In June, 1861, the Lumpkin Law School adjourned for the duration of the war to contribute her quota to the conflict which lawyers had done so much to set going. Between the exhilaration of victories and the despondency of defeats, interspersed with holidays for fasting and prayers, it was not easy to keep up the semblance of an educational atmosphere. In May, 1862, examinations were given to the two remaining seniors, and the other three who had entered the class but who had recently gone to war were given their degrees as a recognition of their patriotism. In July, 1862, there were only 39 students whom the zeal for volunteering assisted by the Confederate draft had left to be educated, and fearing that he might soon be left with no students at all, Lipscomb begged President Davis to allow all students under twenty-one years of age to remain at the University to be trained until they were actually needed on the battlefield. Davis replied that the Confederate executive had no control over the matter. In 1863 there were only twenty students and only one senior. On March 10, 1863, the faculty entered this note on their records: "Thos. Grimes, the only member of the Senior Class, having arrived at the age liable to Conscription, it was resolved to recommend him for a diploma, without examination." In the fall of 1863 the University opened with forty students due to the transfer of the freshman class from "Rock College," where it had been placed in 1862, back to the University; but a few weeks after the University had opened, the

Federals had seized Chattanooga, the nearest the war had yet approached Georgia, and Governor Joseph E. Brown called upon the state guards to enter into active military service. As most of the University community was embraced in this call, the school was closed and when the scare had passed, in February, 1864, it was decided not to reopen the University. Lipscomb was made guardian of the University buildings, and the few remaining professors were granted indefinite leaves of absence and house-rent free. It was in the year 1863 that South Carolina College was also closed; the University of Mississippi had stopped with the outbreak of the war, but the University of North Carolina was able to survive until Reconstruction.[13]

The most convincing proof to many Athenians that something was profoundly wrong with the times was the absence of commencements at the University. Even in 1861 there had been nothing more than a sermon by Chancellor Lipscomb and for the remainder of the war this performance constituted all there was to that once all-absorbing occasion—even after the University had ceased to live it tried to maintain a semblance of life in Lipscomb's annual sermon. With the coming of war the revived celebrations of the Fourth of July were rather illogically considered out of keeping with Confederate principles, and the desolation in Athens became complete. The *Southern Watchman* observed in 1863, "Fourth of July and Commencement both having failed about the same time, leaves the children and negroes almost inconsolable."[14]

Phi Kappa and Demosthenian continued to engage the attention of the students as long as there was life in the University. Imbued with the spirit of the times, both immediately began to pay homage to the Confederacy by electing its generals and statesmen to honorary membership, inviting the latter to become society orators on various occasions, and by discussing the questions of outstanding interest to the Confederacy. The Demosthenians two days after Fort Sumter had been fired upon invited Judah P. Benjamin, a member of Davis' cabinet, to lay down the cares of his office in the most critical period of the Confederacy's existence, to journey to Athens to give the commencement oration. This famous Louisiana Hebrew politely declined on account of "the present conditions of public affairs when we know not what a day may bring forth." The Demosthenians elected to honorary membership Bishop H. H. Kavanaugh of Kentucky, Governor Pickens of South Carolina, and not knowing that the Phi Kappas had elected him in 1838 they elected C. G. Memminger, Confederate Secretary of the Treasury. They also elected generals P. G. T. Beauregard and Albert Sidney Johnston. J. P. Reed, who was elected in 1861, in his letter of acceptance wished the society success "in producing many Demosthenians whose names shall hereafter encircle the 'Confederate States of America' with a halo of enduring glory." Stonewall Jackson was among the honorary members elected by the Phi Kappas.[15]

The Demosthenians in their weekly deliberations and discussions decided that the Southern States should secede if Lincoln were elected; that soldiers should not be required to pay their debts until they should return from war; that the Confederacy should maintain a large standing army; when England was strongly contemplating recognition of the Confederacy, that it was expedient for nations to intervene in each others' affairs; in September, 1862, that conscription should be extended from the age of 35 to 40; and that generals were more responsible for victory than were private soldiers. The visit of Clement L. Vallandigham to Athens in 1863, after he had been banished from Ohio by Lincoln, gave the Phi Kappas an interesting subject for debate. Of course the decision was that his banishment was outrageous. In May, 1861, they decided that the Confederacy should not grant letters of marque and reprisal, though it was decided that the custom was legal, and in 1863 they decided that the Confederacy should not reopen the African slave trade.[16]

As the University weakened, naturally the societies began to languish. The Phi Kappas in 1861 dropped from 50 to 15. In their Annual Report for this year they recorded, "Many of them have gone to war & others intend to do so. May they nobly sustain their country's flag and do honor to the Phi Kappa Society in all the arduous duties of a soldier's life!" Occasionally their numbers were so small that they held no meetings at all. They suggested a union with the Demosthenians, but these ancient aristocrats of the rostrum refused to join their rivals even in a war for Southern independence. Finally in 1863 the Phi Kappas disbanded with only five left on their rolls; in May of this year the Demothenians followed them out of existence.[17]

War enthusiasm in Athens was long in abating. Company after company marched away, proudly bearing the name of its organizer or the name of someone whom it was thought desirable to honor. The Mell Rifles and the Lipscomb Volunteers gave recognition to the University. The former were namesakes of their organizer and the latter were named to honor the Chancellor, who, when not watching his University buildings or delivering his commencement sermon, was likely to be making speeches to the soldiers or presenting them with some flag "made by the ladies of Athens." The Troup Artillery early left for the battlefield and to it fell the honor of firing the signal gun which opened the Battle of Fredericksburg, as well as the gun which set into motion the heroic but pathetic charge of Pickett at Gettysburg. Then there was the Emma Sansom Cavalry, named for the Alabama girl who had helped Forrest. As the war dragged on all sources of men were picked over save the "cradle and the grave," and before the end both of these came forth, armed for the fray. The boys between twelve and sixteen developed a company and called themselves Georgia Rangers. Their chief duty early in the war seems to have been parading through town with the various companies that passed by, such as the Tugaloo Blues, Banks County Guards, Oconee Rangers, and Clarke County Rifles. In the week during March, 1862, seven companies marched through Athens on their way to the front. By 1863 the "Rock College" boys were the greatest source of military strength left in Athens. Here were at this time 103 students from Georgia, South Carolina, Florida, Alabama, and Tennessee, organized for home defense.[18]

But undoubtedly one of the most singular performances that ever attached itself to any war was the half-serious antics of the so-called "Mitchell Thunderbolts" or Colonel Billups' "aged and infirm," as they were also sometimes denominated. Perhaps they were the sour remnants left after recruiting officers had picked over all of those Athenians "capable of bearing arms," who in 1861 drilled back of Old College on Monday, Wednesday, and Friday, "armed with shotgun, rifle or musket." These Thunderbolts were in fact the "Athenian gentlemen of the excessively old school," each a gouty old despot or at least with a disposition that went with such a person, who formed a company for purposes of drill, and yet who acknowledged no authority on earth, neither their own officers nor the War Department of the Confederate Government. Their drill master was Richard Schevenell, a Frenchman, whose commands they heeded not in the least—unless it was to debate whether they should be obeyed. They appeared on the drill ground, armed with every species of weapon the fancy could devise, together with their umbrellas and canes. Some of these military aristocrats brought their Negro servants along to carry their guns and cartridge boxes. The War Department, deceived, perhaps, as to their true character, ordered an inspection to be held. They flatly refused to be inspected and almost precipitated a riot. One of them with a comic-opera blandishment declared, "I had rather see Athens sacked and burned than that my company should be forced to do any act which they do not choose to do." These old gentlemen, half humorous and half serious, were later of some little practical value when they sat around on the edge of the campus, guarding a group of Yankee prisoners quartered there, who instead of wanting to run away were so comfortable that their greatest desire was to remain there as long as possible. Among the higher officers of the war Athens contributed four general officers and seven colonels.[19]

Athens was loyally Confederate from the beginning and on to the devastating end. After June 1, 1861, letters bearing United States stamps were no longer accepted at the post office, and before the Confederacy was four months old the girls at Lucy Cobb Institute, wanting to do something worth while for their new nation, raised $120 with which to "endow" the Confederate Government. A month before the battle of Bull Run, Athens had established the Soldiers' Relief Society, and when the war became old and soldiers were going to and returning from the battlefields, a "Wayside Home" was set up on the campus in Old College. The girls at Lucy Cobb Institute might think they could help save the Confederacy from bankruptcy by bestowing upon it $120; the ladies and little children of Athens felt quite sure they could raise enough money which, added to that obtained from other parts of Georgia, would pay for the building of a gunboat. All the ladies and little girls were begged to bring forward their gunboat money. Soon after the University was suspended the buildings were put to war purposes. Some of them were used as hospitals for soldiers with eye affections—"Eye Infirmaries," as the Athenians called them. The Phi Kappa Society Hall became a depot for quartermaster stores, and New College became the refuge for many families driven out of the lowlands by the invasions of the enemy— from New Orleans, Mobile, Vicksburg, Savannah, Charleston, Memphis.[20]

Athens, being far from the seat of war, developed no war scares until 1864. Now and then strangers were arrested as spies, but no genuine Yankees were ever found. In 1863 two men were arrested and tried for espionage, but they turned out to be in the Confederate service. In June, 1864, Federal raiders were thought to be near, and by August following, many Athenians felt certain that the town would be captured. Soon 431 Federal soldiers appeared in Athens—prisoners taken by General W. C. P. Breckinridge in a clash with Stoneman's raiders. General Williams brought them in on his way to Andersonville, and quartered them on the campus for a few days. The Confederates were given in the College Chapel a banquet as sumptuous as Athens could afford, while the Mitchell Thunderbolts guarded the prisoners. The thrill of having the hated Yankee prisoners in town was too great for one unnamed blustering Southron, who kicked one of them and began cursing him. Another Athenian, who had more of the characteristic gentility about him, greatly disapproved, and years later said of the occasion, "Boy as I was I boiled over with indignation and I felt like apologizing to the prisoner for the whole State of Georgia; and I never saw that man afterwards—and he lived twenty years after the war—that I did not say to myself 'there goes a coward.' " In November, 1864, the railroad to Augusta was cut and the war came one step nearer to Athens. Soon there was much excitement over the approach of Sherman's armies, and many Athenians and refugees from other regions made ready to evacuate the town, but only a few of Sherman's raiders came near enough to see Athens, and none attempted seriously to enter it.[21]

The remoteness of Athens from the lines of battle led to its selection as a location for munitions factories. Shortly before the capture of New Orleans, one of the arms plants there moved its machinery to Athens, where it continued to manufacture muskets, turning out fifty a day as early as August, 1862. Pistols, swords, and bayonets were also made in considerable numbers.[22] The most remarkable engine of destruction turned out at Athens was a mystery gun—a double-barreled cannon. It was hoped that by tying the two cannon balls together with a chain, great slaughter would be dealt out against the enemy. Due to the difficulty of synchronizing the firing of the two barrels, greater destruction was carried out in the rear than in the front. After one trial it was retired, later to grace the public square and to give the city one more claim to fame—the only town in the world with a double-barreled cannon.[23]

Athens had its hardships and its joys, its exhilarations and its depressions. There was not a year during the war that some show-man or singer did not come to afford entertainment—and collect admission fees. Early in 1862 a band of "colored musicians," all slaves except one, performed for Athenians. "What do the invaders of our soil think of this?" asked the *Southern Watchman*. Mr. and the Misses Sloman gave their concert in 1863, and the next year Blind Tom was here again for a series of concerts. But, also, the hardships of war were soon unmistakably here. Before the struggle was a year old print paper was becoming scarce, and the *Southern Watchman* found it necessary to issue only a half-sheet for a time. It remarked that it was unable to find any in the Confederacy, and "We were afraid to go to Doodledom after it." The pine-knot gas which the town had begun to use in the 'fifties to light its streets was turned off in 1863, and darkened streets added to the general desolation. By 1864, even in day-light the town showed little life. Even no longer did stray dogs go yelping down Broadway, "with tin-kettles appended to their caudal extremities." Even "Cat Alley" had gone to sleep. "Nothing disturbs the 'solemn stillness' except now and then a rickety ox-cart whose unlubricated axles make melancholy music! Our great thoroughfare which once was crowded with country wagons laden with the rich products of a generous soil, is now bare and desolate—its stores closed—the noise of trade hushed—nothing to break the stillness, save now and then the voice of some descendant of Abraham 'jewing' " down some countrywoman on her butter and eggs.[24]

The panicky feeling, which so completely seized the people immediately after the election of Lincoln that a servile insurrection was almost inevitable, gradually died down, and all must have seen how utterly they had misjudged their Negro population. One of the greatest assets the Confederacy had was its millions of slaves who labored and produced while the soldiers were fighting at the front. Their friendship for their masters and their servile and tractable nature kept them from seizing the torch and ending the war in quick order. Athenians often complained about the troublesome young Negroes who infested the streets, shouting, boisterously laughing, and throwing stones, and one townsman declared, "We think we may safely venture the assertion that there is more petty thieving carried on in Athens than in any other town of the same size in the United States." Visitors to Athens thought that the Negroes here were uncommonly boisterous and given to stealing. But Athens Negroes were seldom vicious, and never so vicious and dangerous as the mob in 1862 which seized a Negro from the sheriff in the town hall, hurried him about a mile from town, and hanged him.[25]

After four years of pleasures and pains, Athens emerged from the war unscathed by actual invasion but with many vacancies in her families. The University was quiescent if not dead.

CHAPTER XIII

PEACE AND THE PASSING
OF THE OLD SOUTH

Long before Sherman pierced the heart of Georgia it must have been known to wise Athenians that the cause they had so enthusiastically embraced in 1861 would ultimately fail. Their own governor Joseph E. Brown, early showing himself unable to sense the methods of successfully conducting a war, had at times opposed their president Jefferson Davis with almost as much hostility as he displayed toward Abraham Lincoln, the supposed author of all their woes. Sherman presented Savannah to Lincoln as a Christmas gift in 1864, and a few days after Lee surrendered at Appomattox, Federal raiders seized Macon. On May 4 Yankee troops encamped on the streets of Athens, and even the most obdurate rebel now was forced to admit that the war was over— that the Confederacy had been *overpowered*, though not *defeated*. Jefferson Davis and his cabinet were soon fleeing southward, but many of his executive papers made their appearance in Athens, where they were put in charge of Chancellor Lipscomb, there to remain until they were sent to Washington, D. C., with the hope that they might afford evidence to the advantage of the erstwhile Confederate president on trial for treason.[1]

Captain A. B. Cree of Iowa took military charge of Athens, and seizing the *Southern Watchman* office, without formal introduction to his readers, sent out on May 6 the regular issue with nothing to indicate a change in editorship, but Athenians rubbed their eyes in amazement and guessed something had happened when they read the most fulsome praise of Federal arms and of the Union and bitter condemnations of the Confederacy. The *Watchman* was then turned back to John H. Christy, its editor, with the warning that he should ponder carefully what he had to say about the new order. Soon Captain Cree was superseded by Major M. S. Euen of New York, and an Athenian wag returned the trick on the Yankees in this wise: Euen dismounted his horse one day to enter a store and asked this wag to watch the animal; the horse walked away and when Euen chided him he replied, "Well, I did watch him until he went around the corner and I couldn't see him any more then." In the following October Major Euen departed, followed to the station by a parade of soldiers, and Captain Beckwith assumed watch on the Oconee.[2]

Athens was not greatly pleased with her army of occupation, but she had much reason to feel grateful that she did not have the fate of Brunswick and other coast towns where former slaves, in blue uniforms, with shining rifles, administered Anglo-Saxon justice. One of the first acts of the Federal occupiers was to call on the people to surrender immediately all horses and mules branded with the devices "C. S." or "U. S." regardless of any permission that might have been given to keep them. Also with like disregard for parole agreements the people must turn in all firearms, and anyone so devoid of propriety as to appear in a gray uniform should be arrested immediately. Furthermore, all former Confederate officers and non-residents of Athens were given twenty-four hours to leave town. The troops were quartered in all the University buildings except the library, where Chancellor Lipscomb was allowed to stand watch. Demosthenian Hall was made regimental headquarters. The first floor of Phi Kappa Hall housed the quartermaster's department; the second floor was turned into "a place of revelry and riotous amusement," where the soldiers and their Negro satellites staged their social and intellectual activities. The valuable library which Phi Kappas had been collecting for almost a half century was much scattered and scarred. The next year in the society's appeal for aid it said,

"The Hall was much defaced by the occupation of the Federal garrison, and the stove, carpet and some other property of the society was carried off, so that we are considerably in debt, with no prospect of release except through the aid of our honorary friends and brethren." The soldiers carried leaves and rubbish into the University buildings for beds, and only by the kindness of fate did they not destroy the structures by careless fires. The chapel was left in a woeful condition, with its benches burned, windows broken out, walls jabbed with bayonets, and the old Greek columns made targets for pistol fire.[3]

But apart from the ordinary hazards of army occupation, Athens suffered little in property damages. The Federal officers in charge were always amenable to reason, and, in the trying position they filled, commanded the affectionate love of Athenians in comparison to the feeling later vented on the carpetbaggers. True enough, a low-bred Yankee robbed Professor Mell of his watch after threatening to kill him, but on complaint made to the commanding officer the watch was restored. Yet the implacable, unreconstructed, and unrepentant Athenes looked with the greatest disdain on the unspeakable invaders and rather than encounter one they would gather their skirts and cross the muddiest street the town afforded. Such an attitude by the ladies may have suggested to General James B. Steedman the recommendation that all women who made use of the post office should be required to take the oath of loyalty. The women for reasons peculiar to their nature from time immemorial might be excused for their attitude toward Federal soldiers, but young people and street loiterers were informed by the *Southern Watchman* that their hissing at the soldiers must stop.[4]

One of the greatest and most enduring evils incident to the occupation of the South by the soldiers was the feeling it engendered among the former slaves that they were now about to come into an impossible heritage. The criminal provocation of Negro soldiers made itself evident to General Grant on his trip through the South, and he immediately ordered their removal from Georgia. The white troops were not the conscious promoters of this Afro-American *resorgiomento*. People of low standing in the North, who had generally been able to escape the honorable course of a soldier, when peace came hurried to the South to feed on the carcass. They won the name of carpetbaggers, and through the extension of the Union League or Loyal League they played fearful havoc with the peace of mind of the innocent and inoffensive Negroes. They were aided in this work by the minor officers of a well-intentioned organization, the Freedmen's Bureau. Here was perpetrated as great a crime on the Negro as had been worked by his two centuries of slavery. The feeling of profound gratitude the Southern people had in the summer of 1865 for their former slaves, under proper direction, would have led to a course of racial development, unmarred by the generations of bitterness and suspicions that were aroused by supposed friends who utterly misunderstood the nature of the Negroes, and had strangely forgotten the character of Anglo-Saxons. The wrongs of Reconstruction against the whites were great, but no greater than against the Negroes.

When Confederate authority crumbled, the bonds of the slaves were cut asunder, and to prove their freedom the Negroes set out with little or no idea as to where they were going, but always hoping to stumble upon a town. By the autumn of 1865, Athens was overflowing. Asked the *Southern Watchman*, "Can anybody tell where so many idle negroes come from? Like the frogs of Egypt, they seem to be every where and in every body's way." As their orator, Frederick Douglass, said, they had only the dusty road under their feet and the blue sky above. Without the Freedmen's Bureau many would undoubtedly have starved; as it was, an epidemic of thievery broke out in Athens, the intensity of which could have been produced by nothing except hunger. Captain Cree on assuming charge attempted to demobilize the Negroes and induce them to go back into the country to work for their former masters, and the Freedmen's Bureau offered them wholesome advice as to honesty and industry. General David Tillson, the head of the Bureau in Georgia, came up from Augusta and addressed the assembled Negroes in the college chapel, condemning their idleness and thieving. He told them to secure work or he would force them into gainful employment. He told them pointedly that there would be no Christmas present (December 25, 1865) of "forty acres and a mule." Within a few weeks, hundreds of cases of theft were reported to the army. Smoke-houses were broken into; chickens and pigs were constantly being stolen. Everything portable not constantly watched or protected by strong locks was in danger of disappearing. Even the office of the *Southern Watchman* was entered and the type scattered. The editor hoped that the following advertisement would afford some protection: "Wanted immediately at this office Two fierce bull dogs and one thoroughbred bloodhound." The army and the Bureau arrested 150 thieves in one week, and punished them variously. They shaved the head of one downward from the crest, leaving a ridge of wool, and then escorted the culprit out of town at the point of a bayonet. They shaved the head of another, dressed him in a barrel, and hung about his neck the sign "I am a horse-thief," and drove him out of town, followed by the drum and fife corps playing the "Rogue's March." Two other nimble-fingered blacks were labeled, "I will steal" and "I will too," and forced to stand on a barrel for twelve hours.[5]

The boisterous laughter and loud talking of Negroes, especially on Sundays, greatly interfered with church services, and more serious groups sometimes engaged in organized pillaging forays. In the summer of 1865 a band of Negroes who had been slaughtering stolen cattle and hogs was opposed by the sheriff and his posse as they attempted to cross the Oconee River at the Princeton bridge, and about 600 pounds of meat was recovered and thirty Negroes captured. But soon additional forces of Negroes appeared, recovered their booty, and liberated the prisoners. The Loyal League early made its appearance in Athens with its secret ritual, lodge meetings, and regalia parades. Into such an atmosphere E. Remington & Sons sent their advertisements of all kinds of guns and pistols for sale to "the public generally." Near the end of the year 1867, when the Negroes had been further wronged by the unreasoning bestowal of unrestricted manhood suffrage upon them, a few groups began assaults on their white neighbors with bricks. Soon a mob of a hundred blacks gathered, armed with Remingtons and other variously fashioned weapons. J. J. Knox, the Bureau

Agent, dispersed them, but they soon reassembled and refused to retreat until a squad of soldiers with fixed bayonets charged them. Then there grew up the Ku Klux Klan (which strangely enough so many Southerners had never heard of when they were summoned later before the Congressional Committee of investigation), and Negro lodge meetings became more infrequent. Negro mobs gave way to white mobs, and carpetbaggers retreated northward or perchance dangled on the ends of ropes attached to the limbs of trees or to the portico of a courthouse. Some Negroes began to change their minds as to the value of freedom, and according to a vote taken by Major Knox in one of his meetings, he received the disappointing intelligence that from 25 per cent to 50 per cent of his charges preferred ante-bellum bondage to Freedmen's Bureau freedom. Many of the Athens conglomeration of blacks began to migrate westward toward the Mississippi, and the *Southern Watchman* speeded them onward with the news, "*The Bouquet D'Afrique* is not quite so strong on our street corners as it was a few days ago."[6]

When the Confederate Government fell, the people were almost relegated to the mythical state of nature, and were only saved by the timely appearance of Federal armies. During the interregnum the postmaster at Athens issued his own personal postage stamp. President Andrew Johnson, believing that reason and good judgment demanded a return as soon as possible of the states to their former position in the Union, issued his amnesty proclamation and began appointing provisional governors. For Georgia he selected James Johnson, a classmate of Alexander H. Stephens at the University, equally as strong in his Unionism in 1860 and more consistent in it during the war. A new constitution was formed; Charles J. Jenkins was elected governor, and Stephens and Herschel V. Johnson, old University men, were chosen senators—all before the end of 1865. In this new order that the President had attempted to set up, the most intelligent element with Union backgrounds and proclivities was enthroned—Toombs, Cobb, Nisbet, the old secessionists, were conspicuously absent.

How would the University fare in this new order? In the latter part of June the trustees had met, and a few days later Chancellor

Lipscomb preached his customary commencement sermon amidst an atmosphere surcharged with Federal soldiers and freed Negroes. For two years there had been no students, but now with the war over and Georgians still in charge of their state government, could the University not enter into that new day, somewhat modified, which the Chancellor had foreseen in 1861? But the war which had swept away the wealth of the South had left the University prostrate financially. The $100,000 permanent loan to the state, from which the University had been regularly drawing $8,000 annually in interest, had now gone with the Confederate state government of Georgia, and the trustees felt that they should not ask the impoverished state for more. The other funds of the University consisted of $16,000 in the bonds of the defunct Confederate States of America, $1,000 of the former State Bank, $20,000 in bonds of the late Confederate State of Georgia, and $2,400 in individual notes. The immediate value of these evidences of indebtedness was nothing and their ultimate value little more. Professor William H. Waddel suggested that the faculty open the institution on their own initiative, charging $100 a year tuition. The faculty as a unit did not agree to this plan, and the trustees then offered the buildings, the library, and the apparatus to any individual who cared to open private schools in them. There was a strong urge in Athens for the old intellectual atmosphere, which broke out about the end of the war in "Lipscomb's Lyceum," made up of about sixty young men who declaimed, debated, and studied. The army of occupation finally retreated to the outskirts of the town, where it took up quarters in "Rock College," and before the end of the summer Williams Rutherford was preparing to open in New College his school, which he declared would instruct in all subjects from the primary through college, at $5 a month. William J. Magill also prepared to teach in Philosophical Hall surveying, civil engineering, and the higher academy studies. Soon the demand arose that the new constitutional convention provide in the organic law for the permanent support of the University, and also that the legislature continue the $8,000 annual appropriation on the state loan, lost through no fault of the University. The new constitution called for a resumption of University exercises through the establishment of a permanent endowment.[7]

The private schools operating in University buildings were having considerable success, and as the trustees had regarded them as nuclei for the University, it was thought wise to reopen the institution on January 3, 1866. Two days after the opening, 78 students were present and the future of the institution seemed again assured. As the college bell rang again it seemed like music to the ears of Athenians, "awakening reminiscences of the better days of the Republic." A few days later the students called a meeting to express their confidence in the chancellor and faculty and to call on the legislature to grant the University a permanent endowment. The college year was now divided into two terms, the first running from September 1 to December 1 and the second from January 1 to July 1; the trustees also adopted the rule that members of the faculty should be elected every four years and that a professor must have a majority vote to remain.[8]

The character of the students who now entered the University differed much from those who attended before the great cataclysm engulfed the South. There was scarcely one who had not taken some part in the war and who had not come under rules that were not to be questioned. Much of the sterner part of life had taken hold of them and had made them more serious. Their future and the future of the South were yet clouded. Chancellor Lipscomb said of his first class after the war: They "are much more manly in their sympathies and aspirations; much more obedient as to the real spirit of submission to discipline and consequently much more thoughtful and prudent as to matters of personal control; much more under influence and requiring less of stern authority for their government than we ordinarily find in this class of persons." Many young men had been wounded in the war and had become permanently incapacitated in some way. The feeling early grew up that these maimed soldiers should be provided an education by the state, whose life they had sought to preserve; and on December 18, 1866, the state passed a law providing an education "free of charge for tuition, books, board and clothing" for all indigent, maimed soldiers under thirty years of age, to be educated at the University, Mercer, Emory, Oglethorpe, and Bowdon colleges. The expenses for any one were not to be over $300 annually. In return the student, so aided, pledged himself to teach within the state for a period of time equal to the period of state aid. The University, loath to turn away anyone unable to pay his expenses, provided the next year for the education free from tuition of fifty boys willing to teach a period equal to the time spent at the University. Also students preparing for the ministry were granted free tuition. It was now no uncommon sight to see young Confederate warriors hobbling across the campus. "The sight of so many of these mutilated heroes," said the *Southern Watchman*, "has called up many sad and bitter memories, not unmingled, though, thanks to God and their valor! with proud remembrance of a Lost but not Dishonored Cause." J. A. Robson, elected anniversarian by the Demosthenians, had "greatly distinguished himself as a soldier in 'the lost cause,' having alone and unaided captured forty-seven of the enemy at the battle of Cedar Creek, and lost a limb at Hatcher's Run." Nat E. Harris, driven out of East Tennessee by Parson Brownlow's war, came to Georgia and entered the University, though not aided by the state fund. He won the respect and help of Alexander H. Stephens, who, himself, had been aided years before, and when Stephens was later compelled by financial reverses to withdraw his aid, Howell Cobb continued the help until Stephens recovered.[9]

As there was little or no opportunity for the boys of the Civil War days to attend school, most of the soldier students who entered the University were unprepared for college work. They were therefore sent to "Rock College," the high school department of the University, where they constituted practically all the students. The $300 fee from each soldier alone made it possible to continue this department, and when later (March 19, 1869) the legislature, composed of Negroes, carpetbaggers, scalawags, and some conservatives, discontinued the aid, the students as well as the "College" were left in distress.[10]

The Negroes were now free and by the fourteenth amendment they were made citizens of the states and of the nation. Freedom and citizenship demanded unmistakably that they be educated, and Southern leaders, immediately after the surrender of Lee, began to discuss Negro education and to lay plans for it. But the goodwill and understanding that had characterized the relations between the races during the war was soon dissipated by the newly won friends of the Negro. They took complete possession of his affections, his life and his soul, and the incipient plans of the Southern leaders were snuffed out. The Freedmen's Bureau set up schools, and innocent, deluded, self-sacrificing young women "from the 'Heavenly Kingdom' of Doodledom" were soon in Athens armed with exotic notions and impractical educational ideas for the Negroes. Naturally Athenians looked upon them with suspicion, as peddlers of dangerous poisons, and those "pious young females, of the Puritan persuasion" were not long in learning that they were climbing their Golgotha. But they did not sow their ideas in stony ground; they dangled before the Negroes the educational Utopia, and innocently awakened in the African heart longings for what could not be. Again had the Negro been terribly deceived and his feelings been shamefully played with, but by emissaries equally deluded. The Negro had as much right to an education as he had to his freedom, but Rome was not built in a day, neither could Negroes a year removed from slavery be speedily made into polished classical scholars. But the Negroes had a right to think so, for their new friends had so told them. Therefore, one day they decided to storm the citadel of knowledge and capture the heritage of thirty centuries of labor. A motley group of dusky educational warriors collected on the edge of the campus and began to jeer their more fortunate white brothers. The town marshals attempted to drive them off, but with little success; but when the soldier students, clubbing their pistols, made a sally out of the campus, the Negroes fled. This was in 1866. Near the end of 1867 the thirst for higher education gained the ascendancy again among a group of Negroes who, now armed with sticks, clubs, and every kind of weapon obtainable, invaded the campus for the purpose of seizing the buildings. The students, some armed with guns they had carried through the Civil War, gathered to defend their *alma mater*, and a battle was averted only by the plain words of Professor Mell, who told the mob that if they did not depart peaceably, and immediately, not one would get away alive. This was the University's nearest approach to ever having a colored student body.[11]

In the meantime the new government of Georgia had not fared well in her relations with her conquerors. President Johnson soon found that Congress little relished his plan of reconstructing the states, and being a man of plain words and a well-developed temper, he said uncomplimentary things about the Congressmen. They thereupon rejected the Presidential plan, refusing to seat Stephens and Herschel V. Johnson and the other Southern senators and representatives, developed their own plan, which the Southern States rejected, and in 1867 they decided to obliterate the Southern States altogether and divide them into military districts. Georgia was presided over by General John Pope and then General George Gordon Meade, and Athens was made headquarters for one of the Georgia divisions. The Confederate tradition was strong and vigorous, as was only to be expected, and the Georgians, goaded by an almost intolerable Congressional policy, became almost as unreasoning as their conquerors. Joseph E. Brown, as strong a secessionist as ever existed, when the war was over believed the best policy was to accept everything the conquerors imposed as the easiest and quickest way out of a bad situation. Other Georgians thought differently and branded Brown a traitor to his own state and people. Benjamin H. Hill in his "Notes on the Situation" steeled the hearts of Georgia against her conquerors, while Howell Cobb, no friend of Hill's, took a more conservative course.

Athens and the University held as a heritage worth cherishing the War for Southern Independence and the memory of those who carried it on. The fighting was scarcely finished before the town was raising money for a Confederate monument, and the University students aided by raising $800 in a burlesque they gave on May Day. Athens observed Memorial Day first on May 4, 1866, and the next year the town was raising a Davis Benefit Fund by a concert in the town hall—a brilliant event "in the social dullness that reigns so supreme in our staid little town." A Ladies' Memorial Association was organized to see that each year war memories be recalled. And those soldiers who had successfully lived through the four years of destruction organized in 1870 a Mutual Aid and

Benevolent Association. When Howell Cobb dropped dead in a New York hotel in 1868, his remains were brought to Athens and in the college chapel his funeral was held with universal mourning, and two years later when the great Confederate chieftain Lee died, the University held commemorative exercises in the chapel, where Chancellor Lipscomb delivered a eulogy. Charles F. McCay in 1869, who was later to give the University a handsome endowment, now donated to the University library $1,000 to be spent in collecting books on the war.[12]

The University further showed its appreciation for Confederate leaders by electing them to professorships. It offered Custis Lee, a son of the great commander, the new department of civil engineering, and when he rejected it they elected General M. L. Smith of Confederate war fame, who accepted, but who died on his way from Memphis to Athens. Then they chose L. H. Charbonnier, the inevitable Frenchman, a graduate of St. Cyr, who assumed the duties and long directed the work. The trustees created the department of history and political science and in 1868 elected Alexander H. Stephens to keep the records of the past straight for Southern youths. He rejected the offer on account of his health. Benjamin H. Hill was asked to instruct in the mysteries of law, but he never found it convenient to do so.[13]

By 1867 Georgians found themselves under the complete rule of General Pope, and soon discovered that they were no longer a state but merely a part of Military District Number 3. Their hopes and expectations on laying down their arms had vanished. The ancient glamour of the Fourth of July, it seemed, was not to be restored. In 1865 the Athenians had been asked by the Federal troops to help celebrate it, but they declined "in view of our recent humiliation, our great losses of property, and more especially of men." The next year they declined again: "The great objects for which our forefathers fought, bled, and died having failed, so far as we are concerned, we cannot perceive any reasons why this should be a day of rejoicing with us, as formerly. It only serves to call up vividly to our minds a sense of the oppression under which we suffer, and instead of rejoicing, we feel inclined to 'hang our harps on the willows.'" Now in 1867, their humiliation had become deeper and they hung their harps higher upon the willows, for they "could not sing the songs of Zion in a strange land." But the Fourth of July meant much to the new citizens, who this year came to Athens in countless numbers to celebrate. The report had been spread that there was to be a division of goods, chattels, and land, and any Negro who did not come to get his part would be fined $5. "There was a multitude no man could number, from all points of the compass, and some of them from a distance of fifty and sixty miles. They went away empty—hungry—disappointed." Yet the army of occupation enjoyed the day—except one soldier who became greatly enraged when he was arrested by the town marshal for violating the town ordinance forbidding the use of fire-crackers in demonstrating patriotism.[14]

In carrying out the plan of restoring the Southern territory to the Union as states, General Pope first registered those who were to vote—all the Negroes and certain classes of whites. Four hundred and fifty white Athenians were allowed to register, while the names of 675 Negroes were entered, two-thirds of whom it was charged were not residents. "What a mockery," exclaimed the *Southern Watchman*. "And all to gratify the malignity of grinning devils thousands of miles off, who have denounced the Constitution and Bible as a 'covenant with death' and 'a league with hell.'" In the voting for a constitutional convention, Athenians and Georgians generally refrained largely from entering into the farce, as they considered it. Only 21 white Athenians cast their ballots. The convention met, the constitution was made, the new government was elected and inaugurated, and the fourteenth amendment was ratified. The Negroes, aided by Congress, the Federal army, and their carpetbagger friends, had now come into their heritage. Twenty-seven Negroes journeyed to Atlanta to help make laws for the new commonwealth of Georgia. The University of Georgia, Athens, and Clarke County were represented by two of their former slaves and servants. The conservative whites expelled the Negroes and brought additional woes upon the state which made further reconstructing necessary. One of Athens' representatives, Alf Richardson, was done to death by the Ku Klux Klan, and Madison Davis, the other, was so near white that he seems to have escaped the vigilance of the committee which was doing the plucking.[15]

The humiliation of the times was deeply felt, and suppressed emotions were gnawing and corroding the very souls of the people. The Ku Klux Klan, once thought to be a relief, had degenerated into a barbaric mob, yet open protest would have been the greatest folly, in the face of the occupying army. There was left only the unlimited right to secretly hope. John G. Shorter wrote his Demosthenian brothers in April, 1867: "With the liberties of our fathers wrested from us, we have only left the principles on which these liberties were founded, and it rests with us to preserve them inviolate that they may, at some day however distant, serve us, when the uncertain circle of revolutions, may again place our destinies in our own hands." Implacable Robert Toombs, who on returning from Europe in 1867 had said, "I regret nothing in the past but the dead and the failure, and I am ready today to use the best means I can command to establish the principles for which I fought," was elected by the Demosthenians their honorary president at the coming commencement. He found it impossible to be present and Benjamin H. Hill was selected. It was at this commencement, in August, that the assembled crowds burst asunder their subdued spirits and for a short moment were carried away with a wild thrill, unequaled in intensity since the days of Confederate victories. Albert H. Cox of LaGrange had been chosen one of the junior orators, and before a distinguished audience he spoke on the "Vital Principle of Nations." He traced this principle down through Greece and Rome to England, and carried it across the Atlantic to America—and then deftly through intonations and gestures skillfully applied it to the distempers through which the South was going. "As soon as he referred to the South, he struck a chord in the heart of the audience that rung forth in applause." Mindful of the military occupation and of the presence of Major C. F. Trowbridge and his Federal troops, he made no direct references to men and events, but when he had finished, wild applause greeted him and the band played "Dixie"—the audience had perfectly understood him. Benjamin H. Hill, Howell Cobb, and Joseph E. Brown, side by side on the stage but as close in life and sentiment as the three corners of a triangle, heard with varying emotions the young orator. When Cox had finished, Hill grasped his hand and congratulated him; Cobb saw great mischief in the whole performance; and Brown saw in the enraptured audience only lowering frowns for himself. That night, carried away with the excitement, the students collected their brass band and serenaded Hill and Cobb. Hill declared in a half-hour speech that the clouds were still dark but there was a silvery lining far away, and Cobb made a short guarded speech calling on the students not to desert the state in her greatest trial. The newspaper reporter ended his account of the night's performance thus, "P.S.—The students forgot—yes, *really* forgot—to call on Governor Brown."[16]

Cox's speech created a sensation as great as Hill's "Notes on the Situation," and gross exaggerations marked the accounts of it that immediately spread over the state. Cox did not point to Brown when he said "despicable characters" and he did not indicate Hill when he said "moral heroes." The trustees, seeing the dangerous effect that might be produced, passed a resolution introduced by Howell Cobb, requiring the enforcement of the rule "by which, party political subjects are excluded from the speeches of students at Commencement" and requesting the faculty "to exercise under present circumstances more than usual vigilance." The trustees expressed their "sincere regret that any thing should have occurred during the literary exercises of the Commencement to suggest the idea of even an unintentional departure from the established usage of the University." Brown offered an amendment forbidding any student to publish his speech in a newspaper without the permission of the chancellor. The trustees appointed a committee to appeal to Pope for the removal of the military headquarters from Athens, out of consideration for the University. As a general standing counsel to plead the cause of the University before the legislature, all constitution conventions, and the Federal military authorities they appointed Joseph E. Brown, chairman, His Honor Iverson L. Harris, Honorable James. L. Seaward, General James W. Armstrong, and Colonel Benjamin C. Yancey.

When news of Cox's speech reached General Pope, Military Commander of District Number 3, he became greatly enraged and immediately withdrew the $8,000 annuity from the University and ordered its doors closed against further educational use and the buildings converted into army barracks. Howell Cobb said, "The threatened persecution of the College by Genl Pope is raising up friends for it everywhere and we may flatter ourselves with the hope that after all, good will come out of the apprehended evil." Chancellor Lipscomb, who had taken great care to guard his commencement exercises from untoward incidents, hurried to Atlanta to give Pope a true account of what had happened. Many were for ignoring Pope and taking the matter to Washington, where it was hoped there was more justice. James Jackson said, "I am not sure but the best thing for us is to agitate anyway, & let Pope stop the College by force & see how that would go down at W. & the North." There was much correspondence between Georgia and Washington, and Hill made a trip to the capital to see General Grant and President Johnson. The Washington authorities took the side of the University and ordered Pope to cease interfering and restore the annuity. The "Hero of Second Manassas" reluctantly complied.[17]

Lipscomb had in the meantime been attempting to placate Pope but found it difficult to disabuse his mind regarding Hill's part. Pope believed that Hill had inspired the speaker and planned the speech. He wanted Hill to resign from the board of trustees and from his professorship of law; finally he agreed to allow the University to open but he would not restore the annuity. And he gave the warning that if the affair were exploited by the newspapers in attacks on the military authorities or on the Reconstruction policies, "I will not say what I will do." The decision from Washington forced Pope to capitulate completely, and Lipscomb used every effort to prevent the dangers of newspaper discussions.[18]

Hill's part in the controversy and his position in state politics at that time placed the University in a dilemma. He could not be humiliated in any way to please Joe Brown or to gratify Pope, and far would it be from the desires of most Georgians to do so; and yet as long as Pope ruled in Georgia he had the power to do great mischief. Howell Cobb stated the situation thus: "The University occupies a very precarious position at present, and can

only be rescued from the dangers that surround it, by the exercise
of the greatest wisdom. On the one hand we have to encounter
the hostility of Genl Pope, so unfortunately provoked. To remove
this hostility and conciliate his opposition is essential to the present
well being of the University. To that end everything should be
done that will not impair the present usefulness of the College
and jeopardize its future popularity or usefulness. On the other
hand we must not close our eyes to the fact, that a large popular
sentiment in our state is in full sympathy with Mr. Hill, and
nothing should be done to array that sentiment hostile to the University. Looking to the future of the College, it would be most
unfortunate, for the opinion to obtain, that the University had
lent itself to the work of crushing Mr. Hill, that is, had taken part
in the controversy in which Mr. Hill has become involved with
the military authorities."[19]

The brush with the Federal army was a complete victory for
the University. In September it opened with 180 students "& still
they come"—90 more were enrolled in "Rock College." Cox
became a hero of the first magnitude, and the next year when
Chancellor Lipscomb returned from a trip to Europe, Cox was
chosen by the students to welcome the chancellor back. At the
next commencement Cox was again a speaker, but nothing spectacular took place as the faculty had been very careful to closely
censor all speeches.[20]

The perils of war and the uncertainties of Reconstruction had
as profound an effect on the town as they had on the University.
In 1867 the population was 4,073—an increase of 611 during
the past fifteen years. Excluding students, there were 2,313
whites and 1,760 Negroes. The ante-bellum wealth was now gone
and with it and the times went much of that character and spirit
which had so charmed the visitors and given Athens such rare
distinction. Truly the ante-bellum times had departed, the Old
South was gone, and Athens must find itself again. It was always
to remain a college town, largely to revolve around the University
socially and economically. Yet it now sought industrialism and
soon "after the surrender" (from which point time was now
reckoned) certain appreciable prosperity came to the town, as the

Negroes were induced to settle down to work again and the cotton plantations of the hinterland grew white again. In 1869 it was announced that the "large and lofty three-story brick building at the corner of Broad and Thomas streets looms up above all its surroundings, and will be finished in elegant style." In 1870 a street railway was run into town from the Georgia Railroad depot across the river. The cars were for freight only and were pulled by mules. Also street lamps were erected and a heavy fine placed on culprits who threw stones at them. The safety of the citizens was better provided for by ordinances that prohibited the private ownership of gunpowder unless stored in the public magazine, where a rental of one cent a pound per year was exacted, and by the appointment on special occasions of as many as twenty policemen. Individuals and private organizations helped to educate the unfortunate poor, free of charge. Chancellor Lipscomb held night classes in rhetoric and composition weekly; Charbonnier taught mechanics and laboring men the elements of civil engineering and how to draw, and the Episcopal Church gave free instruction in sewing and in other domestic concerns to forty eager pupils. The desire for amusement was born again. Professor C. M. Von Ecklen opened his dancing school; the young ladies gave their cantata, the "Flower Queen"; the Rising Star Division and Young Men's Temperance Debating Society gave a soirée to the largest crowd "since the surrender"; the fire company held its twenty-fifth annual parade (1870), viewed by the young ladies seated on the college chapel portico; the first bicycle, made by a resident Frenchman, rolled down the streets in 1869, and the next year roller skating seized the agile Athenians.[21]

Traveling circuses and amusements again made their appearance. The Stone and Rosston Combination Circus arrived in December, 1865; Robinson's soon followed, and in 1867 Barnum's Museum Collection attracted the biggest crowd that was ever in Athens. Then came Bill Lake's Hippo-Olympiad, admitting that it was "Positively the largest and best show on earth. . . . The 'King Bee' show of the World. The only Traveling Exhibition in the world that do all they Advertise." Times were indeed changing when in 1868 the University permitted the juniors to attend a circus, but with the understanding "that such request should never under any circumstances be granted again." In 1867 the Mr. and Mrs. W. H. Crisp Company played *Macbeth* to an "appreciative audience," but the ancient tastes of Athens had gone if this indictment is to be believed: A highly intellectual amusement appeared and not thirty attended. "Had it been a circus, or a three cent monkey show, or an entertainment for the benefit of the infant Hindoos—to supply them with flannel shirts—or to convert those interesting men and brothers who breakfast on cold baked missionary whenever they have the chance, the rush would have been tremendous. This eminently respectable little 'burg' plumes itself upon the refined and intellectual tastes of its people, but just so long as it allows a false, sickly, spurious morality to taboo and break down all species of amusements that do not tally with its ideas of propriety, just so long will these things be." In 1867 the city put a tax ranging from $10 to $50 on anyone who should "exhibit a caravan of wild animals, or other natural objects of curiosity, a circus, wax figures, rope dancing, legerdemain, puppet shows, theatrical and other public exhibitions for money," excepting lectures of a scientific or literary nature.[22]

Indeed had Athens changed. There was now less leisure and more worry. After a decade of war and reconstructing how could the souls of people be quite the same again? The constant concern at making a living took much of the sweetness out of the lives of many who had learned the secret of how to be useful and valuable to society in a state of leisure. The "old times" now grew mellow quickly, and with little in the future to attract, many Athenians developed the more pleasant pastime of looking backward.

Though the students at the University were more mature and tempered with more seriousness than they had been in ante-bellum times, their having been soldiers or having passed through the furnace of war and Reconstruction did not completely banish lighter moments in their lives. Two months after school opened following the war, "Frederick Lucas having been drunk and riotous in town at night and having made confession thereof, was suspended from College until 1st prox." A month later another student confessed to having inserted a pack of playing cards into the chapel Bible and admitted that he must have been drunk when he did it. For these pranks and others he was expelled, but later re-admitted on the "strictest possible probation." Yet there was not a great deal of drunkenness, considering the sorrows the people had to drown. During the first half of 1867 only three students became drunk, and two of them were expelled.

Violence begets violence and the Ku Klux Klan arose. Some of the students aped its methods when they threatened to drive out of the University Julius L. Brown, a son of the war-time governor, largely because they accused his father of being a traitor to the South. The goodwill of other students prevented this atrocity. Although by the ordinances of Athens no student might play at billiards without his parents' permission, and although there was still a code of University laws for the students to obey, yet the times were fast changing in regard to restrictions. There was no rule that required students to pay their debts owed to the Swiss ice cream vender, who finally after testing out the honesty of five successive generations of college students went into bankruptcy and moved away in 1883. Chancellor Lipscomb said in 1869, "Our present mode of government aims to form in the student habits of self-control by means of self-respect to remove all possible occasions of conflicting feelings between the Professors and themselves; to confine their relations as far as possible to the genial intercourse of teacher and pupil; and above all to develop the sentiment that they are parties pledged by their position to one common interest and bound by right instincts to be co-workers for the same ends." The success of this new order was attested by the chancellor: "I cannot speak too highly of the young men. Taken as a body, they belong to a new race of students, the most hopeful product of these troublous times."[23]

The students began to broaden their interests and to extend their activities. They were now given better opportunities of entertaining *en masse* feminine company. Less than two months after the University had reopened, the students gave an oratorical contest and then "There was promenading, and music, laughing and talking, and, mayhaps, a little love-making, in the spacious

Library of the University." Student theatricals became a continuing interest, and a Students' Tournament Club sprang up in
1868 with its great out-door exhibition. Students on horseback,
gaily dressed in fancy costumes, paraded as various knights
medieval as well as more modern, such as "Knight of the Phi Kappas," "Knight of the Lost Cause," "Knight of the Southern Cross,"
"Knight of the S. A. E." and "Knight of the Chi Phi." They
showed much skill in horsemanship, with young ladies as the
prizes. Outdoor interests were now about to enter into the students' lives, and were to grow and thrive until they threatened
to develop into a Frankenstein. In 1867 three baseball clubs
sprang into existence at the University, the "Franklin," the "University," and the "Adelphian." The craze expressed itself in the
organization of additional clubs at the University, the "Dixie," the
"Champion," and it seemed the business would not end until the
whole body of students would be divided into groups of nine. The
next year some of these clubs became nomadic. One went to
Augusta and in an exciting game defeated its opponents by the
score of 61 runs to 21. The literary activities of the students,
which in ante-bellum times had found expression in the famous
G U M, were resumed in 1870. On February 23rd the first issue of
the *Georgia Collegian* appeared. Religion among the students,
apart from the excitement of camp meetings, was never a dominant
interest, yet by 1870 the Young Men's Christian Association had
made its appearance.[24]

The greatest single interest in the lives of the ante-bellum
Franklin College student, the literary society, was immediately
resumed on the reopening of school. Both Phi Kappas and Demosthenians held their first meetings on January 5th. Secrecy was
still one of their most prized possessions. The attempt of some of
the Phi Kappas to hold an open debate was voted down, and
instead a soirée, to which the Demosthenians were to be invited,
inaugurated the new order. War memories softened the rivalry
of Phi Kappas and Demosthenians to the extent of the two marching arm in arm at the Demosthenian anniversary celebration. The
young ladies at Lucy Cobb Institute and the members of the Par-
thenian Club also participated in the celebration. The war and

the subsequent reconstructing made certain old practices unpleasant and suggested that a house-cleaning would be in order. The Demosthenian constitution required the election of an orator and reader for the Fourth of July celebration, but it did not command the persons so honored to perform. Always with great respect for law and the constitution, the society elected these gentlemen but omitted the celebration. Demosthenians kept close watch on the political developments of their day and felt as outraged as any Athenian at the régime of Loyal Leagues, carpetbaggers, and scalawags. They examined the far-flung roll of their honorary members and passed a resolution expelling any of them who had taken the "iron clad oath" or "voted the abolition ticket." Even Old Sam, who had long been janitor for Demosthenian Hall and had received $1 a month during the interregnum of the Civil War, was accused of having betrayed his trust. He, now known as Freedman Sam, was summoned before the society and quizzed, but the investigation only "succeeded in making him contradict himself." Then they carried his case before the Freedmen's Bureau. Freedman Sam seems to have re-established himself in the confidence of his old friends, but the coming of Negro suffrage in 1867 worked his ruin. The next year the society resolved "to turn off the old freedman servant of the D. Hall, because this negro, basely ungrateful for the numerous favors bestowed upon him by the society during the last twenty years, had voted the radical ticket, and thus declared himself an open enemy to the honor, liberty and life of his benefactors."[25]

There was further evidence that the times were changing. Demosthenians could now put their feet on the rounds of chairs without drawing fines; the societies began (1868) to meet on Friday evenings instead of Saturday mornings; and, most momentous of all, the faculty now (1868) restored to the societies the ancient right of electing junior orators.[26] But all of these changes were ominous signs of coming decadence and dwindling of interest. Instead of needing all day and a night for their exercises, the societies now found they could say what was in their minds in an evening. Decorum was sadly on the wane when feet could be put on chairs with impunity, and now when the societies cared not a great deal about junior orators they were given the right to choose them.

But the practice of electing to honorary membership the outstanding men of the country had not yet ceased, nor had debating vital questions of the day fallen into decay. The Demosthenians crowned with honorary membership Robert E. Lee, who accepted and begged leave "to express thanks to the Society for the compliment," his son General Custis Lee, Zeb B. Vance, the war governor of North Carolina, and General Clement A. Evans, a Georgian. The death of Lincoln, so disastrous for the South, suggested the question as to whether a tyrant's assassination was ever justifiable. The Demosthenians decided in the negative. Directly after the war, when the heart of many Southerners had almost forsaken them and their spirit was subdued, they began to desert their country to try life anew in Mexico and Brazil. The Demosthenians decided the citizens of the late Confederacy should not desert the South "in her present state of affairs." In 1867 they debated the question of Negro suffrage and naturally held it inexpedient, and later with the spectacle of Negro rulers set over them they decided that freeing the slave was not beneficial to the South; yet they held that the Negro should be educated and that the South should encourage his general betterment. With Pope holding registrations of voters for the coming convention in 1867, the Demosthenians decided that the South ought to take no part in the performance. There could be no doubt that the South was thoroughly subdued: The Demosthenians debated in June, 1866, "Would war between the Black Republicans and the Democrats be beneficial?" and decided that it would not. Yet these debaters had not yet come to see that President Johnson was fighting the battles of the South, for they thought Southerners should take no part in Johnson's "Arm-in-arm Convention" at Philadelphia and in February, 1867, that the impeachment of Johnson would be beneficial to the South. In looking over the past four years of war, with a slant on the North, they decided the motto "My country right or wrong" was not right. They also debated, without a decision being recorded, the question, "Is a man justified in disobeying a law of his country, which he feels to be morally wrong?"

In line with their policy of debating the questions uppermost at the time, the Demosthenians started to debate the fifteenth amendment, but on further reflection they decided that such an infamous subject should not be mentioned and they expunged it from their minutes.[27]

In 1866 there crept onto the campus, unobserved, an organization to dispute with Phi Kappa and Demosthenian the affection of the students. All that was known about it was the fact that it displayed the three Greek letters, Sigma Alpha Epsilon; the next year it was followed by another intrusion bearing the letters Chi Phi. Then in 1869 Kappa Alpha appeared, and in 1871 Phi Delta Theta. The University of North Carolina had been beset by such interlopers before the Civil War, but they had died out during the struggle. These organizations were of a literary character and hence were definite and conscious rivals of the old literary societies. In 1870, at the national convention of Sigma Alpha Epsilon in Memphis, the representatives from the University of Georgia, W. D. Trammell and J. B. Smith, won the prizes for the best essay and the best poem, respectively. In 1868 members of these Greek letter fraternities who were also members of Phi Kappa and of Demosthenian sought to disrupt these historic organizations under the pretense of withdrawing to form a new club in which they would have a better chance for debating. Permission for their withdrawal was refused. The appearance of these secret fraternities developed devastating rifts and seams in the solidarity of University students. These groups immediately sought to seize every emolument worth having, and the methods they employed have been left as a heritage of disgraceful and dishonest practices, often referred to as "student politics." These "secret societies," as they were called, soon got control of the *Georgia Collegian,* and finding that they could not disrupt old Phi Kappa and Demosthenian they sought to seize their control. In 1870 an outraged student declared that the campus was now divided into three class: "1st, Secret Societies, who wear badges different from the Literarv Societies; who meet at night in some dark alley, or out house and whose object is known only to themselves. 2nd, Boot Lickers, who are supposed to be hugging and

squeezing the Secret Society men for admission into their organizations. 3d, Anti-Secret Society, who oppose Secret Societies inasmuch as we believe that they unavoidably tend to partisan advance-
ment, regardless of actual merit; that they introduce distrust
and enmity, discord and strife where no such feeling should exist;
and that they are instruments of oppression to the other students."
When he first came to the University he entered into an inspiring
and unified fellowship, but "we have stood and seen those good
old times, which we sigh for again, pass away, and others come
bringing with them changes which render college life disgusting,
and in many instances injurious both to the heart and the mind."
They had introduced such disgraceful methods that when "we have
an election now-a-days you will be asked a dozen times for the
loan of your bowie-knife or revolver." Later the trustees banished
"these purveyors of iniquity and disturbers of the peace" and for
about seven years the campus went about its way undisturbed.[28]

Just as Phi Kappa and Demosthenian had been set on the wane
by the dissipation of student interests into the new intruding fields
of athletics and fraternities with all their attendant distractions, so,
too, that oustanding occasion of all the year, commencement, was
soon to fall on evil days. The first commencement after the reopening of the University was held on July 4, 1866 (perhaps this
day in order to push the "Glorious Fourth" off the calendar), and
a bold effort was made to restore the glamour of ante-bellum
times. There were the distinguished gentlemen and beautiful
ladies—and hours of declaiming, orating, and debating. The war
just past had little effect on the program. Spartacus addressed the
slaves with all the fiery zeal of yore; Regulus harangued the Roman
Senate with great passion; Warren Hastings still defended himself
from the impeachment charges, and Lucifer again addressed Adam.
There was one element in the commencement crowd, out of harmony with the old. Instead of respectful slaves grinning and
bowing under the campus trees, a swarm of noisy Negroes, now
determining with the aid of Federal soldiers to put to practical
use their newly-won freedom, flocked into the chapel. The sheriff
drove them out onto the campus, where they remained undisturbed.
The next year they were warned to stay off the campus entirely.

Only the colored band which made the music was given the freedom of the University, deserving and receiving "the praise of all, for their general good conduct." In 1867 the commencement was changed back to its ante-bellum position on the calendar—the first week in August—a time dictated, some said, by the ladies of Athens, who found in August better peaches and watermelons with which to regale their guests. Confederate generals and statesmen attended the commencements to lend glamour to the occasion, and now and then some student orator fired the crowd as did Albert H. Cox at the commencement in 1867, previously described. In 1870 Nat E. Harris gave one of the senior orations and received this prophetic notice in the *Southern Watchman*, "While all were highly creditable, that of Mr. N. E. Harris, of Tennessee, was generally considered the best. He gives promise of a brilliant future career." The number of graduates at each commencement continued to mount higher. Forty-four received degrees in 1869—the largest number in the history of the University up to that time. The crowd in attendance was the largest "since the surrender," but much smaller than in ante-bellum times. As an attraction, commencement was being outgrown. The lives of the people generally were becoming more crowded with other interests, and no longer did people have to go to a Georgia commencement for excitement or to get into a big crowd. Even the half-fare rates allowed by the Georgia Railroad could not restore the crowds that swarmed to an ante-bellum Georgia commencement.[29]

A new South was undoubtedly approaching; the Old South was dying, though with great agony. There was a new leaven working in the University. Old Franklin College had been only a college, and not a university. Its students had been treated as irresponsible boys, and not as men. It had performed a great service honorably and well, but the new needs of the South demanded more than a small classical college could afford. Many more students were coming than had ever attended old Franklin College at one time. At the end of the school year, 1867-1868, there were 350 students, including the 132 in "Rock College," the preparatory department. At this time Chancellor Lipscomb said, "The year now closing, has been marked by an unusual degree of prosperity. So far as I can see, this prosperity is solid and substantial, indicating a still greater enlargement of the energy and enterprise of the University." Chancellor Lipscomb was a learned man with a broad vision for the future, and in the words of an admirer, "unrivaled for his eloquence, taste and largeness of heart, distinguished in the literary world as a writer and critic." In order to make a real university he would make many changes and additions. Believing the dormitory system to be "the most unmitigated evil connected with college-life," he changed Old College and New College into "Students' Homes," run by families "to give domestic accommodations" and "to afford the advantages of household life." He would have the lecture system used in the classes, and various new schools set up. He would have new and more practical courses introduced into Franklin College. In his report to the trustees in 1869 he said, "We are still cramped by old restrictions, by traditional usages, by fixed boundaries that once acted as limitary lines but now operate as formidable barriers to an intelligent and healthy progress.

"The remnants of the old monastic scheme of education yet exist,—a scheme that denies the name of an educated gentleman to one who happens to prefer the Modern Languages or the physical sciences to the Ancient Classics,—a scheme that sets up an aristocracy of pretensions to culture."[30]

He would have an elective system of courses and not be bound down as a slave to precedent and conformity. As for these short, and narrow-sighted persons, "Like other fashions and their tyrannical prescriptions, the virtue of conformity is the motive that determines their conduct." William L. Broun, who had taken part in the LeConte upheaval in the 'fifties and had left the University, was now back as professor of natural philosophy, with his demand for reform unabated. He ably supported Chancellor Lipscomb. He advocated an elective system and called for higher standards of work. He declared that a college student gets his diploma "though he may be unable to solve a single equation in algebra; unable to translate into correct English an ordinary sentence of Latin or Greek, unable to read the very diploma which declares his proficiency." He bitterly condemned the farcical practice of awarding the Master of Arts degree three years after the Bachelor of Arts to those who applied for it, with a statement that their morality had not suffered since graduation. Broun said this degree was "an award of ignorance, inasmuch as three years of forgetfulness are required for its bestowal." The Demosthenian Society took up the question of transforming Franklin College into a real university and recorded their decision in favor of the change. By 1869 most of the reforms advocated by the Chancellor had been secured. The University was now organized into six departments or schools: The University High School ("Rock College"), Franklin College, Elective Department (leading to the B. S. degree), the School of Agriculture, the School of Civil Engineering, and the Lumpkin Law School. The following degrees were now offered: A.B., B.S., C.E., B.L., and A.M. The Master of Arts degree was conferred only on those who should complete a prescribed course of study, except that it was honorarily bestowed in special cases of distinction. While reorganizing was uppermost, the United States Government tried to introduce military training into the University, but Chancellor Lipscomb, skeptical of mixing military training with other subjects, rejected his government's generosity. The elective principle was extended to the junior and senior classes.[31]

Other signs were fast piling up to show that the new day was breaking fast. In 1867 morning prayers were abolished for Saturdays and Sundays, and two years later the before-breakfast prayers and classes were left out entirely. In the same year oral examinations for seniors were abolished and written ones were substituted. In 1871 Chancellor Lipscomb said, "I begin to see better days for the University." He would have the alumni become better organized and become more closely identified with the University. He thought they should be given a part in governing the University—to have the right to nominate professors to the trustees and to have some voice even in the election of trustees. Benjamin H. Hill at the same time in a speech he made in the chapel heralded the passing of the Old South and the coming of the New South. He laid down three propositions: "1. That the civilization peculiar to the southern States hitherto has passed away, and forever. 2. That no new civilization can be equal to the demands of the age which does not lay its foundations in the intelligence of the people, and in the multiplication and social elevation of educated industries. 3. That no system of education for the people, and for the multiplication and elevation of industries, can be complete or efficient, or available, which does not begin with an ample, well endowed and independent university." To the good counsel of the older generation was added the assent of the new. The Demosthenians debated the once theoretical subject recently given a practical test, whether the pen was mightier than the sword, and decided that the latter had won. In 1870 they also significantly decided that the New South was better than the Old. They, too, would give up "the dusky Helen" and repeat, "Pity we kept the harlot so long!"[32]

The Old South was now gone with the crudities and the charm and the romance that went with plantations. The peculiar character of the college town with its gentlemen of leisure was also fading away; and the college life that had had few distractions from interests beyond the campus was now fast being changed by varied activities that gave a broader outlook, but, perhaps, less depth of learning. The great gulf had been crossed at a terrific sacrifice and the New South lay ahead.

NOTES

Numbers in brackets at the top of the following pages indicate the pages in the text to which these notes refer.

CHAPTER ONE

1. Minutes of the Senatus Academicus, 1799-1842, pp. 1-7. These minutes, in manuscript, are in the University of Georgia Library.
2. *Ibid.*, 14. See also Minutes of the Trustees, 1786-1817, pp. 32, 33. These manuscript minutes are in the University of Georgia Library.
3. S. A. Minutes, 1799-1842, pp. 25, 26. See also *Augusta Herald,* April 15, 1801.
4. Robert and George Watkins, eds., *A Digest of the laws of the State of Georgia from its first establishment as a British Province down to the year 1798 inclusive, and the Principal Acts of 1799* (Philadelphia, 1800), 320. Act of Jan. 26, 1786.
5. George P. Fisher in *A Discourse Commemorative of the History of the Church of Christ in Yale College, during the first century of its Existence* (New Haven, 1858), says that Baldwin came to Georgia in 1781 to assume the presidency of the University. The date of his coming is incorrect and, of course, he could not become president of an institution not yet chartered. See H. C. White, *Abraham Baldwin . . .* (Athens, 1926). For some of the Yale graduates who had come to Georgia, see F. B. Dexter, ed., *The Literary Diary of Ezra Stiles, D.D., LL.D., President of Yale College* (New York, 1901), III, 153.
6. R. M. Johnston, "Early Educational Life in Middle Georgia" in *Report of Commissioner of Education, 1895-96* (Washington, 1897), I, 875.
7. Watkins, eds., *Digest,* 290-95; *The Manual of the University of Georgia* (Atlanta, 1890), 17, 18; Allen D. Candler, ed., *Colonial Records of the State of Georgia* (Atlanta, 1911), XIX, Part II, 300.
8. Johnston in *Report of Commissioner of Education, 1895-96.*
9. *American Almanac and Repository of Useful Knowledge, 1834* (Boston, 1834), 211; E. E. Slosson, *The American Spirit in Education* (New Haven, 1921), 78-84.
10. Stiles, *Diary,* III, 118, 127. The Georgia charter bears no resemblance to the Yale charter either in word or meaning except in the manner provided for calling special meetings of the trustees, and here the evidence is unmistakable that Baldwin had Yale's charter at hand. But it is not surprising that Georgia should not make Yale's charter her pattern, as this document had been granted in 1745 under the King and had no connection with the educational philosophy of the later eighteenth century. For Yale's charter, see *Acts of the General Assembly of Connecticut with other Permanent Documents respecting Yale University* (New Haven, 1901), 9-13.
11. "He originated the plan of the *University of Georgia,* drew up the charter, and with infinite labor and patience, in vanquishing all sorts of prejudices and removing every obstruction, he persuaded the assembly to adopt it." *National Intelligencer* quoted in *Augusta Chronicle,* April 4, 1807. See also *Georgia Historical Quarterly,* X, 4 (Dec., 1926), 326-34.
12. Act of December 5, 1800. MS in University of Georgia Library. The composition and duties of the visitors were later changed again. This body still exists to the present day, without vitality and without reason. [It was abolished with the reorganization of the University in 1931.]
13. P. L. Ford, ed., *Works of Thomas Jefferson* (New York, 1904), IV, 60-65.
14. W. T. Foster, *Administration of the College Curriculum* (Boston, 1911), 39-40. Quesnay de Beauregard was the grandson of Quesnay, the Physiocrat.
15. *American Almanac, 1834,* pp. 218, 219.
16. Watkins, eds., *Digest,* 323; T. Minutes, 1786-1817, pp. 4-8, 18-21; Stiles, *Diary,* III, 296, 543.
17. T. Minutes, 1786-1817, pp. 1-11; A. L. Hull, *A Historical Sketch of the University*

of Georgia (Atlanta, 1894), 10.

18. *Augusta Chronicle,* Nov. 18, 1799; T. Minutes, 1786-1817, pp. 17, 18.

19. Act of December 5, 1800. MS copy in University of Georgia Library.

20. *Augusta Chronicle,* Aug. 8, 1801.

21. Watkins, eds., *Digest,* 575, 576.

22. *Augusta Chronicle,* July 25, 1801; George White, *Historical Collections of Georgia* . . . (New York, 1854), 223, 224.

23. *Georgia Historical Quarterly,* X, 4 (Dec., 1926), 326-34.

24. Ford, ed., *Works of Jefferson,* IX, 96. Jan. 18, 1800.

25. Stiles, *Diary,* III, 127. Stiles was mildly understating the situation.

26. Watkins, eds., *Digest,* 345. Aug. 14. For a convenient source of information about population, see *A Century of Population Growth* (Department of Commerce and Labor. Bureau of the Census), 7, 9, 18.

27. Watkins, eds., *Digest,* 356, 357. Feb. 10.

28. A. O. Hansen, *Liberalism and American Education in the Eighteenth Century* (New York, 1926), 1-43.

29. Stiles, *Diary,* III, 153.

30. *Augusta Chronicle,* Nov. 28, 1801, Dec. 14, 1802.

31. *Ibid.,* July 25, 1801.

32. Wm. M. Meigs, *Life of Josiah Meigs* (Philadelphia, 1887), 11, 16; T. Minutes, 1786-1817, pp. 32, 33, 35, 36; S. A. Minutes, 1799-1842, pp. 22, 23; James Jackson to Baldwin, Nov. 26, 1800, Baldwin MSS (in University of Georgia Library).

33. S. A. Minutes, 1799-1842, p. 14; T. Minutes, 1786-1817, p. 34.

34. Meigs, *Josiah Meigs,* 10.

35. T. Minutes, 1786-1817, p. 98; *Augusta Chronicle,* July 14, 1798; W. Few to Baldwin, Nov. 21, 1799, in Baldwin MSS.

36. S. A. Minutes, 1799-1842, p. 19; *Augusta Chronicle,* Nov. 8, 1800.

37. T. Minutes, 1786-1817, pp. 50, 51.

38. Oliver H. Prince, comp., *Digest of the Laws of the State of Georgia . . . to 1837* (Second Edition, Athens, 1837), 869; S. A. Minutes, 1799-1842, p. 31.

39. A. S. Clayton, comp., *A Compilation of the Laws of the State of Georgia, 1800-1810* (Augusta, 1812), 142; Prince, comp., *Digest,* 869; S. A. Minutes, 1799-1842, pp. 56, 57.

40. T. Minutes, 1786-1817, pp. 44, 57-60; Meigs, *Josiah Meigs,* 45, 47; *Augusta Chronicle,* Oct. 17, 1801.

41. T. Minutes, 1786-1817, pp. 101, 104, 200; Meigs, *Josiah Meigs,* 13; *Augusta Chronicle,* Feb. 1, 1806. For the next fifty years the University came to be familiarly and affectionately called Franklin College. Its name was never officially changed, though in the records Franklin College and the University of Georgia were used interchangeably. For a fuller discussion see E. M. Coulter, "Franklin College as a Name for the University of Georgia," in *Georgia Historical Quarterly,* XXXIV, 3 (September, 1950), 189-94.

CHAPTER TWO

1. T. Minutes, 1786-1817, pp. 46, 56; S. A. Minutes, 1799-1842, pp. 26, 27.

2. For a discussion of academies see E. M. Coulter, "The Ante-Bellum Academy Movement in Georgia" in *Georgia Historical Quarterly,* V, 4 (Dec., 1921), 11-42.

3. *Athens Gazette,* July 6, 1815; T. Minutes, 1786-1817, pp. 74, 89.

4. T. Minutes, 1786-1817, p. 69.

5. Meigs Letter, Oct. 27, 1803. In University of Georgia Library.

6. S. A. Minutes, 1799-1842, pp. 63, 64.

7. *Ibid.,* 16, 17, 95, 113, 114. The curriculum was changed often in minor details.

Soon more English was required.

8. S. A. Minutes, 1799-1842, pp. 39, 40.

9. Meigs, *Josiah Meigs*, 125.

10. A. L. Hull, *University of Georgia*, 15; S. A. Minutes, 1799-1842, pp. 16, 17.

11. Meigs Letter, Oct. 27, 1803.

12. *Georgia Express*, Mar. 31, 1810; *Augusta Chronicle*, Feb. 1, 1806.

13. Meigs, *Josiah Meigs*, 80.

14. S. A. Minutes, 1799-1842, p. 39; T. Minutes, 1786-1817, p. 99; *Augusta Chronicle*, June 23, 1804, Feb. 1, 1808; *Southern Watchman*, April 20, 1870; *Report of Commissioner of Education, 1895-96*, p. 678.

15. Joel Barlow, *The Columbiad, A Poem* (1807). The volume is in the University of Georgia Library.

16. T. Minutes, 1786-1817, p. 154; Meigs, *Josiah Meigs*, 73.

17. Meigs, *Josiah Meigs*, 39, 42, 43.

18. Meigs Letter, Oct. 27, 1803.

19. *Augusta Chronicle*, Aug. 4, 1805.

20. S. Boykin, *History of the Baptist Denomination in Georgia* (Atlanta, 1881), 56-60.

21. S. A. Minutes, 1799-1842, pp. 76-79; T. Minutes, 1786-1817, pp. 134, 141-43, 152; *Southern Watchman*, July 13, 1870.

22. Meigs, *Josiah Meigs*, 56, 57.

23. S. A. Minutes, 1799-1842, pp. 83, 84.

24. *Georgia Express*, July 7, 1810.

25. Meigs Letter, Oct. 27, 1803.

26. S. A. Minutes, 1799-1842, pp. 89, 90; T. Minutes, 1786-1817, pp. 170, 176, 180-87, 188; Meigs, *Josiah Meigs*, 52, 54; *Georgia Express*, Aug. 11, 1810; A. L. Hull, *Annals of Athens, Georgia, 1801-1901* (Athens, 1906), 88-93. Meigs left Georgia and later received through Jefferson's influence an appointment to the land office in Cincinnati. Two years later he received the appointment of commissioner of the general land office and removed to Washington where he died in 1822. His daughter married John Forsyth, who later became a member of Van Buren's cabinet. His grandson, M. C. Meigs, was quartermaster general for the United States armies during the Civil War.

27. T. Minutes, 1786-1817, p. 190.

28. S. A. Minutes, 1799-1842, pp. 89, 90; T. Minutes, 1786-1817, p. 79; *Athenian*, April 18, 1828; Hull, *University of Georgia*, 37.

29. Henry Jackson MSS (In Library of University of Georgia); T. Minutes, 1786-1817, p. 181; *Georgia Express*, Jan. 1813; Hull, *Annals of Athens*, 26.

30. S. A. Minutes, 1799-1842, p. 108; T. Minutes, 1786-1817, pp. 228, 243, 245.

31. S. A. Minutes, 1799-1842, p. 102; T. Minutes, 1786-1817, pp. 132, 228; Prince, comp., *Digest*, 870, 871.

32. *Athenian*, Dec. 15, 1829; Prince, comp., *Digest*, 872.

33. S. A. Minutes, 1799-1842, pp. 57, 64-66; T. Minutes, 1786-1817, pp. 97, 98; *Augusta Chronicle*, July 6, 1805.

34. Isaac V. Brown, *Memoirs of the Rev. Robert Finley, D.D., Late Pastor of the Presbyterian Congregation at Basking Ridge New-Jersey and President of Franklin College, Located at Athens, in the State of Georgia, with Brief Sketches of some of his Contemporaries and Numerous Notes* (New Brunswick, 1819), 138; T. Minutes, 1786-1817, pp. 139, 140.

35. T. Minutes, 1786-1817, pp. 250, 251; Clayton, comp., *Digest*, 457.

36. T. Minutes, 1786-1817, pp. 254, 255, 257, 261; Brown, *Memoirs of Finley*, 111.

37. Brown, *Memoirs of Finley*, 110, 111, 113, 116, 117, 124, 125.

38. Joseph Bevan to Jackson, Dec. 14, 1817 in Henry Jackson MSS; T. Minutes, 1786-1817, pp. 68, 71, 90; *Augusta Chronicle*, Feb. 1, 1806; *Athens Gazette*, March 23, 1815; *A Compilation of the Acts of the Legislature incorporating the*

Town of Athens, Georgia: and a Revision and Consolidation of the Ordinance passed by the Town Council of Athens to the Eleventh of September, 1867 (Athens, 1867), 3; Meigs, *Josiah Meigs*, 46.

39. *Ibid.*, 49.

40. Meigs, *Josiah Meigs*, 72, 73; Hull, *Annals of Athens*, 36.

41. *Georgia Express*, Aug. 21, 1812; *Southern Banner*, Aug. 21, 1851; Hull, *Annals of Athens*, 69-74; Waddel Diary, p. 69 (Oct. 17, 1825). This MS is in the Library of Congress. Moses Waddel with his characteristic minuteness wrote in his diary, Oct. 17, 1825, "saw Indians shooting arrows." Almost a year later he saw them again, and so noted it. *Ibid.*, 89.

42. *Georgia Express*, May 19, 1810, July 9, 1813; *Southern Watchman*, Aug. 10, 20, 1870; Meigs, *Josiah Meigs*, 51.

43. She prohibited it in her constitution of 1798—ten years before she needed to give it up.

44. *Georgia Journal*, June 1, 1819.

45. Waddel Diary, 11 (Oct. 21, 1824); *Georgia Journal*, Sept. 7, 1819.

46. Brown, *Memoirs of Finley*, 75-104, 107.

47. *Ibid.*, 132. July 16, 1817.

48. *Ibid.*, 127-29.

49. *Athens Gazette*, Feb. 1, 1816.

50. *Universal Geography*, 252. By the 'forties many people in the South had come to see that this false philosophy that no gentleman could labor with his hands had done more to retard the progress of the South than all the tariffs combined. See *Southern Whig*, May 31, 1849.

51. T. Minutes, 1786-1817, p. 263; Brown, *Memoirs of Finley*, 126, 128, 129, 142.

52. Brown, *Memoirs of Finley*, 36.

53. *Ibid.*, 120, 121, 131, 132, 140, 141.

54. *Ibid.*, 138-40, 143-51.

55. S. A. Minutes, 1799-1842, pp. 131, 132; Minutes of Trustees, 1818-1834, pp. 1, 2; Brown, *Memoirs of Finley*, 151, 152, 154.

CHAPTER THREE

1. S. A. Minutes, 1799-1842, pp. 133, 134; T. Minutes, 1818-1834, p. 4; Jackson MSS; *Georgia Journal*, Nov. 17, 1818; Brown, *Memoirs of Finley*, 153.

2. S. A. Minutes, 1799-1842, p. 138; Jackson MSS.

3. T. Minutes, 1858-1877, p. 40; Clayton, comp., *Digest*, 456, 457. The composition of the membership of the Senatus Academicus varied; but it was always made up of the two bodies designated the Board of Trustees and the Board of Visitors. The method of composing the Board of Trustees varied from self-perpetuation to enlargements and reductions by the legislature. The Board of Visitors passed through several changes. The University Charter does not indicate the method of their appointment, but after an upper house of the legislature was provided by the Constitution of 1789 the senators became the Board of Visitors. But by the law of December 22, 1808, the senators were relieved of this duty and this Board was now to be composed of the governor, the judges of the superior courts, the president of the senate, and the speaker of the house. In 1811 the senators replaced the judges on this Board, except for the senator residing in the county from which the speaker of the house came. This arrangement continued to the end. In 1831 the Senatus Academicus created a special board of visitors, which it appointed annually, to attend examinations. This board should not be confused with the Board of Visitors which was a part of the Senatus Academicus.

4. T. Minutes, 1818-1834, p. 214; *ibid.*, 1835-1851, p. 188; Prince, comp., *Digest*,

871-874; Hull, *University of Georgia*, 17, 22. The prudential committee was established in 1803.

5. S. A. Minutes, 1799-1842, pp. 36, 37, 49, 113; R. M. Johnston and W. H. Browne, *Life of Alexander H. Stephens* (Philadelphia, 1878), 54; F. Minutes, 1822-1836, p. 4.

6. T. Minutes, 1818-1834, p. 73; *ibid.*, 1835-1857, pp. 5, 72, 73. Various ages were fixed as time went on.

7. S. A. Minutes, 1799-1842, p. 165; T. Minutes, 1818-1834, p. 204; Waddel Diary, 1825, p. 69; *ibid.*, 1828-1829, Oct. 11, 1828; Prince, comp., *Digest*, 872; *Georgia Journal*, Nov. 20, 1821; Hull, *Annals of Athens*, 23.

8. S. A. Minutes, 1799-1842, p. 180; T. Minutes, 1818-1834, p. 336; *ibid.*, 1835-1857, p. 195.

9. *Athenian*, Sept. 14, 1830; *Georgia Journal*, Nov. 2, 1824; Hull, *Annals of Athens*, 374, 375; T. Minutes, 1818-1834, p. 275; *ibid.*, 1835-1857, p. 3; F. Minutes, 1822-1836, p. 191. The missionaries seem to have been responsible for the Greek students in America at this time. *Evangelical and Literary Magazine*, VII, 5 (May, 1824), 266, 267. For an argument favoring the classical languages, see *ibid.*, I, 5 (May, 1818), 193-99.

10. S. A. Minutes, 1799-1842, pp. 252-54. This led to the copying of many of the colonial documents in London, which were brought back to the state.

11. T. Minutes, 1858-1877, p. 42.

12. T. Minutes, 1835-1857, p. 132; *Southern Banner*, Oct. 30, 1840. The Constitution of 1798 did not provide for a supreme court.

13. S. A. Minutes, 1799-1842, p. 255; T. Minutes, 1818-1834, p. 3; *ibid.*, 1835-1857, p. 305-09, 332.

14. S. A. Minutes, 1799-1842, pp. 63, 70, 101; T. Minutes, 1786-1817, pp. 32, 33, 69, 126; Prince, comp., *Digest*, 869; *Georgia Express*, Nov. 18, 1812; *Georgia Journal*, July 14, 1818; Hull, *University of Georgia*, 21.

15. T. Minutes, 1818-1834, pp. 54, 56, 295; *ibid.*, 1835-1857, p. 48; *University of Georgia Catalogue, 1860-1861*, p. 21; *American Almanac, 1841-1842*, pp. 150-53.

16. S. A. Minutes, 1799-1842, p. 45; T. Minutes, 1818-1834, pp. 67, 90-100; *Code of Laws for the Government of Franklin College . . . 1853* (Athens, 1854), 9; *Augusta Chronicle*, June 23, 1804.

17. T. Minutes, 1818-1834, p. 221; *Augusta Chronicle*, June 23, 1804; *Southern Banner*, Mar. 8, 1834; Hull, *University of Georgia*, 55. The University of North Carolina was the first college in America to set up a telescope.

18. *Georgia Historical Quarterly*, X, 4 (Dec., 1926), 326-34.

19. *The Southern Whig* (Athens), May 4, 1848, copied an account from the *New York Express*.

20. The willow still stands weeping over the departed glories of this garden.

21. T. Minutes, 1818-1834, pp. 296, 297; *ibid.*, 1835-1857, pp. 16, 17, 104; *Athenian*, Aug. 9, 1831; *Southern Whig*, May 4, 1848; Hull, *University of Georgia*, 50.

22. T. Minutes, 1835-1857, pp. 289-91.

23. *Ibid.*, pp. 121, 122, 139, 140, 382, 385. The area once covered by the garden is now given over to Negro slums. Some of the shrubs and trees were transplanted to to the University campus.

24. Clayton, comp., *Digest*, 408-22. Dec. 10.

25. Clayton, comp., *Digest*, 414, 415; Prince, comp., *Digest*, 587; Hull, *Annals of Athens*, 65-69; A. B. Longstreet, *Georgia Scenes . . .* (reprint of 1894), 160-67. Though Longstreet included "The Militia Company Drill" in his *Georgia Scenes*, he stated that he did not write it. See John Donald Wade, *Augustus Baldwin Longstreet . . .* (New York, 1924), 178-80.

26. Phi Kappa Minutes, 1835-1853, May 14, 1837; Waddel Diary, 54 (July 4, 1825), 66 (Sept. 27, 1825); *Athenian*, May 18, 1827, July 7, 1829; *Savannah Georgian*, Aug. 13, 1829; Hull, *Annals of Athens*, 132, 133.

27. T. Minutes, 1835-1857, pp. 24, 25; P. K. Minutes, 1835-1853, Mar. 12, 1836; *Georgia Express,* July 10, 1812.

28. T. Minutes, 1818-1834, p. 102; F. Minutes, 1822-1836, p. 59.

29. S. A. Minutes, 1799-1842, pp. 171, 247; T. Minutes, 1835-1857, pp. 7, 26, 31, 57.

30. T. Minutes, 1835-1857, p. 92; P. K. Minutes, 1826-1829, Sept. 9, 1826; *ibid.,* 1835-1853, 1836.

31. T. Minutes, 1786-1817, p. 127 ff.; F. Minutes, 1850-1873, p. 185; S. A. Minutes, 1799-1842, p. 119.

32. S. A. Minutes, 1799-1842, pp. 114, 115; F. Minutes, 1822-1836, p. 30; John N. Waddel, *Memorials of Academic Life: Being an Historical Sketch of the Waddel Family* (Richmond, 1891), 178.

33. S. A. Minutes, 1799-1842, pp. 40, 121, 126, 127; F. Minutes, 1822-1836, p. 172; *Athenian,* Mar. 23, 1830.

34. S. A. Minutes, 1799-1842, pp. 114, 115; F. Minutes, 1822-1836, pp. 27, 28, 116.

35. This was later changed so that the first term began immediately following commencement.

36. S. A. Minutes, 1799-1842, pp. 41, 46, 74, 118, 119, 124, 125; T. Minutes, 1818-1834, p. 179; *ibid.,* 1835-1857, p. 321; *Southern Banner,* Aug. 10, 1854; *University Catalogue, 1860-1861;* F. Minutes, 1850-1873, p. 166.

37. S. A. Minutes, 1799-1842, p. 119; P. K. Minutes, 1835-1853, Mar. 31, 1838; *Georgia University Magazine,* XII, 1 (April, 1857), p. 30; *Autobiography of Joseph LeConte* (New York, 1903), 105. This ambitious city, first known as Terminus and then Marthasville, and finally Atlanta, was the happy accident of two railroads meeting on the Chattahoochee in 1845, preparatory to their extension by the State of Georgia on to Chattanooga. This link was called the Western and Atlantic and was part of the scheme of the Southeast to capture the Middle Western trade.

38. P. H. Mell, *Life of Patrick Hues Mell* (Louisville, 1895), 126, 127.

39. *Athenian,* July 6, 1830; *Georgia University Magazine,* VII, 5 (Aug., 1854), 253; *ibid.,* VIII (April, 1855), 39, 40; *Life and Letters of Stephen Olin, D.D., LL.D.* (New York, 1853), I, 133.

40. S. A. Minutes, 1799-1842, pp. 42, 96; Report Form, 1830.

41. Brown was at this time a superior court judge and was now entering on a career which made him the wartime governor and a stormy figure during Reconstruction.
    Cobb was a prominent lawyer in Athens and was destined to play a decisive part in inducing the state to secede in 1861. He became a general in the Civil War and was killed at the Battle of Fredericksburg.
    Jones was a clergyman interested much in the religious welfare of the slaves and was often called the "missionary of the blacks." He was the father of C. C. Jones, the historian.

42. S. A. Minutes, 1799-1842, pp. 41, 86, 120, 233; T. Minutes, 1786-1817, p. 197; *ibid.,* 1835-1857, p. 200; *Catalogue of Franklin College, 1834,* p. 15; Waddel Diary, 1825, p. 58; *University of Georgia Magazine,* VIII (June, 1855), 119, 120; Prince, comp., *Digest,* 877; *Athenian,* June 24, 1828; *Southern Banner* June 21, 28, 1834; *Federal Union,* July 15, 1856; *Savannah Georgian,* Aug. 22, 1829; William Starr Basinger, MSS, I, 102. The original Board of Visitors, set up in the Charter, continued throughout the life of the Senatus Academicus, as the Senatus Academicus was merely the Board of Visitors and the Board of Trustees meeting as one body. The Board of Visitors which attended examinations was a special group appointed annually by the Senatus Academicus.

43. S. A. Minutes, 1799-1842, p. 124; T. Minutes, 1786-1817, pp. 157, 257.

44. S. A. Minutes, 1799-1842, p. 45; T. Minutes, 1818-1834, p. 45.

45. T. Minutes, 1818-1834, p. 89; *ibid.,* 1835-1857, pp. 64, 65, 286, 316.

46. S. A. Minutes, 1799-1842, pp. 42, 43; T. Minutes, 1818-1834, p. 185; Report Form, April 1, 1833.

47. S. A. Minutes, 1799-1842, pp. 43, 46, 125; T. Minutes, 1818-1834, pp. 124, 186;

Catalogue . . . of the University of Georgia, 1860-1861. In 1807, board was $75 for the year. T. Minutes, 1786-1817, p. 130. The services which the Negro janitor performed for the students led to the erroneous tradition that each student brought to college his own personal slave. Lending strength to this tradition was the presence in Old College of a small bedroom attached to each student's room, where the slave was said to have lived. When Old College was made into an administrative building in the 1940's, these rooms disappeared in the renovation of the interior.

48. T. Minutes, 1818-1834, p. 107; F. Minutes, 1822-1836, p. 124; *Athenian,* Aug. 11, 1829; *Georgia Journal,* July 9, Nov. 19, 1822; *Savannah Georgian,* Aug. 18, 1829; John N. Waddel, *Memorials,* 107.

49. S. A. Minutes, 1799-1842, pp. 155-59, 163, 170.

50. Waddel Diary, July 10, 1822, Oct. 28, 1822; *ibid.,* 1824-1825, pp. 5, 6, 12, 15, 22, 44-46, 57, 64, 96.

51. S. A. Minutes, 1799-1842, p. 15; Waddel Diary, 1824-1825, pp. 2, 43; John N. Waddel, *Memorials,* 114; William B. Sprague, *Annals of the American Pulpit* (New York, 1858), IV, 63-71; T. Minutes, 1818-1834, pp. 205-07.

CHAPTER FOUR

1. S. A. Minutes, 1799-1842, pp. 33, 36, 37, 49, 112-28, 159, 187, 241.

2. *Ibid.,* 40-44, 85, 122, 123; F. Minutes, 1822-1836, pp. 41, 42; T. Minutes, 1818-1834, p. 154; *Code of Laws, 1853,* p. 12.

3. S. A. Minutes, 1799-1842, pp. 34, 35, 38, 39, 44, 85, 94, 95, 116, 122, 146; T. Minutes, 1818-1834, p. 68; F. Minutes, 1822-1836, pp. 17, 62; *University Catalogue, 1860-1;* Report Form, 1830.

4. S. A. Minutes, 1799-1842, pp. 38, 96, 147; T. Minutes, 1818-1834, pp. 147, 152; *ibid.,* 1835-1857, pp. 125, 180, 181; F. Minutes, 1850-1873, pp. 68-71, 80; P. C. Minutes, 1834-1857, p. 73; *Code of Laws, 1853,* p. 3; Report Form, 1830; G. A. Young to Jackson, Sept. 16, 1822, in Henry Jackson MSS; *Autobiography of Col. Richard M. Johnston* (Washington, 1901), 48; *Athenian,* April 12, 1831; W. D. Sullivan Letter; C. S. Hardee Letter.

5. *Georgia University Magazine,* VIII, 3 (June, 1855), 118, 119; Brown, *Memoirs of Finley,* 115, 116.

6. Johnston and Browne, *Alexander H. Stephens,* 53-57; James D. Waddell, *Biographical Sketch of Linton Stephens* (Atlanta, 1877), 11.

7. Johnston and Browne, *Alexander H. Stephens,* 60, 61; John N. Waddel, *Memorials,* 80; Hull, *University of Georgia,* 51; S. F. Tenney Letter.

8. James D. Waddell, *Linton Stephens,* 35; *Autobiography of Joseph LeConte* 48, 49.

9. F. Minutes, 1822-1836, pp. 20-22; T. Minutes, 1818-1842, p. 194; Waddel Diary, April 20, 1824, Feb. 4, 1829; Hardee Letter; Hull, *University of Georgia,* 60.

10. F. Minutes, 1822-1836, pp. 57, 80-90, 129, 174; Johnston and Browne, *Alexander H. Stephens,* 61; J. D. Waddell, *Linton Stephens,* 15; Hull, *University of Georgia,* 43.

11. F. Minutes, 1822-1836, Oct. 1, 1822; *ibid.,* 1850-1873, pp. 9, 160; Hull, *University of Georgia,* 134; *Athens Gazette,* May 8, 1817.

12. F. Minutes, 1822-1836, pp. 220, 221; *ibid.,* 1850-1873, pp. 31, 57, 58, 122, 123; Waddel Diary, Nov. 17, 1824; John N. Waddel, *Memorials,* 104, 105; Sullivan Letter; Hull, *University of Georgia,* 134; Sprague, *Annals of the American Pulpit,* IV, 70; Kemp P. Battle, *History of the University of North Carolina* (Raleigh, 1907); E. L. Green, *History of the University of South Carolina* (Columbia, 1916).

13. F. Minutes, 1822-1836, pp. 185-90.

14. T. Minutes, 1835-1857, pp. 85-91; P. C. Minutes, 1834-1857, pp. 8, 9; *Manual of the University of Georgia,* 43-48; Hull, *University of Georgia,* 186-90. [Calcu-

lations of the amount of money that will have accrued by the time the McCay Fund is available have been revised, because of the lower interest rates of the securities in which the Fund is now invested. In January, 1951, the amount was $267,750. Incomplete information on the twenty-five persons mentioned in the Donation indicates that few if any of them are still in life.]

15. S. A. Minutes, 1799-1842, p. 119.

16. F. Minutes, 1822-1836, pp. 137, 181, 182; *ibid.*, 1850-1873, p. 103; "Diary of James Daniel Frederick, Sept.-Oct., 1849" in *The Georgia Cracker*, Nov., 1921; *Southern Banner*, June 2, 1838.

17. F. Minutes, 1822-1836, pp. 61, 73; P. C. Minutes, 1834-1857, p. 106; Waddel Diary, Dec. 25, 30, 1823, Dec. 24, 1824.

18. F. Minutes, 1822-1836, pp. 20, 24, 25, 59, 156.

19. Waddel Diary, July 23, 1822.

20. F. Minutes, 1822-1836, pp. 106, 107, 141-44, 157-59, 245-48; *ibid.*, 1850-1873, p. 44.

21. F. Minutes, 1822-1836, pp. 80-82, 84, 112, 115; Waddel Diary, Sept. 20, 1825, March 8, 1826; U. B. Phillips, *The Life of Robert Toombs* (New York, 1913), 11-14; *Report of Commissioner of Education*, 1895-96, I, 864; Hull, *Annals of Athens*, 170, 171.

22. F. Minutes, 1822-1836, pp. 9-13, 113, 148, 181, 202; *ibid.*, 1850-1873, p. 25; Sullivan Letter.

23. F. Minutes, 1822-1836, pp. 66, 81, 123, 129; *Autobiography of Richard M. Johnston*, 55; Waddel Diary, March 3, 1829.

24. T. Minutes, 1835-1857, pp. 5, 6; F. Minutes, 1822-1836, pp. 89, 98, 99; *ibid.*, 1850-1873, pp. 6, 7, 159; Waddel Diary, April 26, Nov. 12, 1824; *Southern Watchman*, Jan. 21, 1858; *Southern Banner*, May 18, 1833. A typical college life story was published *ibid.*, April 3, 1845, copied from the *Southern Literary Messenger*.

25. F. Minutes, 1850-1873, pp. 47-49.

26. T. Minutes, 1786-1817, p. 210; F. Minutes, 1850-1873, pp. 4, 85, 101, 104, 105; Waddel Diary, Feb. 14, 1825, Feb. 6, 1826; *Southern Watchman*, Jan. 21, 1858.

27. F. Minutes, 1822-1836, pp. 16, 118; *Georgia University Magazine*, I, 5 (July, 1851), 177-79; IV, 2 (Oct., 1852), 61; W. M. Middlebrooks Letter; John N. Waddel, *Memorials*, 74.

28. S. A. Minutes, 1799-1842, p. 147; F. Minutes, 1822-1836, pp. 15, 68; *ibid.*, 1850-1873, pp. 2, 30, 105, 106; P. C. Minutes, 1834-1857, p. 16.

29. F. Minutes, 1822-1836, p. 114; *ibid.*, 1850-1873, pp. 15, 27, 38, 42, 67, 69, 85, 107, 122.

30. T. Minutes, 1835-1857, p. 261; F. Minutes, 1822-1836, p. 31; *ibid.*, 1850-1873, p. 57; Waddel Diary, Feb. 16, 1829; John N. Waddel, *Memorials*, 83.

31. F. Minutes, 1822-1836, p. 8; *ibid.*, 1850-1873, pp. 24, 43, 115, 131, 146.

32. T. Minutes, 1835-1857, p. 444; F. Minutes, 1822-1836, pp. 3, 90; *ibid.*, 1850-1873, pp. 11, 30, 132; Waddel Diary, Nov., 1825, Feb. 5, 1829.

33. F. Minutes, 1850-1873, pp. 29. 45: Waddel Diary, May 2, 1829.

34. F. Minutes, 1822-1836, pp. 22, 135, 139; *ibid.*, 1850-1873, p. 96; Hull, *University of Georgia*, 35.

35. F. Minutes, 1822-1836, pp. 35, 70, 129, 130.

36. T. Minutes, 1818-1834, pp. 179, 334, 335; *ibid.*, 1835-1857, pp. 124, 125.

37. S. A. Minutes, 1799-1842, p. 164; F. Minutes, 1850-1873, p. 100; Inspector's Book, 1831-1844; Hull, *University of Georgia*, 133; Bliss Perry, ed., *The Heart of Emerson's Journals* (Boston, 1926), 113.

CHAPTER FIVE

1. *Athenian,* March 30, 1827, July 7, 1829; *Autobiography of Joseph LeConte,* 37; [W. T. Thompson], *Major Jones' Chronicles of Pineville: Embracing Sketches of Georgia Scenes, Incidents, and Characters* (Philadelphia, 1843), 18.

2. S. A. Minutes, 1799-1842, p. 38; F. Minutes, 1850-1873, p. 86; *Athenian,* May 12, 1829. The attempt, at first, to foster class distinctions and subordination was copied directly from the Yale College rules. See *Freshman Laws* (New Haven, 1768) in Yale University Library, and reprinted in *Yale News,* Dec. 3, 1926.

3. *Georgia University Magazine,* VII, 5 (Aug., 1854) ; XI, 1 (Sept., 1856), 31, 32; *Athenian,* June 23, 1829.

4. H. A. Scomp, *King Alcohol in the Realm of King Cotton* (1888), 197, 202-21, 257.

5. *Athenian,* June 30, 1829, June 22, July 6, 1830.

6. Phi Kappa Minutes, 1835-1853, June 6, 1840; Demosthenian Minutes, 1840-1847, July 7, 1843; J. D. Waddell, *Linton Stephens,* 39-43; Scomp, *King Alcohol in the Realm of King Cotton,* 355-59, 379, 380; Hull, *University of Georgia,* 141.

7. T. Minutes, 1835-1857, p. 222; P. K. Minutes, 1835-1853, May 11, 1850, June 7, 1851; *Southern Literary Gazette,* I, 3 (May 27, 1848) ; Scomp, *King Alcohol in the Realm of King Cotton,* 409-25.

8. F. Minutes, 1850-1873, p. 36; *Southern Watchman,* Jan. 14, 1858; Scomp, *King Alcohol in the Realm of King Cotton,* 275, 315, 491; Hull, *Annals of Athens,* 146.

9. T. Minutes, 1786-1817, p. 119; *ibid.,* 1818-1834, p. 224; *ibid.,* 1858-1877, p. 248; P. C. Minutes, 1835-1857, pp. 41, 106.

10. T. Minutes, 1786-1817, p. 170; F. Minutes, 1850-1873, p. 21; *Southern Watchman,* July 10, 1867; *Southern Banner,* Sept. 2, 1852; *Compilation of Ordinances of Athens,* 19.

11. T. Minutes, 1786-1817, pp. 119, 242, 269; *ibid.,* 1818-1834, pp. 160, 244, 245; F. Minutes, 1822-1836, p. 214; Waddel Diary, Nov. 12, 1824.

12. T. Minutes, 1818-1834, pp. 122, 285; *Southern Watchman,* July 16, 1857.

13. T. Minutes, 1835-1857, pp. 114, 115, 130, 131, 178, 179; John N. Waddel, *Memorials,* 73.

14. F. Minutes, 1822-1836, p. 150; *Athenian,* Oct. 26, 1830, May 17, 24, 1831.

15. F. Minutes, 1822-1836, pp. 38, 39; *Georgia Journal,* March 23, 1824.

16. T. Minutes, 1818-1834, p. 252; *ibid.,* 1835-1857, p. 235; Thomas Letter.

17. T. Minutes, 1835-1857, p. 38; F. Minutes, 1822-1836, p. 150; Johnston and Browne, *Alexander H. Stephens,* 65; Circular Form, 1831; *Athenian,* Dec. 27, 1831; "Frederick Diary" in *Georgia Cracker,* Nov., 1921.

18. F. Minutes, 1822-1836, pp. 32, 77; "Frederick Diary," in *Georgia Cracker,* Nov., 1921, p. 5.

19. *Georgia University Magazine,* I, 5 (July, 1851), 197; IV, 2 (Oct., 1852), 61; Waddel Diary, Oct. 5, 1824; Johnston and Browne, *Alexander H. Stephens,* 54.

CHAPTER SIX

1. "Wm. Rutherford's Diary" in Demosthenian Letterbook.

2. Demosthenian Minutes, 1840-1847, March 17, 1847; Demosthenian By-Laws (1830), 55, 57; D. Letterbook, Oct. 12, 1847.

3. Phi Kappa Minutes, 1826-1829, Jan. 26, 1828; *ibid.,* 1854-1885, Aug. 5, 1857; Phi Kappa Constitution (1866) ; F. Minutes, 1850-1873, p. 179; *Georgia University Magazine,* I, 5 (June, 1875, N. S.), 239; John N. Waddel, *Memorials,* 74,

4, P. K. Minutes, 1835-1854, July 11, Aug. 3, 1835; July 5, Aug. 3, 1836, Aug. 3, 1837, Aug. 1, 1838, Sept. 16, 1843; D. Minutes, 1829-1839, July 2, 1836; *Southern Banner,* July 9, 1836.

5. P. K. Minutes, 1835-1854, Feb. 7, 1846; *ibid.,* 1854-1885, May 27, 1854.

6. T. Minutes, 1835-1857, p. 227; P. K. Minutes, 1826-1829, Feb. 27, 1828; *ibid.,*

1835-1854 (Annual Report, 1849) ; D. Minutes, 1829-1839, July, 1836; D. By-Laws, 1830; Book of Chronicles, 1853-1854. [The Skull and Bones branch of the Mystic Seven was organized at the University of Georgia in 1846. Its literary production and record, in manuscript, called "The Caldron," for the years 1848 and 1849, is in the possession of the writer. For further information on the Mystic Seven, see Karl W. Fischer, *The Mystics and Beta Theta Pi* (Menasha, Wisc., 1940).]

7. D. Minutes, 1829-1839, June 17, 1834.

8. D. Minutes, 1829-1839, Feb. 5, 1830, Sept. 24, 1831, Mar. 3, 1832, June 8, 1833; *ibid.*, 1854-1860, June 25, 1859; *ibid.*, 1860-1867, Mar. 15, 1862; Demosthenian Loose MSS, July 20, 1833; D. Letterbook; P. K. Minutes, 1826-1829, Feb. 27, 1828; *ibid.*, 1835-1854 (Annual Report, 1852).

9. John N. Waddel, *Memorials*, 191; D. Letterbook; W. S. Basinger's Personal Memoirs, I, 100.

10. P. K. Minutes, 1835-1854, July 11, 1835, Mar. 10, 31, Aug. 18, 1838, Feb. 20, 27, June 5, July 28, 1841, June 15, 29, Aug. 16, 1844, Feb. 18, 1845, Aug. 5, 1847, Sept. 1, 1850, May 3, June 14, 1851; P. K. Name Register, 1855.

11. D. Letterbook, 1831; Demosthenian Loose MSS; P. K. Minutes, 1853-1884, Feb., May 18, 1861.

12. P. K. Minutes, 1835-1854, May 21, 1826, Oct. 26, 1845; *Code of Laws for the Government of Franklin College* . . . (Athens, 1854) ; *University Catalogue, 1856-1857; Savannah Georgian*, Aug. 22, 1829. A student in begging to be allowed to resign wrote the Demosthenians, "I wish it understood nevertheless that I do not withdraw because I cannot appreciate the society, for I consider it among the first advantages of a college life." D. Letterbook.

13. D. Minutes, 1829-1839, Feb. 12, 1831, July 5, 1834; P. K. Minutes, 1835-1854, Mar. 5, 1836, Feb. 13, 1841, May 19, 26, Aug. 25, 1849.

14. P. K. Minutes, 1836-1854, Aug. 19, 1837, June 12, 1841, Feb. 7, 1846, July 13, 1850; D. Treasurer's Book, 1852-1853.

15. P. K. Minutes, 1835-1854, Jan. 28, Feb. 4, 23, 1837, Jan. 3, 1841; D. Minutes, 1847-1854, p. 54.

16. D. By-Laws, 1830, p. 63; P. K. Minutes, 1845-1854, Mar. 14, 1840, Sept. 4, 1841, Annual Report, 1850; T. Minutes, 1818-1834, p. 101.

17. D. Minutes, 1829-1839, March 10, Sept. 8, 1837.

18. P. K. Minutes, 1835-1854, June 10, 1836; D. Minutes, 1829-1839, Aug. 29, 1829 (p. 344), Sept. 10, 1836 (p. 388), Aug. 18, 1838 (p. 456) ; *ibid.*, 1840-1847, Feb. 6, 1841, Feb. 12, Oct. 1, 1842; *ibid.*, 1847-1854, Sept. 16, 1848; *ibid.*, 1860-1867, Oct. 11, 1862.

19. D. Minutes, 1829-1839, July, 1831 (p. 213), pp. 273, 362, Oct. 1, 1836 (p. 391), Apr. 29, 1837; *ibid.*, 1840-1847, Feb. 3, 1844; *ibid.*, 1847-1854, June 12, 1852; *ibid.*, 1854-1860, Sept. 30, 1854, Feb. 3, 10, 1855; P. K. Minutes, 1854-1885, Jan. 27, Feb. 3, 1855, Jan. 7, 1857.

20. D. Minutes, 1829-1839, pp. 130, 146, 299, 366; P. K. Minutes, 1831-1833, May 25, 1833; *ibid.*, 1835-1853, Mar. 11, 1843.

21. P. K. Minutes, 1835-1854, Mar. 25, 1838, Aug. 17, 1839, Sept. 22, 1849; D. Minutes, 1829-1839, pp. 429, 437, Sept. 2, 1854.

22. P. K. Minutes, 1831-1833, Sept. 3, 1831; *ibid.*, 1835-1854, Jan. 26, 1839; D. Minutes, 1829-1839, pp. 211, 290, 304, 459; *ibid.*, 1854-1860; *ibid.*, 1860-1867, p. 96.

23. P. K. Minutes, 1835-1854, Feb. 18, 1837, Apr. 24, 1841; D. Minutes, 1829-1839, pp. 152, 242, 268, 285, 302, 442; *ibid.*, 1854-1860.

24. P. K. Minutes, 1835-1854, Sept. 13, 1835, Feb. 19, 1843, Oct. 4, 1861; D. Minutes, 1829-1839, pp. 141, 334.

25. P. K. Minutes, 1835-1854, Sept. 23, 1843; D. Minutes, 1829-1839, pp. 170, 208, 313, 350, 436, 444.

26. P. K. Minutes, 1831-1833, May 19, 1832; D. Minutes, 1829-1839, pp. 337, 357, April 27, 1844.

27. P. K. Minutes, 1835-1854, Mar. 7, 1836; D. Minutes, 1829-1839, pp. 156, 162, 278; ibid., 1854-1860, Feb. 7, 1857.
28. P. K. Minutes, 1835-1854, Feb. 10, 1838, Aug. 26, 1843, Sept. 17, 1847, May 5, 1855; D. Minutes, 1829-1839, pp. 160, 367; ibid., 1840-1847, May 9, 1840; ibid., 1847-1854, March 11, 1848, Aug. 31, 1850.
29. P. K. Minutes, 1826-1829, Feb. 25, 1826; ibid., 1854-1885, May 28, 1859; D. Minutes, 1829-1839, pp. 124, 332; ibid., 1854-1860, Aug. 19, 1854.
30. P. K. Minutes, 1826-1829, Aug. 11, 1827, Mar. 1, 1828; ibid., 1835-1854, Aug. 29, 1835, Feb. 20, 1836, April 8, 1837; ibid., 1854-1885, Sept. 13, 18, 1858; D. Minutes, 1829-1839, pp. 142, 262, 289, 440; ibid., 1840-1847, May 12, 1843, Sept. 14, 1844; ibid., 1854-1860, Oct. 13, 1855, April 25, 1857, Sept. 15, 1858.
31. P. K. Minutes, 1831-1833, May 26, 1832, Jan. 12, 1833; D. Minutes, 1829-1839, pp. 145, 159, 168, 172, 191, 204, 209, June 15, 1838; ibid., 1840-1847, Jan. 28, 1843.
32. P. K. Minutes, 1835-1854, Aug. 21, 1853; ibid., 1854-1885, Apr. 29, Sept. 11, 1854, Mar. 10, May 19, 1855, Apr. 19, 1856, June 6, 1857, June 2, 1860; D. Minutes, 1829-1839, p. 365; ibid., 1854-1860, Sept. 16, 1854, June 6, 1857.
33. F. Minutes, 1850-1873, p. 83; P. K. Minutes, 1835-1854, Feb. 22, 1836; D. By-Laws (1830), p. 61; Athens Gazette, Feb. 29, 1816.
34. Georgia University Magazine, X, 4 (July, 1856), p. 127; P. K. Minutes, 1835-1854; Southern Watchman, July 9, 1859; Southern Banner, July 9, 1836.
35. F. Minutes, 1822-1836, pp. 194-196; "Frederick Diary" in Georgia Cracker, Nov., 1921, p. 6.
36. T. Minutes, 1835-1857, pp. 7, 8, 141; ibid., 1858-1877, pp. 26, 41, 42; P. K. Minutes, 1835-1854, Mar. 21, Aug. 21, 1836.
37. P. K. Minutes, 1835-1854, Annual Report, 1849; D. Minutes, 1829-1839, pp. 175-197; Demosthenian Loose MSS.
38. P. K. Minutes, 1835-1854, Aug. 4, 1835, Aug. 3, Oct. 8, 1836, April, 1836, Aug. 4, 1841, Jan. 21, Feb. 22, 1843.
39. F. Minutes, 1822-1836, p. 35; P. K. Minutes, 1835-1854, Mar. 5, 1836, June 10, 1837, May 11, 1844; P. K. Constitution (1866), pp. 32, 33; D. Minutes, 1829-1839, pp. 394, 395; D. By-Laws (1830), pp. 20, 21; D. Treasurer's Book, 1838-1839; ibid., 1852-1853.
40. P. K. Treasurer's Book, 1842-1843; D. Minutes, 1840-1847, June 21, 1845; D. Letterbook; D. Treasurer's Book, 1825-1827, pp. 29, 61, 62, 93, 94, 154; ibid., 1832-1835; p. 7; ibid., 1835-1836, pp. 1, 24.
41. P. K. Minutes, 1835-1854, Feb. 24, 1838; ibid., 1854-1885, Apr. 13, 1861; P. K. Librarian's Book, 1840; D. Minutes, 1829-1839, p. 298; D. Librarian's Book, 1826; D. Letterbook.
42. S. A. Minutes, 1799-1842, pp. 185-187; P. K. Minutes, 1826-1829, Nov. 3, 1827; ibid., 1835-1854, Jan. 26, 1839; Annual Report, 1843; May 19, 1849, July 3, 1861.
43. Georgia University Magazine, I, 5 (July, 1851), p. 197; IX, 1 (Oct., 1855), p. 27; T. Minutes, 1835-1857, pp. 273, 311.
44. P. K. Minutes, 1835-1854, Aug. 8, 1835, Apr. 16, 1838, Oct. 5, 1845; D. Minutes, 1829-1839, p. 301; D. Letterbook, Sept. 11, 1839.
45. D. Minutes, 1829-1839, p. 230; D. Letterbook, May 13, 1839, Mar. 14, 1848; Armes, ed., Autobiography of Joseph Le Conte, 45; E. A. Alderman and A. C. Gordon, J. L. M. Curry, A Biography (New York, 1911), 47. While John A. Campbell was a student, his father visited him and took part in a meeting of the Demosthenian Society. Young Campbell riddled his father's argument. H. G. Connor, John Archibald Campbell (Boston, 1920), 7. Joseph A. Blanc wrote in 1860, "Your fraternity has enrolled on its catalogue some of the most distinguished names that have adorned the civil, religious and political history of our widely extended country for the last 30 or 40 years, and without hazard I think I can venture the assertion, that the first flames of that extended patriotism for which they are so eminently distinguished were enkindled while participating in the debates of the Demosthenian Society." D. Letterbook, May 28, 1860. A Fourth of July toast drunk to the societies in 1829 ran, "The Demosthenian and Phi

Kappa Societies.—The 'life and blood' of Franklin College: the seats where genius and eloquence delight to reign in all the pride of primeval greatness, and from their walls has gone forth that flood of light which by its seducing brilliancy has attracted the admiring gaze of the scientific land." *Athenian*, July 14, 1829.

CHAPTER SEVEN

1. *Augusta Chronicle*, June 23, 1804; Meigs, *Josiah Meigs*, 12.

2. T. Minutes, 1786-1817, pp. 116, 128; *ibid.*, 1818-1834, p. 158; *Athens Gazette*, July 21, 1814, July 29, 1815. Of course, there were the salutatory and valedictory speeches.

3. F. Minutes, 1822-1836, p. 137; John N. Waddel, *Memorials*, 168-178; *Southern Literary Gazette*, Aug. 5, 1848; "Frederick Diary" in *Georgia Cracker*, Nov., 1921, p. 5; Hull, *University of Georgia*, 18. A commencement program for 1839 is preserved in the University of Georgia Library.

4. T. Minutes, 1818-1834, p. 274; *ibid.*, 1835-1857, p. 44.

5. *Augusta Chronicle*, June 18, 1808; *Athenian*, Aug. 12, 1828; *Southern Banner*, Aug. 18, 1835; Hull, *Annals of Athens*, 27-29. One of the diplomas issued in 1804 is preserved in the University of Georgia Library.

6. T. Minutes, 1818-1834, p. 265; *Athenian*, July 29, Aug. 25, 1829, Aug. 10, 1830.

7. T. Minutes, 1858-1877, p. 63. By 1951, the University had a much larger auditorium, in the Fine Arts Building, where some features of commencement exercises were held. With a much larger student enrollment, more than 7,000 in 1948, the graduation exercises came to be held in Sanford Stadium.

8. S. A. Minutes, 1799-1842, p. 156; *Georgia University Magazine*, VII, 5, (Aug., 1854), 255; *Athenian*, Aug. 9, 1831; *Augusta Chronicle*, April 21, June 23, 1804, July 26, 1806.

9. T. Minutes, 1835-1857, Aug. 1, 1836; P. K. Minutes, 1835-1854, Aug. 3, 1836; Waddel Diary, 1833-1836, pp. 261, 262; *Athenian*, Aug. 5, 12, 1828, Aug. 31, 1830.

10. T. Minutes, 1835-1857, July 31, 1843; S. A. Minutes, 1799-1842, p. 80; *A Catalogue of the Trustees, Officers and Alumni of the University of Georgia from 1785 to 1876* (Athens, 1876), 54-57. For the regulations concerning honorary degrees see T. Minutes, 1835-1857, p. 18.

11. T. Minutes, 1818-1834, p. 195; P. K. Minutes, 1835-1854, Aug. 3, 1836; *University of Georgia Catalogue, 1860-1861*, p. 25; *Southern Banner*, Aug. 2, 1834, Aug. 6, 1836, Aug. 9, 1839, Nov. 27, 1840; *Georgia Alumni Record*, II, 7, 8 (April, 1922), 174, 175.

12. T. Minutes, 1835-1857, p. 241; *Southern Banner*, Aug. 21, 1851; George R. Gilmer, *The Literary Progress in Georgia. An Address delivered in the College Chapel at Athens . . . 1851* (Athens, 1851).

13. Waddel Diary, 1833-1836, pp. 111, 112; *Savannah Georgian*, Aug. 15, 1829; *Southern Banner*, July 24, 1840; Hull, *Annals of Athens*, 169, 170.

14. S. A. Minutes, 1799-1842, p. 49; T. Minutes, 1818-1834, pp. 97, 98; F. Minutes, 1822-1836, pp. 173, 194; *Southern Literary Gazette*, Aug. 5, 1848; *Savannah Georgian*, Aug. 13, 1829.

15. T. Minutes, 1835-1857, p. 113; F. Minutes, 1822-1836, p. 8; *Athenian*, Aug. 3, 1830; *Southern Literary Gazette*, Aug. 5, 1848; *Georgia University Magazine*, VII, 5 (Aug., 1854), 225, XII, 2 (May, 1857), 63, 64; *Southern Whig*, April 2, 1849; *Georgia Express*, May 13, 1809; *Sullivan Letter* (1856) ; Hull, *Annals of Athens*, 131; *Georgia Alumni Record*, IV, 1 (Oct., 1923), 14; "The Waddel Memoir" in *The Georgia Historical Quarterly*, VIII, 4 (Dec., 1924), 304-24.

16. S. A. Minutes, 1799-1842, pp. 48, 81, 125; T. Minutes, 1818-1834, pp. 227, 271; *ibid.*, 1835-1857, p. 73; F. Minutes, 1850-1873, p. 207; *Augusta Chronicle*, June 6, 1807.

17. *Athenian*, July 1, 1828, May 26, Sept. 15, 29, 1829; F. Minutes, 1822-1836,

p. 118 (June 30, 1828).

18. *Athenian*, Aug. 12, 1828, Oct. 6, 1829.

19. T. Minutes, 1818-1834, pp. 181, 194, 196; P. K. Minutes, 1826-1829, Oct. 1, 1828; *Athenian*, Dec. 9, 1828; Hull, *University of Georgia*, 44.

20. T. Minutes, 1818-1834, pp. 204, 220; *Athenian*, May 19, 26, June 9, 16; Hull, *University of Georgia*, 138, 139. The students at the University of Virginia also adopted a uniform. *Athenian*, Aug. 18, 1829.

21. *Athenian*, March 31, 1829; Hull, *Annals of Athens*, 101. For further information concerning the "Athens Manufacturing Company" see *Athenian*, Feb. 2, 1830, Mar. 22, July 26, 1831; *Southern Banner*, May 11, June 1, Sept. 21, 1833.

22. For a further discussion see E. M. Coulter, "The Nullification Movement in Georgia" in *The Georgia Historical Quarterly*, V, 1 (March, 1921), 3-39.

CHAPTER EIGHT

1. *The Virginia Evangelical and Literary Magazine* (Richmond), II, 11 (Nov., 1819), 529.

2. *American Almanac, 1832*, p. 233.

3. George G. Smith, *The Life and Letters of James Osgood Andrew* (Nashville, 1883), 18-41.

4. Smith, *Life of Andrew*, 18-45; C. C. Cleveland, *The Great Revival in the West, 1797-1805* (Chicago, 1916); *Georgia University Magazine*, X, 5 (August, 1856), 152-55.

5. Slosson, *The American Spirit in Education*, 90.

6. *Virginia Evangelical and Literary Magazine*, III, 6 (June, 1820), 267, 268.

7. T. Minutes, 1786-1817, p. 203; *Georgia Express*, Feb. 21, 1811; Hull, *University of Georgia*, 33; Hull, *Annals of Athens*, 25.

8. *Evangelical and Literary Magazine and Missionary Chronicle* (formerly called *Virginia Evangelical and Literary Magazine*), IV, 12 (Dec., 1821), 692; Waddel Diary, May 6, 1825, p. 44.

9. S. A. Minutes, 1799-1842, p. 178; T. Minutes, 1786-1817, p. 270; Smith, *Life of Andrew*, 199-239.

10. T. Minutes, 1818-1834, pp. 193, 194; *ibid.*, 1858-1877, p. 63; *Southern Watchman*, Dec. 10, 1857; Hull, *Annals of Athens*, 166.

11. *Virginia Evangelical and Literary Magazine*, II, 9 (Sept., 1819), 391-403; *Virginia Evangelical and Literary Magazine and Missionary Chronicle* (a continuation of the publication mentioned above), VII, 10 (Oct., 1824), 555, 556; *Athenian*, Aug. 2, 1831.

12. *Athenian*, Oct. 6, 1829. The onset against the University was carried on by individuals—not by the organized conventions or associations.

13. Perhaps as a sop to the Methodists, the trustees in November, 1829, elected Capers professor of moral philosophy and belles lettres. He did not accept. T. Minutes, 1818-1834, p. 215.

14. *Athenian*, Aug. 4, 25, Sept. 8, 22, 29, 1829; *Southern Banner*, Dec. 28, 1838, March 8, 1834; *Savannah Georgian*, Aug. 13, 1829; S. A. Minutes, 1799-1842, pp. 206, 207.

15. *Athenian*, Sept. 22, 1829; John N. Waddel, *Memorials*, 89.

16. Niles' *Weekly Register*, XL, 150.

17. S. A. Minutes, 1799-1842, p. 227; *Athenian*, Oct. 6, 1829, May 24, 1831; *Southern Banner*, July 12, 1834; *Federal Union*, Sept. 4, 1830; Hull, *Annals of Athens*, 122.

18. *Southern Banner*, Aug. 3, 1833; Hull, *University of Georgia*, 53. The eleven new trustees elected by the legislature on December 21, 1830, were: Thomas W. Murray, Angus M. D. King, James C. Watson, Zachariah Williams, David A. Reese,

Daniel Hook, Jacob Wood, Wilson Lumpkin, Howell Cobb, Stephens Thomas, and James Tinsley. Prince, *Digest*, 876.

19. *Virginia Evangelical and Literary Magazine*, III, 6 (June, 1820), 270; *Report of Commissioner of Education, 1895-96*, I, 882.

20. Henry H. Tucker, *Address Delivered February 3rd, 1875, before the General Assembly of the State of Georgia on the Condition, Interests, and Wants of the University of Georgia* (Atlanta, 1875), 27, 28.

21. *Georgia University Magazine*, Oct., 1855, p. 31; T. Minutes, 1835-1857, pp. 400-402; *Autobiography of R. M. Johnston*, 43-45; J. D. Wade, *Augustus Baldwin Longstreet* . . . (New York, 1924), 259; *Southern Watchman*, March 5, 1857.

22. *Athenian*, Sept. 7, 1830.

23. T. Minutes, 1835-1857, p. 207.

24. Waddel Diary, March 23, 1825, Aug. 28, 1828; John N. Waddel, *Memorials*, 95, 96; *Life of Olin*, I, 138, 141; *Athenian*, Sept. 22, 1829; Hull, *Annals of Athens*, 46; "Frederick Diary" in *Georgia Cracker*, Nov., 1921, p. 16.

25. F. Minutes, 1822-1836, pp. 101, 148, 201, 202; *Athenian*, July 27, Sept. 14, 1830.

26. *Southern Watchman*, April 8, 22, May 6, 20, 1858; *Southern Banner*, May 1, 1840; D. Minutes, 1840-1847, Sept. 11, 1846; D. Letterbook, April 6, 1858; P. K. Minutes, 1835-1854, April 25, 1840; Armes, ed., *Autobiography of Joseph LeConte*, 41-43.

27. *Southern Watchman*, Sept. 9, 1858; P. K. Minutes, 1854-1885, Sept. 8, 1860; W. E. Dodd, *The Cotton Kingdom* (New Haven, 1921), 106, 108.

CHAPTER NINE

1. See E. M. Coulter, "The Ante-bellum Academy Movement in Georgia," in *Georgia Historical Quarterly*, V, 4 (Dec., 1921), 11-42; also E. M. Coulter, "A Georgia Educational Movement during the Eighteen Hundred Fifties," *ibid.*, IX, 1 (March, 1925), 1-33.

2. Prince, *Digest*, 873, 874; *Georgia Journal*, Nov. 20, Dec. 4, 1821.

3. *Athenian*, Nov. 29, 1830, Sept. 9, 1828; *Georgia Journal*, Dec. 21, 1824.

4. Johnston and Browne, *Alexander H. Stephens*, 57; *Savannah Georgian*, Aug. 22, 1829; *Southern Literary Gazette*, April 19, 1848.

5. *Georgia Journal*, Aug. 31, 1819; *Athenian*, Dec. 15, 1829; *Southern Banner*, Aug. 3, 1833.

6. S. A. Minutes, 1799-1842, pp. 209, 231-33; T. Minutes, 1818-1834. p. 81; *Athenian*, Dec. 1, 1829; *Federal Union*, Jan. 15, 1831.

7. S. A. Minutes, 1799-1842, pp. 213-16.

8. *Georgia Journal*, May 13, 1823; *American Almanac, 1834*, p. 210.

9. *Athenian*, Oct. 13, 1829.

10. *Ibid.*, Dec. 15.

11. *Ibid.*, Sept. 8.

12. S. A. Minutes, 1799-1842, p. 212.

13. *Ibid.*, 214.

14. *Athenian*, Sept. 14, 1830; *Savannah Georgian*, May 20, 1823.

15. *Georgia Journal*, June 9, July 28, 1818.

16. *Report of Commissioner of Education, 1895-6*, I; Stephen F. Miller, *The Bench and Bar of Georgia* (Philadelphia, 1858), I, 112, 113.

17. Dec. 15, 1829.

18. Jan. 5, 1830.

19. S. A. Minutes, 1799-1842, p. 225.

20. *Ibid.*, 222, 226, 227.

21. Later the state came to an agreement with the University. S. A. Minutes, 1799-1842, p. 238.
22. Prince, *Digest*, 876, 877; *Athenion*, Dec. 14, 1830, Aug. 9, 1831.
23. S. A. Minutes, 1799-1842, p. 230; T. Minutes, 1818-1834, pp. 277, 366; *Report of Commissioner of Education, 1895-6*, I, 881.
24. T. Minutes, 1818-1834, p. 251.
25. S. A. Minutes, 1799-1842, p. 115.
26. *Georgia Express*, April 1, 1809.
27. S. A. Minutes, 1799-1842, pp. 170, 171.
28. P. K. Minutes, 1826-1829, July 15, 1826.
29. *Georgia Journal*, June 13, 1826; Hull, *Annals of Athens*, 211.
30. *Athenian*, Sept. 27, 1831.
31. Alderman and Gordon, *J. L. M. Curry*, 56; D. Minutes, 1840-1847, May 12, 1841.
32. T. Minutes, 1818-1834, p. 279.
33. Hull, *Annals of Athens*, 123; T. Minutes, 1818-1834, p. 298.
34. F. Minutes, 1850-1873, p. 73; T. Minutes, 1835-1857, p. 227.
35. *Georgia University Magazine*, I, 5, p. 241; S. A. Minutes, 1799-1842, p. 238; *Southern Banner*, Dec. 10, 1841.
36. T. Minutes, 1835-1857, p. 200 (Aug. 5, 1847).
37. S. A. Minutes, 1799-1842, pp. 189, 214, 215; T. Minutes, 1835-1857, pp. 11, 12, 52, 53, 116, 119, 120, 254, 255; *Southern Banner*, Aug. 5, 1842.
38. T. Minutes, 1835-1857, p. 110.
39. *Ibid.*, 150, 151.
40. McIntosh to Jackson, July 31, 1819 in Henry Jackson MSS.
41. S. A. Minutes, 1799-1842, p. 184.
42. *Ibid.*, 176.
43. T. Minutes, 1835-1857, pp. 470, 471.
44. Charles F. Thwing, *A History of Higher Education in America* (New York, 1906), 254, 255; *Georgia Journal*, May 27, 1823; P. K. Minutes, 1834-1857, p. 87.
45. For an account of this interesting but unsuccessful movement see E. M. Coulter, "A Georgia Educational Movement during the Eighteen Hundred Fifties," in *Georgia Historical Quarterly*, IX, 1 (March, 1925).
46. Quoted in *Southern School Journal*, July, 1853, p. 100.
47. D. Letterbook, Aug. 31, 1854.
48. T. Minutes, 1835-1857, pp. 352-80.
49. *Ibid.*, 238.
50. P. C. Minutes, 1834-1857, pp. 102-05.
51. T. Minutes, 1835-1857, p. 388; *Georgia University Magazine*, X, 4 (July, 1856), 110-14.
52. T. Minutes, 1835-1857, p. 393; F. Minutes, 1850-1873, pp. 72, 150; *Southern Watchman*, Oct. 8, 1857.
53. T. Minutes, 1858-1877, p. 65.
54. Robert Fielder, *A Sketch of the Life and Times and Speeches of Joseph E. Brown* (Springfield, Mass., 1883), 152, 154, 157. In 1882 Brown gave to the University $50,000 to be used in aiding students. It was made a loan fund for male students and through skillful management now (1928) amounts to more than $264,000. [In 1951, it amounted to more than $500,000.]
55. T. Minutes, 1858-1877, p. 3; *Southern Watchman*, Feb. 12, 1857.
56. Battle, *History of the University of North Carolina*, I, 644, 645; *American Almanac, 1834*, pp. 210, 216, 226.
57. Thwing, *History of Higher Education in America*, 257; Dodd, *The Cotton Kingdom*, 111, 112.

58. *Report and Memorial of the Trustees . . . to the General Assembly . . .* , 1855, p. 2; John N. Waddel, *Memorials*, p. 172.
59. *Georgia Journal*, Nov. 21, 1821; *Athenian*, Sept. 8, 1829.
60. *Georgia University Magazine*, VII, 5 (March, 1855), 379-81.
61. *Southern Literary Gazette*, May 13, Aug. 19, 1848.
62. *Southern Herald*, Sept. 12, 1850.
63. Ford, ed., *Works of Jefferson*, IX, 78.
64. *Southern School Journal*, Nov., 1854, pp. 171-73.
65. Of course this method of computation gives only an indication. New counties were being created all along, and there were many other variables; but there is nothing to invalidate the main result.
66. Consideration is here given only to the ten representative lists mentioned above. See maps opposite p. 172.
67. *Athenian*, Nov. 2, 1830, Dec. 29, 1829; D. Letterbook, March 15, 1860; *Southern Watchman*, Oct. 1, 1857, Aug. 26, 1858.
68. *Southern Watchman*, Aug. 23, 1855.

CHAPTER TEN

1. *Athenian*, June 30, 1829.
2. Armes, ed., *Autobiography of Joseph LeConte*, 156.
3. T. Minutes, 1835-1857, p. 124; John N. Waddel, *Memorials*, 82; Sullivan Letter.
4. P. K. Minutes, 1835-1854.
5. *Georgia University Magazine*, VII, 5 (Aug., 1854), 256; Richardson Wright, *Hawkers and Walkers in Early America* (Philadelphia, 1927), 129-35. For a further account of this portrait, see E. M. Coulter, "Wanderings of a Painting: The Alonzo Church Portrait," in *Georgia Historical Quarterly*, XXX, 2 (June, 1946), 118-24.
6. "Frederick Diary" in *Georgia Cracker*, Nov., 1921, p. 12.
7. *Southern Banner*, Feb. 15, June 14, July 12, Sept. 27, 1834; *Life of Olin*, I, 41-114.
8. *Southern Banner*, Feb. 27, 1845.
9. *Ibid.*, July 20, 29, 1854.
10. *Georgia Telegraph*, Oct. 23, 1855.
11. T. Minutes, 1835-1857, pp. 188, 198.
12. *Southern Watchman*, Dec. 20, 1855; *Georgia Telegraph*, Dec. 11, 25, 1855; T. Minutes, 1835-1857, p. 347.
13. *Southern Banner*, Nov. 25, 1852; P. C. Minutes, 1834-1857, p. 101.
14. P. C. Minutes, 1834-1857, p. 99.
15. T. Minutes, 1835-1857, p. 299 (July 31, 1854).
16. T. Minutes, 1835-1857, pp. 416-29; Thomas L. Broun, *Dr. William Leroy Broun* (New York, 1912), 43; John N. Waddel, *Memorials*, 89.
17. F. Minutes, 1850-1873, pp. 74-76.
18. Armes, ed., *Autobiography of Joseph LeConte*, 105, 157.
19. Edward J. Thomas, *Memoirs of a Southerner, 1840-1923* (Savannah, 1923), 31-33.
20. *Georgia Telegraph*, Dec. 11, 1855.
21. T. Minutes, 1835-1857, pp. 416-29.
22. *Ibid.*, 338.
23. *Ibid.*, 403-06.
24. *Ibid.*, 346.
25. *Ibid.*, 395-98.

26. T. Minutes, 1835-1857, pp. 97, 414, 415; *Southern Watchman*, Nov. 22, 1855, Dec. 18, 1856; Hull, *Annals of Athens*, 190-93; Armes, ed., *Autobiography of Joseph LeConte*, 156-158.

27. *Report and Memorial of the Trustees . . . to the General Assembly . . .* , 1855, p. 3; T. Minutes, 1835-1857, pp. 350-80.

28. *Report and Memorial*, 3-16.

29. Feb. 24, 1857.

30. *Programme of an Enlarged Organization of the University of Georgia*, 14 pages.

31. T. Minutes, 1858-1877, pp. 13-25, 43-46.

32. Letter from T. R. R. Cobb and H. Hull to Iverson Harris, May 31, 1859, in Miscellaneous MSS.

33. T. Minutes, 1835-1857, pp. 461, 462; *ibid.*, 1858-1877, p. 2; *Southern Watchman*, Nov. 11, 1858.

34. T. Minutes, 1858-1877, p. 52; *Southern Watchman*, May 21, 1862.

35. T. Minutes, 1858-1877, pp. 35, 36, 56; *Southern Watchman*, Feb. 23, 1860; Mell, *Life of P. H. Mell*, 107.

36. F. Minutes, 1850-1873, pp. 152, 153.

37. T. Minutes, 1858-1877, p. 63.

CHAPTER ELEVEN

1. P. C. Minutes, 1835-1857, Nov. 25, 1843.

2. T. Minutes, 1818-1834, pp. 126, 130.

3. A. S. Clayton, comp., *Laws of Georgia, 1801-1810*, pp. 329, 330.

4. *Southern Banner*, March 17, 1838; Hull, *Annals of Athens*, 102, 160.

5. April 21, 1829.

6. James Silk Buckingham, *The Slave States of America* (London, 1842), 11, 113.

7. *Athenian*, March 23, 1827.

8. U. B. Phillips, *A History of Transportation in the Eastern Cotton Belt to 1860* (New York, 1908), 221-51; Hull, *Annals of Athens*, 134; *Georgia Historical Quarterly*, XII, 2 (June, 1928), 173, 174.

9. *Southern Banner*, April 28, 1853; Hull, *Annals of Athens*, 163.

10. *Athenian*, April 26, 1831; *Evangelical and Literary Magazine*, VII, 4, p. 211; *ibid.*, 10, p. 549.

11. *Southern Watchman*, Nov. 24, 1859; Hull, *Annals of Athens*, 163.

12. *Southern Banner*, July 18, 1844, March 27, 1851; *Southern Watchman*, Feb. 4, 1858.

13. *Southern Watchman*, Jan. 25, 1855; Hardee Letter.

14. *Southern Watchman*, Aug. 10, 1870; Hull, *Annals of Athens*, 212.

15. *Southern Banner*, March 27, 1845.

16. T. L. Broun, *Broun*, 7.

17. *Autobiography of R. M. Johnston*, 47.

18. John N. Waddel, *Memorials*, 112.

19. Buckingham, *Slave States of America*, II, 72, 73, 92-94.

20. *Athenian*, June 30, 1829.

21. Buckingham, *Slave States of America*, II, 131; *Athenian*, July 14, 1829, Jan. 18, 1831.

22. Armes, ed., *Autobiography of Joseph LeConte*, 46, 47; Sullivan Letter; Thomas Letter.

23. *Southern Watchman*, Nov. 24, 1869.

24 Buckingham, *Slave States of America*, II, 135; Hull, *Annals of Athens*, 34; *Athenian*, July 1, 1828.

25. "Frederick Diary" in *Georgia Cracker*, Nov., 1921, p. 12.

26. *Southern Banner*, June 22, May 11, 1833.

27. *Athenian*, Feb. 9, 1827.

28. *Southern Banner*, March 31, 1836, July 31, 1840.

29. *Athenian*, June 1, 15, 1827, June 29, July 27, Nov. 9, 1830; *Southern Banner*, July 9, 1836, Aug. 24, 1854; *Southern Whig*, Nov. 25, 1842.

30. *Southern Whig*, June 27, 1850; *Southern Banner*, Dec. 21, 1833; *Athenian*, Jan. 19, 1830.

31. Buckingham, *Slave States of America*, II, 89-91; *Southern Banner*, March 29, 1834, June 17, 1837, March 31, 1838, July 4, 1844; *Athenian*, Aug. 24, Sept. 14, 1827, July 5, 1831.

32. *Athenian*, July 27, 1830, Jan. 11, 1831; *Southern Banner*, July 19, 1834, July 29, 1842.

33. *Athenian*, July 13, 1830, July 12, 1831. In 1809 a celebration was held by "a vast collection of our fellow-citizens." Two balls were held during the evening and the "utmost good order and hilarity prevailed throughout the day and night." *Georgia Express*, July 8, 1809.

34. *Southern Banner*, June 26, 1845.

35. *Athenian*, Feb. 28, 1832.

36. *Georgia Journal*, June 1, 1819; Hull, *Annals of Athens*, 165, 166.

37. *Southern Banner*, March 9, 1854; *Southern Watchman*, Oct. 15, 1857.

38. *Georgia Express*, July 24, 1812.

39. Sullivan Letter.

40. *Southern Whig*, March 28, 1850.

41. *Athenian*, Aug. 5, 1828; *Southern Whig*, March 28, July 25, 1850; *Southern Banner*, May 5, 1838, March 4, 1852, June 8, 1854; *Southern Watchman*, Sept. 13, Dec. 27, 1855, Aug. 26, 1858, Sept. 8, 1859, Dec. 20, 1865.

42. *Southern Banner*, Feb. 22, 1834, Dec. 7, 1839, Nov. 4, 1845, June 23, 1853; *Southern Watchman*, Sept. 6, 1855.

43. *Southern Watchman*, Dec. 20, 1865; P. C. Minutes, 1834-1857, p. 59; T. Minutes, 1835-1857, p. 207.

44. *Southern Banner*, Oct. 24, 1844; *Southern Watchman*, Sept. 6, 1855, July 7, 1859; *Southern Whig*, April 6, Sept. 21, 1828.

45. *Southern Watchman*, May 14, 28, 1857.

46. *Southern Watchman*, April 12, 1855, Feb. 7, 1856, Jan. 28, Feb. 25, 1858, Mar. 10, 1859, March 15, April 5, June 28, Sept. 6, 1860; *Southern Banner*, Aug. 3, 1833, Oct. 21, 1837, June 28, 1838, March 20, July 31, 1840, June 18, 1841, Jan. 29, 1852, March 10, 1853, July 13 1854; Waddel Diary, Oct. 29, 1825.

47. *Athenian*, July 27, 1830, May 3, July 19, 1831; *Southern Banner*, March 17, 1838, May 15, 1840, April 4, 1844; *Southern Watchman*, June 7, 1860; Waddel Diary, 1833-36, p. 261.

48. F. Minutes, 1850-1873, pp. 9, 121; *Southern Watchman*, July 8, 15, 1856.

49. Buckingham, *Slave States of America*, II, 83-87; Andrew Johnson Papers, vol. 65, no. 4009; *Southern Banner*, July 9, 1836, May 11, 1854; Hull, *Annals of Athens*, 152-54, 200, 204, 205. [For a fuller account of this eccentric character, see E. M. Coulter, *John Jacobus Flournoy. Champion of the Common Man in the Antebellum South* (Savannah, 1942).]

50. Buckingham, *Slave States of America*, II, 121; *Athenian*, May 2, 1828, Sept. 7, 1830, July 5, 1831; *Southern Banner*, March 1, 1834, Oct. 22, 1835; *Southern Watchman*, July 14, 1859.

51. Buckingham, *Slave States of America*, II, 129, 130; *Compilation of the Ordinances of Athens*, 21; *Athenian*, Feb. 8, 1831; *Southern Banner*, March 30, 1839; *Southern Watchman*, Jan. 14, 1858, Jan. 19, 1860.

52. *Compilation of the Ordinances of Athens*, 18, 22; Meigs, *Life of Josiah Meigs*, 75; *Southern Banner*, March 27, 1851, May 11, July 27, Oct. 12, 1854; *Southern Watchman*, Sept. 12, 1866.

53. *Athenian*, Feb. 1, 1831; *Southern Banner*, April 3, 1840.

54. Buckingham, *Slave States of America*, II, 114; *Compilation of the Ordinances of Athens*, 22; *Southern Watchman*, May 20, 1858; Feb. 27, 1867. In 1928 the cemetery was a wilderness of briars and weeds, and the tombstones were fast crumbling away under the battering assaults of the children of leisure in the neighborhood. [In 1951 the condition was worse.]

55. *Southern Banner*, May 15, 1851.

56. *Athenian*, March 23, 1830.

57. *Athenian*, April 21, 1829, Jan. 12, July 6, 1830, March 1, 1831; *Southern Banner*, March 31, 1838.

CHAPTER TWELVE

1. *Southern Watchman*, Nov. 8, 1860. For an extensive discussion of the significance of the election of 1860 see Mary Scrugham, *The Peaceable Americans of 1860-1861* (New York, 1921).

2. *Southern Watchman*, Nov. 15, 1860.

3. *Ibid.*

4. *Ibid.*, Nov. 22.

5. *Ibid.*, Dec. 25; Hull, *Annals of Athens*, 218.

6. A preliminary copy of the document in Cobb's handwriting is preserved in the University Library.

7. *Southern Watchman*, June 28, 1860, March 13, 1861.

8. T. Minutes, 1858-1877, July 27, 1860, p. 42; F. Minutes, 1850-1873, Jan. 30, April 30, 1860; D. Letterbook, March 13, 1854; E. J. Thomas, *Memoirs of a Southerner, 1840-1923*, p. 32; Sullivan Letter; Thomas Letter.

9. F. Minutes, 1850-1873, April 15, 22, 1861, p. 167; Thomas Letter; *Testimony taken by the Joint Select Committee to Inquire into the Condition of Affairs in the late Insurrectionary States, Georgia* (Washington, 1872), II, 768; Middle-brooks Letters; *Autobiography of Richard M. Johnston*, 56-58; Hull, *Annals of Athens*, 140, 141.

10. T. Minutes, 1858-1877, July 5, 1861, pp. 68, 69; F. Minutes, 1850-1873; April 22, May 6, 1881, pp. 167, 168; P. K. Minutes, 1854-1885, April 25, 1861; *Southern Watchman*, April 17, 1861; J. D. Wade, *Augustus Baldwin Longstreet*, 339-41.

11. T. Minutes, 1858-1877, pp. 72, 73; F. Minutes, 1850-1873, June 8, 1863, pp. 170-72; Hull, *Annals of Athens*, 407.

12. T. Minutes, 1858-1877, pp. 61, 70-73, 87, 88.

13. T. Minutes, 1858-1877, pp. 84, 92, 100, 120, 121, 123, 124; F. Minutes, 1850-1873, pp. 169, 170; *Southern Watchman*, June 26, 1861, Sept. 9, 1863; Dunbar Rowland, *History of Mississippi the Heart of the South* (Chicago, 1925), II, 485; Green, *History of the University of South Carolina*, 76.

14. P. K. Minutes, 1854-1885, July 31, 1861; *Southern Watchman*, June 26, 1861, July 9, 1862, July 8, 18, 1863, July 6, 1864.

15. D. Letterbook, Mar. 15, 1861; P. K. Minutes, 1854-1885, Oct. 25, 1862.

16. D. Minutes, 1860-1867, pp. 32, 67, 90, 97, 98; P. K. Minutes, 1854-1885, May 25, 1861, April, June, 6, 1863.

17. P. K. Minutes, 1854-1885; D. Minutes, 1860-1867, pp. 105, 118, 119.

18. T. Minutes, 1858-1877, pp. 100-06; *Southern Watchman*, June 17, 1863; Hull, *University of Georgia*, 73; Hull, *Annals of Athens*, 219, 223, 225, 242, 247.

19. *Southern Watchman*, Aug. 14, 1861, Sept. 9, 1863; Hull, *Annals of Athens*,

246, 265-80.

20. T. Minutes, 1858-1877, p. 121; *Southern Watchman*, May 22, 29, June 19, 1861, April 2, 1862, June 29, Oct. 26, 1864; Vestry Book of Emmanuel Parish; Hull, *Annals of Athens*, 260; manuscript written by Miss Alice Rowland, of Athens, Georgia, in possession of the author.

21. *Southern Watchman*, July 8, 1863, June 15, Aug. 3, 10, Nov. 23, 1864; *The Burckmyer Letters, March, 1863-June, 1865* (Columbia, S. C., 1926), 449; Hull, *Annals of Athens*, 263, 264.

22. Workmen excavating for a factory site on the banks of the Oconee in 1924, turned up a quantity of small arms which here had found their hiding place during the Civil War times. The story is told of one of these Athens rifles which performed well for Southern Independence, and when defeat came failed to surrender. Thirty-five years later it was found still opposing the authority of the United States—in the hands of a Filipino. The correspondence with the United States military authorities concerning this rifle was in the possession of the late Dr. Sylvanus Morris of the University of Georgia.

23. *Southern Watchman*, Aug. 20, 1862; Hull, *Annals of Athens*, 254, 280, 282.

24. *Southern Watchman*, Oct. 9, 1861, Jan. 8, 1862, Feb. 11, 1863, Jan. 27, April 27, 1864, June 7, 1865.

25. *Ibid.*, June 21, 1860, June 5, 1861, July 23, 1862.

CHAPTER THIRTEEN

1. Hull, *Annals of Athens*, 306, 307.

2. *Southern Watchman*, June 21, Oct. 25, 1865; Hull, *Annals of Athens*, 300-02, 305, 306.

3. *Southern Watchman*, June 14, Sept. 13, 1865, Dec. 19, 1866; W. W. Thomas to Howell Cobb, Jan. 11, 1866 in Miscellaneous MSS; Hull, *Annals of Athens*, 304-306; T. Minutes, 1858-1877, p. 145.

4. *Southern Watchman*, Sept. 20, 1865, May 8, 1867; Mell, *Life of Mell*, 146; Hull, *Annals of Athens*, 302-304.

5. *Southern Watchman*, June 7, July 26, Aug. 30, Oct. 4, Nov. 15, 1865, June 12, 1867; Hull, *Annals of Athens*, 303. Hinton Rowan Helper in his book, *Nojogue*, advocated the immediate expulsion of the Negroes into the rural districts, then their banishment to Mexico, Central America, or the islands of the seas, and if nature did not speedily bring about their extinction (which he confidently predicted), he would have them done out of existence in some way he did not make clear.

6. *Southern Watchman*, June 14, July 12, 1865, June 20, 27, 1866, Jan. 16, July 10, 31, Dec., 18, 1867; Hull, *Annals of Athens*, 320.

7. T. Minutes, 1858-1877, pp. 139, 140, 143, 145; *Southern Watchman*, June 21, July 5, Oct. 4, Dec. 6, 1865, Jan. 24, 1866.

8. T. Minutes, 1858-1877, pp. 148, 149, 159; F. Minutes, 1850-1873, pp. 172, 173; *University Catalogue, 1865-66*, p. 16; *Southern Watchman*, Jan. 17, 1866.

9. T. Minutes, 1858-1877, pp. 149, 304; F. Minutes, 1850-1873, p. 184; *Acts of Georgia, 1866*, pp. 143, 144; *University Catalogue, 1868-9*, p. 39; *Southern Watchman*, Nov. 29, 1865, Feb. 13, 20, April 10, May 13, 1867, Dec. 1, 1869; *Lexington (Ky.) Observer and Reporter*, Dec. 1, 1866; N. G. Harris, *Autobiography, The Story of an Old Man's Life with Reminiscenses of Seventy-five Years* (Macon, 1925), 145-49, 156-59; *Walter Barnard Hill* (Bulletin of the University of Georgia, Memorial Number, May, 1906, Vol. 6, No. 8), 9, 10; Hull, *Annals of Athens*, 79.

10. T. Minutes, 1858-1877, pp. 198-200; *Southern Watchman*, April 14, 28, 1869.

11. *Southern Watchman*, Jan. 6, 23, 1867; Mell, *Life of Mell*, 223-25.

12. T. Minutes, 1858-1877, pp. 294, 295; F. Minutes, 1850-1873, p. 212; *Southern*

Watchman, Feb. 28, 1866, Feb. 27, 1867, Oct. 21, 1868, Aug. 24, Oct. 19, 1870; Hull, *Annals of Athens,* 317, 371, 372. The results of McCay's liberality have long since departed, if ever secured.

13. T. Minutes, 1858-1877, p. 255; *Southern Watchman,* Aug. 8, 1866; Hull, *Annals of Athens,* 78, 80.

14. *Southern Watchman,* July 5, 1865, July 4, 1866, July 10, 1867.

15. *Southern Watchman,* Aug. 14, Nov. 6, 1867; Hull, *Annals of Athens,* 320, 321; Sylvanus Morris, *Strolls about Athens during the Early Seventies.*

16. T. Minutes, 1857-1877, p. 193; Cobb to I. L. Harris, Aug. 27, 1867, Athens, in Ulrich B. Phillips, Report on the Local Archives of Georgia: The University of Georgia, 124-30; D. Minutes, 1860-1867, pp. 221, 225; D. Letterbook, April 10, 1867; *Daily News & Herald,* Aug. 9, 13, 15, 1867; *Southern Watchman,* Sept. 18, 1867; Hull, *Annals of Athens,* 325-27.

17. T. Minutes, 1858-1877, pp. 190, 203, 208, 215; 216; Cobb to Mrs. Cobb, Aug. 16, 1867 in Miscellaneous MSS; James Jackson to Cobb, Aug. 21, 1867, *ibid.;* W. L. Mitchell to I. L. Harris, Aug. 22, 1867, *ibid.; Southern Watchman,* Aug. 21, 28, 1867.

18. Lipscomb to Cobb, Aug. 19, 1867, in Miscellaneous MSS.

19. Cobb to I. L. Harris, Aug. 27, 1867, in Phillips, Report on Local Archives; Mitchell to Harris, Aug. 22, 1867, in Miscellaneous MSS.

20. F. Minutes, 1850-1873, p. 185; *Southern Watchman,* Sept. 11, 1867, May 6, Aug. 12, 1868.

21. *Compilation of the Ordinances of Athens,* 13, 14, 18; *Southern Watchman,* Dec. 20, 1865, Dec. 25, 1866, March 27, April 10, 24, 1867, Sept. 15, Oct. 20, 1869, April 20, July 20, Aug. 24, 1870; Hull, *Annals of Athens,* 311, 338, 339, 343.

22. F. Minutes, 1850-1873, p. 192; *Compilations of Ordinances of Athens,* 20; *Southern Watchman,* Dec. 20, 1865, Dec. 25, 1866, Oct. 16, Nov. 6, 13, 1867, March 10, 1869.

23. T. Minutes, 1858-1877, pp. 173-75, 260, 261; F. Minutes, 1850-1873, pp. 173, 174; *Compilation of the Ordinances of Athens,* 19; *Athens Daily News & Herald,* Aug. 15, 1867; Hull, *Annals of Athens,* 376; Harris, *Autobiography,* 151-56.

24. F. Minutes, 1850-1873, May 22, 1868; *Southern Watchman,* Feb. 28, 1866; July 17, 1867, May 20, June 10, 1868, Dec. 1, 1869, July 27, 1870; Harris, *Autobiography,* 164, 170.

25. P. K. Minutes, 1854-1885, Feb. 3, 1866; D. Minutes, 1860-1867, pp. 118, 119, 131, 135; *ibid.,* 1867-1882, pp. 22, 30.

26. T. Minutes, 1858-1877, p. 232: D. Minutes, 1860-1867, p. 129; *ibid.,* 1867-1882, p. 38.

27. D. Minutes, 1860-1867, pp. 123, 124, 133, 143, 157, 158, 192, 203; *ibid.,* 1867-1882, pp. 4, 5, 11, 61, 136.

28. D. Minutes, 1867-1882, p. 14; *Southern Watchman,* June 22, July 6, 20, 1870; Harris, *Autobiography,* 156; Mell, *Life of Mell,* 189, 190; *The Pandora* (published by the Fraternities of the University of Georgia) (Atlanta, 1890), 41, 43, 45, 47; Battle, *History of the University of North Carolina,* I, 621.

29. *Southern Watchman,* July 4, 1866, July 8, 1868, Aug. 4, 1869, Aug. 10, 1870; Hull, *Annals of Athens,* 341. Harris later became governor of Georgia and had a distinguished career in the state.

30. T. Minutes, 1858-1877, pp. 152, 177-86, 215, 221, 265; *Southern Watchman,* April 10, 1867, Sept. 15, 1869.

31. T. Minutes, 1858-1877, pp. 186, 187, 238, 266, 294; F. Minutes, 1850-1873, p. 199; D. Minutes, 1867-1882, p. 71; Broun, *Life of Broun,* 107-37; *University Catalogue, 1868-69,* pp. 15, 35, 43, 44.

32. T. Minutes, 1858-1877, pp. 211, 285, 286: D. Minutes, 1867-1882, pp. 47, 115; *Testimony . . . [on] . . . the Condition of Affairs in the Late Insurrectionary States, Georgia,* II, 808; *Southern Watchman,* July 7, 1869.

BIBLIOGRAPHY

BOOKS AND COLLECTED WORKS

Acts of the General Assembly of Connecticut with other permanent Documents respecting Yale University. Fourth edition. New Haven: The Tuttle, Morehouse & Taylor Company, 1901.

Acts of the General Assembly . . . of Georgia, 1840-1872. Published separately for each session.

Alderman, E. A., and A. C. Gordon, *J. L. M. Curry, A Biography.* New York: The Macmillan Company, 1911.

American Almanac and Repository of Useful Knowledge . . . , 1834-1848. Boston: Charles Bowen. Published yearly.

Armes, William D., ed., *Autobiography of Joseph LeConte.* New York: D. Appleton & Co., 1903.

Autobiography of Col. Richard Malcolm Johnston. Second edition. Washington: The Neale Company, 1901.

Barlow, Joel, *The Columbiad, A Poem.* Philadelphia: Fry and Kammerer, 1807.

Battle, Kemp P., *History of the University of North Carolina.* Two volumes. Raleigh: Edwards & Broughton, 1907.

Boykin, Samuel, *History of the Baptist Denomination in Georgia: with a Biographical Compendium and Portrait Gallery of Baptist Ministers and other Georgia Baptists.* Compiled for the Christian Index. Atlanta: Jas. P. Harrison & Co., 1881.

Broun, Thomas L., *Dr. William Leroy Broun.* New York: The Neale Publishing Company, 1912.

Brown, Isaac V., *Memoirs of the Rev. Robert Finley, D. D., Late Pastor of the Presbyterian Congregation at Basking Ridge New-Jersey and President of Franklin College, Located at Athens, in the State of Georgia. With Brief Sketches of Some of his Contemporaries and Numerous Notes.* New Brunswick: Terhune & Letson, 1819.

Buckingham, James Silk, *The Slave States of America.* Two volumes. London and Paris: Fisher, Son & Co., 1842.

Burckmyer Letters, March, 1863-June, 1865. Columbia, S. C.: The State Company, 1926.

Candler, Allen D., ed., *Colonial Records of the State of Georgia.* Vol. XIX, Pt. 2. Atlanta: Chas. P. Byrd, 1911.

Century of Population Growth, A (Department of Commerce and Labor. Bureau of the Census). Washington: Government Printing Office, 1909.

Clayton, Augustin Smith, comp., *A Compilation of the Laws of the State of Georgia, . . . 1800-1810. . . .* Augusta: Adams and Duyckinck, 1812.

Cleveland, C. C., *The Great Revival in the West, 1797-1805.* Chicago:

University of Chicago Press, 1916.

Compilation of the Acts of the Legislature Incorporating the Town of Athens, Georgia: and a Revision and Consolidation of the Ordinances passed by the Town Council of Athens to the Eleventh of September, 1867. Revised and consolidated by Henry Beussee and H. C. Billups. Athens: T. D. Williams, 1867.

Conner, H. G., *John Archibald Campbell.* Boston: Houghton Mifflin Company, 1920.

Coulter, E. M., *John Jacobus Flournoy. Champion of the Common Man in the Antebellum South.* Savannah: The Georgia Historical Society, 1942.

Dexter, Franklin Bowditch, ed., *Literary Diary of Ezra Styles, D. D., LL. D., President of Yale College.* Three volumes. New York: Charles Scribner's Sons, 1901.

Dodd, William E., *The Cotton Kingdom. . . .* The Chronicles of America Series, number 27. New Haven: Yale University Press, 1921.

Fielder, Robert, *A Sketch of the Life and Times and Speeches of Joseph E. Brown.* Springfield, Mass.: Press of Springfield Printing Company, 1883.

Fischer, Karl W., *The Mystics and Beta Theta Pi.* Printed at Menasha, Wisc.: Beta Theta Pi, 1940.

Ford, P. L., ed., *Works of Thomas Jefferson.* Twelve volumes. New York: G. P. Putnam's Sons, 1905.

Foster, William T., *Administration of the College Curriculum.* Boston: Houghton Mifflin Company, 1911.

Georgia Bequest, The. Manolia; or the Vale of Tallulah. By a Georgia Huntsman. Augusta: McKinne & Hall, 1854.

Green, Edwin L., *History of the University of South Carolina.* Columbia: The State Company, 1916.

Hansen, A. O., *Liberalism and American Education in the Eighteenth Century.* New York: The Macmillan Company, 1926.

Harris, Nathaniel E., *Autobiography. The Story of an Old Man's Life with Reminiscences of Seventy-five Years.* Macon: The J. W. Burke Company, 1925.

History of Athens and Clarke County. By various authors. Athens: H. J. Rowe, 1923.

Hull, Augustus L., *Annals of Athens, Georgia, 1801-1901.* Athens: Banner Job Office, 1906.

Hull, Augustus L., *A Historical Sketch of the University of Georgia.* Atlanta: The Foote & Davies Company, 1894.

Johnston, R. M., "Early Educational Life in Middle Georgia," in *Report of the Commissioner of Education, 1895-96.* Vol. I. Washington: Government Printing Office, 1897.

Johnston, R. M., and W. H. Browne, *Life of Alexander H. Stephens.* Philadelphia: J. B. Lippincott & Co., 1878.

Life and Letters of Stephen Olin, D. D., LL. D., The. Vol. I. New York: Harper & Brothers, 1853.

Longstreet, Augustus Baldwin, *Georgia Scenes, Characters, Incidents, &c., in the first Half of the Republic. By a Native Georgian.* Second edition. New York: Harper & Brothers, 1840.

Mallory, C. D., *Memorials of Jesse Mercer.* New York: John Gray, 1844.

Meigs, William M., *Life of Josiah Meigs.* Philadelphia, 1887.

Mell, P. H., Jr., *Life of Patrick Hues Mell.* Louisville, Ky.: Baptist Book Concern, 1895.

Miller, Stephen F., *The Bench and Bar of Georgia. . . .* Two volumes. Philadelphia: J. B. Lippincott & Co., 1858.

Perry, Bliss, ed., *The Heart of Emerson's Journals.* Boston: Houghton Mifflin Company, 1926.

Phillips, Ulrich B., *A History of Transportation in the Eastern Cotton Belt to 1860.* New York: The Columbia University Press, 1908.

Phillips, Ulrich B., *The Life of Robert Toombs.* New York: The Macmillan Company, 1913.

Prince, Oliver H., comp., *Digest of the Laws of the State of Georgia . . . to 1837. . . .* Second edition. Athens, 1837.

Return of the Whole Number of Persons within the Several Districts of the United States. Philadelphia, 1791.

Rowland, Dunbar, *History of Mississippi. The Heart of the South.* Two volumes. Chicago: The S. J. Clarke Publishing Company, 1925.

Scomp, H. A., *King Alcohol in the Realm of King Cotton.* N. P.: The Blakely Printing Company, 1888.

Scrugham, Mary, *The Peaceable Americans of 1860-1861.* New York: Longmans, Green & Co., 1921.

Sell, E. S., *History of the State Normal School, Athens, Georgia.* 1923.

Slosson, Edwin L., *The American Spirit in Education.* The Chronicles of America Series, number 33. New Haven: Yale University Press, 1921.

Smith, George G., *The Life and Letters of James Osgood Andrew.* Nashville: Southern Methodist Printing House, 1883.

Sparks, W. H., *The Memories of Fifty Years. . . .* Third edition. Philadelphia: Claxton, Remsen, and Haffelfinger, 1872.

Sprague, William B., *Annals of the American Pulpit.* Vol. IV. New York: Robert Carter & Brothers, 1858.

Testimony taken by the Joint Select Committee to inquire into the Condition of Affairs in the Late Insurrectionary States. Georgia. Two volumes. Washington: Government Printing Office, 1872.

Thomas, Edward J., *Memoirs of a Southerner, 1840-1923.* Savannah, 1923.

Thompson, C. Mildred, *Reconstruction in Georgia, Economic, Social, Political, 1865-1872.* Volume LXIV, number 1 in *Studies in History, Economics and Public Law.* New York: The Columbia University Press, 1915.

[Thompson, W. T.], *Major Jones's Chronicles of Pineville; Embracing Sketches of Georgia Scenes, Incidents, and Characters.* Philadelphia: T. B. Peterson and Brothers, 1843.

Thwing, Charles F., *A History of Higher Education in America.* New York: D. Appleton & Co., 1906.

Universal Geography, N. P., 1814.

Waddel, John N., *Memorials of Academic Life: Being an Historical Sketch of the Waddel Family. . . .* Richmond: Presbyterian Committee of Publication, 1891.

Waddell, James D., *Biographical Sketch of Linton Stephens. . . .* Atlanta: Dodson & Scott, 1877.

Wade, John D., *Augustus Baldwin Longstreet. . . .* New York: The Macmillan Company, 1924.

White, Henry C., *Abraham Baldwin. . . .* Athens, 1926.

Woolley, Edwin C., *The Reconstruction of Georgia.* Vol. XIII, number 3 in *Studies in History, Economics and Public Law.* New York: The Columbia University Press, 1901.

Watkins, Robert and George, eds., *Digest of the Laws of the State of Georgia from its first Establishment as a British Province down to the Year 1798 inclusive and the Principal Acts of 1799. . . .* Philadelphia: R. Aitken, 1800.

Watterson, Henry, ed., *Oddities in Southern Life and Character.* Boston: Houghton Mifflin Company, 1910.

MANUSCRIPT MATERIAL

All of the following manuscripts are in the University of Georgia Library unless otherwise indicated.

Abraham Baldwin Letters. There are more than a hundred pieces in this collection, consisting of letters both to and by Baldwin and some state government documents.

Andrew Johnson Papers. This extensive collection is in the Library of Congress. Only a few pieces in volume 65 (May, 1865) relate to this study.

Book of Chronicles, 1853-54.

Caldron, The, 1848-49. In possession of the writer.

Demosthenian Literary Society MSS: By-Laws, 1830; Catalogue of all the Books in the Library, 1803-1841; Constitutions (separate books),

1801, 1823, and 1856; Letterbooks, 1830-1870 (being three volumes
arranged without reference to any chronological order and made up
mostly of letters from honorary members expressing appreciation
on election); Librarian's Book, 1833; Minutes, 1829-39, 1840-47,
1847-54, 1854-1860, 1860-67, 1867-82; Treasurer's Book, 1821-22,
1822-25, 1825-27, 1832-35, 1835-36, 1838-39, 1852-53; Loose MSS.
Faculty Minutes, 1822-36, 1836-45, 1850-73.
Henry Jackson MSS. There are about 56 pieces in this collection, consisting of letters to and from Jackson, papers concerning Jackson's
purchases in France for the University, also some papers of a
scientific nature.
Josiah Meigs Letter, October 27, 1803. In glass frame.
Letters from alumni. All of these letters were received during April and
May of 1926. The writers with their addresses and the periods of
time they were at the University follow: C. S. Hardee, Savannah,
Georgia, 1844-48; W. M. Middlebrooks, Atlanta, Georgia, 1860-61;
W. D. Sullivan, Gray Court, South Carolina, 1856-57; S. F. Tenney,
Crockett, Texas, 1860-61; E. J. Thomas, Savannah, Georgia, 1857-60.
These letters are in the possession of the writer.
Miscellaneous MSS. These are unassembled letters.
Moses Waddel Diary, 1824, 1825, 1833-36. These diaries are in the
Library of Congress. A memoir coming down to 1793 is also in the
Library of Congress. It was published in the *Georgia Historical
Quarterly* and is listed in this bibliography under "Pamphlets and
Periodicals."
Personal Memoirs of W. S. Basinger. There are four volumes in bound
ledger books.
Phi Kappa Literary Society MSS: Constitution, 1866; Librarian's Book,
1840; Minutes, 1826-29, 1831-33, 1835-54, 1854-85; Name Register,
1855; Treasurer's Book, 1842-43, 1855-56, 1856-63.
Phillips, Ulrich B., Report on the Local Archives of Georgia: The Uni-
versity of Georgia (133 pages, in possession of writer).
Prudential Committee Minutes, 1834-57.
Senatus Academicus Minutes, 1799-1842.
Trustee Minutes, 1786-1817, 1817-35, 1835-57, 1857-77.
Vestry Book of Emmanuel Parish. In the possession of the Emmanuel
Episcopal Church, Athens, Georgia.
Weekly Record of Absences from Church Prayers & Recitations together
with all Fines imposed by the Faculty of Franklin College beginning
Jany 1834, A. C. F. McCay Secy.

NEWSPAPERS

Athenian. Athens. 1827-32.

Athens Gazette. Athens. 1814-17.

Augusta Chronicle. Augusta. 1786-1841.

Augusta Herald. Augusta. 1799-1806.

Daily News & Herald. Athens. 1867.

Daily Republican. Savannah. 1833-40.

Federal Union. Milledgeville. 1830-31, 1855-56.

Georgia Citizen. Macon. 1856.

Georgia Express. Athens. 1808-13.

Georgia Journal. Milledgeville. 1818-26.

Georgia Telegraph. Macon. 1855-57.

Savannah Georgian. Savannah. 1823-29.

Southern Banner. Athens. 1833-55.

Southern Herald. Athens. 1850. This paper was formerly called the *Southern Whig.* The change in name was made September 12, 1850.

Southern Recorder. Milledgeville. 1832-33.

Southern Watchman. Athens. 1855-71.

Southern Whig. Athens. 1846-50. The name of this journal became the *Southern Herald* on September 12, 1850.

Western Herald. Auraria, Lumpkin County, Georgia. 1833.

PAMPHLETS AND PERIODICALS

Catalogue of Franklin College, 1834-71.

Catalogue of the Trustees, Officers and Alumni of the University of Georgia from 1785 to 1876. Athens, 1876.

Code of Laws for the Government of Franklin College . . . 1853. Athens, 1854.

Coulter, E. M., "The Ante-bellum Academy Movement in Georgia," in *Georgia Historical Quarterly,* V, 4 (Dec., 1921).

Coulter, E. M., "Early Life and Regulations at the University of North Carolina," in *University of North Carolina Magazine,* O. S. Vol. 42, no. 4 (February, 1912).

Coulter, E. M., "Franklin College as a Name for the University of Georgia," in *Georgia Historical Quarterly,* XXXIV, 3 (Sept., 1950).

Coulter, E. M., "A Georgia Educational Movement during the Eighteen Hundred Fifties," in *Georgia Historical Quarterly,* IX, 1 (March, 1925).

Coulter, E. M., "The Nullification Movement in Georgia," in *Georgia Historical Quarterly,* V, 1 (March, 1921).

Coulter, E. M., "Wanderings of a Painting: The Alonzo Church Portrait," in *Georgia Historical Quarterly*, XXX, 2 (June, 1946).

"Diary of James Daniel Frederick. Sept.-Oct., 1849," in *The Georgia Cracker*, Nov., 1921.

Fisher, George P., *A Discourse commemorative of the History of the Church of Christ in Yale College, during the first Century of its Existence*. New Haven: Thos. H. Pease, 1858.

Freshman Laws [at Yale College]. New Haven: Daniel Bowen, 1768. These laws were reprinted in *Yale Daily News*, Dec. 3, 1926.

Georgia Alumni Record, II, 7 and 8 (April, 1922); IV, 1 (Oct., 1923).

Georgia University Magazine, I-XII (1851-57).

Gilmer, George R., *The Literary Progress of Georgia. An Address Delivered in the College Chapel, at Athens . . . 1851*. Athens: Wm. N. White & Bro., 1851.

Manual of the University of Georgia, 1890. Printed by order of the trustees. Atlanta: Jas. P. Harrison & Co., 1890.

Morris, Sylvanus, *Strolls about Athens during the early Seventies*.

Pandora, The, IV. Published by the Fraternities of the University of Georgia. Atlanta, 1890.

Programme of an Enlarged Organization of the University of Georgia. May, 1859.

"Reminiscences of Charles Seton Henry Hardee," in *Georgia Historical Quarterly*, XIII, 2 (June, 1928).

Report and Memorial of the Trustees of the University of Georgia to the General Assembly of the State. Adopted by the trustees, November 9, 1855.

Report Form. 1830, 1833.

Southern Literary Gazette. 1848. Published at Athens, 1848-1849 and at Charleston, 1850-1853.

Southern School Journal, 1853, 1854. Published successively at Columbus, Macon, and Madison, Georgia.

Tucker, Henry H., *Address delivered February 3rd, 1875, before the General Assembly of the State of Georgia on the Condition, Interests, and Wants of the University of Georgia*. Atlanta: Jas. P. Harrison & Co., 1875.

Virginia Evangelical and Literary Magazine. Edited by John H. Rice. I, 1 (Jan., 1818). Richmond. With volume IV the name was changed to *Evangelical and Literary Magazine and Missionary Chronicle*.

"Waddel Memoir," in *Georgia Historical Quarterly*, VIII, 2 (June, 1924).

Walter Barnard Hill. Bulletin of the University of Georgia. Memorial Number. VI, 8 (May, 1906).

INDEX

This index refers to the University of Georgia and
the State of Georgia unless otherwise indicated.

Academies, feeders for University, 14
Academy of Columbia County, 1
Agricultural education, promoted, 39
Alabama Polytechnic Institute, 199
Alexander, Peter W., alumnus, 161
Allen, Harriet, teacher, 27
Altamaha River, claims of South Carolina south of, 22
Alumni, control of University by suggested, 189-90
Alumni Society, organized, 139
American Colonization Society, 28
Andersonville, 245
Andover, Mass., 33
Andrew, James O., Methodist bishop, 153
April Fool's Day, 85
Armstrong, James W., 262
Asbury, Francis, visits Georgia, 150
Athenian, projected magazine, 139-40
Athenian, quoted, 56, 99, 205; on legislature, 176; Athens newspaper, 230
Athens, founded, 7; citizens pilfer University wood, 21; growth, 24-25, 204-31, 205, 264; female education, 27; newspapers, 27, 230; religious conditions in 1817, pp. 30-31; families housing students, 55; liquor shops, 79; taxes liquor, 94; and temperance, 97; Presbyterian congregation, 152; Methodist congregation, 152-53; Baptist congregation, 153; Episcopal congregation, 153; government, 205; railroad connections, 206; lighting facilities, 207; culture of citizens, 207-14; influence on students, 211-13; music, 214; education, 214-15; celebrations, 216-18; fire department, 218-19; circuses and other amusements, 219-26; local characters, 226-27, city ordinances, 228-29; hotels, 230-31; in Civil War, 233-34, 236, 241, 243-47; officers contributed to Confederacy, 244; Federal prisoners in, 245; Sherman's approach, 245-46; munitions works, 246; wartime conditions, 246; occupied by Federal troops, 248-51; economic and social development after war, 265; amusements after war, 265-66; cemetery, 295 n.; rifles made in, 296 n.

Athens, Greece, 38
Athens Cattle Show, 216
Athens Debating Club, 215
Athens Fair Society, 216
Athens Female College, 216
Athens Gazette, 27
Athens Guards, 236
Athens Harmonic Society, 104, 214
Athens Hotel, 230
Athens Independent Lyceum, 215
Athens Manufacturing Company, 289 n.
Athens Society for the Improvement of Sacred Music, 214
Athletics, 100, 268
Atlanta, varying names, 282 n.
Augusta, 71, 155
Augusta Baptist Church, 156
Augusta Chronicle, news on University, 134; quoted, 141

Bachelor of Arts, 202
Bachelor of Laws, 202
Bachelors' Club, 215
Baldwin, Abraham, comes to Georgia, 3; on first board of trustees, 4; writes University charter, 4-5, 277 n.; elected president of University, 5; in Federal Constitutional Convention, 6; on committee to locate University, 6-7; resigns University presidency, 10-11; favors agriculture, 41
Baltimore, Md., 71, 95
Banks County Guards, 243
Baptists, fear of, 18; organize temperance society, 94; number in Georgia, 149, 150; and University, 153, 154-62; on educating ministers, 154; joined by students, 164
Baptist State Convention, 112
Barber, G. W. town wit, 226
Barlow, Joel, classmate of Meigs, 11; receives honorary degree, 17, 139
Barnard, Frederick A. P., 186
Bartow, Francis S., alumnus, 160; on secession, 234; and organization of Confederacy, 235
Baseball, 268
Bath houses, 97

307

dent, 23; receives willow, 42; attracts
students, 85; at Athens tariff meeting,
145, 147

Cree, A. B., 248, 249

Crittenden, John J., honorary Phi Kappa,
109

Cumming, William, makes donation, 41

Curriculum, of University, 15-16

Curry, Jabez L. M., and literary society,
113; activities in literary society, 132;
on literary societies, 133; student, 179;
alumnus, 161; and organization of Confederacy, 235

Dances, 142-43

Darwin, Charles, 116

d'Autel, G. L. Jules, 209

Davis, Jefferson, honorary Phi Kappa,
109; on student deferment in war, 240;
president of Confederacy, 235

Davis, Madison, Negro politician, 260-61

Davis Benefit Fund, 258

Dawson, William C., alumnus, 160

Dearing, William, accused of vandalism
and challenged to duel, 71

De Beauregard, Quesnay, works out system of education, 5

De Clairville, Petit, professor of French,
17; leaves University, 19

De Fleur, Baron, 110

Demerit system, adopted, 203

Demosthenes, 103

Demosthenian Literary Society, 103-33;
founded, 103; relations with rivals, 105-
11; honorary members, 108, 110-11;
meeting time, 111-12; character of
meetings, 112-15; subjects debated, 115-
24; celebrations, 124-25; part played in
commencement exercises, 126-29; decorum requested in meetings, 129-31;
library, 131-32; adjourns for camp
meeting, 163; during Civil War, 241-
43; disbands, 243; hall occupied by
Federal troops, 249; after the war, 268-
71; subjects debated after war, 270-71,
276

De Nemours, Dupont, works out system
of education, 5

d'Estaing, Count, 208

"Dialectic Adelphic Society," 27

Diomatari, John D., Greek student, 38

Diplomas, 136

Doctor of Divinity, 202

Doctor of Laws, 139

Doctor of Medicine, 202

Doctor of Philosophy, 202

Dodge, Henry, honorary Phi Kappa, 109

Dormitory accommodations, 55

Douglas, Stephen A., presidential candidate, 232

Douglass, Frederick, 251

Dow, Lorenzo, visits Georgia, 150

"Dramatic Caps," 105

Duels, forbidden by University, 60; duel
averted, 71

Dupré, Lucien J., member of Confederate
Congress, 235

Dwight, Theodore, 18

Dwight, Timothy, 18

Early, Peter, friend of Meigs', 20; made
president temporarily, 23

Early, Thomas, student, 74

Easley, Daniel, resident of Jackson County, 7; sells land for locating University,
7; builds house for University president, 12

Easter, John D., becomes professor, 199

Eatonton Academy, 192

Echols, Joseph H., member of Confederate Congress, 235

Education, for the people, 9

Emerson, Ralph W., 88

Emma Sansom Cavalry, 243

Emory College, 159, 161, 255

Empire State, 188

Episcopal Church, decline, 9; and University, 153; in Athens, 265

Etowah River, 26

Euen, M. S., 249

Evans, Clement A., honorary member of
literary society, 270

Examinations, for entrance, 36; nature,
52-53

Faculty, first, 17; methods of teaching by,
49; enforcement of rules, 59-89; duty
to watch student conduct, 63-65; houses,
99; salaries, 181; revolt, 193-99; dismissal, 199; and Civil War, 239

Fairfield Jockey Club, 216

"Fantastiques," 225-26

Federalists, 18

Greek, language, 35
Green, William, professor, 20-21
Greene, Nathanael, settles in Georgia, 3
Greene County, selected as location of University, 2; Francis Asbury in, 150
Greensboro, laid out as a town, 6; residence of Andrew, 153
Griffin, Davies, 152
Grimes, Thomas, 240
Grivot, M., French professor, 20
Gunboat fund, 245
Gunn, James, benefactor of University, 11
Gunther, Charles, 110
Gymnasium, at University, 100

Hall, Lyman, favors a university, 3; trustee, 4
Hammond, Harry, professor, 197
Hampden-Sydney College, 136
Hancock County, University lands in sold, 12
Haralson, Hugh A., alumnus, 160
Harden, Edward, opens law school, 39; on professors as ministers, 162
Harden, Mary, 209
Harris, Iverson L., alumnus, 160
Harris, Jeptha V., at Semi-centennial, 140
Harris, Nat E., student, 256; wins praise for oratory, 273
Harris, Robert, student, 68
Harris, Wiley P., and organization of Confederacy, 235
Harrison, William Henry, commemorative exercises for, 179
Harvard University, 182
Hawaiian Islands, 41
Hayne, Robert Y., declines invitation, 128
Haynes, Thomas, burned in effigy, 179
Helper, Hinton R., 296 n.
Henrico College, in Virginia, endowed with land, 4
Hill, Benjamin H., on literary societies, 133; alumnus, 161; and organization of Confederacy, 235; during Reconstruction, 258; elected to law professorship, 259; on Cox affair, 261-64; advocates New South, 275-76
Hillyer, Granby, student, 75-76; activities in literary society, 131
Hillyer, Junius, student, 75-76; alumnus, 160; trustee, 200

Hillyer, Shaler G., alumnus, 160
History, promoted by Church, 38; as course in curriculum, 39; Stephens to teach, 259
History of Georgia, 39
Hodges, Rev. John, editor, 27
Hoffman, Professor, music master, 214
Hog Mountain, 26
Holidays, 83-84, 97
Holmes, Oliver W., author, 226
Homespun, worn by students, 144, 145, 146, 147, 178
Honorary degrees, 17-18, 139
Hook, Daniel, University trustee, 290 n.
Hopewell Presbytery, 152
Hopkins, Benjamin B., and student prank, 66
Houses, for professors, 99
Hull, Asbury, defeated for legislature, 170
Hull, Henry, student nickname for, 66; declines chancellorship, 203
Hull, Hope, Methodist preacher, 47; builds chapel, 104; preaches, 150, 152
Hull, William Hope, alumnus, 160

Immigration, subject of discussion by literary society, 121
Indians, visit University, 25-26, 280 n.; rumors that they would attack University, 26; removal, subject of discussion by literary society, 123; removed from state, 123
Indian Springs, 51
Ingersoll, Joseph R., honorary Phi Kappa, 109
Irvin, Isaiah Tucker, alumnus, 160
Italian, language, 37
Ivy, Richard, preacher, 150

Jack, S. S., toast on bachelors, 216
Jackson, Andrew, and literary society, 109; burned in effigy, 159; memorial exercises for, 217
Jackson, Henry, elected professor goes to France, 20; returns from France, 24; and presidency, 33; favorite of students, 64, 66
Jackson, Henry R., declines chancellorship, 203
Jackson, James, student nickname for, 66; and students, 67; and literary so-

cieties, 108; resigns, 194, 195

Jackson, Judge James, alumnus, 160; on Cox affair, 263

Jackson, Stonewall, honorary member of literary society, 242

Jackson, William H., trustee, 200; and tree, 226-27

Jackson County, location of University, 2, 6

Jefferson, Thomas, on education, 5; on location for a university, 8; congratulates Meigs, 16; praised by Meigs, 18; on religion, 151; founds University of Virginia, 162; on legislatures, 187; letter, 187-88

Jenkins, Charles J., governor, 253

Jews, 86

Johnson, Andrew, honorary Demosthenian, 110; receives letter from Flournoy, 226; Reconstruction policy, 253, 258; and Cox affair, 263

Johnson, Herschel V., presides at meeting, 129; alumnus, 160; argues for support for University, 183; trustee, 200; on secession, 234; member of Confederate Congress, 235; chosen United States Senator, 253, 258

Johnson, James, provisional governor, 253

Johnston, Albert Sidney, honorary member of literary society, 242

Johnston, Richard M., professor, 39, 161, 199; on patrolling students, 64; shows how to handle students, 78-79; honorary Demosthenian, 110; comments on Athens, 209; and secession, 238

Jones, A., chemist, 207

Jones, Charles C., on Board of Visitors, 53; clergyman, 282 n.

Jones, Charles C., Jr., 282 n.

Jones, Henry H., alumnus, 161

Jones, Joseph, professor, 199

Jones, Noble W., in land dispute, 22

Jones, Welden, student, 152

Jones, William, language professor, 17

Jones, William L., liberal professor, 193; resigns, 194, 195

Josephine, Empress, 208

"Junior Exhibition," 126-27

Junior orators, at commencements, 135

Kappa Alpha, 271

Kavanaugh, H. H., honorary member of literary society, 242

Keowee River, in boundary dispute, 22

King, Angus M. D., University trustee, 289 n.

Know Nothing Party, debated by literary societies, 117

Knox, J. J., 252-53

Kollock, Henry, refuses presidency of University, 19

Ku Klux Klan, 253, 260-61

Ladies' Memorial Association, 258

LaGrange, 261

Lamar, Lucius Q. C., makes address, 125, 128

Lanier House, 231

Law, Henry M., student, 96

Law, Joseph, student soldier, 45

Law, William, declines invitation, 120

Law School, private, 39; promoted by University, 39; established, 202, 203; in Civil War, 238; closed during war, 240

Leathers, Joel, mountain man, 100

LeConte, John, alumnus, 160; liberal professor, 193; resigns, 194; nature of quarrel, 194-96

LeConte, Joseph, refuses to patrol students, 64; on literary societies, 133; alumnus, 160; joins church, 163, 165; comments on President Church, 192; liberal professor, 193, 197; resigns, 194, 196, 199

Lee, Custis, offered professorship, 259; honorary member of literary society, 270

Lee, Daniel, professor, 39; re-elected professor, 199

Lee, Robert E., death mourned, 259; honorary member of literary society, 270

Legaré, J. M., honorary Phi Kappa, 109

Lehman, William, language professor, 37; dismissed, 181

Lewis, Addin, professor, 17

Lewis, David W., alumnus, 160; member of Confederate Congress, 235

Lexington, attraction for students, 85, 86

Liberty County, 108

Library, appropriation, 40; lottery, 40; number and kind of books, 40; gift of books by Gilmer, 40; gift by British